WAGNER

WAGNER

A DOCUMENTARY STUDY

compiled and edited by

Herbert Barth · Dietrich Mack

Egon Voss

Preface by Pierre Boulez

with 296 illustrations, 73 in colour

THAMES AND HUDSON · LONDON

Authors' note

At the time of the selection of literary material for inclusion in this documentary study, only those extracts from the Diaries of Cosima Wagner (see pp. 247–50) which had previously been published in the *Bayreuther Blätter*, 1936–38, were available to the authors, publication of the greater part of the diaries being prevented by testamentary provisions. The town of Bayreuth, as the owner of the copyright in the complete diaries, would like it to be known that a complete edition is in preparation and that the first volume is expected to appear in 1976; the diaries will be published in Germany by R. Piper & Co. Verlag, Munich, and will also appear under the imprint of Harcourt Brace Jovanovich, Inc., New York.

Documents translated by P. R. J. FORD and MARY WHITTALL

Editorial collaboration: SIGRID WIESMANN

First published in German under the title *Wagner: sein Leben und seine Welt in zeitgenössischen Bildern und Texten*

This edition first published in Great Britain in 1975 by Thames and Hudson Ltd, London

Illustrations printed in the Netherlands by Druckerij de Lange/Van Leer, Deventer and London; text printed in West Germany by Universitätsdruckerei H. Stürtz AG, Würzburg

Contents

Authors' Note

Although few other composers can have had as much written about them as has Richard Wagner, one notable omission to date has been a comprehensive coverage of his life and work based on contemporary documents and illustrations. In attempting to fill this gap, the present book also takes account of the fact that in recent years there has been a considerable upsurge of interest in the nineteenth century and in Wagner especially. Based entirely on contemporary material, this book is intended to assist the reader in understanding both the character of the composer and his creative work.

In making a choice of documentary material the emphasis has been on Wagner's works as the basic criterion, and as his œuvre is for the most part intended for the stage it demands a much more extensive documentation than does that of most other composers. We therefore found ourselves obliged to omit much of an anecdotal nature – i.e. biographical material – relating not only to Wagner's friends, patrons and members of his family, but also to the places in which he lived at various stages of his career. Some of the illustrations have not been previously published, and many are here reproduced in colour for the first time. In this respect the book enjoys a definite advantage over the much more detailed volume by Robert Bory – long since out of print.

The sequence of both illustrations and documents is basically chronological; thus, for example, the first prose sketch for *Die Meistersinger von Nürnberg* (1845) follows directly on *Tannhäuser* (ills. 57–67) rather than in the context of its later development and completion from 1861 on, thus avoiding the creation of a false sense of homogeneity. Conversely, if particular associations of subject matter seemed to demand otherwise, strict chronology has been dropped, e.g. in the case of parodies and caricatures which may have appeared later than the work or performance which gave rise to them.

The captions to the illustrations include, wherever appropriate, a cross-reference to assist the reader in locating a related document, while firm dating is confined to known cases. Unless otherwise noted, autograph scores are in Wagner's own hand; musical examples have had to be severely restricted for reasons of space and in only one work – *Lohengrin* – are the stages of its development shown in detail. For the most part we have had to be content with examples combining the visually obvious and the musicologically relevant, and in many cases such a combination was equally successful in reverse.

On the whole, the choice of documents leaves out the theoretical writings of Wagner – they are easily accessible in other books – and in any case extracts from them tend to be arbitrary; however, for the first time in a book, we have included extensive extracts from Cosima Wagner's diaries. We were naturally concerned to present the reader with less familiar material, and in cases where selection by combination was not practicable we hope that it will be evident that our choice depended on the readability of the documents quoted.

Regrettably, we were unable to obtain illustrative material from the Richard Wagner Museum in Eisenach, nor were we able to reproduce in colour the portrait of Minna Planer by Otterstedt (ill. 24) in the Burrell Collection, Philadelphia. However, we are especially indebted to Herr Wolfgang Wagner for his wholehearted support in this venture, and to Frau Gertrud Strobel of the Richard Wagner Archive in Bayreuth for her help in providing information. Thanks are also due to the individuals, collections, museums and institutions through whose courtesy both illustrations and certain documents appear in this book. For a list of the sources of illustrations see p. 145; documentary sources are given at the end of each passage quoted.

1975

HERBERT BARTH
DIETRICH MACK
EGON VOSS

Preface

DIVERGENCES: THE MAN AND HIS WORK

Hagiography seizes greedily upon those figures who have contributed the most to creating the image of a given era. It raises men to the status of heroes, heroes in turn become saints, gods even, disappearing progressively beyond the misty sea of myth. If some imprudent person ventures to seek out the primary truth, he is rebuffed as indiscreet, not to say indecent or immoral. Biography must adapt itself to the work: a Titan knows no weaknesses. The unity of a man's life and work is one of the most indisputable articles of faith, with few exceptions. One such exception is Richard Wagner: will the passions he arouses never abate? I refer to the passions felt, not concerning his music, but about what he represents in the society of his day. While one can make light of the champion of vegetarianism, it is difficult to look upon Wagner's anti-semitism as something to be ignored. Further, if his political ideas smack of amateurism, his views on reforming musical education should warrant serious consideration. What strikes one today, over and over again, about Wagner's career is its inextricable mixture of ambition, of ideologies and of accomplishment: an illusory ambition in fields where he believed himself the master; an ideology somewhat confused, if one compares it to the philosophical trends of his time, and to Marx in particular; an artistic accomplishment of the first order which brings into question and revolutionizes the musical language as well as music in the theatre. He doubtless regarded himself as having been chosen to be a prophet much more than an artist – the prophet, having received the light and grace, assumes the right to speak out boldly and as an authority on any and every subject. The artist as redeemer possesses intuitively universal knowledge; his worldly mission is to bring revealed solutions.

Before Wagner, indeed not such a long time before, the artist was still a servant – the spiritual servant of a community, or the temporal servant of a patron. He became a token of timid independence, even if he had to enter into a society which accepted him, for better or worse, as an exception. Then the artist sought to become the leader, the saviour, the one who by his intuition and genius reveals the destiny of mankind. In the eighteenth century, the philosophers had played this role on a rationalistic and political plane; especially, the French *philosophes* in the age of the enlightenment who set themselves the task of instructing the people, of leading them towards a better future, towards a society founded on reason and justice. After the upheaval of the Revolution and its consequences, a far-reaching and fateful reaction sets in. To be sure, the philosophers continue to delve deeper in their analysis of society, and the revolutionary ferment manifests itself here and there, as a more or less permanent feature. The artist, however, rejects the rationality of this attitude and would seek to become the

symbol of redemption, whereby disillusionment comes to his aid. Yet the more disillusioned he becomes with this ideal, the more the artist withdraws and develops his imagination in the direction suggested by his own particular gifts. Meanwhile he vents his pessimism against this society which refuses to accept him as a prophet, for it is bitter, this disenchantment, caused by having to give up reforming the world in favour of restricting himself to 'artistic' reforms or revolutions. The artist is then made aware of his own limitations; he is in some way denied the universality of his thought, he is forced to restrict his field of action, to abandon the present for the future; now he merely has a privileged role, one that is gladly accorded him within a society over which he has no influence. At the point in history where we find ourselves today this fiction and this contradiction have not yet disappeared, unless there has sometimes been a return to the idea of the artist as servant – not to a patron or a community, but to the aims of the State. Through sacrifice, submission or by force, ideology is accepted as being a general condition in which the artist has no part to play except to follow and obey decisions, in the taking of which – far from having helped – he has often had no part, others – regarded as more efficient and more political – having robbed him of this essential responsibility.

Was Wagner himself a servant of society, after having wished to be its prophet? Was he not obliged, more and more, merely to play a part, having once attempted to live it? How often the change effected during his life has been described before: from destroying angel to master of ceremonies, from utopian, even confused revolutionary to the bitter and disillusioned conservative trying to deal on equal terms with kings and emperors, keeping up this façade of the power of the artist – a sort of religious power at odds with temporal power, cruelly deceived when, plainly, he is regarded as a mountebank: as a man of the theatre, living in a world of illusions and myth and not in that reality which rates these dreams as of no account, as games left to the artist with no responsibility. The simple fact that Bayreuth, after the brilliant inauguration of the Festival, attended by all the ruling aristocracy in 1876, was condemned to silence from 1877 to 1882, with the première of *Parsifal*, left Wagner bitter and, even more so, perplexed. Was his dream of a national art premature, or was it a mere illusion? How distant and unattainable seems the enchanted communion of Greek tragedy ... The society which he wanted to endow with a unique self-identity derives a few moments' amusement from this intention and then forgets it, temporarily, until a series of misunderstandings converts his work into a narrow-minded symbol of nationalism and of racism: a posthumous phenomenon of sordid irony! Stripped of this hideous mask, Wagner's œuvre continues to exercise its fascination, for that is the crux of the matter: an œuvre – and a theatre. The duality of this legacy is a true enough reflection of the measure of his revolutionary accomplishment. The œuvre has been, and still is, an essential leaven in musical life even more than in theatrical life; and not without reason, for, possessing a universal significance, it has had universal consequences, and without it the musical language as we know it today is simply unthinkable. But what about the theatre? And the practical aspects which this theatre implies through its architecture and its general conception – choice of location, change of the limits of action, of its functions, of its modalities – have these practices changed nothing? In this area the block is almost complete. The diatribes which Wagner was writing over a century ago have a complete relevance today – concerning the dullness of the repertory theatre, its deficiencies and defects, its operations defying all logic, the random choice of works, the chance casting of singers and musicians, the lack of rehearsals, the routine of every man for himself. As for architecture, the model of Bayreuth has remained a dead letter – we still live with the Italian-style theatre. The proportions, however, have become totally ridiculous, notably the pit enlarged out of all recognition to accommodate ever bigger orchestras. Beyond this vast pool, in which one can view, during the performance, that microcosm known as the orchestra, the singer's voice attempts to penetrate the wall of sound raised before it: a vain struggle which regularly gives rise to dubious – even disastrous – results. Both visually and acoustically, we continue to witness this permanent failure of the theatrical concept, without the slightest improvement derived from Bayreuth. The comprehensive answer proposed by Wagner has remained an individual and isolated response, absorbed into the general context which has itself remained basically unchanged.

And yet it is the totality of the solution to be found which was Wagner's lifelong passion; this is the justification of his life even in its most ambiguous and least acceptable aspects. We see the musician in turn defining his objectives, determining his line of action with growing precision and then gradually uniting every intellectual and artistic preoccupation at the centre of a world essentially bounded by music – so that this frontier is no less coercive, being accepted simply as a lesser evil. In the early days there was nothing exceptional, far from it: a desire to 'become a member of the club'. Certainly, the influences, early on, were 'irreproachable'; but they dominate, in equal measure, the best of Wagner's contemporaries. Gluck, Beethoven and Weber: this same trinity also dominates the early work of Berlioz. If we think of the theatre, its models, its everyday repertoire, the competitive struggle was much less commendable. If we now think of Wagner, of his accomplishment with regard to history, we are inclined to think that he could not be otherwise, that a genius of such compass, of such quality, endowed with such will-power and at the same time with exceptional vitality and uncommon vigour should inevitably give rise to spectacular results. Taking a closer look at his writings, we see on occasion how fragile and lacking in assurance are the transitions which lead him from the uncertainty of youth to the absolute self-confidence revealed in the completion of his creations. These documents strengthen our impression, not that their content is

insincere, but that where Wagner regards himself as a figure of public interest even his most personal writings seem to be written with an eye to posterity. It is interesting to note how spontaneous are the exchanges of youthful ideas between friends – with all the world still to conquer and with no constraint with regard to history; later, when the situation changed, how calculated the relationships became between 'powers', when people have become personalities, creating the image they would wish posterity to have of them, of their existence and their activities. The rhetoric of passion often develops into bombast, being degenerates sometimes into appearance. The letters to Ludwig II of Bavaria are the most obviously symptomatic of this illusion, the more so in that they run counter to the sought-after goal: instead of raising their creator to 'glory', they reveal the mechanics of deception – the excess of noble feeling proclaims the artificiality of the role being played, reveals the parody of this dialogue – conceived as an exchange between pope and emperor at the time of the Holy Roman Empire – turning it into a dialogue between masqueraders, each seeking to convince the other of the authenticity of his disguise. But while the verbal pageantry is given free rein, a faithful and imperious wife keeps vigil. Respect and admiration force her to record the sayings and doings of the Master – even to his slightest utterances: not the least curious paradox of this fierce and unbounded devotion is the fact that we owe to it the most striking, the least 'improved', and the most revealing documents. The man no longer on his guard, not seeking in such moments to build his own statue for eternity – we thus see his true dimension developing, infinitely greater than that propounded by him in public, and detect the true basis of his personality, infinitely more resistant and robust than that pasteboard illusion which he sought to inflict upon us.

Perhaps Wagner himself provides the best analysis of his own personality. This 'projection' is imprinted like a watermark on many of his writings. Being adventurous – even irrational – and extremely analytical by nature, Wagner reveals to us, in his correspondence and his writings, an extraordinary perception of his own development and importance, of his impact, as well as of the mechanics of his creative process. Such introspection furnishes us with incredibly perspicacious views on the salient points of his inventiveness, on the cardinal aims of his quest. Indeed, in *Tristan* he describes what we find most obvious in this work, but in addition, and most precisely, he sees the quality which makes it unique in history: a music of transition and not of repetition and retrospection. These thoughts on continuity and transition as indelible stamps of the music of the future are seen again many years later in an arresting conversation with Liszt, in which he states his desire to regenerate the symphony in accordance with the following principle: as Beethoven had exhausted the possibilities of antagonism, of the opposing of themes, so the future would belong to their fusion and their transformation. Such analytical ability and inventiveness based on analysis are truly fascinating. Especially with regard to Beethoven, to whom he felt a particularly close affinity by inheritance, his private conversations are revelations of the manner in which he accepted his inheritance. Alongside this 'Germanic orthodoxy', we note on many occasions a mixture of fascination and amusement vis-à-vis Italian opera – not the works of his contemporary Verdi, but those of popular composers at the beginning of the nineteenth century. Although well aware of the superficiality of their musical content, he was none the less envious of their melodic invention and expressive power; we note his resolve to reconcile the two approaches – the German symphonic tradition and the expressiveness of Italian *bel canto*. Speaking more generally, he refused to sacrifice expression to polyphony, but endowed each voice forming this polyphony with great expressive power to the point where there is almost a conflict of interest: everything is melody, unending melody. The sensuality and density of his writing, as well as its continuity on such a wide scale, were the characteristic qualities which most disturbed his contemporaries – especially in opera, a field in which the listener was not particularly discerning. And what of his harmonic invention, resulting equally from his need for continuity and his striving for endless transition? The more he advances, the more often he reaches towards areas in which certainty of language is lost for long periods: the uncertainty of development, the fickleness of the transient solution, the discovery of twilight zones in which outlines dissolve – these become more and more his fundamental preoccupations. He abandons the known absolute of the musical language only to discover a much wider, more gripping absolute. He abandons established forms in order to create the fundamental unity of the work in which each successive moment blends into the next, thanks to our recollection of individual motifs, each with an unmistakable identity, which are repeated and metamorphosed to suit the occasion.

Is this the theatrical vision which gave rise to such a wealth and proliferation of ideas and concepts? It seems difficult to give an affirmative answer, because the levels of our reading of Wagner are very different, depending on whether his literary or his musical invention is in question. While the music strides boldly and forcefully into the future, the theatre looks back obstinately into the past; which is not to say that in the context of opera in his own day Wagner did not undertake a vast amount of refining and renewal. Indeed, in the face of the then dominant pseudo-historical junk he invested archetypal characters with a mythical dimension, bringing to his theatre an inexhaustible wealth of expression. Meanwhile, we must note that the place where these myths were born – an ideal of the Middle Ages in which so much of his work is set – belongs to the beginnings of Romanticism. With his literary creation practically complete by 1850, at least in its themes, there remained thirty years more during which Wagner's music developed in a more and more striking and singular manner, while his theatrical world remained unchanged, even if – as he frequently emphasized – the perspectives were transformed. When after a bitter struggle the work was finally completed and concentrated within itself, literature and poetry had left Wagner behind. One of the most striking contradictions of his theatre lies in the force of the myths and symbols he created, contrasted with their obsolescence at the time of being formalized in the final composition. In this sense, one is justified in speaking of Wagner 'the Gothic', as had formerly been done in the case of Bach 'the Gothic'. Yet an extremely powerful nationalist impulse sufficed to enable certain ambiguous aspects of Wagnerian myths to provide an alibi, even a cultural justification.

In the second half of the nineteenth century, Europe, after oscillating between revolutionary activism and conservative repression, lurched in the direction of a patriotic chauvinism, aggravated by the conscious awareness of each nation, whether free or oppressed, of its own individuality. Wagner did not escape this swing of the pendulum and – in the same way as many other creative artists did – sought to give his œuvre a sound ethnic foundation. This became something of an obsession, as the many references to a 'German art' show. Is there not in this a means of reassuring himself in the face of the cosmopolitanism to which he had eagerly subscribed up to that point. He was a cosmopolitan, certainly, but was he a true revolutionary? The statements by Bakunin, dry and laconic, hardly speak in his favour, any more than his associations with the German exiles in Zurich show him to be devoted to the revolutionary cause. Above all, he puts on theatrical airs, dramatizing the conflicts and utilizing them to his own advantage, in order to nurture his work. For him, as creator, i.e. egoist or at least egocentric artist, the order of priority will be maintained: first and foremost stands the work to be created. For this reason, we should not be at all surprised by the second priority: to base the work on a solid foundation, and to anchor it to that base which goes beyond its individual realization. If the revolution provided the impulse, nationalism brought its elaboration. Therein lies a mixture of opportunism and idealism which are reflected even in the smallest details. German art would of course mean the performing of Wagner's operas, and in addition the creation of a German school of singing whose purpose would be to train young singers in the performance of Wagner. This pedagogical concern is easily understandable: convinced of the importance of his work in the context of German culture, he had to face up to the impossibility of fitting his creation into the existing musical framework, whose practices and customs he lamented. In order to present 'correct' interpretations of his works, he had to begin by educating the performers. These plans never came to fruition because he died before he could realize them. Thus, German art could never come to know its first school, and before long Bayreuth, instead of revealing something alive, was jealously preserving it instead. German art was to become the booty of a satiated society scarcely concerning itself with daring. Later, when political ideology took hold of Wagner's work and raised it by force as its own banner, the original ideal was brought to its lowest point. Perhaps this purification through shame was necessary for the myths and symbols to take on their true meaning, removed from the fortuitous nature of their origins.

There does remain, however, the undisguised anti-semitism, the strangest example of which is the episode between Wagner and the conductor Hermann Levi during the preparations for the première of *Parsifal*: the conflict, which would be laughable but for its unpleasantness, between the boastful stance of Wagner the committed Christian, à propos the purity of his religious ideal, and the interest of Wagner the composer in not losing the services of an outstanding conductor; the desire to have control over a weaker character while humiliating him.

(But was this not equally true of Hans von Bülow?) To explain this militant anti-semitism solely by reasons of personal jealousy towards Mendelssohn or Meyerbeer seems somewhat shortsighted, even if there was for Wagner an apparent dislike of what these two composers represented: the usurpation of German art by a too superficial or too adroit hand. We should not forget that anti-semitism had been an endemic disease of Christian Europe for centuries, and that nationalist feeling merely exposed more pointedly what was already there in a latent form, before the 'national' concept had taken on the force and significance it acquired at the end of the nineteenth century. In France the Dreyfus affair was soon afterwards to show up these feelings, and there was no lack of declared anti-semitic French musicians – one example is the case of Vincent d'Indy seeking to provide, in his composition course, a 'rational' explanation why a Jew would be incapable of composing music of any worth. Down the centuries, the Jewish cultural heritage had not been taken into account, even though the Jewish religion had been the object of ostracism and persecution. The Jews were thus closely confined in ghettoes and their beliefs were a danger to nobody. But when a Jewish intelligentsia developed and when the European nations began to take shape, the Jewish culture represented a tradition which could not be reduced from a cosmopolitan form and brought within the limitations of national ideals, and above all it revealed its powers of resistance to any attempts at enforced assimilation. The Jewish community remained unchanged by outside pressures, forming the cracks in the walls thrown up to separate one state from another. Wagner, steeped in the romantic idealism of medieval myth, adds to the political and cultural reaction of the nineteenth century the prejudices of a militant Christian. If he was no exception among anti-semitic intellectuals, Wagner does represent an amalgam of concepts on which it was only too easy to draw in order to label him the

leader of a particularly vicious crusade. He was of course aware of this – a victim of his own image – for the Nordic myths which he helped to revive were included, willy-nilly, in an ideological panoply for which they were clearly never originally intended. From Greek tragedy to outspoken racism – this was a debasement for which we can consider him only partially responsible, but responsible none the less. For this reason it becomes difficult, not to say practically impossible, to banish this mist, these clouds, this night.

Thus, hagiography cannot ever totally grasp the character of Wagner: he remains vulnerable on account of various basic aspects of his life. But the documents provide us with a clear view of that opaque amalgam which produced one of the most headstrong geniuses who ever lived: through the youthful uncertainties, through the joys and disappointments of experience, the mystery and the mastery were forged, to the point at which self-confidence established an etiquette of behaviour, comparable to an etiquette at Court. At the same time we detect an impatience to realize his plans; and note that at the point when he was striving for a German art he withdrew to Italy to pursue his dreams there. Does this not lead us to the conclusion that, having once created the constraint of Bayreuth, he contrived to flee from it, fearful of the responsibilities it imposed because they might hamper his inventive powers? An impatient ruler of a domain conquered after a long drawn-out struggle, his lot – almost his choice – was restless unease. Was this end so surprising? He completed his œuvre, thinking that he had written everything that lay within his power to create; his mind turned to the symphony . . .

We are left with this problematical character and this all-important œuvre. The character of the man has not yet become lost behind the œuvre he created. Can this ever come to pass?

PIERRE BOULEZ

Wagner's Autobiographical Sketch

Richard Wagner described his life up to the year 1842 in an 'Autobiographical Sketch'; this sketch appeared (in two instalments) in the Leipzig journal *Zeitung für die elegante Welt* on 1 and 8 February 1843. It was prefaced with an introduction by the paper's editor, Heinrich Laube, whom Wagner had known since 1833.

Heinrich Laube writes in his introduction to Wagner's autobiographical sketch:

Launched by Fate into strange adventures, which took him as far afield as Russia, he disappeared from my view for a while, and I was not a little surprised to see him appear, out of the blue, in my room in Paris in the winter of 1838 [1839]. That was the typical madcap wantonness of the artist. Takes his wife, an opera and a half, scarcely two coins to rub together and a terribly big and terribly hungry Newfoundland dog and sets off through storm and sea straight from the Dvina to the Seine to make his fortune in Paris! In Paris, where half Europe is competing for fame and fortune, where everything, however deserving, must first be bought, or at least paid for, before it can appear on the market and thus have any chance of being noticed. Heine, otherwise so carefree, folded his hands in prayer at so much blind confidence in a German. Well, he did not succeed, but he did not fail either, and two years later, outwardly poorer but inwardly enriched, the wandering musician was back in his native Saxony, where he was welcomed as he deserved. Now, in order to introduce my friend to a wider public I asked him to send me . . . a sketch of his life, which I intended to expand and publish. But the pressure of life in Paris has in a short space of time turned the musician into a writer too: I should only spoil the sketch if I tried to alter it. . .

Wagner's autobiographical sketch:

My name is Wilhelm Richard Wagner and I was born in Leipzig on 22 May 1813. My father was a police registrar and died six months after my birth. My stepfather, Ludwig Geyer, was an actor and painter; he also wrote a few comedies, one of which (*Der bethlehemitische Kindermord* ['The Massacre of the Innocents']) was successful. My family moved to Dresden with him. He wanted me to become a painter, but I was very poor at drawing. My stepfather, too, soon died – I was only seven. Shortly before his death I had learned to play *Üb' immer Treu und Redlichkeit* and the *Jungfernkranz*, which was quite new then, on the piano. The day before he died I had to play both pieces to him from the next room; then I heard him say to my mother in a weak voice: 'Do you think he perhaps has musical talent?' Next morning, after he had died, mother came into the nursery and said something to each of the children. To me she said: 'He wanted to make something of you.' I remember thinking for a long time that something would become of me. When I was nine I started at the Kreuzschule in Dresden. I wanted to study and there was no thought of music: two of my sisters learned to play the piano well, but I only listened, without having piano lessons myself. Nothing else appealed to me as much as *Der Freischütz*. I often saw Weber go past our house on his way home from rehearsals; I always gazed at him with holy reverence. A tutor, engaged to elucidate Cornelius Nepos to me, finally had to give me piano lessons too. I was scarcely beyond the first five-finger exercise, when I secretly learned the overture to *Der Freischütz*, at first without the music; my teacher heard it once, and said nothing would become of me. He was right. I have never in my life learned to play the piano properly. Now I just played for myself, nothing but overtures, and with the most hair-raising fingering. I was incapable of playing any passage without mistakes and I therefore acquired a great antipathy to all passage-work. Of Mozart I liked only the overture to *The Magic Flute*; *Don Giovanni* I disliked because of its Italian text: it struck me as silly. But this interest in music, though substantial, was only a sideline: my main concern was with Greek, Latin, Mythology and Ancient History. I also wrote poems. Once one of our classmates died, and the teachers set us the exercise of writing a poem on his death. The best one would be printed: – mine was, but only after I had eliminated a great deal of bombast from it. I was eleven years old then. Now I wanted to become a poet: I planned tragedies modelled on the Greeks, inspired by the discovery of Apel's★ tragedies: *Polyidos, Die Ätolier* ['The Aetolians'] etc. I had by then a reputation for letters in the school: as a fourth-former I had already translated the first twelve books of the *Odyssey*. Once I learned English, too, simply in order to get to know Shakespeare properly: I translated Romeo's monologue into metric verse. I soon dropped English again, but Shakespeare remained my idol. I sketched out a great tragedy which consisted more or less of *Hamlet* and *King Lear* rolled into one. The plan was quite stupendous: forty-two people died in the course of the play and I found myself obliged to bring most of them back as ghosts, since otherwise I should have run out of characters in the later acts. This play occupied me for two years. In the meantime I left Dresden and the Kreuzschule and went to Leipzig. In the Nikolaischule there I was put in the fourth form, whereas in Dresden I had already been in the fifth: this circumstance so embittered me that I lost all interest in philological studies. I became lazy and uncouth: only my great tragedy still interested me.

★ Johann August Apel (1771–1816)

While I was completing it I had, at the Leipzig Gewandhaus concerts, my first taste of Beethoven's music: the effect was shattering. I came to like Mozart, too, especially his Requiem. Beethoven's incidental music to *Egmont* so excited me that I would not for anything in the world launch my now completed tragedy unless accompanied by similar music. I has absolutely no doubts about being able to write this so necessary music myself, but I nevertheless considered it would be worthwhile reading up a few of the main rules of harmony and counterpoint beforehand. In order to do this quickly I borrowed Logier's *Methode des Generalbasses* for a week and applied myself eagerly to its study. However, my studies did not bear fruit as quickly as I had imagined; the difficulties in fact stimulated and fascinated me, so I decided to become a musician. Meanwhile my great tragedy had been discovered by my family: they became greatly disturbed since it was obvious that I had thoroughly neglected my school-work over it and I was sternly warned to get back to my studies and work hard at them. In the circumstances I kept quiet about this secret discovery of my musical calling, but that did not stop me secretly composing a sonata, a quartet and an aria. When I felt myself sufficiently advanced with my private musical studies I eventually came into the open and revealed them. Of course I now had to fight an uphill battle, since my family could not but regard my inclination for music, too, as no more than a passing fancy, the more so since it was not supported by any preliminary studies, such as an already acquired skill in playing an instrument. I was then in my sixteenth year and moreover was stirred to the wildest mysticism by reading Hoffmann: in the daytime, while dozing, I had visions, in which root, third and fifth appeared and revealed their great significance to me: what I wrote down was raving nonsense. Eventually I was accorded instruction from a qualified musician.★ The poor man had a hard time with me. He had to explain that what I took to be strange figures and forces were intervals and chords. What could be more disconcerting for my family than to discover that I proved negligent and irregular in this study too? My teacher shook his head and it looked as though nothing worthwhile would become of me here, either. My desire to study became weaker and weaker and I preferred to compose overtures for large orchestra, one of which was performed once in the Leipzig Theatre. This overture was the culminating point of my idiocies; I had actually wanted to write it in three different inks to make things easier for anyone who might want to study the score: the strings in red, the woodwind in green and the brass in black. Beethoven's Ninth was to be but a Pleyel sonata compared to this wonderfully complex overture. What did me most damage during the performance however was a fortissimo drum-roll which recurred regularly every three bars throughout the piece. The public, surprised at first at the stubbornness of the timpanist, soon became undisguisedly irritated but fell finally into a state of mirth which saddened me deeply. This first performance of a work of mine left a deep impression on me.

But now came the July Revolution [Paris 1830]. At a stroke I became a revolutionary, and acquired the conviction that any tolerably resolute man should concern himself exclusively with politics. I now felt at ease only in the company of political writers: I also began an overture which had a political theme. So I left school and entered the University [February 1831], no longer in order to read for a degree – for I was now destined to become a musician after all – but to follow the lectures on philosophy and aesthetics. This opportunity to acquire an education was almost entirely lost on me; I did however take part in all the student excesses, and indeed with such lightheadedness and such abandon that I soon became sick of them. My family at this time had great difficulties with me: my music I had almost completely abandoned. But I soon came to my senses: I felt the need to begin again with a strictly ordered study of music, and Providence led me to the right mentor, who was to inspire me with new love for my art and to purify it through the most painstaking course of instruction. This man was Theodor Weinlig, precentor at the Thomasschule in Leipzig. While I had already had a go at writing fugues, it was with him that I first began a proper study of counterpoint, which he had the happy knack of being able to turn into child's play for his pupils. It was at this time that I first acquired a true understanding and love of Mozart. I composed a sonata in which I freed myself of all excess and adopted a natural and unforced style of writing. This extremely simple and modest piece of work was printed and published by Breitkopf & Härtel [1832]. My studies with Weinlig were ended in less than six months: he himself dismissed me after he had brought me to the point where I was capable of resolving with ease the most difficult problems of counterpoint. 'What you have acquired from this dry study,' he said to me, 'is called independence.' In the same half-year I also composed an overture in the style, now somewhat better understood by me, of Beethoven; this was played to encouraging applause at one of the Leipzig Gewandhaus concerts. After several other efforts I finally had a go at writing a symphony: my principal model, Beethoven, was joined by Mozart, especially his great C-major symphony. Clarity and power, with some strange aberrations, were my aim. With the finished symphony I set off in the summer of 1832 on a journey to Vienna, for no other purpose than to make a fleeting acquaintance with that city of such musical renown. What I heard and saw there did not impress me much: wherever I went all I heard was [Hérold's] *Zampa* and Strauss's potpourris on *Zampa*. Both – especially at that time – anathema to me. On my way back I spent some time in Prague and there made the acquaintance of Dionys Weber and Tomaschek.★ The former had several of my works, including the symphony, performed in the Conservatoire. While there I also wrote a tragic opera text: *Die Hochzeit* ['The Wedding']. I cannot remember now where I got the medieval subject from: a frenzied lover climbs to the bedroom window of his friend's bride, where she is waiting for her bridegroom; the bride struggles with the madman and finally hurls him into the courtyard below, where he breaks his

★ Christian Gottlieb Müller

★ Dionys Weber (1766–1842), and Wenzel Johann Tomaschek (1774–1850), composers

neck and dies. At his funeral the bride with a cry sinks lifeless upon his corpse. When I got back to Leipzig I immediately composed the first number of this opera, which included a grand sextet that pleased Weinlig very much. But my sister disapproved of the libretto; I destroyed it without trace. In January 1833 my symphony was performed at a Gewandhaus concert and was received with very encouraging applause. It was at that time that I got to know Laube.

I travelled to Würzburg to visit one of my brothers,* and I stayed there for the whole of 1833; my brother was important to me as an experienced singer. It was here that I composed a three-act romantic opera, *Die Feen* ['The Fairies'], the libretto of which I wrote myself after Gozzi's *La Donna serpente*. Beethoven and Weber were my models: there was much successful stuff in the ensembles, and especially the finale of the second act promised to be very effective. But the individual solos lacked that independent free melodic line, which alone enables the singer to come across; instead the composer robs him of all spontaneous effectiveness by petty detailed declamation. Drawback with most Germans who write operas. Selected excerpts from this opera were performed with success at Würzburg concerts. With high hopes for my completed work, I went back to Leipzig at the beginning of 1834 and offered it to the director of the theatre there for performance. Despite his initially declared willingness to fulfil my wishes, I very soon encountered the same difficulty which nowadays every German opera composer must come to terms with: thanks to the success of the French and the Italians we are looked down upon on our own stages, and the performance of our operas is a favour we must beg for. The production of my *Feen* was postponed. In the meantime I heard Devrient** in Bellini's *Montecchi e Capuletti* – I was astonished to see such an extraordinary accomplishment with such utterly insignificant music. I began to have doubts about the choice of means that would lead to great success; I was far from according any merit to Bellini, but nonetheless, the material of which his music was made up seemed to me more felicitous and more likely to radiate warmth than the anxious and meticulous conscientiousness thanks to which we Germans can mostly create no more than a tortured pseudo-truth. The sloppy characterlessness of our Italians of today, along with the frivolous levity of the latest French composers seemed to me a challenge to the serious and conscientious German to acquire for himself the better chosen and better developed musical material of his rivals, in order to prove himself decisively better than them in creating true works of art.

I was then twenty-one, inclined to enjoy life and with a happy view of the world; [Wilhelm Heinse's] *Ardinghello* and [Heinrich Laube's] *Das junge Europa* filled my veins: Germany seemed to me only a very tiny part of the world. I had emerged from my period of abstract mysticism and I came to love material things. Beautiful materials, wit and spirit were wonderful things to me: as far as music was concerned I found both amongst the French and the Italians. I abandoned my idol, Beethoven; his last symphony seemed to me the summit of a great era of art,

beyond which no one could progress and within whose shadow none could achieve independence. I felt Mendelssohn had sensed this too when he came out with his smaller-scale orchestral compositions, leaving the great consummate form of the Beethoven symphony untouched. It seemed to me that he wanted to begin with a smaller, quite independent form and then create his own larger structures. Everything around me seemed to be in ferment, and the most natural thing to do seemed to be to join the ferment. On a beautiful summer journey to the spas of Bohemia I conceived the plan of a new opera: *Das Liebesverbot* ['Forbidden Love']. I took the material from Shakespeare's *Measure for Measure*, but with the difference that I eliminated its serious elements and thus modelled it in the true spirit of the Young Europe: free and open sensuality overcame puritanical hypocrisy simply by being itself. In the summer of the same year, 1834, I accepted the post of musical director of the Magdeburg Theatre. The practical application of my musical knowledge to the job of conducting soon worked out: the peculiarities of dealing with singers behind the scenes and before the footlights fitted in well with my inclination for merriment and diversion. The composition of my *Liebesverbot* was begun. At a concert I performed the overture to my *Feen*; it was very well received. Still I began to become dissatisfied with this opera and since I could not in any case pursue the matter in Leipzig personally, I soon decided not to bother about it any more – which is as good as saying I gave it up. For a festival on New Year's Day 1835 I composed a piece in no time, and it was quite well received. Such easy successes considerably strengthened my view that to succeed one must not be too scrupulous in one's choice of means. In this spirit I carried on with work on my *Liebesverbot*, taking not the slightest trouble to avoid French or Italian influences. I was interrupted for a while but resumed the composition in the winter of 1835/36 and finished it shortly before the dispersal of the opera company of the Magdeburg Theatre. I had only twelve days before the departure of the principal singers; so if I wanted them to perform it they had to prepare for it in this time. With more recklessness than good sense, I had the opera – which had some very big parts – on the stage after ten days of rehearsal; I was relying on the prompter and my own baton. But I could not help the fact that the singers scarcely knew half their parts by heart. The performance was like a dream to all concerned, no one had a clue what it was all about; still, the parts that went more or less right were suitably applauded. For a variety of reasons there was no second performance. Meanwhile, I had encountered the serious side of life. My speedily acquired outward independence had led me into all sorts of foolish enterprises, and debts and pecuniary embarrassment threatened me from all sides. I decided I had to risk something extraordinary to avoid getting into the common rut of poverty. With no prospects whatever, I went to Berlin and offered my *Liebesverbot* to the director of the Königstädter Theatre. I was at first received with the best promises, but after long delays I came to realize that none of them was honestly meant. I left Berlin in the most serious situation to apply for the post of musical director of the theatre at Königsberg in Prussia, which I later duly received. I was married there in the autumn of 1836, although at the time I was in the most difficult financial circumstances. The year I spent in Königsberg was completely lost to my art, owing to the most petty material cares. All I wrote was a single overture: *Rule Britannia*.

In the summer of 1837 I visited Dresden for a while. Reading Bulwer [-Lytton]'s novel *Rienzi* there revived a favourite idea I had had for some time, that of making the last Roman Tribune the hero of a tragic grand opera. But I was so beset with financial problems that I was not able to work on the project. That autumn I went to Riga to become the first musical director of the new theatre there which had just been opened under Holtei.* There I found outstanding forces assembled for opera and I set to work employing them with great gusto. I composed several arias for individual singers at that time for insertion into other operas. I also prepared the text for a two-act comic opera, *Die glückliche Bärenfamilie*, the idea for which I took from one of the stories from the Arabian Nights. I had already composed two numbers for it when I realized with horror that I was once again on the way to composing music à la Auber; my spirit and my deeper feelings were desperately hurt by this discovery. I abandoned the work in disgust. My daily study and conducting of the music of Auber, Adam and Bellini then finally made their own contribution to making me heartily sick of my frivolous enjoyment of it.

Since the theatre audiences of our provincial cities are utterly unqualified to pass a first judgment on a new work of art – they are only used after all to performances of works which have already been judged and approved elsewhere – I was determined not to permit a première of a major work of mine in a small theatre at any price. So when I once again felt the urge to undertake a major work, I resigned myself completely to the idea of not getting it performed locally or quickly; I took it for granted that some great theatre would perform it one day and for the time being did not bother myself with the where and the when. And so when I wrote the scenario for a grand tragic opera in five acts, *Rienzi, der Letzte der Tribunen* ['Rienzi, the Last of the Tribunes']; from the very beginning I planned it on such a grand scale that it would be impossible to perform it in a small theatre – at least for its première. Apart from that, the powerful story itself did not admit of any other treatment, so the latter was more a question of necessity than of design. In the summer of 1838 I wrote the full libretto. At this time I was preparing with great delight and enthusiasm a production of Méhul's** *Jacob and his Sons* with our opera company. When I began the composition of *Rienzi* in the autumn I had at the time no preconceived notions, but was determined to let the subject dictate the composition. I had no model in mind, I abandoned myself completely to the feeling which consumed me, the feeling that I had now reached the point where I could demand something significant from the development of my artistic powers and expect to get a not insignificant result. The thought of being consciously shallow or trivial, even for a single bar, horrified me. I continued the composition in the winter, full of enthusiasm, so that by the spring of 1839 the first two big acts were

finished. At this time my contract with the theatre director expired and I had various reasons for not wanting to stay in Riga any longer. In fact, for two years I had been planning to go to Paris. With this in mind, I had already sent Scribe* from Königsberg a sketch of an idea for an opera libretto, with the suggestion that if it appealed to him he should write the full libretto for his own account and then in return obtain a commission for me to compose the work for Paris. Of course, Scribe had as good as disregarded this. Nevertheless I did not give up my plans, indeed in the summer of 1839 I tackled the project with gusto and it was not long before my wife and I were aboard ship and sailing for London. This sea journey will remain eternally engraved on my memory; it lasted three and a half weeks and was beset by accidents. Three times we were caught in the most violent storms and once the captain was forced to take shelter in a Norwegian harbour. Sailing between the Norwegian reefs made a striking impression on my imagination; the legend of the Flying Dutchman, as recounted to me by the sailors, took on a very definite and individual colouring in my mind such as only my adventures at sea could inspire. We spent eight days in London recovering from this extraordinarily harrowing journey. Nothing interested me as much as the city itself and the Houses of Parliament. I did not visit any of the theatres. I stayed four weeks in Boulogne-sur-Mer; there I first made the acquaintance of Meyerbeer, to whom I showed the two completed acts of my *Rienzi*; he promised me most cordially his support in Paris. With very little money, but with the highest of hopes, I now reached Paris. Since I had no recommendations whatsoever I was completely dependent on Meyerbeer; he was most extraordinarily considerate in setting everything in motion that could possibly serve my purpose, and I am sure I should soon have achieved my goal had it not been my misfortune that throughout my stay in Paris Meyerbeer was away most of the time. He did in fact try to assist me from a distance, but he had himself warned me that efforts by letter were unlikely to bear fruit where constant personal intervention alone had any chance of success. At first I approached the Théâtre de la Renaissance, which at that time performed both plays and operas. For this theatre I felt my most suitable score was *Das Liebesverbot*; moreover the somewhat frivolous story would have been easy to adapt for the French stage. I had been recommended so strongly to the director of the theatre by Meyerbeer that he had no option but to make me the best promises. As a result one of the most prolific Parisian stage-writers, Dumersan, offered to take on the translation of the libretto. Three numbers, which were chosen for audition, Dumersan translated so aptly that my music fitted the new text even better than the original German – it was just the sort of music the French most readily comprehend, and everything was set for a great success when, suddenly, the Théâtre de la Renaissance went bankrupt. Thus, all my efforts and all my hopes had been in vain. During that same winter period (1839–40), apart from an overture to Goethe's *Faust*, Part I, I composed several French songs, among others a French translation

43-49
34
36

---

* Karl von Holtei (1798–1880), actor, playwright and author
** Etienne Nicolas Méhul (1763–1817)

* Eugène Scribe (1791–1861), dramatist and librettist

that was done for me of H. Heine's 'The Two Grenadiers'. I never considered the idea of putting on *Rienzi* in Paris because I foresaw that I should certainly have had to wait at least five or six years before such a project could be realized, even under the most propitious circumstances. In any case the translation of the text of the already half-completed opera would have presented unsurmountable difficulties. So I began the summer of 1840 with no immediate prospects whatever. My acquaintance with Habeneck,* Halévy, Berlioz, etc. led to no closer friendships: in Paris no artist has time to make friends with another, everyone is always in a mad rush on his own behalf. Halévy, like all Parisian opera composers of our time, was inspired with enthusiasm for his art only so long as he was struggling to achieve a major success. As soon as this was his and he entered the ranks of the privileged musical lions, the only thing that interested him was turning out operas and taking in the money. Fame is everything in Paris, the joy of composers and their

downfall. Berlioz, despite his repugnant nature, attracted me far more: he is as unlike his Parisian colleagues as chalk is to cheese, for he does not compose for the money. But he too cannot write for pure art's sake, he lacks any sense of beauty and with few exceptions his music is a grimace. In his style he is completely isolated: beside him he has only a crowd of admirers who, devoid of any sense of judgment, shallowly proclaim him the creator of a brand new musical system and quite turn his head as a result; everyone else avoids him as though he were a lunatic. The final blow to my earlier facile views on musical means was dealt by – the Italians. These most highly vaunted heroes of song, Rubini** at their head, made me feel completely disgusted with their music. The public they sing to made its own contribution to my reaction. The great Paris opera was a complete disappointment, with not a drop of genius in any of its performances: everything very ordinary and mediocre. The *mise en scène* and the décor are, frankly, the best part of the whole Académie Royale de Musique. The Opéra Comique was much better placed to satisfy me: it has the best talents and the performances there have an individuality and a sense of unity which is unknown to us in Germany. But what is written for this theatre at the moment is amongst the worst that has ever been produced in times of artistic decay. What has become of the charm of Méhul, Isouard, Boïeldieu*** and the young Auber in the face of the abject quadrille rhythms which are the only sound to be heard clattering through this theatre today? The sole things of consequence that Paris offers the musician today are the orchestral concerts in the concert-

hall of the Conservatoire. The performances of German orchestral music at these concerts made a deep impression on me and reintroduced me to the wonderful mysteries of true art. Anyone who really wants to get to know Beethoven's Ninth Symphony properly must hear it performed by the Conservatoire Orchestra in Paris. But these concerts are like an oasis; all the rest is desert.

I had very little contact with musicians; I spent my time with intellectuals, painters and so on, and I had many pleasant friendships in Paris. Being so completely without immediate prospects in Paris, I once again took up the composition of my *Rienzi*. I now had Dresden in mind for it, firstly because I knew the best forces were available at this theatre, including Devrient, Tichatschek* etc., and secondly because I had reason to hope that my connections from my earliest time there would help me gain an entrée quickly. My *Liebesverbot* I now more or less gave up completely. I felt I could no longer regard myself as the composer of this work. But I was able to follow my true artistic conviction all the more freely as I continued the composition of my *Rienzi*. Manifold anxieties and dire need beset my life at this period. Suddenly Meyerbeer reappeared in Paris for a short while. He asked, with the most sympathetic concern, about the state of my affairs and helped me where he could. He now put me in touch with the director of the Grand Opera, Léon Pillet: the objective being a two- or three-act opera, which this theatre was to commission from me. With such an opportunity in mind I had already equipped myself with a draft scenario. The Flying Dutchman, whose intimate acquaintance I had made at sea, occupied my imagination constantly. In addition I came across H. Heine's remarkable version of this legend in one part of his *Salon*. In particular the truly dramatic treatment of the redemption of this Ahasuerus of the oceans, which Heine invented, gave me all I needed to adapt the legend into an operatic story. I came to an arrangement with Heine himself, wrote the sketch and handed it to M. Léon Pillet with the suggestion that he should have a French libretto written for me. So everything was in hand when Meyerbeer left Paris again, leaving the fulfilment of my wishes in the hands of Fate. I was soon astonished to hear from Pillet that he liked my scenario so much that he wanted me to sell it to him. Apparently he was obliged by an earlier promise to provide another composer with a libretto as soon as possible: the sketch I had prepared struck him as eminently suitable and I would probably have no hesitation in agreeing to give the work up when I considered that I could not possibly hope to receive a direct commission to compose an opera for at least four years, since he had to satisfy several other applicants to the Grand Opera first; clearly I would not want to be working on this story all that length of time – I would find another subject by then and would surely be able to console myself for my sacrifice. I resisted this outrageous proposal stubbornly but was unable to achieve more than a postponement of the question. I counted on Meyerbeer's coming back soon and kept quiet. During this period I was invited by Schlesinger** to write for his *Gazette Musicale*. I supplied several detailed articles: 'On German music', 'Virtuosity and free composition', etc. A little short story I wrote, 'A Pilgrimage to Beethoven', was particularly well received. These works contributed quite a lot to making my name better known and respected in Paris. In the November [1840] I had completely finished the score of my *Rienzi* and sent it post-haste to Dresden. This period saw the culmination of my extremely unfortunate situation. I wrote a short

* François Antoine Habeneck (1781–1849), conductor of the Conservatoire orchestra
** Giovanni Battista Rubini (1794–1854), known as the 'king of tenors' (*il re dei tenori*)
*** Niccoló Isouard (1775–1818) and François-Adrien Boïeldieu (1775–1834)

* Joseph Tichatschek (1807–86), tenor
** Maurice Schlesinger (1798–1871), music publisher

story for the *Gazette Musicale*: 'The end of a German musician in Paris', in which I let the unfortunate hero die with the following declaration of faith: 'I believe in God, Mozart and Beethoven.' It was a good thing my opera was now completed, for I now found myself obliged to drop all artistic work for an indefinite period. I had to undertake musical arrangements for Schlesinger for every instrument under the sun, even for the *cornet à pistons*, as the only means of slightly alleviating my financial straits. I thus spent the winter of 1840/41 in the most inglorious way possible. In the spring I moved out to the country, to Meudon. As the warmth of summer approached I began to long for work to occupy my mind again: and an opportunity was to present itself more quickly than I expected. For I learned that my sketch of *The Flying Dutchman* text had already been passed on to a poet, Paul Fouché, and I saw that if I did not agree to sell the sketch I should soon simply lose it entirely on some pretext or other. So at last I gave my consent and accepted a certain sum for the scenario. I now had no more urgent task than to translate the story into German verse myself. In order to compose it I needed a piano, for after a nine-month interruption of all musical output I had first to try to get myself back into a musical frame of mind: so I hired a piano. When it arrived I ran around in a terrible fright – I was afraid I should now discover that I was no longer a musician at all. I began first

with the sailors' chorus and the spinning song: everything went like a charm and I jumped for joy at the inner realization that I was still a composer. In seven weeks the whole opera was composed. But at the end of this time I was overwhelmed by the meanest of material cares, and it was two full months before I could write down the overture to the completed opera even though I was carrying it around in my head almost complete. Naturally my first concern now was to get the opera performed quickly in Germany. From Munich and Leipzig I received rejections: the opera was not suitable for Germany, they said. I had been fool enough to think it was suitable only for Germany, since it strikes chords which will resound only in a German heart. In the end I sent my new work to Meyerbeer in Berlin, begging him to obtain its acceptance at the Court Theatre there. This he did, quite quickly. Since my *Rienzi* had already been accepted for the Dresden Court Theatre, I could now look forward to performances of two of my works at leading German theatres and I could not help thinking that in some strange way Paris had been of the greatest use to me for Germany. For Paris itself I now had no prospects for some years: and so I left in the spring of 1842; for the first time in my life I saw the Rhine, – and with tears in my eyes I, a poor artist, swore eternal faith to my German fatherland.

Zeitung für die elegante Welt, Leipzig, 1/8 February 1843

1 Brühl in Leipzig, watercolour, 1840; on the left is the house 'Zum Roten und Weissen Löwen' (the 'Red and White Lion'), in which Wagner was born on 22 May 1813.

Wagner's father was a lawyer and police registrar; Friedrich Wagner (1770–1813) had artistic leanings and a great love of the theatre; many artists would come to visit his house. He died on 23 November 1813 from typhoid fever, in the epidemic which broke out in Leipzig; no portrait of Friedrich Wagner is known.

2 Johanna Rosine Wagner (1774–1848), *née* Pätz, mother of the composer; portrait in oils by Ludwig Geyer, 1813.

Wagner was the youngest of the nine children of the marriage, and after his father's death his mother married the actor and painter Ludwig Geyer, a long-standing friend of the family. Friedrich Wagner had supported Geyer financially as an artist and helped him in many ways to develop his acting skills.

3 Ludwig Geyer (1779–1821), self-portrait in oils, *c.* 1806.

It has frequently been claimed that Geyer was the natural father of Richard Wagner, but no evidence exists to prove this.

4 The Battle of the Nations, Leipzig: battlefield north of Gohlis; coloured drawing by Strassberger, 1813.

In this battle, from 16 to 19 October, Napoleon was defeated by the German Confederation.

5 The Nikolaischule (St Nicholas' School) in Leipzig; coloured lithograph, c. 1840.

Wagner attended this school from 1828 to 1830, having previously (1822–27) been a pupil at the Kreuzschule in Dresden. At this time he completed the tragedy 'Leubald und Adelaïde', begun in Dresden, which was notable for the large number of characters who are killed and who return as spirits in the final act. Taking Beethoven's *Egmont* as his model, Wagner studied Johann Bernhard Logier's *Methode des Generalbasses*, borrowed for a week, in order to help him write incidental music for his play.

6 St Thomas' Churchyard, Leipzig; coloured lithograph.

In the Thomaskirche (St Thomas' Church; right), Wagner was baptized Wilhelm Richard on 16 August 1813. He attended St Thomas' School (centre) from 1830 to 1831; to the left of the school is the so-called Schneiderherberge (Tailor's Inn) in which the 'Euterpe' music society, led by Christian Gottlieb Müller, played Wagner's Symphony in C major on 15 December 1832.

7 Christian Gottlieb Müller (1800–63), who was Wagner's first composition teacher, from 1828 to 1831; photograph.

At first, Wagner's family was unaware of the lessons that Müller, a member of the Leipzig Gewandhaus orchestra, was giving him.

8 Christian Theodor Weinlig (1780–1842); photograph of a lost oil painting.

Weinlig, who was Precentor of the Thomaskirche, gave Wagner a thorough musical grounding in 1831–32. Cf. p. 152.

9, 10 Carl Maria von Weber's 'Freischütz' ('Marksman'); copper engravings in the *Orphea-Taschenbuch*, Leipzig 1824.

11 Opening of the score of Weber's overture to *Der Freischütz*, in a piano version by the composer.

Der Freischütz, first performed in Berlin in 1821, and soon after (1822) in Dresden, was one of the most profound influences of Wagner's youth. Cf. p. 151.

12, 13 Heinrich Marschner's 'Vampire'; copper engravings in the *Orphea-Taschenbuch*, Leipzig 1831.

The first performance of *Der Vampyr* ('The Vampire') was given in Leipzig on 29 March 1828; Marschner's opera *Der Templer und die Jüdin*, first performed in Leipzig in 1829, was another important experience of Wagner's youth, as was Wilhelmine Schröder-Devrient's intepretation of Leonora in Beethoven's *Fidelio*, Leipzig, April 1829.

14 Wagner's score of the Allegro for Aubry's aria in *Der Vampyr*, composed for his brother Albert, Würzburg 1833.

15 Opening of Wagner's piano transcription of the last movement of Beethoven's Ninth Symphony.

This is one of the first documents that reveal the inspiration which Wagner derived from Beethoven's music; this continued unabated throughout his life. Cf. p. 152.

16 Adolf Wagner (1774–1835), the composer's uncle; drawing, 1832.

The philologist and writer had a considerable influence on Richard Wagner; several of his essays, e.g. 'The Theatre and the Public', are pointers to the later writings of Wagner's Bayreuth period. Cf. p. 149.

17 Riots in Leipzig, September 1830, by G. E. Opiz; water-colour.

Wagner took part in the riots, and wrote in his autobiography *Mein Leben*: 'The historical world began for me from this day; and naturally I was wholeheartedly for the revolution.'

18 Wagner's Sonata for Piano in B major, 1831; this was the first of Wagner's compositions to appear in print (1832).

Written during Wagner's period of instruction from Theodor Weinlig, the work was dedicated to him, and was published at his instigation.

19 The arrival of fleeing Poles in Leipzig, 1831; woodcut. Cf. p. 153.

Wagner's concern over the fate of the Poles under Russian domination was reflected in his overture *Polonia*, written only in 1836. Cf. ill. 29.

20, 21 *Die Feen* ('The Fairies'), title page of the composition sketch and page 45 with the note (right), 'Today, 22 May 1833, I became 20 years of age'.

This 'grand romantic opera' is in the tradition of Beethoven, Weber and Marschner. The libretto derives from Carlo Gozzi's play *La Donna serpente*. Wagner's attempt to have the work put on in Leipzig was unsuccessful, and it was first performed – after the composer's death – at Munich in 1888.

22

23

22, 23 Wilhelmine Schröder-Devrient as Romeo in Bellini's opera *I Capuletti ed i Montecchi*, which was based on Shakespeare's *Romeo and Juliet*; drawings by Carl Heidelhof, Nuremberg 1835.

Wagner had earlier seen the singer in this role in Leipzig, 1834. Cf. p. 13.

24 The actress Minna Planer (1809–66), whom Wagner married on 24 November 1836 at Königsberg, having first met her in 1834 at Lauchstädt; photograph from a painting by Otterstedt, 1835.

24

25 Richard Wagner, silhouette by an unknown artist, Magdeburg 1835.

Wagner was engaged as director of music at the Magdeburg Theatre from October 1834 to April 1836.

26

27

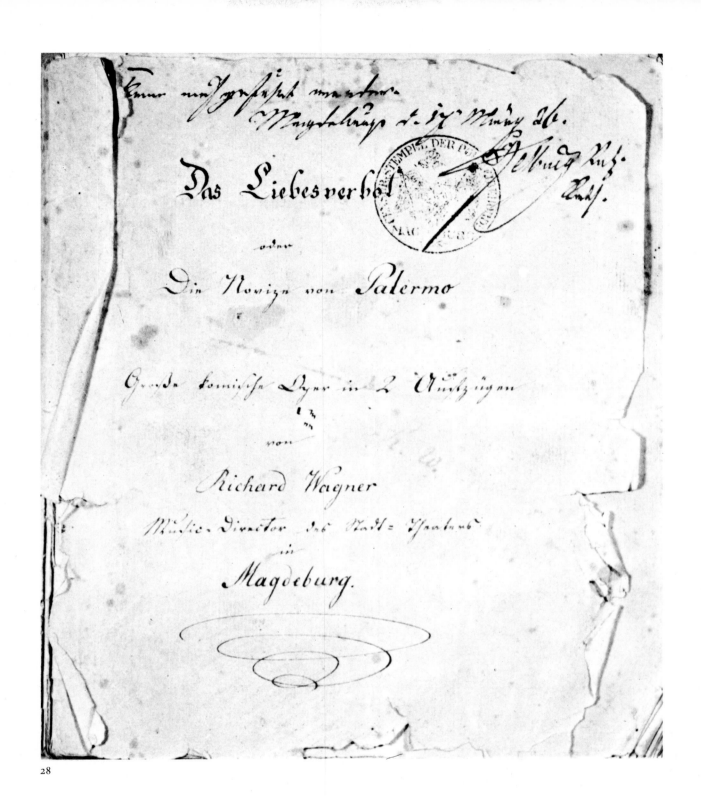

26 Lauchstädt, interior of the theatre; photograph.

Wagner's first operatic production – Mozart's *Don Giovanni* – was given here; the design of this theatre shows several similarities with the later Festival Theatre at Bayreuth.

27 Concert hall in Magdeburg; woodcut.

28 *Das Liebesverbot* ('Forbidden Love'), title page of the text endorsed by the censor's office in Magdeburg, 17 March 1836.

Wagner based his libretto on Shakespeare's *Measure for Measure*, and was influenced by the ideas of the 'Young German' movement. His models for the score included Adolphe Adam, Auber and, in particular, Bellini. The 'grand comic opera' was first performed, under Wagner's own direction, on 29 March 1836 in Magdeburg. A second performance had to be abandoned on account of a row between members of the cast. Wagner tried, unsuccessfully, to have the work staged in Paris in 1840.

29 Page 49 of the score of Wagner's overture *Polonia*, Berlin 1836. Cf. illus. 19 and p. 153.

30 The theatre at Königsberg, where Wagner spent a few weeks in 1837 as director of music.

30

31 Announcement of a concert given on 19 March 1838, at the Riga Theatre, where Wagner was director of music from August 1837 to March 1839; the programme included his own overtures *Columbus* and *Rule Britannia*. Cf. pp. 159–60.

32 Announcement of a performance at the Riga Theatre of P. A. Wolff's play *Preciosa, das Zigeuner-Mädchen* ('Preciosa, the Gipsy Girl'), in which Minna Wagner played the lead as a guest artist, 11 April 1839; for financial reasons, she was obliged to undertake further guest performances after Wagner lost his job there.

31

32

33 Concert hall of the Paris Conservatoire.

Performances by the orchestra of the Conservatoire under François Antoine Habeneck (1781–1849) renewed the inspiration which Wagner derived from Beethoven's music.

34 The composer Giacomo Meyerbeer (1791–1864); lithograph.

As a result of Meyerbeer's efforts on his behalf Wagner hoped to have his opera *Rienzi* performed in Paris, but the attempt failed. Meyerbeer was, however, instrumental in arranging the première in Dresden, 20 October 1842. Cf. p. 163.

35 *Rienzi*, list of characters in the French translation of the libretto.

(Salle des Concerts du Conservatoire.)

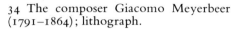

34   35

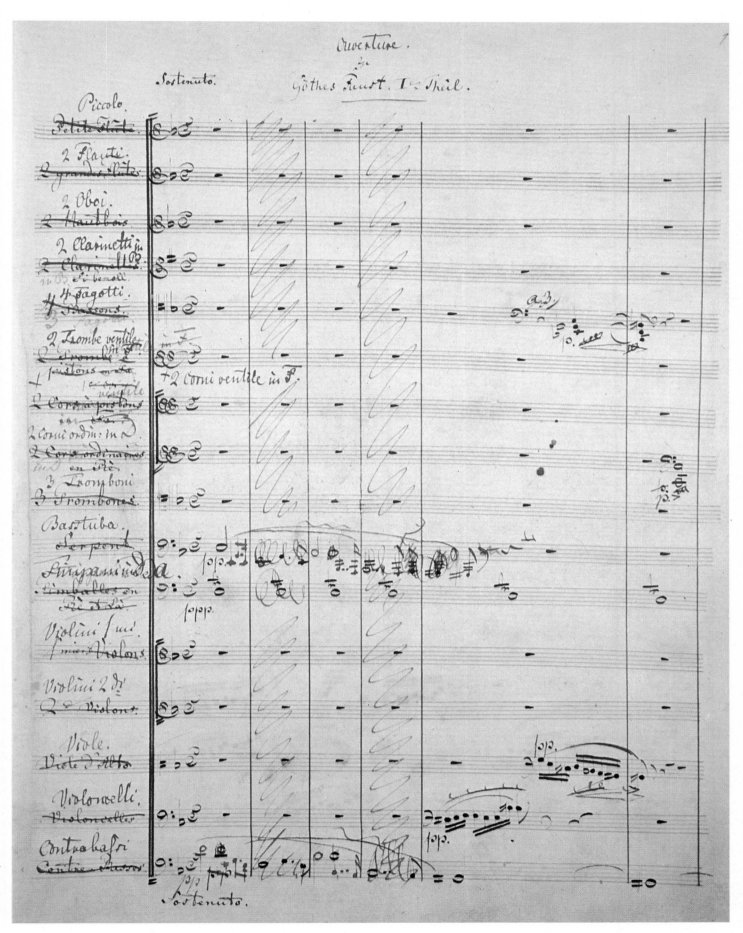

36 Wagner's Overture to Goethe's *Faust*, Part I, page 1 of the autograph score, Paris 1839–40.
The heading 'Overture', added later, is evidence of Wagner's own statement that he originally wanted to write a 'Faust Symphony' (of which this would have been the first movement). Wagner planned changes to the score while still in Paris; he revised the work in 1855, after which it was published under the title *A Faust Overture*.

Introduction.

37 *Rienzi, der Letzte der Tribunen* ('Rienzi, the last of the Tribunes'), page 1 of an outline for the Introduction to Act I, Riga, 7 August 1838. The date (top right) – '26 July' – refers to the Russian calendar.

38 The poet Heinrich Heine (1797–1856), whom Wagner first met in Paris in 1840 at the home of the writer Heinrich Laube – his friend since 1833; drawing by J. Diez, 1842.

39 Title page of Wagner's setting of Heine's poem 'The Two Grenadiers', reprint of the first publication (of which no copy is known to survive) by B. Schott's Söhne, Mainz; the drawing is by Ernst Benedikt Kietz.

38

à Mr Henri Heine

LES DEUX GRENADIERS

(Die beiden Grenadiere)

Mélodie de

RICHARD WAGNER

L'Aurore Nº 22.

Collection de morceaux de chant moderne avec acc. de Piano.

Nº 6231.   Pr. M 1.25

Propriété pour tous pays

MAYENCE CHEZ LES FILS DE B. SCHOTT

Bruxelles Schott frères   Paris Maison Schott   Londres Schott & Cie

Dépôt général de notre fonds de Musique

LEIPZIG. C. F. LEEDE.

Enregistré aux Archives de l'Union

au Ministère de l'Intérieur de France et à Stationers Hall

39

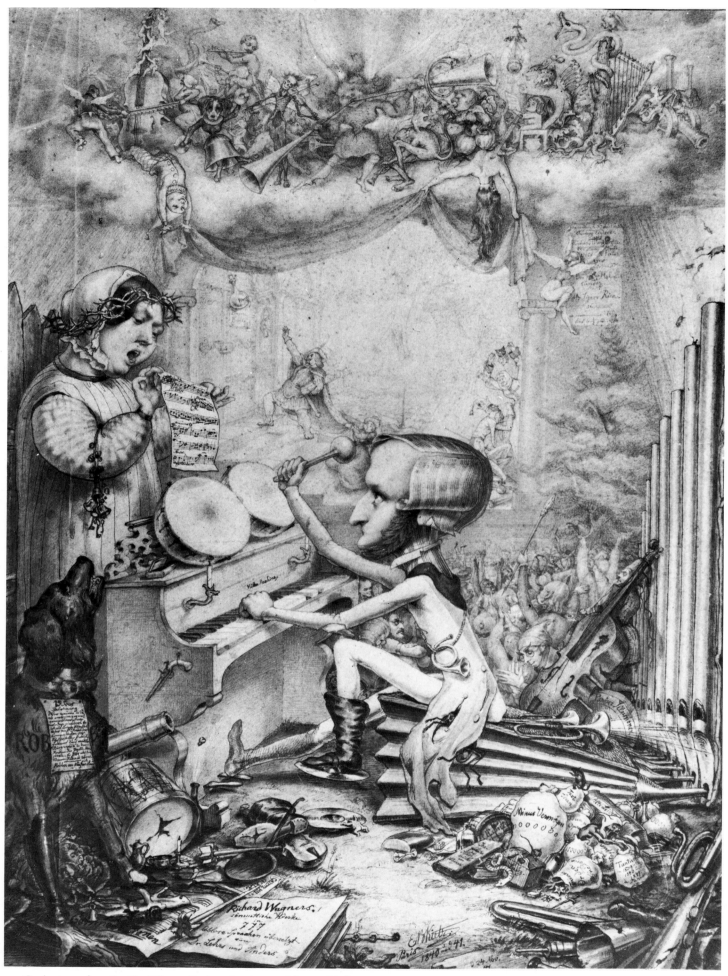

40 Caricature by E. B. Kietz, Paris 1840/41, with multiple
allusions to the life and work of Wagner.

41 The Court Theatre, Dresden, built by Gottfried Semper; hand-coloured lithograph, *c.* 1841.

In this theatre Wagner's operas *Rienzi*, *Der fliegende Holländer* ('The Flying Dutchman') and *Tannhäuser* received their first performances. Wagner was Kapellmeister to the Royal Saxon Court in Dresden from 2 February 1843 until his flight from that city in May 1849.

42 Interior of the Court Theatre, Dresden; coloured lithograph.

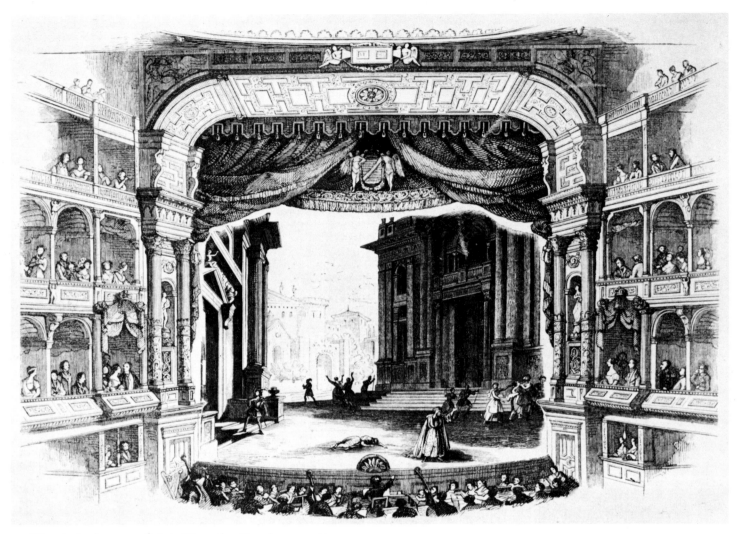

43 *Rienzi*, final scene of Act IV at the Dresden première, 20
October 1842 (*Illustrirte Zeitung*, Leipzig, 12 August 1843).
Cf. p. 163–5.

The conductor at the première was Wagner's predecessor as
Kapellmeister to the Royal Saxon Court, Carl Gottlieb Reissiger.
Although the 'grand tragic opera in five acts' proved too long and
had to be extensively revised and cut subsequently, the première
itself was a great success, bringing Wagner fame almost overnight.

44

46

44–48 *Rienzi*, characters and cast at the première: (44) Cola Rienzi – Herr Tichatschek; (45) Irene – Fräulein Wüst; (46) Adriano – Madame Schröder-Devrient; (47) Orsini – Herr Wächter; (48) Colonna – Herr Dettmer (*Illustrirte Zeitung*, Leipzig, 12 August 1843).

45

47

48

49 *Rienzi*, finale of Act II; watercolour by Baron von Leyser.

This rendering shows a later performance (1843), in which the part of Adriano was sung by Henriette Kriete, with Joseph Tichatschek as Rienzi.

50 *Der fliegende Holländer*, page 120 of the autograph score (Senta's ballad in Act II, the central point of the action), written at Meudon, near Paris, in 1841.

1ste Vorstellung im vierten Abonnement.

Königlich Sächsisches Hoftheater.

Montag, den 2. Januar 1843.

Zum ersten Male:

Der fliegende Holländer.

Romantische Oper in drei Akten, von Richard Wagner.

Personen:

Daland, norwegischer Seefahrer. — — — Herr Risse.
Senta, seine Tochter. — — — Mad. Schröder-Devrient.
Erik, ein Jäger. — — — Herr Reinhold.
Mary, Haushälterin Dalands. — — — Mad. Wächter.
Der Steuermann Dalands. — — — Herr Bielezizky.
Der Holländer. — — — Herr Wächter.

Matrosen des Norwegers. Die Mannschaft des fliegenden Holländers. Mädchen.

Scene: Die norwegische Küste.

Textbücher sind an der Casse das Exemplar für 2½ Neugroschen zu haben.

Krank: Herr Dettmer.

Einlaß-Preise:

Ein Billet in die Logen d. 3 ersten Ranges und das Amphitheater . . . 1 Thlr. — Ngr.
"   "   Fremdenlogen des zweiten Ranges Nr. 1. 14. und 29. 1 " — "
"   "   übrigen Logen des zweiten Ranges . . . — " 20 "
"   "   Sperr-Sitze der Mittel- u. Seiten-Gallerie des dritten Ranges— " 12½ "
"   "   Mittel- und Seiten-Logen des dritten Ranges . . . — " 10 "
"   "   Sperr-Sitze der Gallerie des vierten Ranges . . . — " 8 "
"   "   Mittel-Gallerie des vierten Ranges . . . . . . — " 7½ "
"   "   Seiten-Gallerie-Logen daselbst . . . . — " 5 "
"   "   Sperr-Sitze im Cercle. . . . . — " 20 "
"   "   Parterre-Logen . . . . — " 15 "
"   " das Parterre . . . . — " 10 "

Die Billets sind nur am Tage der Vorstellung gültig, und zurückgebrachte Billets werden nur bis Mittag 12 Uhr an demselben Tage angenommen.

Der Verkauf der Billets gegen sofortige baare Bezahlung findet in der, in dem untern Theile des Rundbaues befindlichen Expedition, auf der rechten Seite, nach der Elbe zu, früh von 9 Uhr bis Mittags 12 Uhr, und Nachmittags von 3 bis 4 Uhr statt.

Alle zur heutigen Vorstellung bestellte und zugesagte Billets sind Vormittags von 9 Uhr bis längstens 11 Uhr abzuholen, außerdem darüber anders verfüget wird.

Der freie Einlaß beschränkt sich bei der heutigen Vorstellung blos auf die zum Hofstaate gehörigen Personen und die Mitglieder des Königl. Hoftheaters.

Einlaß um 5 Uhr.   Anfang um 6 Uhr.
Ende gegen 9 Uhr.

51

52

51–56 *Der fliegende Holländer*, première at Dresden, 2 January 1843.

51 Theatre poster.

52 Final scene as depicted in the *Illustrirte Zeitung*, Leipzig, 7 October 1843.

53 The Helmsman's Song (*Illustrirte Zeitung*, 15 July 1843).

54–56 Characters depicted in the *Illustrirte Zeitung*, 7 October 1843: (54) the Dutchman; (55) Erik; (56) Senta.

53   54

55   56

57

58

59

60

57–60 *Tannhäuser*, première at Dresden, 19 October 1845. Copies of designs by Flinzer: (57) Tannhäuser; (58) Elisabeth; (59) Landgrave; (60) Wolfram.

61

61, 62 *Tannhäuser*, première.

61 Sepia drawing made by F. Tischbein after the première, showing Wilhelmine Schröder-Devrient as Venus and Joseph Tichatschek as Tannhäuser.

62 Act II, scene 2, after a watercolour by Wilhelm Heine.

The 'grand romantic opera', originally entitled 'The Venusberg', became the most frequently played of Wagner's operas in the 1850s. In 1852 he wrote a treatise 'On the Performance of *Tannhäuser*. A Report for Conductors and Performers of this Opera', with powerful hints as to its interpretation.

62

63 *Tannhäuser*, page 1 of the prose sketch, entitled 'The Venus-berg', begun on the Schreckenstein near Aussig on 22 May 1842.

64 *Tannhäuser*, page 300 of the score 'printed on stone as written in the hand of the composer', Dresden 1845: Tannhäuser's 'Venuslied' from the Singing Tournament in Act II.

65–67 Parodies of *Tannhäuser*

65 Johann Nestroy (1801–62) as Landgrave Purzel in his farce *Tannhäuser*; pencil drawing by Theodor Rothang, 1858.

66 Title page of the parody by Carl Binders (1816–60), Vienna 1857.

67 Title and cast of the parody by Levitschnigg and Suppé, Vienna 1852.

Many parodies of Wagner's works appeared in the 1850s as a reaction against his growing fame – resulting from the success of his operas, his theoretical writings (1849–51) with considerable pretensions, and public support from friends and associates, e.g. Franz Liszt and his circle.

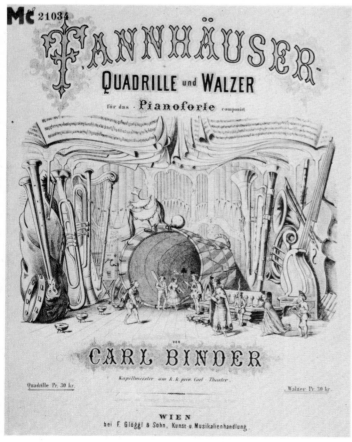

66

67

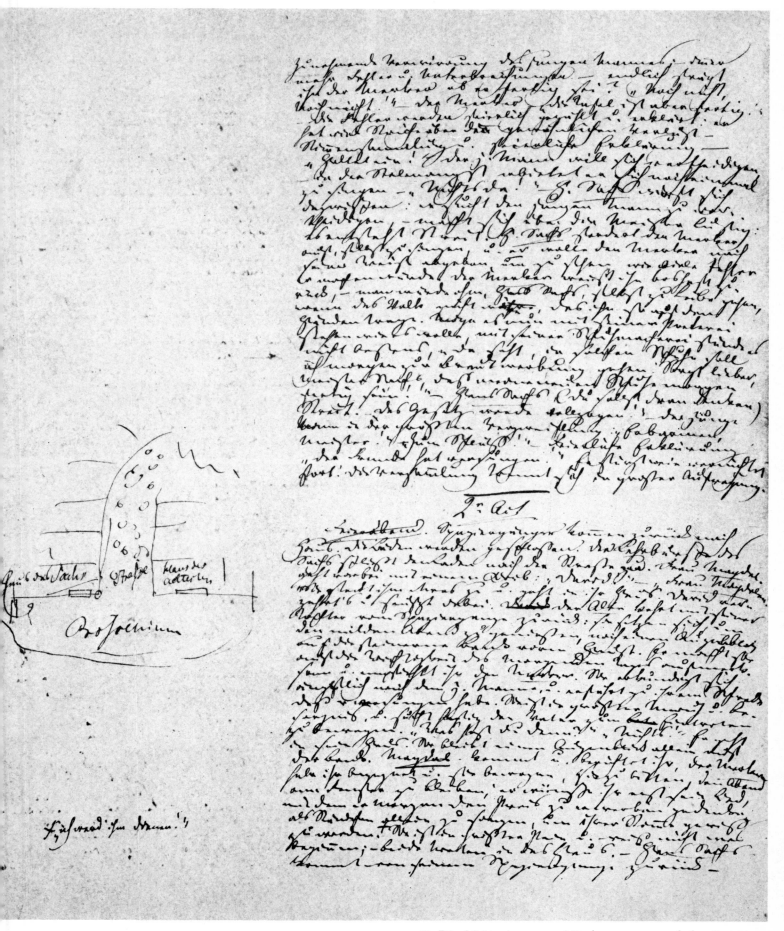

68 *Die Meistersinger von Nürnberg*, page 3 of the first prose sketch, with an outline of Act II, Marienbad, July 1845.

The sketch remained in this state until 1861, when Wagner resumed work on the composition.

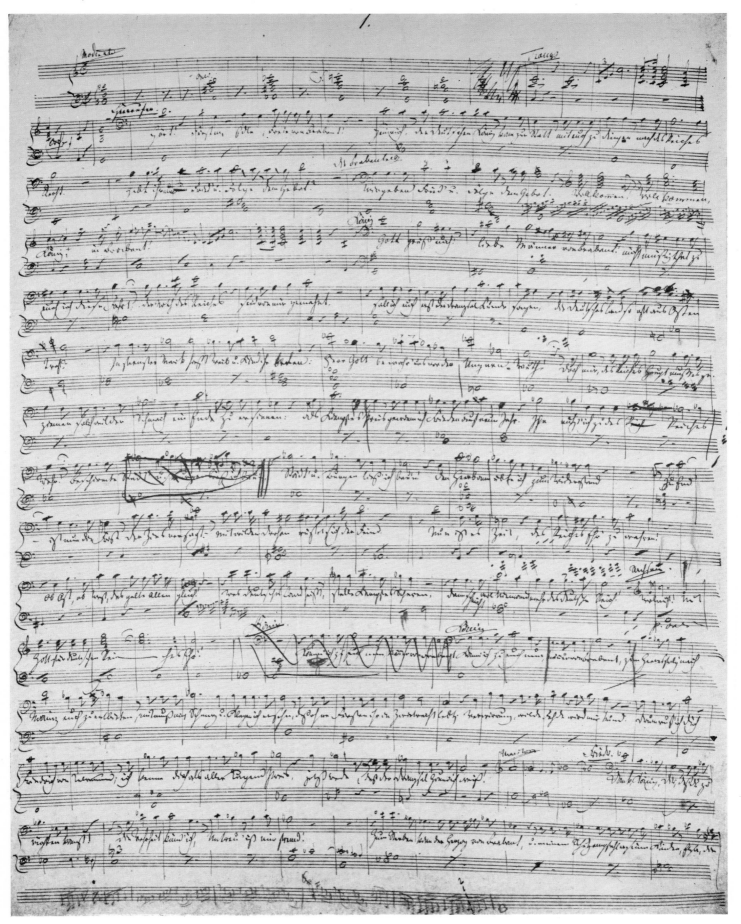

69 *Lohengrin*, composition sketch written for the opening of Act I, 1846.

Early on, Wagner developed an individual manner of composing, which remained virtually unchanged throughout his life. First, he set the words to music in the form of a comprehensive sketch confined to singing voice and bass line (composition sketch), then he worked over the whole again in full length (orchestral sketch), the final stage being the orchestration itself (autograph score).

70 *Lohengrin*, orchestral sketch for the opening of Act I, Dresden,
12 May 1847.

71 *Lohengrin*, autograph score of the opening of Act I, Dresden, 1
January 1848.

72 *Siegfrieds Tod* ('Siegfried's Death'), page 1 of the original poem, Dresden, 12 November 1848; after a photocopy.

From this drama Wagner developed his tetralogy, *Der Ring des Nibelungen* ('The Ring of the Nibelung'), *Siegfrieds Tod* being adapted to become *Götterdämmerung* ('Twilight of the Gods').

2

Act. I.

(: Tiberias in Galiläa. – ein überdeckter weiter raum – gleich einem grossen schuppen –, nach hinten ganz offen auf das freie ausgehend: zur seite führt es in das innere des wohn= hauses des zöllners Levi (Matthäus.). Nacht.:)

Judas Ischarioth und Barrabas kommen im gespräch. Barrabas beabsichtigt einen auf= stand in Judäa gegen das römische joch: die römische macht sei zu dieser zeit ausser= ordentlich schwach, der erfolg gewiß, wenn es gelänge das volk zu einer entscheidenden erhebung zu drängen: nun wäre in Jerusalem alles voll von dem sohne Davids der sich in Galiläa rundgezogen; man erwarte sich in ihm den Messias. Barrabas komme nun sich davon zu überzeugen, was von Jesus zu erwarten sei. Judas giebt auskunft von Jesus wirken und wandeln, von seiner heilkunst und von dem grossen anhange den er im volke gewonnen habe: er selbst nenne sich den erlöser, noch habe er (Judas) aber noch nicht klarheit darüber erlangen können, wie Jesus seinen beruf zu erfüllen ge= denke: herzlich wünsche auch er, daß Jesus die zügel des volkes ergreifen möge, um als könig der Juden frei und offen die errettung des auserwählten volkes zu bewirken. – Der zöllner Levi, da er vernommen daß Jesus in der nähe von Tiberias sich aufhalte, habe nach ihm gesandt, um sein dem tode nahes töchterchen zu retten; Judas sei ihm dem nahenden vorausgesandt um seine ankunft zu melden. – Judas pocht an der thür, – der zöllner tritt jammernd heraus:, sein kind sei soeben verschieden. – Laute klage er= hebt sich im hause: frauen bringen auf einer baare das 12 jährige mädchen heraus, nachbarn stellen sich ein. Mit anbrechendem tage erscheint Jesus mit den jüngern und tritt dem trauerzuge entgegen: man ruft ihm zu:, meister, du kommst zu spät, das kind begraben wir jetzt. Jesus betrachtet das kind genau:, begrabt die todten doch nicht die lebendigen: diese schläft. – Schrecken und verwunderung: Jesus festlegt der scheintodten seine hände auf die schläfe, u. spricht dann:, deine tochter ist von schwerer krankheit genesen: bringt sie in das haus und pfleget sie wol. – Er folgt ihnen in das haus. Volk ist von aussen neugierig hinzugedrungen: es verbreitet sich die kunde, Jesus von Nazareth sei eingetroffen, – er habe eine todte erweckt; – die jünger nehmen dem aufruhr, – viele eilen fort es in der Stadt zu verbreiten. – Jesus tritt wieder aus dem hause, – der zöllner hält ihn beim kleide fest, schluchzend und ausser sich wirft er sich ihm zu füssen:, herr, wie habe ich deine gnade verdient: mein kind lebt, du hast es vom tode erweckt. Jesus:, was lebte, habe ich dem leben erhalten: öffne dein herz, daß ich dich vom tode erwecke! d. zöllner:, was soll ich thun Herr, daß ich dir gefalle? Jesus:, höre meine lehre und befolge sie. – Der zöllner bittet Jesus mit den jüngern zu verweilen und ein frühmal bei ihm einzunehmen: Jesus nimmt es an. Seine jünger beschicken ihm, – er ermahnt sie. –

Ein pharisäer tritt auf: er macht Jesus vorwürfe über seinen vertrauten umgang mit zöllnern und sündern. Abfertigung ✠ (: über den sabath und das gesetz.) – Barrabas sucht ✠ Jesus zu erforschen. (: der kaiserzins.) Enttäuschung des Barrabas.

Aufruhr auf der straße: man schleppt eine ehebrecherin herbei um sie zu stei= nigen; andere verlangen man solle sie vor Jesus stellen: der Pharisäer entscheidet für die letzteren um Jesus zu versuchen: Maria Magdalena wird hereingebracht, das volk dringt mit ihr herein; alles berichtet wild durcheinander von dem ärgerlichen, hoch= müthigen wandel und von dem verbrechen Maria's, die mit einem grossen von Herodes häuse, zur schmach der Juden, denen sie angehöre, in einem sündigen verhältnisse gelebt habe. (: Freisprechung: – alles zieht sich beschämt zurück. – Jesus mit Maria allein. –) (: Joh: VIII.)

Das mal wird bereitet: – die jünger, verwandte des zöllner's und leute aus dem volke nehmen daran theil; Jesus entwickelt seine lehre von der liebe. Beseligen= der eindruck auf alle. Das volk hält den raum und die strassen dicht gedrängt besetzt. Jesus wird benachrichtigt, seine mutter und brüder suchten ihn und könnten nicht herzu, er möchte zieht das volk weichen lassen. Jesus:, dies ist meine mutter, u. dies sind meine brüder.' –

(: Pilatus ist im einver= ständnis mit Maria von Magdala. –)

Apostel.
Simon. } br.
Andreas. }
Jacobus. } br.
Johannes. }
Philippus.
Bartholomäus.
Thomas.
Matthäus (Levi.)
Jacobus. Alphäus
Lebbäus (Thadäus.)
Simon v. Kana.
Judas Ischarioth. /
Jesu brüder:
Jacob. u. Joses

(: Der kann in folge eines aufrührerischen Herodes. des vorleben' wegen u. der bejahung der griechen gelten. – Maria hatte den ganzen zorn ihrer stamms= genossen wegen ihres umganges mit den fremden griechen auf sich geladen.)

✠ wegen der fasten: ihr möget die hochzeitsleute nicht zum fasten treiben, so lange der bräutigam bei ihnen ist. Es wird aber die zeit kommen, da der bräutigam von ihnen genommen ist, dann werden sie fasten. (: der bräutigam: das leben.)

74

73 'Jesus of Nazareth', page 1 of the prose sketch for a drama, Dresden, January 1849; in this sketch Christ is treated as a social revolutionary.

74 The February Revolution, Paris, 1848: the storming of the throne room in the Tuileries; *Illustrirte Zeitung*, Leipzig, 18 March 1848.

75 Wagner's article 'Die Revolution', published anonymously in the Dresden paper *Volksblätter*, 8 April 1849. Cf. pp. 170–3.

This article was one of several written by Wagner and published – all anonymously – in this journal; Wagner was sympathetic towards the revolution, or at least towards August Röckel, editor of *Volksblätter* since August 1848.

14.

Volksblätter,

von

A. Röckel.

Dresden, Sonntag, den 8. April 1849.

Dieses Blatt erscheint alle Sonnabende und ist durch alle Postanstalten des In- und Auslandes zu beziehen.

Preis vierteljährlich 4 Ngr. Durch die Post 5 Ngr.

Man abonnirt in der Expedition: große Brüdergasse Nr. 13. und in Neustadt bei Otto und Behmann, Heinrichstraße.

Die Revolution.

Sehen wir hinaus über die Länder und Völker, so erkennen wir überall durch ganz Europa das Gähren einer gewaltigen Bewegung, deren erste Schwingungen uns bereits erfaßt haben, deren volle Wucht bald über uns hereinzubrechen droht. Wie ein ungeheurer Vulkan erscheint uns Europa, aus dessen Innerem ein beständig wachsendes, drängsigendes Gebrause ertönt, aus dessen Krater dunkle, gewitterschwangere Rauchsäulen hoch zum Himmel empor steigen und, Alles rings mit Nacht bedeckend, sich über die Erde lagern, während bereits einzelne Lavaströme, die harte Kruste durchbrechend, als feurige Vorboten, Alles zerstörend sich ins Thal hinabwälzen.

Eine übernatürliche Kraft scheint unsern Welttheil erfaßt, aus dem alten Gleise herausheben und in eine neue Bahn schleudern zu wollen. Ja, wir erkennen es, die alte Welt, sie geht in Trümmer, eine neue wird aus ihr erstehen, denn die erhabene Göttin Revolution, sie kommt daher gebraust auf den Flügeln der Stürme, das hehre Haupt von Blitzen umstrahlt, das Schwert in der Rechten, die Fackel in der Linken, das Auge so finster, so strafend, so kalt, und doch, welche Glut der reinsten Liebe, welche Fülle des Glückes strahlt Dem daraus entgegen, der es wagt, mit festem Blicke hinein zu schauen in dies dunkle Auge! Sie kommt daher gebraust, die ewig verjüngende Mutter der Menschheit, vernichtend und beseligend fährt sie dahin über die Erde, und vor ihr her saust der Sturm und rüttelt so gewaltig an allem von Menschen Gefügten, daß mächtige Wolken des Staubes verfinstern die Lüfte erfüllen, und wohin ihr mächtiger Fuß tritt, da stürzt in Trümmer was in eitlem Wahne für Jahrtausende erbaute, und der Saum ihres Gewandes streift die letzten Ueberreste hinweg! Doch hinter ihr, da eröffnet sich uns, von lieblichen Sonnenstrahlen erhellt, ein nie geahntes Paradies des Glückes, und wo ihr Fuß vernichtend gewaltet, da entsprossen duftende Blumen dem Boden und frohlockende Jubelgesänge der befreiten Menschheit erfüllen die noch vom Kampfestoße erregten Lüfte!

Nun blickt hier unten um Euch her. Da seht Ihr den Einen, den mächtigen Fürsten, wie er mit ängstlich klopfendem Herzen, mit stockendem Athem dennoch eine ruhige, kalte Miene zu erheucheln und sich selbst und Andern wegzulügen sucht, was er doch klar erkennt als unabwendbar. Da seht Ihr den Andern, mit dem von allen Lastern durchfurchten Antlitz, wie er mit emsiger Thätigkeit all seine kleinen Gaunerkünste streift die ihm so manches Titelchen, so manches Ordenskreuzlein eingebracht, aus-

kramt und spielen läßt, wie er mit diplomatisch-lächelnder, geheimnißvoller Miene den ängstlich zum Riechsfläschchen greifenden Dämchen und den zähneklappernden Junkerlein Beruhigung einzuflößen sucht durch die halboffizielle Mittheilung: daß höchstgestellte Personen dieser fremdartigen Erscheinung bereits ihre Aufmerksamkeit zu widmen geruhten, daß Couriere mit Cabinetsbefehlen nach verschiedenen Seiten abgegangen, daß selbst das Gutachten des weisen Regierungskünstler Metternich von London unterwegs sei, daß die betreffenden Behörden rings umher Instructionen erhalten haben, und somit der hochgebornen Gesellschaft die interessante Ueberraschung vorbereitet wird, beim nächsten Hofballe diese gefürchtete Landstreicherin, Revolution, — natürlich im eisernen Käfig mit Ketten beladen, — in genauen Augenschein nehmen zu können. — Dort seht ihr den Dritten, wie er spekulirend das Nahen der Erscheinung beobachtet, auf die Börse läuft, bemißt und berechnet das Steigen und Fallen der Papierchen, und schachert und feilscht, und immer noch ein Procentchen zu erhalten strebt, bis mit Einemmale sein ganzer Plunder in die Lüfte zerstäubt. Da seht ihr hinter dem verstaubten Aktentische eins der eingerosteten, verrosteten Räder unserer jetzigen Staatsmaschine lauern, wie es seine alte, abgestumpfte Feder über das Papier kratzen läßt, und fort und fort den alten Haufen der papiernen Weltordnung zu vermehren strebt. Wie getrocknete Pflanzen liegen zwischen diesen Stößen von Dokumenten und Verträgen die lebendigen Herzen der lebendigen Menschheit und verdorren zu Staub in diesen modernen Folterkammern. Dort herrscht gewaltige Emsigkeit, denn das über die Länder gesponnene Netz ist an manchen Stellen zerrissen, und die überraschten Kreuzspinnen, sie drehen und weben neue Fäden durcheinander, um das Gelockerte wieder zu festigen. Dort dringt kein Strahl des Lichtes hinein, dort herrscht ewige Nacht und Finsterniß, und in Nacht und Finsterniß wird das Ganze spurlos versinken. — Von jener Seite aber, da klingt helle kriegerische Musik, es blitzen Schwerter und Bajonette, schwere Kanonen rasseln herbei und dichtgedrängt wälzen sich die langen Reihen der Heere heran. Die tapfere Heldenschar, sie ist ausgezogen, den Strauß zu bestehen mit der Revolution. Der Feldherr läßt marschiren rechts und links, und stellt dahin die Jäger, dorthin die Reiterei, und vertheilt nach weisem Plane die langen Heeressäulen und die zerschmetternde Artillerie; und die Revolution, das Haupt hoch in den Wolken, kommt herangeschritten, — und sie sehen sie nicht und warten auf den Feind; und sie steht schon in ihrer Mitte, und sie sehen sie nicht, und warten auf den Feind; — und

75

76 Michael Bakunin (1814–76), the Russian anarchist whom Wagner first met in Dresden in 1848. Cf. pp. 169, 177.

77 August Röckel (1814–76); photograph.

Röckel was director of music at the Court Theatre, Dresden, 1843–48. For his involvement in the Dresden Uprising in May 1849, he spent thirteen years in Waldheim prison.

78 The architect Gottfried Semper (1803–79); lithograph by Franz Hanfstaengl, 1848.

Like Wagner, Semper was forced to flee Dresden after the May uprising in which he also took part. At Wagner's instigation, Ludwig II of Bavaria commissioned Semper on 29 December 1864 to draw up plans for a Festival Theatre in Munich, but these were not executed.

79 The May uprising, Dresden 1849: the old Opera House and the Zwingerstrasse burning; lithograph.

The uprising was triggered off by a breach of the constitution by Friedrich August II of Saxony; it was suppressed with the help of Prussian troops summoned to aid the king. Cf. p. 169.

80 Warrant for the arrest of Wagner, published in Dresden on 16 May 1849. Cf. p. 174.

81 Document granting Wagner a full amnesty, issued in Dresden on 28 March 1862.

77   78

Aktientheater in Zürich. **Montag den 18. November 1850.**

5. Vorstellung im 2. Abonnement.

Don Juan, oder: Der steinerne Gast.

Große Oper in 2 Akten von Mozart.

Mit neuer Bearbeitung des Dialogs und mit Recitativs von Richard Wagner.

Personen:

Don Pedro, Gouverneur	. . Hr. Windwart.	Leporello, Don Juans Diener . Hr. Ubrich.
Donna Anna, seine Tochter	. Fr. Rauch-Wernau.	Masetto, ein junger Bauer . . Hr. Feistmantel.
Don Oktavio, ihr Geliebter	. Hr. Wihrler.	Zerline, seine Braut . . . . Fr. Dupont.
Don Juan	. Hr. Dupont.	Ein Gerichtsdiener . . . Hr. Richter.
Donna Elvira, Don Juans Geliebte	Frl. Kral.	Bauern und Bäuerinnen.

Die Scene ist in Spanien.

Der Feuerregen am Schlusse der Oper ist von Hrn. Schweizer angefertigt.

Kassaeröffnung halb 6 Uhr. — Anfang 6¼ Uhr. — Ende vor 9 Uhr.

Der Besuch auf der Bühne bei Probe und Vorstellungen ist Jedermann, der nicht daselbst beschäftigt, untersagt.

82 Theatre in Zurich; watercolour.

After fleeing from Dresden, Wagner lived in Zurich until 1858; he frequently appeared as a conductor.

83 Announcement in the *Tageblatt der Stadt Zurich* of a performance on 18 November 1850 of Mozart's *Don Giovanni* adapted by Wagner for the Aktientheater, Zurich.

84 Title page of the first impression of Wagner's *Kunstwerk der Zukunft* ('The Work of Art of the Future'), 1850.

85 The opening of Wagner's article 'Das Judentum in der Musik' ('Jewry in Music') in its original publication in the *Neue Zeitschrift für Musik*, 3 September 1850, under the pseudonym 'K. Freigedank'. Cf. pp. 217–8.

86 Title page of the first impression of Wagner's *Die Kunst und die Revolution* ('Art and the Revolution'), 1849.

87 Title page of the first impression of Wagner's *Oper und Drama* ('Opera and Drama'), 1852.

Das
Kunstwerk der Zukunft.

Von

Richard Wagner.

Leipzig,
Verlag von Otto Wigand.
1850.

Neue

Zeitschrift für Musik.

Verantwortlicher Redacteur:
Franz Brendel.

№ 19.

Verleger:
Robert Friese in Leipzig.

Dreiunddreißigster Band.

Den 3. September 1850.

Von dieser Zeitsch. erscheinen wöchentlich 2 Nummern von 1 oder 1½ Bogen. || Preis des Bandes von 52 Nrn. 2½ Thlr. Insertionsgebühren die Petitzeile 2 Ngr. || Abonnement nehmen alle Postämter, Buch-, Musik- und Kunsthandlungen an.

Inhalt: Das Judenthum in der Musik. — Drei Tage in Weimar. — Intelligenzblatt.

Das Judenthum in der Musik. *)

Von
K. Freigedank.

Kürzlich kam in dieser Zeitschrift ein „hebräischer Kunstgeschmack" zur Sprache: eine Anfechtung dieses Ausdruckes konnte, eine Vertheidigung durfte nicht ausbleiben. Es dünkt mich nun nicht unwichtig, den hier zu Grunde liegenden, von der Kritik immer nur noch versteckt oder im Ausbruche einer gewissen Leidenschaftlichkeit berührten Gegenstand endlich zu erörtern. Dabei wird es sich nicht darum handeln, etwas Neues zu sagen, sondern die unbewußte Empfindung, die sich im Volke als innerlichste Abneigung gegen jüdisches Wesen kundgiebt, zu erklären, somit etwas wirklich Vorhandenes deutlich auszusprechen, keineswegs aber etwas Unwirkliches durch die Kraft irgend welcher Einbildung künstlich beleben zu wollen. Die Kritik verfährt gegen ihre Natur, wenn sie in Angriff oder Abwehr etwas anderes will.

*) Bei mangelhafter äußerer Gestaltung haben wir immer als einen Vorzug Deutschlands, als ein Resultat seiner großen Wissenschaft, die geistige Freiheit desselben wenigstens auf wissenschaftlichem Gebiet betrachtet. Wir nehmen diese Freiheit in Anspruch, wir stützen uns auf dieselbe, indem wir obigen Aufsatz drucken, wünschend, daß man ihn in diesem Sinne aufnehmen möge. Mag man die darin ausgesprochenen Ansichten theilen, oder nicht, Genialität der Anschauung wird man dem Verf. nicht abstreiten können.
D. Red.

Da wir den Grund der volksthümlichen Abneigung auch unserer Zeit gegen jüdisches Wesen uns hier lediglich in Bezug auf die Kunst, und namentlich der Musik erklären wollen, haben wir der Erläuterung derselben Erscheinung auf dem Felde der Religion und Politik gänzlich vorüber zu gehen. In der Religion sind uns die Juden längst keine hassenswürdigen Feinde mehr, — Dank unsern Frömmlern und Jesuiten, die allen religiösen Volkshaß auf sich allein nur noch gelenkt haben, so daß mit ihrem dereinstigen Falle die Religion nach ihrer jetzigen Bedeutung (welche vielmehr die des Hasses als der Liebe war) vermuthlich ebenfalls untergegangen sein wird! In der reinen Politik sind wir mit den Juden nie in wirklichen Conflict gerathen; wir gönnten ihnen selbst die Errichtung eines jerusalemischen Reiches, und hatten in diesem Bezuge eher zu bedauern, daß Hr. v. Rothschild zu geistreich war, um König der Juden werden zu wollen, wogegen er bekanntlich vorzog, der Jude der Könige zu bleiben. Anders verhält es sich da, wo die Politik zur Frage der Gesellschaft wird: hier hat uns die Sonderstellung der Juden unter anderen Staatsangehörigen seit eben so lange als Aufforderung zu menschlicher Gerechtigkeitsübung gegolten, als in uns selbst der Drang nach socialer Befreiung zu deutlicherem Bewußtsein erwachte. Als wir für Emancipation der Juden stritten, waren wir aber doch eigentlich mehr Kämpfer für ein abstractes Princip als für den concreten Fall: wie all unser Liberalismus ein luxuriöses Geistesspiel war, in dem wir für die Freiheit des Volkes disputirten ohne Kenntniß dieses Volkes,

---

Die Kunst und die Revolution.

Von

Richard Wagner.

Wo einst die Kunst schwieg, begann die Staatsweisheit und Philosophie: wo jetzt der Staatsweise und Philosoph zu Ende ist, da fängt wieder der Künstler an.

Leipzig,
Verlag von Otto Wigand.
1849.

Oper und Drama.

Von

Richard Wagner.

Erster Theil.

Die Oper und das Wesen der Musik.

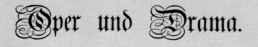

Leipzig,
Verlagsbuchhandlung von J. J. Weber.
1852.

88 Franz Liszt (1811–86), portrait in oils by Miklós Barabás, 1846. Cf. p. 177.

Wagner and Liszt had been acquainted since 1840 and had become friends. As a result of this friendship, Liszt helped Wagner to escape from Dresden in 1849 and, while Wagner was in exile in Switzerland, had his *Faust Overture* and *Tannhäuser* performed. He also made preparations for the première of *Lohengrin* at the Court Theatre, Weimar, on 28 August 1850, and three years later conducted a Wagner week there.

89 Announcement of the première of *Lohengrin*, 28 August 1850. Cf. pp. 177–80.

Hof-Theater.

Weimar, Mittwoch den 28. August 1850.

Zur Goethe-Feier:

Prolog

von Franz Dingelstedt, gesprochen von Herrn Jaffé.

Hierauf:

Zum Erstenmale:

Lohengrin.

Romantische Oper in drei Akten,
(letzter Akt in zwei Abtheilungen)
von Richard Wagner.

Heinrich der Finkler, deutscher König,	Herr Höfer.
Lohengrin,	Herr Beck.
Elsa von Brabant,	Fräulein Agthe.
Herzog Gottfried, ihr Bruder,	Frau Hettstedt.
Friedrich von Telramund, brabantischer Graf,	Herr Milde.
Ortrud, seine Gemahlin,	Fräulein Fastlinger.
Der Herrufer des Königs,	Herr Pätsch.

Sächsische und Thüringische Grafen und Edle.
Brabantische Grafen und Edle.
Edelfrauen.
Edelknaben.
Mannen. Frauen. Knechte.

Antwerpen: erste Hälfte des zehnten Jahrhunderts.

Die Textbücher sind an der Kasse für 5 Sgr. zu haben.

Preise der Plätze:

Fremden-Loge	1 Thlr. 10 Sgr. — Pf.	Parterre-Loge — Thlr. 20 Sgr. — Pf.	
Balkon	1 — —	Parterre — 15 — —	
Sperrsitze	1 — —	Gallerie-Loge — 10 — —	
Parket	— 20 —	Gallerie — 7 6	

Anfang um 6 Uhr. **Ende gegen 10 Uhr.**

Die Billets gelten nur am Tage der Vorstellung, wo sie gelöst worden.

Der Zutritt auf die Bühne, bei den Proben wie bei den Vorstellungen, ist nicht gestattet.

Das Theater wird halb 5 Uhr geöffnet.

Die freien Entréen sind ohne Ausnahme ungültig.

90, 91 *Lohengrin*.

90 Title page of the poem of the 'romantic opera in three acts', Weimar 1850.

91 Arrival of Lohengrin in Act I, scene 2; *Illustrirte Zeitung*, Leipzig, 12 April 1851.

92

93

94, 95 Portraits of Wagner and his wife Minna by Clementine Stockar-Escher, Zurich, 1853; both watercolour.

92 Mariafeld, oil painting by R. Buhlmann, 1835.

In 1852 Wagner became closely acquainted with the benevolent François and Eliza Wille through the writer Georg Herwegh. He often visited their house – Mariafeld – overlooking Lake Zurich. Later, threatened with arrest for debts incurred in Vienna, he left Austria and took refuge here in spring 1864. Cf. p. 204.

93 The Hotel Baur au Lac, Zurich; coloured engraving.

Here on four successive evenings (16–19 February 1853), Wagner gave readings of his tetralogy, *Der Ring des Nibelungen*. Cf. p. 182.

96 Cosima, Blandine and Daniel Liszt, the composer's children; drawing by Friedrich Preller.

Wagner first met the three children of Liszt and Countess d'Agoult in Paris in October 1853. Cosima, born in 1837 on Lake Como, married the pianist and conductor Hans von Bülow in 1857, and they were divorced in 1870, leaving Wagner and Cosima free to remarry (Minna Wagner having died in 1866). A clandestine relationship between Wagner and Cosima had developed in the early 1860s, and their first child (Isolde) was born in 1865, at which point von Bülow was still unaware of his wife's association with Wagner; from May 1866, Cosima lived almost continuously with Wagner and their children at Triebschen (cf. ill. 162).

97 Page 1 of the fair copy of the Album Sonata for Mathilde Wesendonck, bearing the words 'Wisst ihr wie das wird?' ('Knowest thou how it will be?'), June 1853.

This was Wagner's first composition since the completion of *Lohengrin* in 1848.

98 Hans von Bülow (1830–94); portrait in oils by W. Streckfuss, 1855.

Wagner had supported von Bülow in his desire to become a musician; for a while he was Wagner's pupil in Zurich, and later he conducted the premières of *Tristan und Isolde* and *Die Meistersinger von Nürnberg*.

99 Mathilde Wesendonck and her son Guido, by E. B. Kietz, Paris, December 1856; pastel.

Wagner met the wealthy businessman Otto Wesendonck (cf. ill. 104) and his wife Mathilde in Zurich in 1852; cf. pp. 185–9. He was captivated by the beautiful Mathilde and an intimate friendship grew up between them; this mutual sympathy, suspected by Minna Wagner as well as Otto Wesendonck, has often been cited as the motivating force for the poem and musical composition of *Tristan und Isolde*. Although no such direct cause and effect can be established, a clear connection does exist.

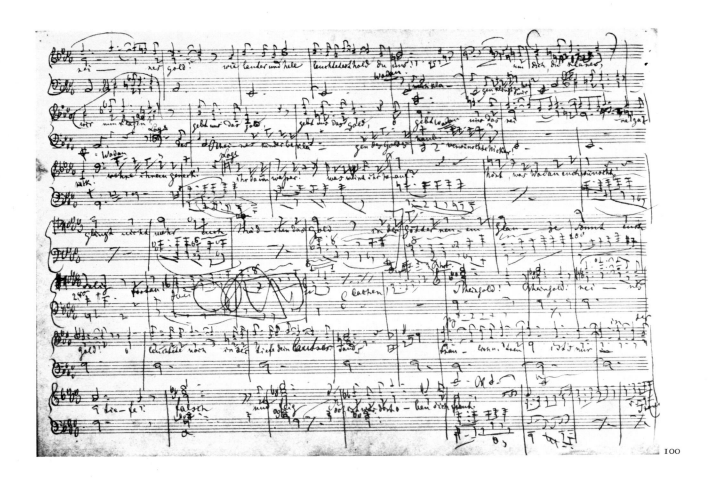

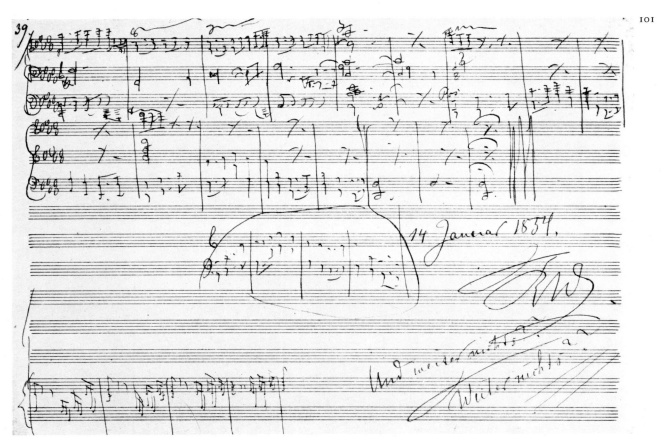

100, 101. *Das Rheingold* ('The Rhinegold'), the last two pages of the composition sketch, completed on 14 January 1854 with the comment 'und weiter nichts?? Weiter nichts??' ('and nothing more?? Nothing more??').

102 *Die Walküre* ('The Valkyrie'), page 389 of the first draft of the
Fire Scene preceding Wotan's farewell in Act III, early 1856.

ſo — werf' ich den Brand
in Walhall's prangende Burg.

Sie ſchleudert den Brand in den Holz-
ſtoſs, der ſich ſchnell hell entzündet.
Zwei Raben ſind vom Uſer aufgeflogen,
und verſchwinden nach dem Hintergrunde
zu. — BRÜNNHILDE *wendet ſich noch*
einmal zurück.

Ihr, blühenden Lebens
bleibend Geſchlecht:
was ich nun euch melde,
merket es wohl! —
Saht ihr vom zündenden Brand
Siegfried und Brünnhild' verzehrt;
ſaht ihr des Rheines Töchter
zur Tiefe entführen den Ring:
nach Norden dann
blickt durch die Nacht!
Erglänzt dort am Himmel
ein heiliges Glüh'n,
ſo wiſſet all' —
daſs ihr Walhall's Ende gewahrt!

Verging wie Hauch
der Götter Geſchlecht,
laſs' ohne Walter
die Welt ich zurück:
meines heiligſten Wiſſen's Hort
weiſ' ich der Welt nun zu. —
Nicht Gut, nicht Gold,
noch göttliche Pracht;
nicht Haus, nicht Hof,
noch herriſcher Prunk;
nicht trüber Verträge
trügender Bund,
noch heuchelnder Sitte
hartes Geſetz:
ſelig in Luſt und Leid
läſst — die Liebe nur ſein! —

Zwei junge Männer führen das
Roſs herein; Brünnhilde faſst es,
und entzäumt es ſchnell.

Grane, mein Roſs,
ſei mir gegrüſst!

Weiſst du, Freund,
wohin ich dich führe?
Im Feuer leuchtend
liegt dort dein Herr,
Siegfried, mein ſeliger Held.
Dem Freunde zu folgen
wieherſt du freudig?
Lockt dich zu ihm
die lachende Lohe? —
Fühl' meine Bruſt auch,
wie ſie entbrennt;
helles Feuer
faſst mir das Herz:
ihn zu umſchlingen,
umſchloſsen von ihm,
in mächtigſter Minne
vermält ihm zu ſein! —
Heiaho! Grane!
grüſse den Freund!
Siegfried! Siegfried!
Selig gilt dir mein Gruſs!

Sie hat ſich ſtürmiſch auf das Roſs
geſchwungen, und ſprengt es mit einem
Satze in den brennenden Scheithauſen.
Sogleich ſteigt praſſelnd der Brand hoch
auf, ſo daſs das Feuer den ganzen
Raum vor der Halle erfüllt, und dieſe
ſelbſt ſchon zu ergreifen ſcheint. Ent-
ſetzt drängen ſich die Frauen nach
dem Vordergrunde. Plötzlich bricht das
Feuer zuſammen, ſo daſs nur noch eine
düſt're Gluthwolke über der Stätte
ſchwebt; dieſe ſteigt auf und zertheilt
ſich ganz: der Rhein iſt vom Uſer her
mächtig angeſchwollen, und wälzt ſeine
Fluth über die Brandſtätte bis an die
Schwelle der Halle. Auf den Wogen
ſind die DREI RHEINTŒCHTER *herbeige-*
ſchwommen. — HAGEN, *der ſeit dem*
Vorgange mit dem Ringe in wachſender
Angſt Brünnhilde's Benehmen be-
obachtet hat, geräth beim Anblicke der
Rheintöchter in höchſten Schreck; er
wirft haſtig Speer, Schild und Helm von
ſich, und ſtürzt wie wahnſinnig mit dem

*Rufe: **Zurück vom Ringe!** fich in die Fluth.* **WOGLINDE** *und* **WELLGUNDE** *umfchlingen mit ihren Armen feinen Nacken, und ziehen ihn fo zurückfchwimmend mit fich in die Tiefe:* **FLOSSHILDE,** *ihnen voran, hält jubelnd den gewonnenen Ring in die Höhe. — Am Himmel bricht zugleich von fern her eine, dem Nordlicht ähnliche, röthliche Gluth aus, die fich immer weiter und ftärker verbreitet. — Die Männer und Frauen fchauen in fprachlofer Erfchütterung dem Vorgange und der Erfcheinung zu.*

Der Vorhang fällt.

ENDE.

103 *Siegfrieds Tod* ('Siegfried's Death'), the closing pages of Wagner's personal copy of the first impression with textual corrections made as a result of reading (in 1854) Schopenhauer's philosophical writings.

G. Meyer Mei.
1851. Enge. bij Rieters Villa.

104 Otto Wesendonck (1815–96); photograph, c. 1860.

105 The writer Gottfried Keller (1819–90); pastel drawing by Ludmilla Assing, 1854. Cf. pp. 185–6.

106 Wagner's 'refuge' (the house close to the Wesendonck villa near Zurich) bought by his benefactor and placed at his disposal; pencil drawing, c. 1857.

Wagner lived here from April 1857 to August 1858.

107 *Siegfried*, page 88 of the orchestral sketch (end of Act II), 9 August 1857.

At this point Wagner broke off the composition of the *Ring* cycle in order to write *Tristan und Isolde*.

108

108 View of Zurich with the Wesendonck
villa at the left; watercolour, 1857.

110

109 The Palazzo Giustiniani, Venice; coloured engraving.

While living here from August 1858 to March 1859, Wagner continued the composition of *Tristan* begun in Zurich.

110 The Hotel Schweizerhof, Lucerne; coloured lithograph, *c.* 1860.

Here *Tristan* was completed on 6 August 1859.

109

111 *Tristan und Isolde*, page 1 of the original draft of the poem,
with an outline of the Mariner's Song, August/September 1857.

112 *Tristan und Isolde*, page 1 of the orchestral sketch for Act III, Lucerne, 1 May 1859.

113 Portrait of Wagner, February/March 1860; photograph by Petit et Trinquart, Paris.

Wagner moved to Paris in September 1859, and busied himself with arranging performances of his own works. He conducted three concerts (on 25 January and 1 and 8 February) at the Théâtre des Italiens; these enjoyed a great success, especially among Paris intellectuals.

114 Princess Pauline Metternich, after a portrait by Winterhalter.

The wife of the Austrian Ambassador in Paris, Prince Richard von Metternich, persuaded Napoleon III to order the performance of *Tannhäuser* (March 1861). Cf. pp. 189, 194–7.

115 Emile Ollivier (1825–1913), portrait in oils by Gustave Courbet, *c.* 1860.

Ollivier, a lawyer, was the son-in-law of Franz Liszt; he gave Wagner financial support in Paris.

116 Hector Berlioz (1803–69); portrait in oils by Gustave Courbet, *c.* 1860. Cf. p. 189–93.

117 Charles Gounod (1818–93); portrait in oils by Ary Scheffer (1795–1858).

118

119

120

118 Gustave Doré (1833–83), painter and illustrator; photograph by Nadar, Paris, 1859.

119 Jules Champfleury (1821–89), French writer; photograph by Nadar, 1859(?).

120 Camille Saint-Saëns (1835–1921); photograph. Cf. p. 235.

Berlioz, Gounod, Doré, Champfleury and Saint-Saëns were members of Wagner's circle of artistic friends in Paris, and met regularly at his home.

121

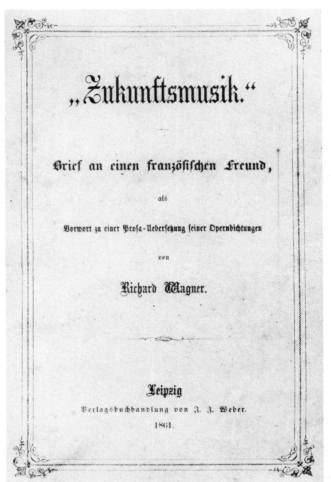

122

121 Gioacchino Rossini (1792–1868); photograph, Paris 1860.

In March 1860 Wagner visited Rossini, and had a theoretical discussion with him (see E. Michotte, *La Visite de R. Wagner à Rossini*, Paris 1906); in 1868 Wagner published 'A Remembrance of Rossini'.

122 Title page of the German first edition of Wagner's 'letter' to Frédéric Villot, Curator of the Louvre, who was a close friend of Eugène Delacroix (cf. ill. 128).

123–126 *Tannhäuser*, drawings by Alfred Albert of characters for the Paris production of 1861: (123) Venus;

(124) Tannhäuser; (125) Elisabeth; (126) member of the chorus. Cf. pp. 193–7.

127 *Tannhäuser*, design by Philippe Chaperon for Act II, scene 3, of the Paris production, 1861.

128 'Tannhäuser and Venus'; gouache, signed (lower left) 'Eug. Delacroix'.

129

130

RICHARD WAGNER

ET

TANNHAUSER

A PARIS

PAR

CHARLES BAUDELAIRE

PARIS

E. DENTU, ÉDITEUR

LIBRAIRE DE LA SOCIÉTÉ DES GENS DE LETTRES

PALAIS ROYAL, 13 ET 17, GALERIE D'ORLÉANS

—

1861

129 *Tannhäuser*, the Singing Tournament in Act II, scene 4; drawing by M. Rouargue, Paris 1861.

130 The poet Charles Baudelaire (1821–67); photograph by Nadar, Paris 1859. Cf. p. 193.

131 Title page of the first edition of Baudelaire's essay 'Richard Wagner and *Tannhäuser* in Paris', 1861, the inspiration for which came in part from the scandals caused by the production of this opera. Cf. p. 196.

131

132 Portrait of Wagner by L. Pierson, Paris, October/November 1867.

133 Pencil drawing by Auguste Renoir (1841–1919), after the photograph by Pierson, formerly in the possession of Claude Monet.

The Renoir drawing is undated, but the artist appears to have portrayed the composer six times in all; cf. ill. 238. A second drawing after the Pierson photograph can be found reproduced in Adolphe Jullien, *Richard Wagner, sa vie et ses œuvres*, Paris 1886, p. 157.

134

134 Ludwig II of Bavaria (1845–86); coloured photograph presented by the king to Wagner.

Ludwig II succeeded his father, Maximilian II, on 10 March 1864. He summoned Wagner to Munich, where the two met for the first time on 4 May in the royal palace (Residenz). The king's adulation and the friendship that developed became the object of much anger and ridicule, both in public and in private. Cf. pp. 204–6.

135 Title page of the first edition (1871) of Wagner's *Huldigungsmarsch* ('Homage March').

Dedicated to Ludwig II, the march was composed in 1864 in honour of the king's birthday in August.

136 Schloss Berg on Lake Starnberg; coloured lithograph.

In the summer of 1864 Wagner stayed at a house overlooking the lake placed at his disposal by the king to enable them to meet daily at the castle.

135

136

137 The royal palace (Residenz) and Court Theatre, Munich; lithograph.

On 7 October 1864 Ludwig II formally commissioned Wagner to complete his *Ring* cycle.

138 Wagner and friends, Munich, 17 May 1865: (from the left) Friedrich Uhl, Richard Pohl, H. von Rosti, August Röckel (seated), Wagner (with his dog Pohl), Auguste de Gasperini, Hans von Bülow, Adolf Jensen, Carl Gilla, Franz Müller, Felix Draeseke, Alexander Ritter, Leopold Damrosch, Heinrich Porges, Michael Moszornyi; photograph by Joseph Albert.

This circle of friends grew up at the time of the rehearsals for the première of *Tristan und Isolde*.

139, 140 *Tristan und Isolde.*

139 Page 1 of the printed score.

140 Announcement of the première on 10 June 1865 at the Court and National Theatre, Munich; the conductor was Hans von Bülow.

An earlier attempt to have the opera performed in Vienna had been abandoned after many rehearsals.

Tristan

141

Isolde

142

143

Melot

144

141–146 *Tristan und Isolde*, designs for the première, 10 June 1865.

141–144 Designs for costumes by Franz Seitz: (141) Tristan; (142) Isolde; (143) Melot; (144) Brangäne.

145, 146 Stage designs by Angelo Quaglio II: (145) Act III; (146) Act I.

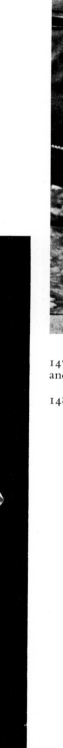

147 Ludwig and Malvine Schnorr von Carolsfeld in the roles of Tristan and Isolde, Munich 1865; photograph. Cf. pp. 207–8.

148 'Tristan', marble statue by Caspar Zumbusch, 1866.

149 Caricature on the relationship between Wagner and Cosima and Hans von Bülow during the Munich *Tristan* period, with the remark 'And I carried her off, it is already there in Homer! Richard Paris'.

150 Announcement of a parody on *Tristan und Isolde – Tristanderl und Süssholde* – to be staged in Munich in response to 'much demand', June 1865.

München.
Isar-Vorstadt-Theater
in der Müllerstraße.
Eigenthümer und Direktor Max Schweiger.

Heute Donnerstag den 8. Juni 1865:
Auf vieles Verlangen.

Tristanderl und Süßholde.

Dramatisches Verslein mit Worten ohne Melodie, gegenwärtige Parodie von einer Zukunfts-Oper in 3 Aufzügen, wo drüber viel losgezogen wird, und einem Vorspiel des Vorspielers, von Richard, Wagnermeister und Stückschreiber, sowie musikalischen Dramatisirer. Satyrisirt und in Scene gesetzt von **Ferdinand Fränkl.**

Musik von H. Rauchenecker.

Personen.

Tristanderl, Floßknecht von Ammerland und Vetter des Hopfenkönigs Marke, Bräuer zu Benried	Hr. Eisenmann.	Kuhwenzel, ehemaliger Viehtreiber, der sich aber jetzt mit Tristanderl umeinander treibt	Hr. Weber.
Süßholde, eine reiche Bäckerstochter von Wolfrathshausen	Hr. Preis.	Melotte, erster Pfannenknecht des Marklbräu	Hr. Seeberg.
Brangäuschen, ihre Gespielin in Mariage und Sechs und sechzig	Fr. Kummerer/Scholz.	Ein Schweinhirt und Schalmeienbläser, blasirt wie normal ein ComponTenor	Hr. Dot.
	Frln. Ehrenstein	Ein Steuermann, der zukünftige Opern über Bord halten soll	Hr. Baierdorf

Bräuknechte, Schiffsvolk, unnöthige Kranzljungfern und nöthige Hochzeitsgäste.

Die Handlung spielt in der Vorzeit und ist in der Gegenwart zu Allem reif, theils zu Wasser, theils zu Land, weßhalb auch der Text bald zu schlüpferig und bald zu trocken ist. Textbücher werden keine ausgegeben, weil der Text doch nicht hier so recht verstanden wird.

Für dieses Stück sind nur 3 Vorstellungen angesetzt, wenn es das Publikum aushaltet und die Schauspieler nicht umbringt, wird man schon sehen, was noch weiters geschieht, vor der Hand wurden einmal die Preise erhöht, damit das Stück mehr an Werth gewinnt.

Auswärtige Bestellungen auf Logen und Sperrsitze werden aus der alten und neuen Welt angenommen und bittet man den Betrag derselben in den landesüblichen Briefmarken franco einzusenden.

Aller Anfang ist schwer, mit dem Ende wird es leichter gehen.

Besonders zu bemerken ist noch, daß die 30 Sperrsitze in erster Reihe bleiben, die Frauenzimmer ohne Erröthen hinein und auch wieder herausgehen können, der freie Eintritt aber für Alle, selbst für die Freunde des Verfassers aufgehoben ist, weil, was man umsonst kriegt, nicht viel werth ist.

Anfang Nachmittags 4 Uhr. Abends 8 Uhr.

Preise der Plätze:

Eine ganze Gallerie-Loge 6 fl. — ein Logenplatz 30 kr. — Eine ganze Parterre-Loge 7 fl. und eine 6 fl., ein Logenplatz 36 kr. und 24 kr. Gallerie-Sperrsitz 30 kr. Gallerie 18 kr. — Parterre-Sperrsitz 24 kr. — Erstes Parterre 12 kr. — Zweites Parterre 6 kr.

Der freie Eintritt ist für Jedes ohne Ausnahme aufgehoben.

Billets für Logen und Sperrsitze sind in meiner Wohnung, Frauenhoferstraße Nr. 4/a zu haben. **Max Schweiger,** Direktor.

151 View of the Venus grotto built for Ludwig II in Linderhof seen under red lighting; detail of watercolour by Heinrich Breling, 1881.

The grotto itself was decorated by August Heckel, and the boat was the work of Franz Seitz.

152 Portrait of Wagner in oils by Friedrich Pecht, Munich 1864/65.

The portrait, now in The Metropolitan Museum, New York, was painted for Ludwig II, whose bust is seen at the right. Pecht had been a friend of Wagner since 1839/40.

153, 154 *Die Meistersinger von Nürnberg*

153 Title page of the appendix to Johann Christoph Wagenseil's *Chronicle of the Free City of Nuremberg*, 1697; this 'Book of the most gracious Art of the Mastersingers' was the source of Wagner's knowledge about the historic Mastersingers of Nuremberg.

154 Wagner's sketch for the prize-song in *Die Meistersinger*, 'Morgendlich leuchtend in rosigem Schein' ('Morning dawn glowing in rose-coloured light'), 1866; the note at the bottom states '28 Sept. afternoon while waiting for C. (R)'.

The words of the song were written later, at Christmas 1866.

155 *Die Meistersinger von Nürnberg*, page 111 of the orchestral score at the end of Act II (the so-called Cudgel Scene), summer 1866.

Eva. 2 Anzug.

156

Walther Stolzing 5 Anzug.

157

158

156–160 *Die Meistersinger von Nürnberg*

156, 157 Costume designs for the première (21 June 1868) by Franz Seitz: Eva and Stolzing.

158 Stage design for Act III, scene 5 (the open meadow) by Heinrich Döll, Munich 1868.

159 Announcement of the première. Cf. pp. 214–6.

The conductor at the première was Hans von Bülow and, although considerable private and personal tension existed between the two men during the rehearsal period, the opening night was a great success. Wagner described as 'perfect' the performance, which he saw from the royal box in the company of Ludwig II, an unprecedented privilege at the time.

160 Act I, scene 1, drawing by Theodor Pixis, Munich 1868.

161 *Die Meistersinger von Nürnberg*, oil painting by Eduard Ille, 1866; formerly in Ludwig II's castle, Schloss Berg.

The king commissioned many similar renderings of subjects from history and mythology; they were based on the subject matter of Wagner's operas without following them in precise detail.

162 Triebschen, overlooking Lake Lucerne; copy of a lost watercolour.

The house called Triebschen (centre) was occupied by Wagner – after his enforced departure from Munich in 1865 – from April 1866 to April 1872, the rent being paid by Ludwig II. Cf. p. 213.

163 Portrait of Wagner by Joseph Bernhardt (detail), Munich 1868.

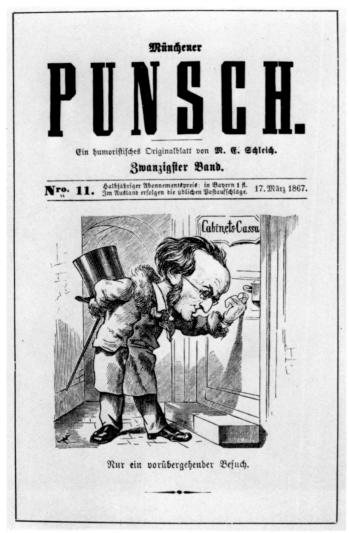

164, 165 Caricatures of Wagner: 'Just a passing visit' (to the royal treasury) published in Munich, 1867; and attacking the eardrums of the public with his 'music of the future', Paris 1869.

The campaign to have Wagner banished from Munich was in part the result of large sums of money being paid to him – or so public opinion would have it – from treasury funds. When he revisited Munich in 1867, Wagner obtained 12,000 gulden in damages for the *Punsch* cartoon.

166 Certificate recording Wagner's election as a member of the Royal Academy of Arts in Berlin, 4 June 1869.

On 28 April 1871 Wagner read a paper at the Academy, 'The Destiny of Opera'.

167 *Siegfried*, page 1 of the orchestral sketch for Act III, composed at Triebschen, 25 January 1869.

München.

Königl. Hof- und National-Theater.

Mittwoch den 22. September 1869.

119ᵗᵉ Vorstellung im Jahres-Abonnement:

Zum ersten Male:

Das Rheingold.

Vorspiel zu der Trilogie: „Der Ring des Nibelungen", von Richard Wagner.

Regie: Herr Dr. Hallwachs.

Personen:

Wotan,			Herr Kindermann.
Donner,	Götter		Herr Heinrich.
Froh,			Herr Nachbaur.
Loge,			Herr Vogl.
Alberich,	Nibelungen		Herr Fischer.
Mime,			Herr Schlosser.
Fasolt,	Riesen		Herr Bayer.
Fafner,			Herr Bausewein.
Fricka,			Fräulein Stehle.
Freia,	Göttinnen		Fräulein Müller.
Erda,			Fräulein T. Seehofer.
Woglinde,			Fräulein Kaufmann.
Wellgunde,	Rheintöchter		Frau Vogl.
Floßhilde,			Fräulein Ritter.
Nibelungen.			

Neue Decorationen:

Erstes Bild: In der Tiefe des Rheines, entworfen und ausgeführt von dem kgl. Hoftheatermaler Herrn Heinrich Döll.

Zweites Bild: Freie Gegend auf Bergeshöhen am Rhein gelegen, entworfen von dem kgl. Hoftheatermaler Herrn Christian Jank, ausgeführt von demselben und dem kgl. Hoftheatermaler Herrn Angelo Quaglio.

Drittes Bild: Die unterirdischen Klüfte Nibelheims, entworfen von dem kgl. Hoftheatermaler Herrn Christian Jank, ausgeführt von demselben und dem kgl. Hoftheatermaler Herrn Angelo Quaglio.

Textbücher sind zu 18 kr. an der Kasse zu haben.

Preise der Plätze:

Ein Galerienoble-Sitz	3 fl. 30 kr.
Ein Parket-Sitz	3 fl. — kr.
Parterre	1 fl. — kr.
Galerie	— fl. 30 kr.

Die Kasse wird um sechs Uhr geöffnet.

Anfang um 7 Uhr, Ende um halb zehn Uhr.

Der freie Eintritt ist ohne alle Ausnahme aufgehoben und wird ohne Kassenbillet Niemand eingelassen.

Beurlaubt kontraktlich vom Schauspielpersonal: Frau von Bulyovszky bis 31. Oktober.
vom Opernpersonal: Herr Bachmann bis 4. Oktober.
Beurlaubt auf ärztliche Anordnung vom Schauspielpersonal: Herr Rüthling für unbestimmte Zeit.
Krank vom Opernpersonal: Fräulein Therese Seehofer.

Der einzelne Zettel kostet 2 kr.

Kgl. Hofbuchdruckerei von Dr. C. Wolf & Sohn.

168–170 *Das Rheingold*

168 Announcement of the première, 22 September 1869. Cf. p. 217.

This performance was ordered by Ludwig II, against Wagner's wishes, and the composer pointedly stayed away. The conductor was Franz Wüllner, whom Wagner considered unsuited to the task; a year later Wüllner also conducted the première of *Die Walküre*, in an exactly similar situation.

169 Drawing by Theodor Pixis, Munich 1869.

170 Drawing by Theodor Pixis published in the *Illustrirte Zeitung*, Leipzig, 23 October 1869.

169

171, 172 *Die Walküre*, drawings by Theodor Pixis for Act II,
scene 4, and Act III, scene 2, Munich 1870.

173, 174 The *Siegfried Idyll*, fair copy of title page and opening.

Wagner wrote this work (at the end of 1870) for Cosima to commemorate the birth of their son Siegfried on 6 June 1869.

175 View of Lucerne; coloured engraving, after 1870.

176 Announcement of the wedding of Wagner and Cosima, 25 August 1870.

177 Wagner and Cosima; photograph by Fritz Luckhardt, Vienna 1872.

178 Friedrich Nietzsche (1844–1900); portrait in oils by an unknown artist, 1869, commissioned by Comte de Claussade. Cf. pp. 216, 224–5, 230.

Wagner and Nietzsche met in Leipzig in 1868. Their friendship did not last long, however, and they broke with each other in 1876; their last meeting took place in Sorrento on 28 October 1876.

DIE

GEBURT DER TRAGÖDIE

AUS DEM

GEISTE DER MUSIK.

VON

FRIEDRICH NIETZSCHE,

ORDENTL. PROFESSOR DER CLASSISCHEN PHILOLOGIE AN DER
UNIVERSITÄT BASEL.

LEIPZIG.
VERLAG VON E. W. FRITZSCH.
1872.

179 Title page of the first edition of Nietzsche's *Die Geburt der Tragödie aus dem Geiste der Musik* ('The Birth of Tragedy from the Spirit of Music'), the writing of which was influenced by Wagner and his works.

180 'The Balance-sheet for 1871', by Honoré Daumier (1808–79); lithograph.

The course of the Franco-German War of 1870–71, leading up to the surrender of the French army on 2 September at Sedan, was followed closely by Wagner, who in January 1871 wrote a poem in praise of the German victory, 'To the German army outside Paris', which he sent to the Chancellor, Otto von Bismarck. Previously, in November 1870, he had attacked the French in a 'comedy in the ancient manner', entitled *Eine Kapitulation* ('A Surrender').

181 Report from Berlin published in the *Basler Nachrichten*, 3 September 1870.

Formerly in Wagner's possession, this report reads:
Berlin 3 Sept. (official) Telegram from the King to the Queen, sent from Sedan at 1.30 p.m. on 2 Sept.
  Surrender terms just agreed with General Wimpffen, commander replacing the wounded Marshal MacMahon, under which the entire army at Sedan is taken prisoner.
  The Emperor has surrendered to me alone, since he is not in command and has handed all powers to the Regency in Paris.
  I will establish his whereabouts after I have spoken to him at a meeting to be held immediately.
  What a turning-point through God's guidance. (signed) Wilhelm

Berlin 3. Sept. (Offiziell.) Telegramm des Königs an die Königin aus **Sedan** 2. Sept. Nachmittags 1½ Uhr.

  Kapitulation, wodurch die ganze Armee in Sedan kriegsgefangen, ist soeben mit General Wimpffen geschlossen, der an der Stelle des verwundeten Marschalls Mac Mahon das Kommando führt.

  Der Kaiser hat nur sich selbst mir ergeben, da er das Kommando nicht führt und alles der Regentschaft in Paris überläßt.

  Seinen Aufenthaltsort werde ich bestimmen, nachdem ich ihn gesprochen habe in einem Rendez-vous, das sofort stattfindet.

  Welch eine Wendung durch Gottes Führung!

  Unterzeichnet: Wilhelm.

182 Proclamation of the German Empire, 18 January 1871, at Versailles, as depicted in the *Illustrirte Zeitung*, Leipzig, on 25 February.

183 Wagner's *Kaiser March* with popular chorus 'Hail to the Kaiser, King Wilhelm, saviour and protector of the freedom of all Germans! . . .', written at Triebschen, February/March 1871.

184. Portrait of Wagner, December 1871; oil painting by Franz
von Lenbach.

185 General view of Bayreuth; coloured steel engraving, c. 1870.

Wagner decided on Bayreuth as the site for his Festival Theatre in 1871, and the formal announcement of the project was made on 12 May. Cf. pp. 218–22.

186 Interior of the Margraves' Opera House, Bayreuth; oil painting by Gustav Bauernfeind, 1879.

Here, on 22 May 1872, Wagner conducted Beethoven's Ninth Symphony for Patrons who attended the laying of the Festival Theatre's foundation stone. Cf. pp. 220–1.

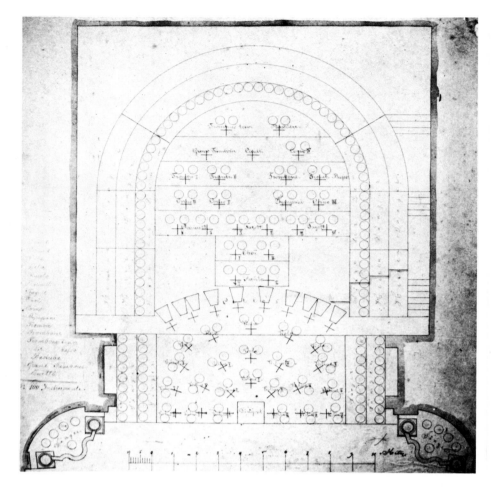

187, 188 The performance of Beethoven's Ninth Symphony on 22 May 1872 in Bayreuth.

187 Seating plan for orchestra and chorus.

188 The performance in the Margraves' Opera House with Wagner conducting, as depicted in the *Illustrirte Zeitung*, Leipzig, 15 June 1872.

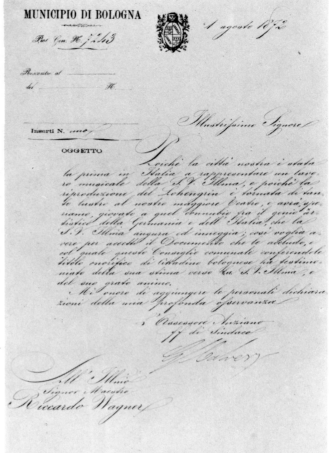

189 Certificate of Wagner's nomination as an Honorary Member of the Imperial Russian Music Society, 18 May 1872.

190 Document according Wagner honorary citizenship of Bologna, 1 August 1872.

191 Letter according Wagner citizenship of Bayreuth, 1 December 1872.

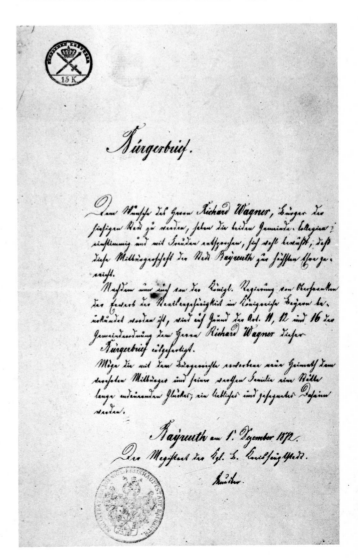

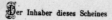

PATRONAT-SCHEIN

Nro. *N.*

Der Inhaber dieses Scheines

hat durch die hiemit quittirte Einzahlung von **300 Thalern** die Rechte eines Patrones der in

Bayreuth

zu bewerkstelligenden drei vollständigen Aufführungen des Bühnenfestspieles

„Der Ring des Nibelungen"

erworben, als welche Rechte ihm die unbedingte Verfügung über einen bequemen Sitz-
platz für jeden der zwölf Abende, in denen die dreimalige Aufführung des viertheiligen
Werkes bestehen wird, sowie ferner die Betheiligung an der Bildung einer Patronat-
Commission zuerkannt sind, welcher die Verfügung über 500 Freiplätze für jede der durch
die Beisteuer der Patrone ermöglichten Festaufführungen zustehen soll, und in welcher
der Inhaber dieses Scheines sich für eine Patronatstimme durch Delegirung vertreten
lassen wird.

BAYREUTH.

1 Februar 1872. *Richard Wagner*

Als Bevollmächtigte und Verwalter:

Feustel   Muncker   Mappler

192 A Patron's Certificate issued in return for a subscription of 300 thalers to the Bayreuth Festival undertaking.

The construction of the Festival Theatre and the staging of the first festival in 1876, at an estimated cost of 300,000 thalers, were financed through the sale of these certificates, which guaranteed the purchaser the right to attend the performances of the *Ring* cycle.

193 Design for the front elevation of the Bayreuth Festival Theatre by Otto Brückwald, 1873, bearing Wagner's comment 'Die Ornamente fort!' ('Away with the ornaments!').

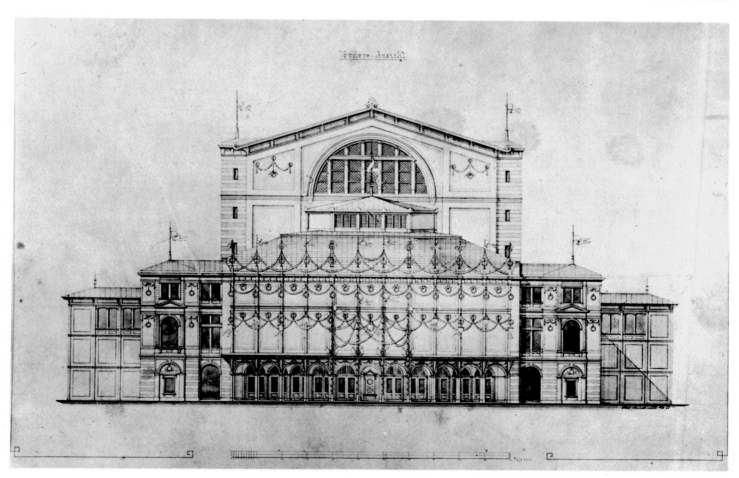

194 Title page of Wagner's manuscript *Der Ring des Nibelungen*, with dedication to Ludwig II, 1873.

195 Dedication page of Anton Bruckner's Symphony No. 3 in D major. Cf. pp. 222, 224.

Bruckner, who almost worshipped Wagner, visited Bayreuth in 1873 to seek the master's acceptance of the dedication of one of his symphonies. Given the choice of No. 2 or No. 3, Wagner opted for the latter.

196, 197 Wahnfried, Wagner's house built, largely at Ludwig II's expense, in 1873–74 and occupied by him on 28 April 1874: detail showing the sgraffito by Robert Krausse above the entrance, and general view. Cf. p. 225.

198 *Götterdämmerung*, final page of the score with the note
'Completed at Wahnfried, 21 November 1874. I say nothing
more!'.

199 200

201 202

199 Wagner conducting; drawing by Gustav Gaul, Vienna, 27 February 1875, at a concert rehearsal.

200 Announcement of a concert in Budapest, 10 March 1875, featuring works by Liszt and Wagner.

201 Silhouette inscribed: 'R. Wagner. Music Society, Vienna, 14. III. 1875'.

202 Portrait of Wagner; drawing by Gustav Gaul(?), Vienna 1875(?).

203 Caricature of Wagner by K. Klic, published in *Humoristische Blätter*, Vienna.

204 The Opernring, Vienna; coloured lithograph by Franz Alt, Vienna 1872.

In 1875 Wagner gave five concerts in Vienna to raise funds for the building of the Festival Theatre in Bayreuth, as well as rehearsing *Tannhäuser* and *Lohengrin*. Cf. p. 226.

203

204

205 The Festival Theatre, Bayreuth; photograph 1876.

206 View of Bayreuth from the Festival Theatre; photograph.

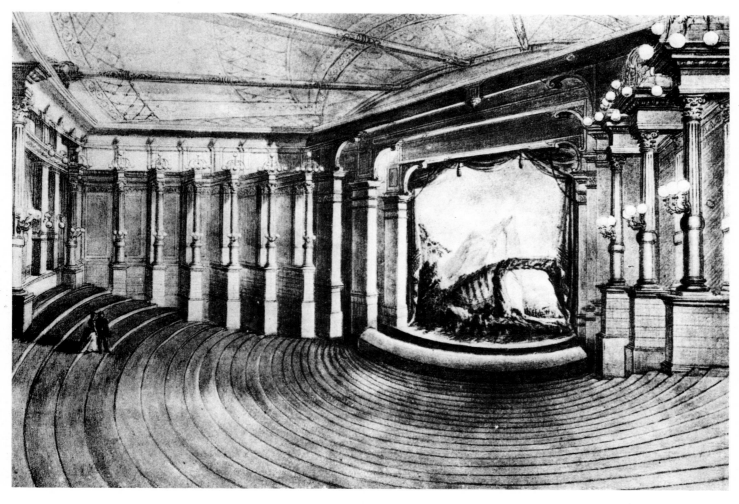

207 Wagner on the stage of the Festival Theatre during preliminary rehearsals; drawing by Adolph von Menzel (1815–1905), 8 September 1875.

208 Wagner's Last Request to my dear Colleagues', a handwritten notice dated 13 August 1876, the day of the first performance at Bayreuth, posted at the entrance to the Festival Theatre. Cf. p. 232.

209 Interior of the Festival Theatre; drawing 1875/76.

210–213 *Der Ring des Nibelungen*; designs by Joseph Hoffmann (1831–1904). The coloured originals are lost.

210 *Das Rheingold*, fourth scene.

211 *Die Walküre*, Act I, final scene.

212 *Siegfried*, Act II, scene 2.

213 *Götterdämmerung*, final scene.

212

213

214 *Die Walküre*, Act III; slide for use in a magic lantern.

215–218 *Der Ring des Nibelungen*, designs by Carl Emil Doepler.

215 Valkyries

216 Wotan

217 Siegfried

218 Norns

215

216

217

218

219–222 Characters in *Der Ring des Nibelungen*, 1876; photographs by Joseph Albert: (219) Alberich – Karl Hill; (220) Brünnhilde – Amalie Materna; (221) Siegfried – Georg Unger; (222) Norns – Johanna Jachmann-Wagner, Friederike von Sadler-Grün and Josephine Scheffzky.

223–226 *Der Ring des Nibelungen*, drawings by Knut Ekwall, done after the first performances at Bayreuth, published in the *Illustrirte Zeitung*, Leipzig, 16 and 30

September 1876: (223) *Das Rheingold*, first scene; (224) *Die Walküre*, Act II, scene 5; (225) *Siegfried*, Act III, scene 3; (226) *Götterdämmerung*, Act III, scene 2.

227 'Frou-frou Wagner', caricature by F. Grätz in *Der Floh* ('The Flea'), Vienna, 24 June 1877.

This is a caricature based on the contents of Wagner's letters to his Viennese milliner, published by Daniel Spitzer, which reveal the composer's liking for velvets and satins. Costly fabrics and sumptuous garments seem to be a prerequisite to his artistic creations.

228, 229 Caricatures from *Der Ulk* ('The Joke'), Berlin, 1876, inspired by the publicity surrounding the first Bayreuth Festival.

228 'From the modern mythology: the apotheosis of Wagner at Bayreuth'.

229 'Aeschylus and Shakespeare . . . pay their respects to the Master in the prescribed manner'.

230 *Richard Wagner at his Home in Bayreuth*, oil painting by W. Beckmann, 1882, showing (from the left): Cosima and Richard Wagner, Liszt, and Hans von Wolzogen (cf. ill. 233).

WAGNER FESTIVAL,

ROYAL ALBERT HALL, LONDON,

Monday Evening,	May	7.	Monday Evening,	May	14.
Wednesday ,,	,,	9.	Wednesday ,,	,,	16.
Saturday Morning,	,,	12.	Saturday Morning,	,,	19.

WAGNER .... Conductor.

WILHELMJ .... Leader of the Orchestra.

DANNREUTHER .... Conductor of Rehearsals.

Programme.

LONDON:

HODGE & ESSEX,

Directors,

6 and 7, ARGYLL STREET, REGENT STREET, LONDON, W.

BAYREUTHER BLÄTTER.

Monatschrift

des

Bayreuther Patronatvereines

unter Mitwirkung Richard Wagner's redigirt von H. v. Wolzogen.

Verlag von **Ernst Schmeitzner** in Chemnitz.

Januar. **Erstes Stück.** **1878.**

Inhalt: — Zur Einführung. Von Richard Wagner. — Unsere Lage. Von Hans von Wolzogen. — Geschäftlicher Theil. I. Bekanntmachungen: An die Vorstände der lok. Wagnervereine. Von R. Wagner. — Erklärung des Verwaltungsrathes. — Bitten der Redaktion. — Erklärung des Verlegers. — II. Statistik: Einnahmen des Vereines vom 16. September 1877 bis zum 1. Januar 1878. — Verzeichniss der Vertretungen.

Zur Einführung.

Wiederholt bin ich vor meinen Freunden als Schriftsteller erschienen, noch nicht aber an der Spitze einer Zeitschrift. Gab zu dem Ersteren mir der Drang der Umstände die Veranlassung, so hat auch den letzteren Entschluss mehr der Zufall als ernstere Erwägung hervorgerufen: durch seine Ausführung soll vorläufig die Verbindung, welche die Freunde meiner Kunst zum Zwecke der Förderung der praktischen Tendenzen derselben vereinigt, in möglichst erspriesslicher Weise erhalten und sinnvoll befestigt werden.

Ich kann, als den betreffenden Vereinen wohlbekannt, die letzte Veranlassung zur Herausgabe dieser „Bayreuther Blätter" übergehen; wogegen ich auf meine Eröffnungen vom 15. September des verflossenen Jahres mich zu beziehen habe, um für jetzt zu bestätigen, dass von dem, dort in weit ausgedehntem Plane vorgelegten Entwurfe, nur die Herstellung eben dieser Blätter zunächst als ausführbar sich bewährt hat.

Die Wunder unserer Zeit produziren sich auf einem anderen Gebiete als dem der deutschen Kunst und deren Förderung durch die Macht. Ein Wunder unerhörtester Art wäre es aber gewesen, wenn mein vorgelegter Plan zur Ausbildung einer vollkommen tüchtigen musikalisch-dramatischen Künstlergenossenschaft, welche die andauernde Pflege eines uns Deutschen durchaus

231 Programme for a series of eight Wagner concerts at the Royal Albert Hall, London, May 1877.

These concerts, conducted by Wagner himself, were held to raise funds to offset the deficit at the 1876 Bayreuth Festival, the final cost being considerably in excess of the estimated 300,000 thalers.

232 'The Music of the Future', cartoon in *Vanity Fair*, London 1877.

233 Photograph of the Bayreuth supporters Heinrich von Stein (1857–87), Carl Friedrich Glasenapp (1847–1915) and Hans von Wolzogen (1848–1938).

234 Page 1 of the monthly *Bayreuther Blätter*, January 1878, edited by Hans von Wolzogen until 1938; with Wolzogen's death the paper ceased publication.

235 *Parsifal*, sketch for the Song of the Flower Maidens (Act II), Bayreuth, 9 February 1876; the inscription 'Wanting to be American' (right) in Cosima's hand refers to the composition of Wagner's 'Grand Festival March . . . for the Centenary of the United States'.

236 Judith Gautier-Mendès (1846–1917), the attractive French writer with whom Wagner conducted a secret and intimate correspondence while composing *Parsifal*; photograph by Nadar, Paris 1875. Cf. pp. 239–40.

236

237 Cosima Wagner, portrait in oils by Franz von Lenbach, 1879.

238 Portrait of Wagner by Renoir, Palermo, 15 January 1882; Louvre, Paris.

A finished studio portrait by Renoir (1893) was based on this rapidly executed oil sketch. The circumstances of Renoir's visit to Wagner in Palermo in 1882 are explained by him in a letter to a friend; cf. pp. 240–1.

239 *Parsifal*, the final page of the autograph score, bearing the inscription and dedication in Wagner's hand: 'Palermo, 25. Dezember 1881. Für Dich ['For you', i.e. Cosima]'.

This page was written before the completion of the opera on 13 January 1882, so that Wagner could present the work to Cosima on her birthday.

240 Wagner with his son Siegfried; photograph by P. Biondi e Figlio, Naples, 1 June 1880.

241 The cathedral at Palermo, winter 1881/82; drawing by Siegfried Wagner.

This drawing by Siegfried was done during one of the family's several visits to Italy during the last years of Wagner's life to escape the rigours of winter in Germany. Cf. p. 240.

242 Interior of Siena cathedral; coloured lithograph, *c.* 1865.

On a visit here in 1880, Wagner was moved to tears; cf. p. 249. He took the building as the model for the Temple of the Grail in *Parsifal*.

243, 244 *Parsifal*, Klingsor's enchanted garden (Act II) and the Temple of the Grail; oil paintings by Max Brückner based on designs by Paul von Joukovsky (1845–1912).

245 *Parsifal*, announcement of the first performances for patrons and public at the Bayreuth Festival Theatre, July/August 1882.

At the last performance of the series on 29 August, Wagner climbed into the orchestra pit during Act III, and took over from the conductor Hermann Levi. This was the only occasion when Wagner personally conducted at the Festival Theatre.

246 The orchestra at the Bayreuth Festival during a rehearsal, 1882; coloured drawing by a member of the orchestra.

The orchestra was seated according to a precisely determined plan in the sloping pit which was invisible to the audience.

247 The orchestra at the Bayreuth Festival, 1882, with (centre) the two conductors – Franz Fischer and Hermann Levi; postcard.

246

247

248, 249 *Parsifal*, costume designs by Paul von Joukovsky
for the part of Kundry in Act II.

250 *Parsifal*, costume designs by Paul von Joukovsky for
the Flower Maidens in Act II.

251 Charlotte Wolter (1834–97), the leading tragedienne of her day, as Messalina (in *Arria und Messalina* by A. Wilbrandt); oil painting by Hans Makart (1840–84), Vienna 1875.

Arria und Messalina was specially written for Charlotte Wolter, who appeared at the Burgtheater, Vienna, from 1861; the undoubted influence of Makart's style is reflected in ill. 252.

252 *Parsifal*, Kundry – played by Marianne Brandt – in Act II; photograph by Hans Brand, Bayreuth 1882.

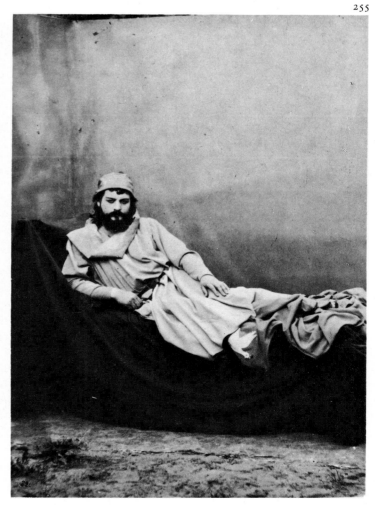

253 *Parsifal*, design by Paul von Joukovsky for the closing scene of Act III.

254, 255 *Parsifal*, photographs by Hans Brand of the 1882 production at Bayreuth, showing Gurnemanz, Kundry and Parsifal (played respectively by Emil Scaria, Amalie Materna and Hermann Winkelmann), and Amfortas (played by Theodor Reichmann).

256 Page 71 of the score, written by Anton Seidl, of Wagner's rediscovered Symphony in C major, with additions in the composer's own hand. Cf. p. 244.

This early symphony, lost since 1836, was rediscovered in 1877, and the score reconstituted by the young conductor Seidl from the instrumental parts; this was revised sporadically by Wagner. The work was performed at the Teatro la Fenice in Venice, Christmas 1882, as a birthday offering to Cosima.

257 The Teatro la Fenice, Venice; coloured steel engraving.

258 View from the canal of the Palazzo Vendramin-Calergi, Venice, in the garden wing of which Wagner lived from 18 September 1882 until his death on 13 February 1883; coloured engraving.

259 Wagner and Cosima in front of the Palazzo Vendramin-Calergi (land side); anonymous oil painting, winter 1882/83.

260 Wagner's last letter to Ludwig II, Venice, 10 January 1883.
Cp. pp. 244–5.

261 Portrait drawing of Wagner by Paul von Joukovsky, inscribed by Cosima, 'R. reading, 12 Febr. 1883'.

Overleaf
262 Wagner's death-mask, by Augusto Benvenuti, Venice, 14 February 1883.

SOURCES OF ILLUSTRATIONS

DOCUMENTS

Wilhelm Richard Wagner was born in Leipzig in 1813, the year of the Battle of the Nations, on 22 May; he was the ninth child of Friedrich Wagner (1770–1813), a police registrar, and his wife Johanna Rosine, *née* Pätz (1774–1848).

In the year 1813 the writer Ernst Theodor Amadeus Hoffmann was in Leipzig as musical director of Seconda's opera troupe. Here he made the acquaintance of Wagner's father, the police registrar and theatre enthusiast Friedrich Wagner, and of his brother the philologist and essayist, Adolf Wagner (1774–1835).

E. T. A. Hoffmann in his diary, 17 June 1813:

Evening in the Grüne Linde, *Registrar* Wagner, an exotic fellow, taking off Optiz, Iffland et al. – and very cleverly, at that – he seems to belong to the better school, too, *un poco exalt*[*ato*] after a great deal of rum.

E. T. A. Hoffmann, *Tagebücher*, ed. Friedrich Schnapp, Munich 1971, p. 213.

E. T. A. Hoffmann in his diary, 31 December 1813, about Adolf Wagner, who exercized a decisive influence on his nephew Richard from 1828 until his death:

Up late till 1.30 drinking punch at Keller's / but no real atmosphere . . . the punch was wretched and the company dreary! – Adolph Wagner – a learned man – speaks 1,700 languages – but it does not work out right –

Ibid., p. 241

In his autobiography Mein Leben, *begun in 1865, Wagner describes his mother Johanna Rosine Wagner (née Pätz), daughter of a master-baker from Weissenfels:*

A portrait of her which Geyer painted in the course of her first marriage represents her external features to great advantage. From the time that she enters at all clearly into my own memory constant headaches had already obliged her to wear a bonnet all the time, so that I never had an image of her as a youthful and attractive mother. The anxieties and pressures of bringing up a large family (of which I was the seventh living member), the difficulties in obtaining all we needed, and at the same time satisfying, despite her very limited means, a certain inclination for

ostentation robbed her of that warm tone of motherly tenderness for her family; I can hardly ever remember being cuddled by her, in fact there were never any displays of tenderness in our family; whereas a certain restless, almost wild, boisterousness appeared very natural. Under these circumstances I remember it seemed quite out of the ordinary when, one evening when I was put to bed very tired and looked up at my mother with tears in my eyes, she looked at me approvingly and spoke about me with a certain tenderness to a visitor who was present. What appealed to me most about her was the strange eagerness of the almost pathetic tone in which she spoke about the great and the beautiful in art. But to me in particular she said she never meant theatrical art by this, only poetry, music and painting, and she often used almost to threaten to curse me if I, too, should ever want to go into the theatre. At the same time she was very religiously inclined; she often addressed us in long sermon-like speeches, full of expressive pathos, about God and the divine in mankind, in the middle of which however she would sometimes suddenly lower her voice and deliver herself a joking rebuke. In later life, expecially after the death of my stepfather, she gathered the remaining members of the family around her bed each morning while she drank her coffee – but not before one of us had read aloud a song from the hymn-book. The choice of text was not taken too seriously until once, by accident, my sister *Klara* recited a 'prayer in the distress of wartime' with such emotion that mother interrupted her with the words 'Tch, come off it now! God forgive me my sins but we're not quite suffering wartime distress yet!'

Mein Leben, p. 19

A close friend of the Wagner family was the portrait painter and Dresden Court actor Ludwig Geyer (1779–1821). When Friedrich Wagner died Geyer took charge of the family. On 28 August 1814 he married Johanna Wagner. Geyer's close relationship with the Wagner family has given rise to the theory that Geyer might be Richard Wagner's natural father. There is no proof for this; but the possibility cannot be entirely discounted.

3

Als ein Opfer seines Berufs starb am 23sten Nov., im 41sten Jahre, mein Gatte, Carl Friedrich Wilhelm Wagner, erster Actuarius im Königl. Polizeyamte, viel zu früh für mich und meine acht un-erzogenen Kinder. Was er gegolten hat, als Mensch, als Freund, das hat mir jetzt die überaus zarte Sorgfalt seiner Freunde für mein und meiner Kinder Wohl besonders bewiesen, mir aber auch die Grö-ße meines Verlastes um so fühlbarer gemacht. Leipzig, den 6. Dec. 1813.
Johanne Wagner.

Notice of the death of Friedrich Wagner, the composer's father, in the *Leipziger Zeitung*, 11 December 1813.

Ludwig Geyer writes to Johanna Wagner from Dresden on 14 January 1814, after hearing the news of the recovery of her eldest son Albert from illness:

Dear Friend,

From the bottom of my heart I thank the Heavens for Albert's recovery and for the peace of mind that you will regain with this happy omen. Poor, good woman! Heaven has really marked you out to suffer, but it has also endowed you with the strength to bear it and your joy that your pleas for Albert's life have been heard must now be truly cheering and uplifting. I have certainly really shared your horror, for Albert could not be nearer to my heart if he were my own son, so I wish you and myself and Albert happiness in the new-won life, which now means so much more to all of us.

Your kind concern for me and my health deserves my hearty thanks, but, praise God, I am well, like all of us here who are close to you, and it is only because I have been occupied in the theatre every day so far and had to learn several difficult parts by heart that I have become so ill-mannered as to leave a letter unanswered. And now don't immediately jump to the wrong conclusion again, be kind and tolerant, and forgive me . . .

You will be very pleased with me when I tell you I now have no more debts, except the remainder of the tailor's bill for 10 florins Rhenisch*, 1 groschen, which 8 florins will settle; so now I can breathe quite freely, too. . .

Tell the faithful souls Jettchen and Luischen** I wish to be as high in their regard as they are in mine. And to the Cossack: his wildness cannot but be divine, for the first window he breaks he shall have a silver medal.

God keep you! Love and kisses to all my friends, and my Albert, from your

ever faithful friend

Geyer

Burrell-Briefe, pp. 586–87

3 *From August Böttiger's obituary of Ludwig Geyer, in the* Abend-Zeitung, *Dresden:*

If one considers the obstacles and constraints the strikingly talented man had to overcome right from his youth, one will be fair in one's assessment of his art and will be entirely convinced that only genuine and unremitting hard work could have achieved such eminence in two branches of art. His calling to painting was the earlier and more decisive. Had he had the opportunity to devote himself exclusively to portrait-painting his works would be preserved in the galleries, not only for their much-appreciated life-like accuracy but also as genuine works of art.

Born on 21 January 1780 in Eisleben, where his father was employed as an actuary in the Tax Inspectorate, he spent his childhood in Artern, whither his father was transferred as a magistrate. His talent for painting developed early. A painter from Leipzig, who was living in Thuringia at the time, taught all he knew to the receptive and quick-witted boy. His feeling for painting grew daily. But his conscientious father regarded this as an unsteady art, decided on jurisprudence for him and sent him to the grammar school at Eisleben in preparation for the University. After four years' preliminary schooling he went to Leipzig in 1798 to complete his studies. But his career was interrupted the very next year by the death of his father. On his way back from Dresden, where he had been offered a better-paid position, his old father was injured in a crash of the heavily laden stage-coach, was brought ill to Leipzig and died there despite the care of his tender and loving sons. Robbed of the means to continue his studies, the youth nevertheless joined his equally magnanimous brother to help take care of his family by devoting himself from now on entirely to portrait-painting. He attended the Drawing Academy in Leipzig at the same time and earned his living by doing small portraits. In the exercise of his art he spent some years visiting small provincial towns, painting young girls and old men in the spas, and returning to Leipzig in 1801. It was here that the muse of dramatic art first attracted him. His performances in a private theatre won applause, and he was further encouraged by a circle of friends who shared his passion. The hope of being able to obtain a secure position impelled him to seek employment as a professional actor on the public stage. From now on he devoted the same eager passion to his career as an actor, without however bidding farewell to his earlier love of painting. His first part was Don Carlos. It was only later that he discovered his true genre – character roles, especially in high comedy, and cloak-and-dagger parts. To begin with he tried romantic and cavalier parts. He was helped throughout by his gift of subtle observation and his quick grasp of facial expressions, and since his talent as a painter opened the door for him to the most select family circles and he thus learned to move with dignity in the highest society, it became quite easy for him to represent on the stage what he had seen in real life. The collapse of Prussia in 1806 [following the defeat at Jena] had a disastrous effect on the Stettin stage, a respected member of which he had been since 1805. Breslau, which had just paid the price of resistance, accepted him as an actor in 1807 and appreciated him as a painter. His old nostalgia for Saxony reawakened here with new strength. The affable Franz Seconda, at that time director of the Court Theatre, offered him guest appearances during the Michaelmas Fair in Leipzig in 1809. He was well received and now joined the Leipzig company, where he remained an outstanding performer until his death. The terrible war year of 1813 robbed him of his closest friend, the Leipzig police-registrar Friedrich Wagner, to whom he had always ascribed the most beneficial influence on his theatrical career and who had stood by him as friend and adviser on every subject. He had absolutely no thought for his own needs. Trusting in God and his own talents, he offered his hand to the penniless widow of the man who had been true to him unto death, and thus became father to seven orphans. He himself had only one child from this marriage, a sweet little girl.* From now on he spared no effort in and out of his artist's studio, which was often packed with

---

* Florins, same as guilders
** Richard Wagner's sisters; 'the Cossack' is presumably a reference to Richard himself

* Wagner's step-sister Cäcilie

people wanting their portraits painted, in order to raise the money to bring up and educate such a numerous family. For he had never given a thought to his own self-interest, and money was to him only a means to the most noble ends. Two of his step-children have already begun their artistic careers, Albrecht [Albert] Wagner as a singer at the Breslau Theatre and Rosalie Wagner as a beautiful young actress at the Dresden Court Theatre, both blessing the ashes of a father whose every thought, day and night, had been for their proper artistic training.

He took his art seriously, but enjoyed life so long as fresh vitality and vigorous energy flowed in his veins. He was the heart and soul of a lively circle of friends of both sexes, whom the hospitable man liked most of all to entertain in his own home and who were kept in constant good humour by his merry sparkling wit. Little family parties turned into imaginative puppet shows, and later even dramatic performances, all of which he organized himself, making the costumes and writing the texts. The success of these comic sketches, which were at first intended only for social entertainment, encouraged him to try his hand at bigger works and verse-plays. And so it came about that for some years before he died the few hours of leisure that his exertions in his studio and on the stage left him were spent on his writing, so that he finally succeeded in having some of his own works of this kind performed on the public stage. His humour was inexhaustible, although the wittiest ideas, the sparks of humour that crackled the most, depended for their effect on very specific knowledge of people or places, and, divorced from these, they lost their subtle pointedness. Three plays, which have either already appeared or will soon appear in print have become known through public performances and were reviewed at the time in these pages: *Die Braut aus der Fremde* ['The Bride from Abroad'] *Der Aerntekranz* ['The Harvest Wreath'] and *Der Bethlehemitische Kindermord*. . . .

The rather over-used device of a paint-brush poking through a palette with an actor's mask hanging lightly beside it would be most appropriate to him but only if it were laid upon a myrtle-wreath bedewed with tears.

Abend-Zeitung, Dresden, 29/30 October 1821

9–11 One of the most important impressions on the young Wagner was that made by Carl Maria von Weber, who was employed from 1816 as the musical director of the Deutsche Oper in Dresden and was friendly with the Wagner family. *Der Freischütz* was first performed in Berlin in 1821 and was repeated in Dresden the following year.

Ferdinand Avenarius, the son of Wagner's step-sister Cäcilie Geyer, on the young Wagner's enthusiasm for Der Freischütz:

At that time the boy's whole mind was full of *Der Freischütz* – one example among many will prove this. Among other things Richard had a theatre in his room. As soon as he had seen *Der Freischütz*, he had to put it on immediately. It was – naturally – the scene in the wolf's glen that the boy felt was most suitable. So out came the papier-mâché and the glue in order to produce the necessary

equipment. His school-friends had to join in the work. Scenery and curtains, fireworks and animals – everything was produced; my mother particularly admired a great boar, which was rolled in on a plank looking with its fearful tusks horribly like the Prince of Hell in person. The performance was to be staged at a friend's. Richard played Caspar, but Max hadn't learned his part, and when Richard whispered his disapproval he at first laughed, then swore. And the others laughed and jeered, too.

Ferdinand Avenarius, 'Richard Wagner als kind. Nach Erinnerungen seiner Schwester Cäcilie Avenarius und anderer Jugendgenossen,' *Allgemeine Zeitung*, Munich, 15 March 1883

In 1829 Wagner saw the singer Wilhelmine Schröder-Devrient in Leipzig playing Leonora in Beethoven's *Fidelio*. Her interpretation had a lasting influence on Wagner's ideas on musico-dramatic performance.

Wagner in *Mein Leben:*

But now the time came when my interest in the theatre again seized me passionately. A new company had been formed under very propitious auspices in my home town, thanks to the efforts of the Dresden Court Theatre management, which had also taken over the direction of the Leipzig theatre for three years. My sister Rosalie had joined this company; through her I could always get in easily to the performances, and the interest which in my childhood had been no more than the curiosity of a vivid imagination now became a more thoroughgoing and conscious passion. *Julius Caesar, Macbeth, Hamlet,* Schiller's plays and finally Goethe's *Faust* filled me with excitement and enthusiasm. The Opera put on the first performances of Marschner's *Vampyr* and *Der Templer und die Jüdin*. The 12, 13 Italian opera company came from Dresden and delighted the Leipzig audiences with demonstrations of their extraordinary virtuosity. I, too, was almost on the point of being swept away by the fever which they excited throughout Leipzig – even to the extent of eclipsing the impressions which Signor Sassaroli* had imprinted on my mind as a child – when another miracle occurred, which also came to us from Dresden and which gave my artistic feelings a decisive new direction that was to be of life-long significance.

This was a short season of guest appearances by Wilhelmine Schröder-Devrient, who was then at the very peak of her artistic career – youthful, with a warmth and beauty such as I have never seen in any woman on the stage since – she appeared in *Fidelio*.

When I look back on my whole life I can think of hardly any event which I could set beside this as being comparable in its effect on me. Any man who can remember this wonderful woman from that period of her life must somehow be able to bear witness to the almost primeval warmth which such a humanly ecstatic performance as that of this incomparable artiste must certainly have radiated over him. After the performance I raced round to one of my acquaintances to write a short letter in which I declared irrevocably to the great artiste that from that

* An Italian castrato

day my life had acquired its true meaning, and if one day in the world of art she should hear my name mentioned with praise, she should remember that on this evening she made me what I hereby swore I intended to become. I delivered this letter to the singer's hotel and fled into the night like a madman. When I went to Dresden in 1842 for the première of *Rienzi*, I frequently visited the house of this warm-hearted singer; once she surprised me by an accurate recitation of that letter, which seemed to have impressed her too, since she really had preserved it.

Mein Leben, pp. 48–49

Wagner decided to be a musician and composer. At first he tried to teach himself the necessary knowledge; in 1828 he took secret lessons from the composer Christian Gottlieb Müller (1800–63), a violinist in the Gewandhaus orchestra. Once his family accepted his determination to become a musician, Wagner's lessons with Müller became official. In the autumn of 1831 the precentor at the Thomasschule, Christian Theodor Weinlig (1780–1842), took Müller's place. Although he followed his composition lessons very closely, Wagner attached little importance to learning an instrument, which he neglected and finally abandoned. His piano-playing remained inadequate throughout his life.

The Leipzig Gewandhaus violinist Robert Sipp about his one-time pupil Richard Wagner:

He was quick to grasp things, but he was lazy and did not bother to practise. He was my worst pupil.

Burrell-Briefe, p. 30

Wagner in a letter of March 1834(?) to the Leipzig producer Franz Hauser, about his lessons with Christian Gottlieb Müller and Theodor Weinlig:

I had the good fortune to have the strictest and most candid of teachers; my lessons with Herr Müller were a series of almost depressing indications of a well-nigh pedantically strict frankness; he hardened me against the most damaging and discouraging outbursts of my youthful energy by making me realize that they were only the edifying proofs of sincerity, even if the latter did not always spring from the most untarnished source. When I had finished learning harmony from Herr Müller and began to tackle counterpoint, I felt – and others I asked also felt – that this teacher would no longer be adequate for me, and so I continued my studies with Herr Weinlig. This man, to whom I owe more than any achievements of mine will ever be able to repay, now saw at once what I needed. To start with, he suspended the study of actual counterpoint in order to assure me of a completely secure base in harmony; so first he put me through the strict style of classical harmony and did not move on until he felt I had fully mastered it, for in his opinion this strict style was the first and only starting-point, not only in order to use free and rich harmony but definitely also in order to learn counterpoint. He now started me off on the study of counterpoint with the clearest directions and according to the strictest principles, and when he felt he had provided me with the surest foundations by bringing me to perfection in this, the last and most difficult stage of general

152

musical study, he dismissed me with the following words: 'I hereby release you from your studies, as a master does his apprentice when he has learned all that the master can teach him.'

I felt immensely strengthened by this deep and serious study; I felt myself to be in possession of the means which enabled me to go forward and educate myself in the world. To this end, both my teacher and I believed I should tread the path of a public career since it is this that holds the key to a universal education. Thus even in the course of my studies Herr Weinlig was not only against the performance of the instrumental compositions I had worked on at that period, he positively desired their performance and indeed promoted them vigorously. And so, during and after this time, several overtures and finally a symphony of mine were performed at our subscription concerts, and I am pleased to be able to say that it never did me any harm: on the contrary, I enjoyed not only the advantage of hearing my pieces and thus of obtaining greater clarity in matters of musical technique but also that of being in the public eye.

Sämtliche Briefe, vol. 1, pp. 150–51

Through Christian Gottlieb Müller Wagner got to know the works of Beethoven. It was the Ninth Symphony which left the most lasting impression on him. He copied it out with the greatest care and began preparing a piano arrangement. On 6 October 1830 he offered this score to the Mainz publishers, B. Schott's Söhne, who were the original publishers of Beethoven's symphony, but his score was turned down.

Wagner to the publishers, B. Schott's Söhne:

Honoured Sir,
I have long made Beethoven's magnificent last symphony the object of my most attentive study, and the more I realized the greatness of the work the more it saddened me to think that it is still so neglected, so completely unknown to the greater part of the musical public. Now what would make this masterwork more accessible would be an arrangement for the piano, which to my regret I have never yet come across (for the four-handed arrangement by Czerny will obviously not serve this purpose). In my enthusiasm I have therefore dared to attempt myself to produce a version of this symphony for *two hands*, and so far I have succeeded in arranging the first – probably most difficult – movement with the greatest possible clarity and fullness. I therefore apply now to your resp. publishing company to enquire whether you would be interested in bringing our such an arrangement (for of course I should not be inclined to continue with such a laborious task without this certainty). As soon as I receive your confirmation I shall immediately set to work to complete what I have begun. I should therefore be most grateful for a speedy reply; as for myself, honoured Sir, you may be assured of my most earnest diligence.

My address: Your
Leipzig, im Pichhof before the   obedient servant
Halle Gate, 1st staircase   Richard Wagner

Sämtliche Briefe, vol. 1, p. 117

The revolution which broke out in Paris in July 1830 strengthened the movements for national liberation in many European countries. Wagner followed it with intense sympathy. He was particularly excited by the struggle of the Polish people for liberation from Russian domination, which ended in the Battle of Ostrolénka on 26 May 1831. In the autumn of that year Polish refugees arrived in Leipzig.

Wagner in his autobiography:

My short but intense student life had more or less swamped not only my impulse for my artistic development but also my interest in anything else, spiritual or secular. However, while I never quite lost touch with my music, as I have shown, it was with the reawakening of my interest in political events that I felt the first shudder of disgust with the senseless dissolute student life, which was soon to be forgotten altogether, like a bad dream. It was the *Polish liberation movement* against Russian domination which quickly filled me with growing enthusiasm. The successes which the Poles achieved for a short while in the month of May 1831 filled me with amazement and ecstasy: it seemed to me as though the world by some miracle had been re-created. But then the news of the Battle of Ostrolénka made me feel as though the world had once again come to an end . . .

Of course my excitement knew no bounds when the first columns of the remnants of the Polish army passed through Leipzig on their emigration to France, and I shall never forget the sight of one of the first companies of these unfortunates, who were lodged in the Grünes Schild in the Fleischergasse. But if this had made me feel very dejected, this feeling was soon to give way to enthusiastic enchantment, for in the foyer of the Leipzig Gewandhaus, where Beethoven's C-Minor Symphony was to be played

Letter from Wagner to the Mainz publishers, B. Schott's Söhne, 6 October 1830 offering his piano version of Beethoven's Ninth Symphony (for translation see text).

that evening, I was able to observe with great interest a group of heroic figures which consisted of several of the most distinguished leaders of the Polish uprising. I was immensely attracted by the uncommonly powerful figure and thoroughly manly physiognomy of a man like Count *Vincenz Tyskiewics* who combined a quiet, dignified air with a self-assurance and poise which had been quite unknown to me until then. The sight of a man of such royal bearing in his jerkin and red velvet cap destroyed at a stroke any trace of admiration which I had had until then for the affected fighting-cock pose of the heroes of our student world. I was delighted soon after to come across precisely this man at the home of my brother-in-law *Friedrich Brockhaus* and to meet him there frequently as though at home for a long time after. For my brother-in-law was outstanding in his most passionate devotion to the unfortunate Polish fighters: he headed a committee which made them its constant concern, and he himself proved his sympathy over a long period by very consider-able sacrifices. The Brockhaus' house thus became a great attraction for me . . .

Now the 3rd of May approached. Eighteen Poles who were still in Leipzig got together for a celebration dinner in a restaurant outside the city: there they were to celebrate the first anniversary, so dear to Polish remembrance, of the founding of their Constitution. Only the officers of the Leipzig Polish Committee, and, out of special consideration and love, myself too, were invited to it. It was an unforgettably moving day. The men's dinner became a feast: a brass band from the town played Polish folk-songs non-stop, in which, led by a Lithuanian by the name of *Zàn*, the whole company joined – jubilant or lamenting. Especially the fine 'Third of May Song' aroused shattering enthusiasm. Tears and shouts of joy built up into a thunder-ing tumult until the groups spread out on to the lawns in the garden and broke up into individual loving couples, in whose passionate exchanges the word '*Oiczisna*' (father-land) was the inexhaustible motto, until at last the veil of serene intoxication hid everyone in the night. The dreams of that night I later developed into an orchestral composition in the form of an overture with the title '*Polonia*'.

Mein Leben, pp. 74–77

In the spring of 1832 Wagner's lessons with Theodor Weinlig came to an end. His first major work was a symphony in C major. It had its first performance at the Prague Conservatoire in November 1832 during Wagner's journey to Prague and Vienna. Further performances took place on 15 December 1832 at the Leipzig 'Euterpe' Music Society and on 10 January 1833 at the Gewandhaus.

Clara Wieck, later Schumann, reports in a letter to Robert Schumann from Leipzig, 17 December 1832:

On Saturday father went to the 'Euterpe'.★ I say, Herr Wagner has outstripped you; they played a symphony by him which is supposed to have resembled the A major

★ The 'Euterpe' Music Society was run by Wagner's first composition teacher, Chr. G. Müller

Was man sich nicht bis zur Form ausgebildet hat, das besitzt man auch noch nicht.

Heinr Laube.

Heinrich Laube (1806–84), Wagner's friend and editor of the Leipzig paper *Zeitung für die elegante Welt*. Drawing by Friedrich Pecht, Paris 1840, Museum für Geschichte der Stadt Leipzig.

symphony of Beethoven to a tee. Father said: the symphony by F. Schneider,* which was done in the Gewandhaus could be compared to a horse and cart which took *two days* to get to Wurzen, kept straight on the road and a dozy old driver with a big peaked cap kept muttering to the horses, 'Come on, gee up, giddyup, giddyup'. But Wagner drove his gig up hill and down dale and was in the ditch every minute. But he got to Wurzen in *one day*, even though he was black and blue all over.

Berthold Litzmann, *Clara Schumann*, vol. 1, Leipzig 1902, p. 55

The writer Heinrich Laube on Wagner's symphony:

The same dominant attitude that I have already described with respect to other things, naturally also influences their judgment of artistic performances. This is especially

* Friedrich Schneider (1786–1853), a highly regarded composer in his time

narrow-minded, limited, petty-bourgeois in relation to the theatre. Which is the more remarkable here, inasmuch as under Küstner's directorship Leipzig long had an outstanding theatre, Mostly they lack any refinement of taste and their reactions are pretty predictable. This even applies to many connoisseurs, who assess art according to stereotyped formulas, and thus for all their knowledge, their judgment still lacks taste. Of course, there are exceptions; I am talking about the *general* impression. In view of this state of affairs, the *subscription concerts* which are performed at the Gewandhaus under the direction of *Pohlenz*, the musical director, really astonished me by their excellence, both in the choice of programmes and in their execution; and there, apart from those for whom music is just a means of whiling away a few hours and the concert-hall a place to meet people, you also find those who enjoy music and are delighted by it, and love it because it is beautiful. Admittedly you have to seek them

Wagner's Symphony in C major:
opening of the first violin part, by a
Parisian copyist, 1832.
Staatsbibliothek (Preussischer
Kulturbesitz), Berlin.

out amongst the large circle of those who only love music because they understand it. But these *Gewandhaus* concerts are an expression of the best and most refined taste. The symphonies of the humorous eccentric, the musical poet made sad by the world's happiness, Beethoven, who wrote his scores in his own blood, his symphonies are at home here, and the flood of poetry that pours from them really does affect most of the audience with joy. In the course of the winter I heard there another symphony, conceived and written in the same genre, by a young composer, *Richard Wagner*, which aroused in me the most sympathetic interest in the works of the young musician. There is a pert and lively energy in the thoughts which intertwine in this symphony, he storms boldly from one end of the work to the other, and yet there is such a virginal naivety in the conception of the basic themes that I place great hopes in the musical talents of the composer.

Zeitung für die elegante Welt, Leipzig, 27 April 1833

In January 1833 Wagner moved to Würzburg. There, through the influence of his brother, the singer and producer Albert Wagner (1799–1874), he obtained the post of chorus-master at the theatre. Wagner stayed in Würzburg for a year.

Text of Wagner's contract of employment in Würzburg:

Under the personal guarantee of Frau Johanna Geyer, of Rosalia Wagner, actress, resident in the Pichhof, Leipzig, and of Herr Albert Wagner, singer, actor and producer, resident in Würzburg, for the punctuality and obedience of the Minor Richard Wagner, until now student of music in Leipzig, son of the actor's widow Johanna Geyer, the said Richard Wagner is taken on as chorus-master for the Stadttheater in Würzburg, from the first day of his activity until Palm Sunday 1834. Richard Wagner will be employed principally as chorus-master. If need be, however – and for this both he and the guarantors of his

155

diligence have given their permission and consent – he is to make himself useful as required in walk-on and spoken parts in plays and tragedies and in mimed groups in the ballet. In the event of indiscipline or irregularities the management shall have the right to punish Herr Richard Wagner in accordance with the theatre regulations. If the case should arise that Richard Wagner's income is insufficient to pay any fines that may be imposed, the above-mentioned guarantors undertake to pay them to the theatre management on his behalf. Richard Wagner will put his complete energies and the services required of him at the disposal of the management of the Stadttheater at all times; in return for the punctual fulfilment of his obligations, he will be paid a monthly fee of 10 guilders, in writing ten guilders Rhenish, by the management.

Allgemeine Musik-Zeitung, Berlin, 14 October 1910

Wagner on his activity in Würzburg in 1833:

My brother Albert, who now entered my life as something of a stranger . . . obtained for me . . . occasional work as chorus-master at the theatre, for which I received 10 guilders a month. So I devoted the rest of the winter to my first practical experience of conducting: in the quite short time still available we had to learn two big new operas, in which the chorus has a major part to play, namely Marschner's *Vampyr* and Meyerbeer's *Robert le diable* . . . My brother, who was singing in Bellini's *Straniera*, wanted to include in it a cavatina from that composer's *Pirati*, the orchestral score of which was unobtainable; so he asked me to orchestrate it for him. From the piano version I was quite unable to recognize the noisy, thick instrumentation of the – musically so extraordinarily thin – ritornelli and interludes, and the best that the composer of a grand symphony in C major with fugal finale could manage here was flutes and clarinets playing in thirds. In the orchestral rehearsal the cavatina sounded so terribly empty and ineffective that my brother decided to do without it and reproached me bitterly for the wasted copyist's expenses. But I had my revenge: I added a new allegro to Aubry's tenor aria in Marschner's *Vampyr*, for which I wrote both words and music. My piece came over as demonic and effective and earned me the applause of the audience and the encouraging approval of my brother.

In the course of that year (1833) I then composed the music of my *Feen* in the same German style.

Mein Leben, pp. 91–92

In the summer of 1834 Wagner became musical director of Heinrich Bethmann's theatre company in Magdeburg. He made his début with Mozart's *Don Giovanni* in the summer theatre in Bad Lauchstädt. There he made the acquaintance of the actress Minna Planer, later to become his wife.

Wagner on his first engagement as musical director and his first meeting with Minna Planer:

My family had been waiting impatiently for my return to tell me that I had been offered the post of musical director with the *Magdeburg* theatre company. This com-

The opening of Wagner's first printed work, his essay on 'The German Opera', which appeared in the Leipzig *Zeitung für die elegante Welt*, 10 June 1834.

pany was at the time making summer guest appearances at *Bad Lauchstädt* . . .

In the time of Schiller and Goethe this little spa had achieved wide fame and importance; the wooden theatre was constructed to a design by Goethe; it was there that his play *Die Braut von Messina* had had its first performance. I repeated all this to myself and yet the place still made a dubious impression on me. I enquired after the house of the theatre manager; he had gone out: a dirty little boy, his son, was to take me to the theatre to find 'Daddy'. But he met us before we got there, an elderly man in a dressing gown and a cap on his head. His pleasure at meeting me was interrupted by complaints that his stomach was very upset, to overcome which he sent his son to fetch a schnaps from a nearby stall, handing him – with some ostentation for my benefit – a genuine silver *groschen* for the purpose. The manager was Heinrich Bethmann, widower of the famous actress, who had belonged to the golden age of German theatre and had won the favour of the king of Prussia so whole-heartedly that even her husband continued to enjoy it for a long time after her death. Bethmann always drew a good pension from the Prussian Court and enjoyed the latter's protection, and for all his bohemian and disreputable behaviour, he never quite managed to alienate this patronage entirely. At that time his continuous theatre management schemes had already brought him down to a very low ebb; his language and manners bespoke the genteel elegance of a bygone age, while all that he did and everything around him bore witness to the most unworthy decay. He led me back to his house, where he introduced me to the Frau Direktorin who, lame in one foot, lay on a weird couch, while an oldish bass – regarding whose excessive devotedness Bethmann complained to me without ceremony – sat beside her smoking his pipe. From there the director took me to meet the producer, who lived in the same house, and left him to make all necessary arrangements. The producer, Herr *Schmale*, who was involved in consultations about the repertoire with the theatre factotum, a toothless old skeleton, shrugged smilingly and assured me that it was just typical of the manager to dump everything on him and to concern himself with nothing: there he was sitting now and had been discussing with *Kröge* for a whole hour as to what they could put on next Sunday; he might well have performed *Don Giovanni* but how could he arrange a rehearsal, since the Merseburg town band, who constituted the orchestra, would not come over to rehearse on a Saturday? While he was explaining this, Schmale was constantly reaching out through the open window to the branch of a cherry tree, picking and eating from it non-stop, and spitting the stones out with uncommon energy. It was particularly the latter which had a decisive effect on me, since I strangely have an inborn dislike of fruit. I declared to the producer that he need not worry about *Don Giovanni* that Sunday, since I for my part, if they had been counting on my making my début at this performance, had no alternative but to upset the director's plans myself, since I was obliged to return at once to Leipzig to clear up my affairs there. This polite circumlocution of my complete refusal of the post, which I had immediately determined upon, involved me in some further dissimulation, as a result of which I ended up having to attend to a number of matters while in Lauchstädt, which in view of my determination not to return, was really rather unnecessary. They offered to help me find accommodation, and a young actor whom I happened to know from my time in Würzburg took it upon himself to be my guide. He said to me that by taking me to the best lodging that he knew of he would be making me the neighbour of the prettiest and nicest girl to be found in Lauchstädt at that time: namely the company's leading lady, Fräulein *Minna Planer*, of whom I would undoubtedly already have heard.

As chance would have it the lady in question met us in the doorway of the house itself. Her appearance and bearing were in most striking contrast to all the unpleasant impressions of the theatre, which I had just received that fateful morning: of very charming and fresh features, the young actress stood out through the great sedateness and earnest assurance of her movements and demeanour, which endowed her warm features with a pleasantly arresting dignity; her neat and modest mode of dress completed the striking impact of this most unexpected encounter. When I was introduced to her in the hallway of the house as the new musical director, she studied me with surprise that, for one so young, the newcomer should enjoy such a title, but then she recommended me to the landlady for good lodgings and went out across the road with a proud and unhurried step to go to the theatre rehearsal. I took the rooms on the spot, sent word that I would conduct *Don Giovanni* on Sunday, regretted not

having brought my luggage with me from Leipzig and returned to fetch it as quickly as possible, in order to hurry back to Lauchstädt quicker still.

Mein Leben, pp. 105–108

Wagner to Minna Planer, Magdeburg, 8 November 1835:

Yesterday I had no letter from you, my dear bride; – I beg and implore you, write to me every day during your present absence; if you really love me, I am sure that however much your gallant visitors impose on your time, you will always find a half-hour, a quarter of an hour even, which you can devote to your poor Richard, for whom this is now the only solace, the one and only comfort in his terrible sufferings; oh, don't deprive him of it; – for all I look forward to is your letters, – in the end they must bring me your consent to my most ardent requests and pleas; it cannot be otherwise; it will not be otherwise; – I shall sooner get used to the idea of an early death than a separation from you. Well, I'll not touch on this subject today, what else is there to say after my earlier letters; the girls whose innermost heart is not reached by these pleas, these representations, these addresses, – that girl's heart will never be reached by anything – except – a sharp knife. Well, I'll be still today and tell you about me.

My life?! – Almighty God, can there be a more wretched, more miserable life! I am alone here in this town, alone, deserted as if dead; not a soul, not a thing which arouses the tiniest spark of interest in me; everything for me is cold and empty! It was only because of you that I came here and took on this job; you were the focal point of my existence here, for it was only through you that these houses and streets interested me; it was thinking of you that I carried out my duties, for I well knew you were up in the box while I was down at the conductor's desk: I knew that you liked me so, and this vanity made me feel so good; – And now, – Everything gone! – With what horrible indifference I go on to the stage, where your dear face will no longer appear before me; how disdainfully I think of my work, and, oh, with what feelings I enter your house; I now never open the right-hand parlour door, if I were to knock, there would be no sweet inviting 'Come in!', would there? I go into the left-hand room, which I could never stand before; I see your sister in *your* dressing-gown, opposite me *Otterstedt's* picture, I drink alone from the glass from which I only ever drank together with you; your mother pours me my coffee in your cup, so that I don't forget you; O Heavens! And now to cap it all, such stupid, indifferent people like this fellow Schreiber, who now – almost as though he meant to mock me – gets more and more importunate with Amalie; I have to watch them kissing. Minna, – Minna, – and you expect me to put up with this misery for long? It is appalling! You know how soft-hearted I am, you have seen my tears often enough and kissed them away from my eyes; doesn't it upset you to think of me now? – I work all the harder as an antidote to my grief; I get up at seven and write to you; then I work through to one o'clock at my opera, which is now welling up powerfully inside me again, intimately tied up with my union with you; then I have lunch, then pop over quickly to my sisters, and then back home again; at work again until seven; then over to your family – my family – again, and finally back home to my sad and lonely bed.

But how long can one stand this sort of life; in the end I shall simply go to pieces! I am getting quite clottish, and shy of contact with others; I have forgotten how to love and to hate and am going under; that is my lot, an awful lot that was surely not meant for me. O, and don't deceive yourself into thinking that time will soothe and cure my grief; time has a quite different effect on me. Instead of gradually dulling and weakening my love for you the passage of time has only made it firmer and more enduring; and the same would happen to my wretchedness at our separation; I can already feel it gnawing away at my heart.

But you won't let me sink, you'll come back to me, we'll belong to one another again and never separate again! It cannot, it will not be otherwise! It is only this hope that sustains me! – God greet you, my angel!

Your
Richard

Sämtliche Briefe, vol. 1, p. 240ff.

Wagner to Robert Schumann, Magdeburg, 19 April 1836:

Dearest Friend,
I am enclosing a sort of report on MAGDEBURG; actually there isn't much to say, and all in all I haven't said much either. At one point I have addressed you personally, if you don't like it change it however you like. With the best will in the world I could not avoid saying something about myself – firstly because in a musical report on MAGDEBURG I have to be mentioned anyway since I am musical director here; secondly it would be silly to suppress myself (since I don't deserve it), and the reason thirdly why I have written about my opera is that no one else will write about it and I would particularly like something to be said about it. It is terrible how one has to help oneself out! Not that I feel I have said too much about myself, though. Still you will certainly see that my name must not be mentioned – not to anyone, otherwise woe is me!

I shall probably see you again soon in Leipzig one day; God knows, I am really looking forward to it. There are nothing but bloody Philistines here! Adieu, dearest Schumann!

Your
Richard Wagner

Sämtliche Briefe, vol. 1, pp. 260–61

Wagner's anonymous report in Robert Schumann's musical journal (see preceding document):

27 From Magdeburg
(The intrigues – The Opera)
Magdeburg – Tell me frankly and honestly, what is Magdeburg doing in a musical journal? I have not often had the opportunity of finding out, and that precisely is the problem, for I can tell you *secretly* – for the *public* just would not believe it – that sometimes they really do play good music here; but the fact that not even the citizens of Magdeburg, let alone visitors, notice it – that precisely is the curse which seems to hang over every violin string and

every vocal chord unfortunate enough to be cast away here. The degree of indifference shown by the local populace is surely unlawful – they should have the police in to stop it for here it is becoming subversive. I bet it is a cover for seditious political machinations and it would be a true public service to draw the attention of the highest authorities to all those private parties, card-clubs etc. and to cast suspicion on them from time to time; for they cannot be hatching anything very worth while. But people hide the really dangerous purpose of their gatherings from the eyes of the uninitiated with such polish that one cannot help admiring them. Consider the ploy of beginning one of these subversive meetings with a concert – very subtly done: the invite good-natured souls like myself to come and hear the concert. I go into a well-lit hall, everything is laid on as you would expect, they play symphonies, concertos, overtures, they sing arias and duets and spare no effort to make you think it is a genuine concert. But a politically trained eye soon notices something wrong: the indifference, the boredom, the restlessness in the auditorium; you realize that the whole thing is a blind, set up to deceive the spies and informers; the nearer the concert gets to the end the more eagerly the eyes of the conspirators are turned to a great closed door. What is behind it? During the adagio of the symphony you can hear plates being rattled in the next room. The restlessness begins to spread; at this moment happily the orchestra lets loose a real furore; it seems as though they have been paid to stifle the shuffling, coughing and sneezing of the conspirators, so as to distract our attention from these sweet signals. The concert is over, everyone gets ready to go, respectable people like myself take their hats, and then the suspicious door is opened and tell-tale smells float into the hall, the conspirators throng through the door together – I am politely turned away – the whole deception is now clear. How can anyone doubt that something dastardly is going on? For my part I am surprised at the forbearance of the police. But what is the use of my warning – the police do not read musical journals, so they will not see this warning, either.

Still, let me assure you once again that occasionally there is serious music to be heard at these concerts. An orchestra with a full complement of instrumentalists, which, when it pulls itself together, is capable of outstanding achievement, a good soprano, Mme Pollert, released for these suspicious concerts by kind permission of the theatre manager, a conductor full of fire and newly-wed passion – what more can one want? I will go further and say what more can you want when I assure you that there was an opera season this winter as never seen here before? But what of the fact that everyone here granted this fact – and still no one went ot the opera? What of the fact that this opera-company was unable to survive and had to be disbanded before the winter season was even finished? What about that, then, eh? But joking apart, it was a sorry story; hard work, chance and good luck finally produced, as I say, an opera ensemble here such as we could scarcely hope to improve on. For example, I should like to see another theatre that could easily fill the three soprano parts in [Auber's] *Lestocq* better than we could with Mesdames Pollert, Limbach and Schindler – Elisabeth, Catherina and Eudoria. We had a reliable first tenor, Freimüller, a second, Schreiber, with a charming, youthful

158

chest-voice, and a good bass, Krug, who also made a good job of training the chorus. Add to this the fact that a young and gifted artist, the conductor Richard Wagner, shaped the whole ensemble with great skill and imagination and you will not be surprised to hear that altogether we were offered some really enjoyable performances. Amongst these I include three new productions: *Jessonda, Lestocq* and *Norma*. The season ended with a new opera by R. Wagner – *Das Liebesverbot oder die Novize von Palermo* ['Forbidden Love, or The Novices of Palermo']. The disaster had already happened, the ensemble was already breaking up and it was only under the most disastrous circumstances that the composer was able to rush this opera on to the stage at the last moment. So the performance was very rough and ready – or rather not ready – but even allowing for this it is hard to see what on earth can have impelled the composer to choose Magdeburg for the première of a work such as this opera. I regret in fact that I cannot yet offer a full review of the piece; what is a single performance – and that only half intelligible? – the performers on stage did not even know their parts. But one thing I do know: if the composer manages to get his work performed in a better theatre it will succeed. There is a great deal in it, and what I particularly like about it is that it all sings, it is so musical, tuneful, which I am afraid is more than can be said for our other German operas today.

But I can see clearly from Herr Wagner and the likes of him and me what a torment it is to feel energy and movement in every nerve and every fibre and have to live in a place like this city of soldiers and merchants. Life here is very upright and very vague – there is not even a really definite air of reaction, which would at least represent some kind of movement, and if things went backwards long enough there would be a chance of a return to some primeval state, which might make a pleasant change; but no – things just stand still. I feel moreover an inner confidence that it will never be different here, so you have no need to worry that you will receive many reports of this kind from me; nothing does any good.

Neue Zeitschrift für Musik, Leipzig, 3 May 1836

After the bankruptcy of Bethmann's theatre company Wagner left Magdeburg. Although unemployed, he followed Minna Planer, to whom he was now engaged, to Königsberg. There he married the actress on 24 November 1836. On 1 April 1837 Wagner became musical director of the Königsberg Theatre.

Minna Planer as Amalia in Schiller's Die Räuber – *review in the Königsberg* Unterhaltungsblätter, *23 November 1836:*

Miss Planer as Amalia. – When you see the *great artist* in one role it is hard to imagine her in any other, and yet at the same time you cannot help thinking how her magic would carry her through any part. When she first appears on stage, even before she begins to unfold the melody of her speech and the burning flower of passion, she stands there like the statue of an ancient goddess descended from her pedestal. You wish you could always see her in this state of calm, wish the storm of heart-rending passions would never darken her beautiful brow. But as soon as

she begins to act you are amazed to see that not only does her sweet mouth become even more beautiful when she smiles, she still radiates grace even in her anger. In her fury at the devilish Franz Moor her brows contract, her eyes, which can radiate the heavens, darken and roll with anger. But as the ancient Greek sculptor could imbue even the terror and agony of Niobe with a feeling of grace – without by any means weakening the expression – in the same way one such as Miss *Planer* blends the most varied elements into an evening blooming laurel-wreath which crowns her divine brow. How she enlivens Hermann's narration, with such a wealth of different movements, of beautiful, expressive poses and significant gestures! How magnificent she was in the scene where she tears Franz's sword from him and again where she melts into Carl's arms! There is not a moment which she does not fill with added meaning. And yet all this passion is controlled with divine composure. What is the muse? A mere figment of the imagination. But here Nature has stamped her ideal in glorious reality and presented sculptors eith their most perfect model.

[signed] Sph—x.

Burrell Collection, no. 74., Curtis Institute of Music, Philadelphia, Pa.

Announcement in the Königsberg Unterhaltungsblätter, *23 November 1836:*

Today, Wednesday 23 November.
Benefit performance for Miss Planer.
Die Stumme von Portici★
Who will refuse his presence today to the artist who has spared no effort to give pleasure to others through her charming and remarkable performances? When she appears this evening in a production for her own benefit, she is sure to repay her audience with a particularly outstanding achievement. Miss Grosser and Miss Planer will vie with each other, the former as a great soprano, the latter as an unsurpassable mime. May they both win the crown of fame, which they are both so worthy to share. Herr M.D. [Musikdirektor] Wagner★★ will conduct the opera and will certainly strive to deserve his own share of the applause which will crown this fine performance.

Burrell Collection, no. 74, Curtis Institute of Music, Philadelphia, Pa.

The theatre's bankruptcy again cost Wagner his post. In August 1837 he became conductor at the theatre in Riga.

The theatre building at Riga:

In fact the . . . auditorium of the old Riga Stadttheater in the Königstrasse was a pretty gloomy place by today's standards. It had only one block of stalls, immediately above which was the gallery, which was much frequented by middle-class families, and both younger and older ladies, equipped with their knitting and the necessary

★ Minna Planer in the part of the dumb girl
★★ Wagner was appearing as guest-conductor

refreshments, could be seen arriving early (the places being unnumbered) to assure themselves of a comfortable seat, preferably on the balustrade, and there to await what was to follow. With regard to this auditorium, the cellist Arved Poorten, who was born in Riga, interrupted the Master to call it a stable, a barn, and asked, 'How on earth, Master, were you able to conduct there?' To which Wagner replied very seriously: *three* things had stuck in his memory as being particularly remarkable about this 'barn': firstly the steeply rising stalls, rather like an ampitheatre, secondly the darkness of the auditorium, and thirdly the surprisingly deep orchestra pit. If he ever succeeded in building a theatre to his own plans, he would have regard to these three features, and that was something he had *already decided on at the time.*

Carl Friedrich Glasenapp, *Das Leben Richard Wagners*, 4th impression, Leipzig 1905, vol. 1, pp. 288–89

The conductor and composer Heinrich Dorn in a 'musical report from Riga':

Of the local forces the following gave *concerts* which all enjoyed large audiences: Musical director Löbmann, the opera singers Köhler and Wrede and the conductor *Richard Wagner*. The latter produced two overtures composed by himself, one on *Rule Britannia*, the other entitled *Columbus*. These compositions, especially the latter, consisted of very disparate parts. The conception and execution one can only call Beethovenian: great, beautiful ideas, bold rhythmic structures, the melody less prominent, the development broad and in intentionally ponderous tempi, the length almost tiring – while on the other hand the technique is highly modern, almost Bellini-like, and I promise you it is the naked truth when I tell you that *Columbus* employs two valve-trumpets, whose parts together fill fourteen and a half closely written pages; and on top of that pretty well every other spectacular and unusual effect. If such a combination of kernel and *shell* is not unthinkable *per se* – here at least it failed and simply sounded like a Hegelian in the style of Heine. I can still well remember when I was in Leipzig and Wagner brought me his first overture (in B♭ major, in 6/8 time) and asked me to perform it in the theatre.* I did, too; the orchestra could scarcely contain its laughter at the rehearsal and in the evening the audience were at once troubled and quite dumbfounded. But there was something in this composition which had won my respect and I consoled the visibly disillusioned composer out of my confidence in his future. His next symphony already aroused general and well-deserved attention in the Gewandhaus and was widely reviewed; I doubt if there has ever at any time been a young composer who was better acquainted with the works of Beethoven than the then 18-year-old Wagner. The Master's overtures and major orchestral works he owned for the most part in scores which he had himself copied, he went to bed with the sonatas and got up with the quartets, the concertos he whistled (for he never could make much progress himself at the piano), in short it was a *furor teutonicus*, which, allied with a thorough

* The performance of this overture in B-flat took place at Christmas 1830; at that time Dorn was conductor at the Leipzig Theatre

technical training and an extraordinary mental alertness, promised to father powerful progeny; to finish with, old Weinlig introduced the inner secrets of double-counterpoint and left it up to Father Time to polish up the rough edges. Time polished rather hard, though. For Wagner turned to opera, and while he was now waving his arms about in scores by every Tom, Dick and Harry and yet at the same time kept his feet firmly rooted in the works of Beethoven, his still too youthful heart was swept along by the waves of emotion, first this way and then that, while his head swung like a pendulum between the two B's, Bach and Bellini. But you cannot serve God and the devil at the same time and he who is not for me is against me. From the bottom of my heart I abhor those boring men who, having once discovered that this or that is the best thing there is, now devote a fanatical energy to denying everything else. And if such a man is a conductor, to boot, he is the ruin of the theatre that employs him since, for the sake of his own chosen favourites, he neglects those of other people, and the public, as is known, is a many-headed monster whose throat must be stuffed with many different kinds of nourishment. But to try to unite every possible style and fashion in one's own compositions with a view to having everyone on one's own side is the surest way of upsetting everyone; and were I not convinced that it is a man of *great talent* who has embarked on this doleful course, be sure I should not have written such a long discourse in a widely-read journal about the conductor of the Riga theatre.

Neue Zeitschrift für Musik, 24 July 1838

Wagner lost his post in Riga to Heinrich Dorn. On 9 July 1839 he left Riga, his destination Paris, the musical capital of Europe. There he hoped to make his name through the protection of Giacomo Meyerbeer, and to perform his grand opera *Rienzi, der Letzte der Tribunen* (*Rienzi, the last of the Tribunes*). After a long and eventful journey aboard the sailing ship Thetis he arrived in England on 9 August. On 17 September he reached Paris. However, Wagner's hopes for success were not realized and he had to earn his living from musical arrangements and newspaper articles. For the *Revue et Gazette Musicale* in Paris he wrote short stories including 'A Pilgrimage to Beethoven', 'The End of a German Musician in Paris' and 'A Happy Evening', along with the essays 'On German Music', 'The Virtuoso and the Artist', 'On the Overture', 'The Artist and the Public', '*Der Freischütz* in Paris', and 'Halévy and *La Reine de Chypre*'.

34

The painter Friedrich Pecht on his acquaintance with Wagner in Paris:

Heinrich Laube, whom I met soon after I arrived in Paris in the autumn of 1839 (he had just come back from a tour of France) wanted to spend the winter in Paris with his wife, full as he was of his admiration for the French and French art – indeed he constantly over-estimated them both, much to my dismay. Anyway, he had rented an apartment on the Boulevard des Italiens, where I often visited both him and his wife. One day I was to take them round the Louvre. When I arrived he told me that we should be joined by a young musician, the brother-in-law of Friedrich Brockhaus, whom I had been friendly with earlier, along with his wife, and while we were waiting he told me that the musician had come to Paris from Riga with the idea of getting an opera performed. His name was *Richard Wagner*.

It was not long before the young man appeared, strikingly elegant, indeed aristocratic in his appearance, despite his somewhat short legs, and with such a strikingly beautiful woman on his arm that she alone would have sufficed to make the couple interesting, if Wagner himself had not had such an arresting head that one's attention was involuntarily fixed upon him. Looking at the paintings, however, he was often distracted and obviously far away, but soon pulled himself together and developed such a witty vivaciousness that we quickly became friends, the more so since, being a Leipziger by birth, he in any case had many points of contact with me, as I already knew of his sisters. After our tour of the gallery we all ate together in a restaurant and here he told us – in his own way of speaking, where the words came pouring out like driven snow – the story of his adventures on the journey here, how he had set sail in a little boat and had been driven off course to Norway by the gales. Then how the whistling of the wind in the frozen rigging had made such a strangely demonic impression on him, indeed had sounded to him like pure music, so that once, when a second ship had suddenly appeared before them in the storm and then vanished again in the darkness as quickly as it had come, he immediately thought of the Flying Dutchman and had since constantly been thinking of the story and composing music to it. I was attracted by the irresistible charm of his company and soon became closely acquainted with him; and since I had all sorts of interests in common with him, as I, like him, was seeking my fortune in Paris, I often visited him in the little fourth-floor flat which he had rented in the Rue du Helder and which he had straight away furnished – on credit, of course. For he clearly also had an innate talent for running up debts – perhaps it was because of his old actor's blood. Well, here I now saw and heard gradually taking shape the opera which had instigated our acquaintance. Unfortunately he was much too bad a pianist, and I much too poor a musician for me ever to be able to make out for certain whether he really possessed creative genius. But all the more certain were his magical power of attraction and his quick superiority in every other matter, combined with the innate nobility of his nature, which made sure that for all his boisterous passion and bubbling wit he never appeared common or trivial.

Allgemeine Musik-Zeitung, Berlin, 20/27 July 1894

Wagner on Meyerbeer in Paris:

I begin with an obituary! The Paris Grand Opera will die at any moment. It awaits its salvation from the German
Messiah, from *Meyerbeer*; if the latter delays his rescue 34
much longer the death rattle will very soon begin. The tragedy is this: *Auber* has become old before his time, and *Halévy* has not made an effort for three years; but *Meyerbeer*, who only plays the fame-game here with big and well-considered moves, has his own reasons for

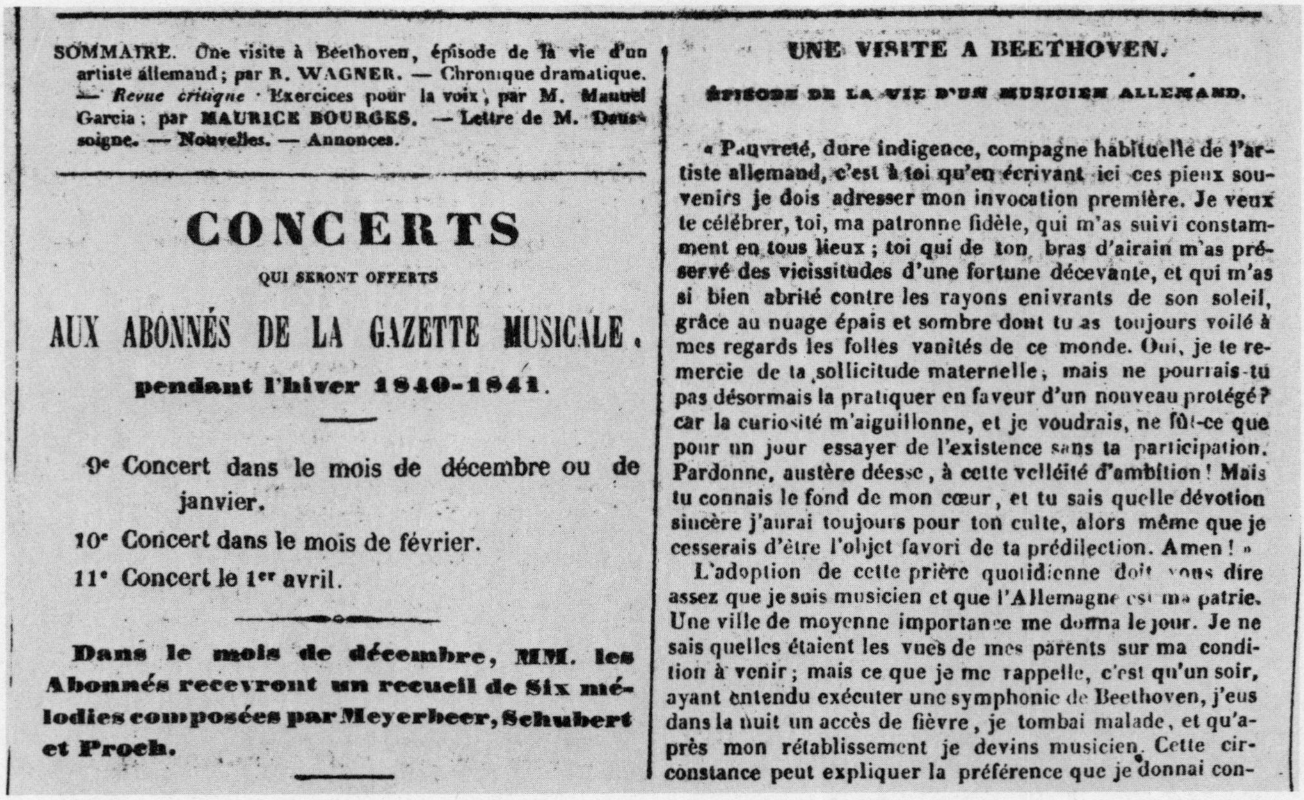

SOMMAIRE. Une visite à Beethoven, épisode de la vie d'un artiste allemand; par R. WAGNER. — Chronique dramatique. — *Revue critique* · Exercices pour la voix, par M. Manuel Garcia; par MAURICE BOURGES. — Lettre de M. Dussoigne. — Nouvelles. — Annonces.

CONCERTS

QUI SERONT OFFERTS

AUX ABONNÉS DE LA GAZETTE MUSICALE.

pendant l'hiver 1840-1841.

9e Concert dans le mois de décembre ou de janvier.

10e Concert dans le mois de février.

11e Concert le 1er avril.

Dans le mois de décembre, MM. les Abonnés recevront un recueil de Six mélodies composées par Meyerbeer, Schubert et Proch.

UNE VISITE A BEETHOVEN.

ÉPISODE DE LA VIE D'UN MUSICIEN ALLEMAND.

« Pauvreté, dure indigence, compagne habituelle de l'artiste allemand, c'est à toi qu'en écrivant ici ces pieux souvenirs je dois adresser mon invocation première. Je veux te célébrer, toi, ma patronne fidèle, qui m'as suivi constamment en tous lieux; toi qui de ton bras d'airain m'as préservé des vicissitudes d'une fortune décevante, et qui m'as si bien abrité contre les rayons enivrants de son soleil, grâce au nuage épais et sombre dont tu as toujours voilé à mes regards les folles vanités de ce monde. Oui, je te remercie de ta sollicitude maternelle; mais ne pourrais-tu pas désormais la pratiquer en faveur d'un nouveau protégé? car la curiosité m'aiguillonne, et je voudrais, ne fût-ce que pour un jour essayer de l'existence sans ta participation. Pardonne, austère déesse, à cette velléité d'ambition! Mais tu connais le fond de mon cœur, et tu sais quelle dévotion sincère j'aurai toujours pour ton culte, alors même que je cesserais d'être l'objet favori de ta prédilection. Amen! »

L'adoption de cette prière quotidienne doit vous dire assez que je suis musicien et que l'Allemagne est ma patrie. Une ville de moyenne importance me donna le jour. Je ne sais quelles étaient les vues de mes parents sur ma condition à venir; mais ce que je me rappelle, c'est qu'un soir, ayant entendu exécuter une symphonie de Beethoven, j'eus dans la nuit un accès de fièvre, je tombai malade, et qu'après mon rétablissement je devins musicien. Cette circonstance peut expliquer la préférence que je donnai con-

The opening of Wagner's 'A Pilgrimage to Beethoven', published in four instalments in the *Gazette Musicale de Paris*, the first on 19 November 1840; the paper was edited by Maurice Schlesinger. Bibliothèque Nationale, Paris.

holding back his newest work, upon which every hope rests. So the Opera is labouring and has been obliged for some time to seek its salvation with mediocrities. However the public has the whim of only wanting to applaud excellence, and I must confess that in this particular regard they have won my full esteem. Directors and impresarios are impressed only by brilliant reputations and famous names; but the public are not dazzled by these. And the result is that only what is genuinely excellent can really hold its place. Which is why we keep on seeing *Robert* and the *Huguenots* reappearing whenever some second-rate piece has to be withdrawn. In fact *Robert le diable* seems to possess a strange, almost uncanny quality, and if I were M. Donizetti, M. Rualtz or one of the other countless musicians 'who have already met their fate in this same risky gamble', then I should hate this Robert as if he were a real devil. For this is the opera which is the decisive barometer of success or failure for these gentlemen's works; for if a new opera is not successful after a

few performances, out comes *Robert le diable* again, and if you see this name on the posters then you know that the preceding new opera was a failure. Robert is immortal! Despite the often scandalous standards of performance, despite the fact that now even Duprez has at last done his very best to sing the title role badly and like a circus clown, despite the fact that the décor and the dances have become faded and lifeless under the immense wear and tear of two hundred and thirty performances – in spite of all this, I tell you – *Robert* is still – beside the *Huguenots* – the one and only successful box-office draw.

Abend-Zeitung, Dresden, 19 March 1841

Friedrich Pecht on Wagner's acquaintance with Heinrich Heine in Paris: 38

When we got to know Wagner then, his distracted air in fact was all too understandable, since he had arrived in the

New Year's Eve, Paris 1840; drawing by E.B. Kietz, 1841. Richard Wagner Archiv, Bayreuth.

The party depicted in Kietz's drawing is referred to in Wagner's autobiography *Mein Leben*: 'Supper turned into a bacchanalian carousal when, after the champagne, the punch too began to have its effect. I gave an outspoken address which, because of the ceaseless laughter it provoked among the friends present, went on and on . . . I was already standing on a chair, and finally I climbed on to the table itself . . .'

strange city without any means of support, indeed with no real command of the language even, and he was at his wits' end, as he soon revealed to us when we got to know him better. This happened quickly, for we often met one another at Laube's. For all his abruptness Laube was a stout fellow, always helpful and friendly and he soon introduced us both to Heine, whose acquaintance we were both of course very anxious to make. Our first meeting took place at a dinner which we all had together in the then famous Italian restaurant Brocci's in the Rue Lepelletier, opposite what was then the Grand Opera. Heine, who had been friendly with Laube for a long time, was at that time, if I remember rightly, just writing his 'Wintermärchen', or it might have been the 'Atta Troll'; at any rate he was at the height of his creative powers and showed as yet no trace of illness. Now Laube was just the man to animate him by contradicting him, for when we first met he appeared blasé and indifferent but regularly came to life when attacked. Heine brought his wife with him, who was then a delectable beauty and who, merry and naive as a child, was a wonderful sight for sore eyes and even outshone the beautiful Frau Wagner. For she had the most stunning satin-like complexion, magnificent black hair and beautiful teeth that you could ever hope to see, and a really voluptuous figure.

But it was the witty sweetness of Iduna Laube, who was better than any woman I have ever met at loosening the tongues of even the slowest of men, which finally did the trick and drew a brilliant firework display of immortal ideas from Heine, who, on such occasions at least, in stimulating company, was in any case the wittiest man alive and certainly, unlike many another author, was just as funny in the flesh as in his books. It was only when he began shooting his verbal darts in every direction that his splendid poet's head became apparent, with his broad Jove-like brow and his aquiline nose above a constantly quivering voluptuous mouth. However, it was not his style to conduct a connected conversation, but rather he peppered a whole subject with lightning flashes of wit, which, in fact, he clearly often prepared in advance. Under this cascade Wagner, too, who had been very reserved until then, soon thawed out and now demonstrated that wonderful resilience he possessed, the rare gift of preserving the most absolute freedom and the highest flights of the imagination even in the midst of the most oppressive material poverty and despair. He was a very good story-teller, he had the finest eye for comic traits, the sharpest ear for the sounds of nature and the surest feeling for everything beautiful, including the plastic arts.

Friedrich Pecht: 'Aus Richard Wagner's Pariser Zeit', supplement in the *Allgemeine Zeitung*, Munich, 22 March 1883.

Wagner on Heinrich Heine:

You have to admit, we Germans are a generous race! We see a talent arise from our midst, the like of which Germany has little to offer; we rejoice at his fresh, bold development, we shout our applause and bravos as he rouses our young spirits from complete lethargy and sacrifices his own fulfilment to break new ground and to show the way which the regenerating forces of our literature must take to reach new and unknown, but necessary, goals. Any youngster who picks up his pen today, for good or ill, consciously or unconsciously, tries to imitate *Heine*, for never before has a writer who appeared so suddenly, so quickly and so quite unexpectedly come to dominate his field so irresistibly as *Heine* has his. But it is not enough that we should then look on without demur as our police hound this splendid talent out of the land that bore him, not enough that our quickly tiring attention should overlook the fact that he has been brutally uprooted from the only soil that can nourish his genius, so that we just notice before we fall back to sleep that in Paris friend *Heine* seems to have lost the knack of writing travelogues, that our indifference has finally made him blasé towards himself, that we have forced him to stop being a German – while he has no hope of ever becoming a Parisian – not enough that we have so utterly cut the ground from beneath his feet that – perhaps unintentionally – we have left him no other outlet for his pulsating energy than to turn his wit on the most feeble subjects – not enough that we sit by *indifferent* and pusillanimous and watch the desiccation of a talent which, better tended, would have developed into the equal of the greatest names in our literature; no! we are actually *glad* and clap with glee when this man *Heine* is finally treated the way we are accustomed to handling the critics of a tuppenny newspaper!

Abend-Zeitung, Dresden, 4 August 1841

Letter of recommendation from Giacomo Meyerbeer to the General Manager of the Dresden Court Theatre, Baron Wolf von Lüttichau, Dresden(?), 18 March 1841:   41, 42

Your Excellency will forgive me for troubling you with these lines, but I am too keenly aware of your constant benevolence towards me for me to be able to refuse an interesting compatriot who, perhaps with too flattering a confidence in my influence with Yr Ex., has asked me to support his application by writing to you. Herr Richard Wagner from Leipzig is a young composer endowed not only with a sound musical education but also with much imagination; he possesses moreover a wide-ranging literary culture and his situation in every respect deserves a great deal of sympathy from his native country. His greatest desire is to have the opera *Rienzi*, for which he has composed both text and music, performed on the new Royal stage in Dresden. I found various pieces which he played to me from this work full of inspiration and of powerful dramatic effect. May the young artist enjoy the protection of Yr Ex. and have the opportunity of seeing his fine talent more generally recognized.

Wilhelm Tappert, *Richard Wagner*, Elberfeld 1883, p. 20

In order to prepare for the première of *Rienzi* (20 October   43–48
1842) Wagner left Paris on 7 April 1842 and moved to Dresden. The success of *Rienzi* led to the first performance of *Der fliegende*   51–56
Holländer (*The Flying Dutchman*) shortly afterwards, on 2 January 1843. A month later Wagner was appointed Conductor to the Royal Saxon Court. He held this office until 1849. In this period *Tannhäuser* and *Lohengrin* were written. The première of *Tannhäuser* took place on 19 October 1845.   57–62

Letter from the Dresden costume-designer Ferdinand Heine to the painter Ernst Benedikt Kietz about the first performance of Rienzi:

Dearest friend Kietz,

I shall try to leave aside all enthusiasm and all partisan interest for our friend Wagner and report to you only genuine unadulterated facts about this *Rienzi* performance. In the first piano and quartet rehearsals I do not know who cursed most – the singers or the musicians – about the unreasonable difficulties of the music; but as soon as they began to get the hang of it, there arose an enthusiasm which grew with every rehearsal, and soon spread throughout the whole orchestra and to every singer, right down to the last member of the chorus, in a way I have never seen in my life. The wildest praise came from Tichatschek and the leader of the orchestra, Lipinsky, who could not find words strong enough to express their delight. I must say that, as the rehearsals progressed, so many difficulties arose that I rather think that without the untiring patience of our chorus-master, old Fischer, nothing like the same standard of performance would have been achieved. I really enjoyed Schröder-Devrient. *Comme à l'ordinaire*, she was the last one to get her – admittedly very difficult – part – Adriano – right, in fact Wagner was quite shattered and we had trouble consoling him. All the more stupendous was his surprise on the evening of the première when quite out of the blue she produced before his spellbound eyes one of her most stunning performances. I never left his side the whole

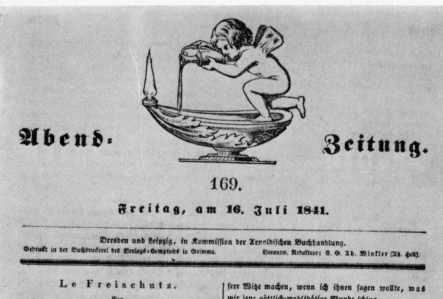

The opening of Wagner's report on the Paris première of Weber's *Der Freischütz*, published in five instalments in the *Abend Zeitung*, Dresden; the first instalment appeared on 16 July 1841.

evening, and did not know what to marvel at most – the rapture and jubilation of the audience, or Wagner's own astonishment at this incomparable effect of his creation. Our magnificent theatre was full to bursting, despite the increased prices. From the very first note of the overture there was a hushed silence, which was followed by thunderous applause that became more and more intense until the simply soul-stirring end of the fourth act, which was followed by a deep silence, turning into all the more deafening applause after the fifth act. The opera lasted until half-past eleven, but no one went home early. The Dresdeners were no longer Dresdeners. I was the old Paul Pry. In the entr'actes I wandered through the foyer, the boxes, the buffet and the stalls to hear what people were saying, and often I did not know whether to believe my ears. There they were, the old minim-mongers and counterpoint-codgers, putting their heads together and declaring roundly that with this opera Wagner had earned his place amongst the most worthy classics; then again, such sickening Italian-fanatics as the fat Count Solms and his cronies, who spat on Beethoven, Mozart, Weber and Marschner as though they were dirt, were saying things like 'even better than the divine Donizetti'. I could have gone mad with joy!

But what a performance! Tichatschek was a new man, a hero! Despite his Raoul, Adolar and all his other brilliant interpretations, I should never have believed him capable of such dramatic power. You could honestly say he was inspired! – and Schröder-Devrient, too, and Dettmer, all of them, every one! Especially the choruses, too. Really, Fischer is a choral director of the first order; you cannot imagine the degree of precision and subtlety, despite the immense forces and the difficulties! I cannot help repeating muself – we have never seen anything like it!

And please do not believe, dear Kietz, that this is a partisan account, for wherever you go you hear the same ecstatic reaction.

Wagner himself declared that if by some magic spell he could transport this whole production to Paris just as it stands, he would be made for life. Be that as it may – I think he is made for life anyway, with or without Paris.

What a pity the king could not come – he had fallen from his horse in the morning and hurt his knee. But the princesses were there right to the end and Princess Amalie, the poetess, several times said that no composition had ever made such an impression on her and she had constantly felt as though some precious silken cloth inlaid with gold and pearls were being spread out before her. (We learned this the next day from Friederici, her lady-in-waiting.)

The king (Friedrich August) has let it be known that he, too, will hear the next performance, right to the end. When Lüttichau drew his attention to the fact that the opera is very long, the king answered: No matter, a work like that you have to hear properly, I shall stay the night in town. (Because he is still living in his vineyard out at Wachwitz.)

Your busy little elf, too, did not disgrace himself and is proud to have set before the Dresdeners costumes such as they have not set eyes on before. But, my God! how tiny and pitiful one feels beside the composer. When people paid me compliments about my costumes I always felt sorry I had no tail to hide between my legs like a dog! For the next performance Wagner has decided to shorten the opera considerably to make it run until a quarter past ten. Admittedly it is a pity for every lost bar; but what can one do – the net result will be an even more lasting and general success; for at present no German stage could dare to make such demands on its singers. Of course, the strange – and flattering – thing is that Wagner is meeting the strongest opposition and difficulties over his cuts from the singers themselves. Tichatschek has declared with tears in his eyes that he will not suffer a single note to be cut from his part. Despite the increased prices the next two performances are three or four times over-subscribed, so that Wagner cannot even get as many tickets as he wants for his relatives. I'd love to know what his fee is!

Only one thing worries me: *Rienzi* has completely eclipsed *Les Huguenots* and I am afraid that Meyerbeer, who is so immeasurably influential for Wagner in both Berlin and Paris, will in the end become green with envy. He is so ambitious.

Kietz, pp. 6–11

Hector Berlioz on Dresden, Rienzi *and* Der fliegende Holländer:

The Dresden orchestra, which was for a long time directed by the Italian Morlachi and the famous composer of *Der Freischütz*, is now conducted by Messrs Reissiger and Richard Wagner. We know more or less nothing by Reissiger in Paris except a gentle melancholy waltz, published under the title of *Weber's Last Thought*; while I was in Dresden they played one of his religious works, which was spoken of with the highest praise. I was unable to join in this acclaim; the day of the service during which this work was performed I was confined to my bed by the most cruel pains and I was thus unfortunately prevented from hearing it. As to the young *maître de chapelle*, Richard Wagner, who lived for a long time in Paris without succeeding in becoming known other than through several articles published in the *Gazette musicale*, it was at the rehearsals of my own works that he first took charge of the orchestra; he assisted me eagerly and very willingly. The swearing-in ceremony and his presentation to the orchestra had taken place the day after my arrival and I found him in a very understandable state of happy excitement. Having put up with a thousand privations and all the miseries of obscurity while he was in France, Richard Wagner returned to Saxony, where he was born, and had the audacity to undertake, and the pleasure of completing, the composition of both words and music for a five-act opera (*Rienzi*). This work was a brilliant success in Dresden. Soon after came the *Dutchman*, an opera in three acts, for which he also wrote both words and music. Whatever opinions one may have of the merits of these works, it must be admitted that men capable of twice performing this double literary and musical feat successfully are not common, and that Mr Wagner has demonstrated a talent more than adequate to attract both attention and interest. The king of Saxony well realizes this; and the day that by giving his chief conductor Richard Wagner as his assistant the king secured the latter's existence, art-lovers could have said to His Majesty what Jean Bart replied to Louis XIV when the latter told the fearless old sea-dog that he had put him in charge of a squadron: 'Sire, you have done the right thing!'

43–48
51–56

The opera *Rienzi*, being much longer than the duration normally allotted to operas in Germany, is now no longer performed whole; they play the first two acts on one evening and the last three on another. It is only this second part that I saw performed; hearing it once only I was not able to get to know it well enough to be able to express a considered opinion about it; I remember only a beautiful prayer sung in the last act by Rienzi (Tichatschek), and a triumphal march well modelled, without slavish imitation, on the magnificent march in [Spontini's] *Olympia*. The score of the *Dutchman* I thought remarkable for its dark coloration and certain storm-effects perfectly motivitated by the story; but I could not help noticing as well an excessive use of the *tremolo*, which is the more disturbing in that it had already struck me in *Rienzi* and that it implies a certain intellectual laziness on the part of the composer, against which he is not sufficiently on his guard. Of all orchestral effects, sustained *tremolo* is the one you get tired of most quickly; what is more, it requires no imagination at all on the part of the composer when there is no striking idea above or below it.

Be that as it may, we must, I repeat, give all honour to the royal thought which, by giving him complete and active protection, has so to speak saved a young artist gifted with precious faculties.

The Dresden theatre management went out of their way to secure the most brilliant performances possible of Wagner's two works; the décor, the costumes and the production of *Rienzi* are close to the best that Paris has achieved in this direction. Mme Devrient, of whom I shall have occasion to speak more fully à propos of her performances in Berlin, plays in *Rienzi* the part of a young boy; her somewhat matronly figure is no longer very suited to this sort of role. She seemed to me much better cast in the *Dutchman*, despite certain affected poses and the *spoken* interjections she feels obliged to introduce everywhere. But a really immaculate and rounded, genuine talent, which impressed me most vividly, is that of Wächter, who played the part of the accursed Dutchman. He has one of the most beautiful baritone voices I have ever heard and he uses it with consummate skill: it is one of those voices which is both smooth and resonant at the same time and which can be very expressive if the artist puts both his heart and his head into his singing; and Wächter does both, to a very high degree. Tichatschek is elegant, passionate, brilliant, heroic and thrilling in the role of Rienzi, in which his fine voice and his great fiery eyes serve him marvellously. Mlle Wiest [correctly, Wüst] plays Rienzi's sister, who has hardly anything to say. The composer in writing this part has tailored it perfectly to the abilities of the singer.

'Premier voyage en Allemagne', in *Mémoires de Hector Berlioz*, Paris 1870, pp. 272–4

The author Eliza Wille describes Wagner's appearance:

I had got to know him in 1843 in Dresden at a soirée given by Major Serre, who later founded the Schiller Institute. It had remained a fleeting encounter . . . But Wagner's features had impressed themselves on my mind: his elegant, supple figure, the head with the mighty brow, the acute eye and the energetic lines around his small and tightly closed mouth. A painter who was sitting next to me drew my attention to his straight, protruding chin, which

166

seemed to be carved out of stone, giving the face a special character. Wagner's wife had attractive features; she was merry and talkative and seemed to feel particularly at her ease in society. He himself was very lively, self-conscious but naturally affable.

Wille-Briefe, pp. 28–29

Marie Schmole, the daughter of the costume-designer Ferdinand Heine, remembers Wagner's early years in Dresden:

Although I was only ten years old at the time, I clearly remember the first visit Wagner and his wife paid to my parents. It was in the summer of 1842. I came home from school and went to find my parents in the garden; there I found them with a gentleman with elegant features, and, what impressed me, light-coloured kid gloves. I noticed later that in fact they had been washed rather often, and were badly worn on the inside. Although in quite straitened circumstances, he still always maintained a neat and elegant appearance; Wagner and his wife had already had their full measure of poverty and deprivation of every kind during their stay in Paris. There Richard had often slipped out towards evening with a few sheets of manuscript and tried to sell straight away what he had perhaps barely finished writing.

When they both lived in Meudon they sometimes used to walk along garden walls at dusk and knock down walnuts from any overhanging branches, because – they were starving.

His wife, too, who at that time was a very beautiful lady, won my heart through her kindly nature. When I was presented to them both he greeted me as the little Marie who had got over such terrible illnesses while he was still in Paris. From then on the Wagners came several times every week to have supper with us in the garden, where Richard found a vine-arbour that really appealed to him. It was not until later that I realized why he used to gaze so appreciatively at the simple food which was set out on the table. For I heard once that Minna Wagner often used to tell my mother that on many a day this had been their first proper meal since breakfast. As we stood ready to sit down to eat he would say to his wife: '*Minel, nun wollen wir aber pampen*' (which in proper German would mean to eat until they were really full).

His greatest delight was something we had before the cold meats: new potatoes in their jackets with herring in a piquant sauce – 'pickle' he called it.

Burrell-Briefe, pp. 165–66

Friedrich Pecht on Wagner's time in Dresden:

I now met my old friend Richard Wagner rather less, simply because I was not really very musical, although I honestly did admire his works and saw straight away that *Tannhäuser*, the first performance of which I saw in Dresden, would clearly conquer the world. But it was highly interesting to see how this ball of fire was constantly involved in all sorts of projects. But since he was incapable of any kind of restraint he was equally for ever involved in financial embarrassments and by the beginning of 1848 he had already built up debts amounting, it was said, to more than 20,000 thalers. For he somehow did not know

57–62

even how to take full advantage of his author's rights, which even at that time would already have brought him in a great deal. Instead he regularly entered into the most disadvantageous contracts, which always left him the loser, for the simple reason that he invariably sold his grain on the stalk. And so, while his operas were winning the most enthusiastic applause and were gradually becoming established throughout Germany, he had got himself into an untenable position, which certainly contributed not a little to his kicking over the traces so abruptly a short time later. How this insatiable nature soaked up ideas from every quarter may be judged from the following experience I had with him around this time. One day when I called on him I found him burning with passion for Hegel's Phenomenology, which he was just studying, and which, he told me with typical extravagance, was the best book ever printed. To prove it he read me a passage which had particularly impressed him. Since I did not entirely follow it, I asked him to read it again, upon which neither of us could understand it. He read it a third time and a fourth, until in the end we both looked at one another and burst out laughing. And that was the end of phenomenology.

Friedrich Pecht, *Aus meiner Zeit*, Munich 1894, vol. 1, pp. 293–94

Letters from Robert Schumann on Tannhäuser:

(a) to Felix Mendelssohn-Bartholdy, Dresden, 22 October 1845:
Now Wagner's got another opera ready – he's certainly a live-wire, full of terrific ideas and as bold as brass – the aristocracy are still crazy about him since *Rienzi* – but honestly he just cannot write or think four bars together which are *even good* music, let alone beautiful. The simple harmony, the plain four-part technique are just not there. So what can come of it in the long run! And now here we are with the whole score nicely printed – fifths and octaves and all – and now he would like to start changing and re-writing it – but it's too late! Enough now! The music is not a lot better than *Rienzi*, rather flatter, more artificial! But if you say anything of the sort the reaction is simply – 'ah, jealous', so I shall say it only to you, for I know you have known it for a long time.

(b) to Felix Mendelssohn-Bartholdy, Dresden, 12 November 1845:
Tannhäuser I hope to tell you about verbally soon; *I must take back* much of what I wrote to you after reading the score; on the stage everything appears quite different. I was quite moved by much of it.

(c) to the conductor and composer Heinrich Dorn, Dresden, 7 January 1846:
I wish you could see Wagner's *Tannhäuser*. It contains some deep, original stuff, absolutely *a hundred times better* than his earlier operas – although some of it is still trivial. In short, he may turn out to be a great composer for the stage, and if I know him he certainly has the courage. The technique, the orchestration I find outstanding, incomparably more masterly than before. He already has a new text ready: *Lohengrin*.

Robert Schumanns Briefe, new series, ed. F. Gustav Jansen, 2nd impression, Leipzig 1904, pp. 252 (a), 254 (b), 256 (c)

'Another view of Tannhäuser*'*:

It is high time something frank and candid were said about the panegyrics with which the composer of *Rienzi* and *Tannhäuser* is being proclaimed to the world as the new Messiah of opera. Of course, no one who has any idea of the methods of journalism, and how certain private connections operate, will be surprised that it is possible for so many different journals to be blowing the same trumpet of praise; yet one cannot but express surprise at the improvidence of such a manoeuvre, since everyone knows that excessive praise always calls forth even harsher criticism and that an inept friend often does more harm than a thoughtful foe. You would think that the experience with *Rienzi* would have dictated a note of caution, for this opera has long since been back on dry land after being swept along like some Noah's ark by a veritable flood of adulation. Or are we witnessing a desperate effort to achieve with *Tannhäuser* what incorruptible Nemesis denied to *Rienzi*? But *Tannhäuser will share the fate of Rienzi*, despite such preposterous assertions as this one: '*Mozart's operas are mere formalistic routine stuff, whereas it has fallen to Wagner's free, independent and genial originality to create sound-pictures for all times.*' Now a man who can write that sort of thing may be an expert on certain philosophical catchwords and high-sounding aesthetic theories, but he does not know the true nature of music, either as an artist or as a philosopher, otherwise he would know that the part played in other arts by material space and the revelation of the idea to the conscious intellect is replaced in music by time and the emotional experience of the idea in time, and that music is therefore more dependent on a precise form because its elements are so intangible. Let that reporter first study the folk-song, let him study Mozart, Weber and the operas of other important composers, let him study the works of other great masters of the past which have stood the test of time down to our own age and will delight generations yet to come, just as the works of Gluck, for example, delight us; and then let him judge! They are trying to tell us now, after four performances, that you must hear the opera several times in order to be able to appreciate all its endless beauties, now, that is, that the *vox populi*, which is usually also the *vox dei*, has already crystallized into decided opposition to all these paeans of praise. What is the point of this? *Does a corpse come to life if you put rouge on its cheeks?*

Much play is made of the fact that the composer wrote his own text. Let us not assert that it is impossible for one man to achieve mastery both as a composer and as a poet; as yet we have nothing to go by. Certainly not *Tannhäuser* or *Rienzi*. The moral lesson of the story is ruined by an *all-too-pretentious exhibition of sin*, and at the same time you cannot overlook the intention, evident in all the external trappings of the production, to play up to the lasciviousness of the public for the sake of cheap applause. The manner in which the author lets virtue win in the end is no doubt psychologically right, but *because heaven and hell are mobilized in mere theatrical effects the conclusion appears intellectually cold and calculated,* so that it is a lie for anyone to claim that this moral satisfaction has any lasting beneficial effect; for it is only too true: 'When you can feel the intention its effect is lost!' Like the text, the music, too, is not the result of an irrepressible creative urge, although both certainly reveal a talented and, especially, a speculative mind. Just as the introduction of the Singers' Tournament into the Tannhäuser legend is obviously a good idea, so also we must justly praise individual neat combinations, many a clever effect and piquant turn; but unfortunately these individual polished ideas become lost in the exaggerated, supposedly inspired, musical style. One effect kills the other.

Signale für die musikalische Welt, Leipzig, 19 November 1845

On the effect of Wagner's operas on the Dresden public:

It is an interesting and noteworthy phenomenon that the cool and unexcitable Dresden theatre public has been transformed by Wagner's operas into a fiery and enthusiastic body, such as may be seen nowhere else in Germany. When has it ever been known for the composer of an opera that has been in the repertoire over a year to be called on to the stage three times at the end of a performance, as happened after the most recent performance of *Tannhäuser*?

Signale für die musikalische Welt, Leipzig, 17 February 1847

Robert Schumann in a letter to Felix Mendelssohn-Bartholdy, Dresden, 18 November 1845, about a circle of artists in Dresden to which Wagner also belonged:

To our surprise Wagner yesterday showed us his new opera text, *Lohengrin* – a double surprise for me as I have been thinking about the same story – or a very similiar one about the Knights of the Round Table – for more than a year, and I must now consign it to oblivion. Most of them liked the text very much, especially the painters. We now all meet regularly once a week – Bendemann, Rietschel, Hübner, Wagner, Hiller, Reinick* – there's always plenty to relate or read aloud and it's always quite lively.

Robert Schumanns Briefe, idem, p. 255

The writer Karl Gutzkow's reminiscences of Wagner's time as Kapellmeister in Dresden:

Actually this idol of all the uncertainties of our age was not unfavourably disposed towards me. He was by then already quite a famous personality and one day he came to me and invited me to follow the same path as himself. The second and fourth acts of my *Uriel Acosta*, he said, proved my capabilities. And there I had certainly cast no doubt on the compatibility of opera and drama. After a few words of thanks I fell back on my doubts about the possibilities of a lasting union of the two branches of art; every hybrid art form, I said, went against the grain with me. Opera must stay opera and drama drama. The latter, after all, must appeal to reason and judgment, and at the same time to a very definite, specifically stimulated excitement of the heart; quite unlike music, whose effect was always directed to the general and indefinite, so that it remained nebulous and unclear. Admittedly both forms had to appeal to the imagination. Had I already had any

idea of *Götterdämmerung*, of *Das Rheingold*, of *Der Ring des Nibelungen* and of the Bayreuth Theatre, I should rather have said: to appeal only to the imagination is mere sensuality and makes a whole nation effeminate! As my acquaintance with music was not entirely superficial, since the excellent piano-playing of my wife, a pupil of Aloys Schmitt, daily kept me in touch with musical impressions, I said quite frankly, if not to Wagner, at least to others, that the *Tannhäuser* overture appeared to me like some offensive and at times tasteless canon; I compared it with that Shakespearean canon which 'might winch the soul from one's body'; the eternally recurring sextuplets I called nerve-racking. With the exception of the charming polonaise I found *Tannhäuser* boring. But to the author himself I said once on the Dippoldiswalder Platz: 'Why did you do without Klingsohr in your Wartburg tournament? Surely he belongs to the story? You would have gained a powerful bass role like Bertram in *Robert le diable* and for the action you would have acquired a representative of the demonic forces to exercize a dramatic influence on Tannhäuser! For the idea that everything should come from Tannhäuser himself, that is, from his reminiscences, is really not dramatic.' After this piece of candour no further meeting took place. But at every performance of a Wagner opera that I heard (I was present later at the first performance of *Lohengrin* in Weimar) I heard the most exaggeratedly demonstrative applause, the beginning of this claque which has been organized throughout Germany and which Wagner, Liszt and others will one day have to answer for in the history of art. Behind me in the audience there was a German-Russian family, literally going crazy with wild fanaticism and making an unbelievable contribution to the Wagner cult. In Dresden they set the tone for this adulation. Women in high society, licentious natures, and men of effeminate character then made the propagation of Wagnerian music in other places and in the same manner their particular concern.

Karl Gutzkows ausgewählte Werke in zwölf Bänden, ed. Heinrich Hubert Houben, vol. 11, pp. 353–4

Letter from Wagner to the Viennese critic Eduard Hanslick, Dresden, 1 January 1847; at first Hanslick encouraged Wagner but later became one of his most outspoken critics:

Do not underestimate the power of reflection: the work of art which is produced by unconscious inspiration belongs to periods which lie far away from our own: the art of the highest period of culture cannot but be produced in the conscious realm. The Christian poetry of the Middle Ages, for example, had this unconscious spontaneity: but the wholly valid work of art was not created then – that was reserved for Goethe in our age of objectivity. That only the most richly endowed human spirit can achieve this marvellous combination of the power of the reflective spirit – that is why the highest achievement is rare, and if we are right to doubt whether we shall so easily find such a talent in the realm of art which we are discussing, we must at the same time presuppose at least the existence of a more or less felicitous conjunction of both qualities in any artist worth his salt – and we must regard the disjunction of these gifts – properly speaking – as an obstacle to the higher goal.

---

* Bendemann, Hübner and Reinick were painters, Reitschel a sculptor; Hiller was the composer and conductor Ferdinand Hiller

What keeps you and me worlds apart is your reverence for Meyerbeer; I can say this without embarrassment, for Meyerbeer is a close personal friend and I have every reason to esteem him as a pleasant and sympathetic person. But, if I have to summarize what I object to in the way of inner frivolity and outward ponderousness in operatic music-making, I am inclined to lump everything together under the heading 'Meyerbeer', the more so because I can see in Meyerbeer's music a great gift for outward effectiveness, which weakens the deeper nobility of art all the more because – for all its denial of inner values – it still tries to satisfy the listener with every trick of colouring: a composer who slips into triviality will atone for it in terms of his nobler self. But a composer who seeks triviality on purpose is – lucky: he does not have to atone for it at all.

Sämtliche Briefe, vol. 2, pp. 538–9

In a letter to Freiherr von Biedenfeld, Dresden, 17 January 1849, Wagner explains his aesthetics:

. . . I have always objected to seeing the whole vast apparatus of dramatic action, situation and plot, supported by the most energetic use of every conceivable kind of artistic endeavour, such as painting, sculpture, choreography etc., being used solely for the purpose of putting across to the public so many pretty tunes. I became convinced that the only goal which could justify all this effort could be nothing less than the dramatic work of art itself, and that opera surpassed the stage play in dramatic art because apart from all the normal means of expression it also incorporates that richest, most varied and most inexhaustible expressive element, music. Now the Greeks, and possibly in some measure also the drama of the Middle Ages, were able to make use of an element of musical expression for the benefit of the drama without essentially altering the latter. But in our time, the heroes of absolute music – that is, music independent of poetry culminating in Beethoven – have raised the expressive power of this art especially through the orchestra, to an entirely new and previously – even to Gluck – almost undreamed-of artistic potential. As a result the influence of music on drama is bound to be substantial since it will now naturally expect to develop this potential. Thus the expressive capacity of the drama itself has to be expanded and it seems to me that it is only the musician who can discover and develop this capacity in line with the expressive potential of music. If in the process I have turned the musician into a poet as well, at the same time this meant that I had all the more reason not to let him lose sight of the real objective, the drama, for it was of course only for the benefit of this highest of all artistic goals that his particular art – music – was brought in. And so it seemed to me to follow that his proper task was, while remaining completely sure and deeply conscious of the power of musical expression, to desire drama and nothing but drama, but naturally that drama which can only arise from the poet's musical consciousness. To make myself completely clear about this, let me refer to one of the principal scenes of my *Tannhäuser*, the Singers' Tournament; now here, obviously, only the dramatic idea could and must predominate, particularly as the catastrophe had to be brought about by this scene; to have

the singers outdoing one another in vocal virtuosity, trills and cadenzas might well have been the purpose of a musical competition, but not of a dramatic battle of ideas and emotions; but at the same time the dramatic effect of this contest of poets, involving the very essence of all those taking part, could not have been achieved without that highest and most abundant force of musical expression which I am talking about, and I have been very pleased to see that it has been precisely this so daring scene which has claimed the liveliest and most intent interest of the audience at every performance: I thus achieved the triumph of holding the audience through an *idea* and not merely through the *emotions* – something to which they are unfortunately not all accustomed to in *opera*.

To repeat it again briefly: I have chosen my path as a musician whose confidence in the inexhaustible wealth of the art of music leads him to seek the highest works of art, namely *drama*. I say to *seek* to indicate my objective; whether I *can* reach it I cannot judge, but if I fail this can only be because of my lack of ability, not because my genuine desire is wrong.

Sämtliche Briefe, vol. 2, p. 636ff.

The February Revolution in Paris in 1848 once again revived the movements for liberty and democracy throughout Europe which had been suppressed by the Restoration of 1815. Wagner followed these developments with great interest. On 18 May the long-awaited German National Assembly was constituted in St Paul's church, Frankfurt. This first German parliament passed a National Constitution, without, however, being able to implement it. After the Prague Revolt (Whitsun 1848) the Russian anarchist Michael Bakunin (1814–76) came to Dresden and lodged with Wagner's friend August Röckel. The latter's political activities led to his losing his post as Wagner's assistant at the Hoftheater (Court Theatre) in the summer of 1848. On 26 August the first number of Röckel's newspaper *Volksblätter* appeared. In this paper Wagner published anonymously several political articles. On 30 April 1849 the king of Saxony, Friedrich August II, dissolved the 'Chambers', thus breaking the constitution. This led to the Dresden May Uprising, which was put down by Saxon troops, with the help of Prussian units. Whereas Michael Bakunin and Otto Leonhard Heubner – a member of the Provisional Government formed by the rebels – were arrested, Wagner managed to escape. Using a false passport, obtained with the help of his friend Franz Liszt, he fled to Switzerland. Only in 1862 did he receive a full amnesty.

74
76
77
79
88

Robert Schumann in a diary (so-called 'household book') on Wagner's political activity:★

15.5.48. At Wagner's in the morning – his theatre-republic.
20.5.48. At Wagner's in the morning, visits by Wagner. His political poem.
19.6.48. Richard Wagner's political coup.

Georg Eismann, *Robert Schumann*, vol. I, Leipzig 1956, p. 159

★ 'His theatre-republic' must refer to Wagner's 'Plan for the organization of a German National Theatre for the Kingdom of Saxony' which he had handed in to the Ministry on 11 May, while the 'political poem' is probably the 'Greeting from Saxony to the Viennese' which Wagner had in fact written in March after the troubles in Vienna and which had been published in the *Allgemeine Österreichische Zeitung*. 'Political coup' is Schumann's description of Wagner's speech at the Dresden Vaterlandsverein on the subject of 'what is the attitude of the republican effort towards the Monarchy'; the speech appeared as a supplement to the *Dresdener Anzeiger*, although without any indication of its author's identity

Letter from Wagner to Professor Franz Jacob Wigard, a member of the Frankfurt National Assembly, Dresden, 19 May 1848:

I fear there will be a lot of trouble if the German Parliament does not first of all decide upon the following:

1. The German *Bundestag* of hitherto is dissolved, the Parliament thus assumes sole constitutional authority and has the right to derogate executive power to a commission nominated from amongst its members.

2. Immediate arming of the populace in the manner we have discussed.

3. *Defensive and offensive pact with France.*

These three measures will be enough to give the inevitable struggle a definite direction, in every province, in every town, the two distinct parties will emerge: the Frankfurt (German) Party and the Special Government Party. This way the matter will be brought to a head.

The fourth step must now be: the territorial question of the German states. If the Frankfurt Assembly has the task of drawing up a constitution that will unite Germany, it must first grapple with the problem of the inequality of the various inner German states. It must set up a commission to work out proposals for a rational and natural distribution of the territories of the constituent German states, on the principle of no longer tolerating states with a population of less than three or more than six million.

This in the end is the decisive point, and without it our whole effort would be mere patch-work. *It will then be up to the Princes to decide their own lot by their actions: if they start protesting and objecting they should all be put straight into the dock and the indictment against them should be founded on a completely historical basis.*

Only after these questions have been decided and these battles fought should the Assembly get down to the constitutional task, for this cannot be undertaken until we have *clear ground* beneath our feet. How useless a constitution would be in the present state of Germany! *The Parliament must first completely revolutionize the individual states*, and that it will do by its first decrees for it is through these decrees that the parties will get the necessary guidelines which they lack at present.

If you could share my opinion and rouse all possible forces to get the Assembly moving along these lines, your achievement would be immortal. *No softer measures will achieve our aims!*

I wish you every success.

Your
obedient
Richard Wagner.

Sämtliche Briefe, vol. 2, pp. 589ff.

75 '*The Revolution*', *an anonymous newspaper article by Wagner:*

If we look out over the nations and peoples of Europe we see everywhere the ferment of a mighty movement, whose first ripples have already reached us and whose full weight threatens to engulf us soon. Europe appears to us like some immense volcano, from within which a constantly growing, alarming roar can be heard; from its crater dark, stormy pillars of smoke are already rising into the sky and forming heavy blankets of cloud, plunging the surrounding earth into darkness, while individual rivers of lava have already broken through the crust and go pouring down into the valleys, destroying everything in their path, fiery harbingers of the coming eruption.

A supernatural force seems to be about to seize our continent, to lift it from its well-tried course and hurl it off on to another track. Yes, the old world, we can see, is about to collapse; from it a *new* world will arise, for the sublime Goddess of *Revolution* comes thundering in on the wings of the storm, lightning flashing round her august head, a sword in her right hand, torch in her left, her eye so dark, so vengeful, so cold; and yet what a glow of the purest love, what abundant happiness it radiates *upon him* who dares to look straight and unswerving into this sombre eye! She thunders down upon us, the ever-rejuvenating mother of mankind, destroying and blessing she sweeps across the earth; and before her the howl of the storm, shaking so violently all that man has fashioned that vast clouds of dust darken the air; wherever her mighty foot treads what vain presumption built to last a thousand years crashes in ruins, and the hem of her robe sweeps away its last remains! But behind her there is revealed to us, bathed in glowing sunshine, an unsuspected paradise of happiness, and where her foot has passed in destruction, sweet-scented flowers spring from the ground and the joyful hallelujahs of liberated mankind fill the air, which is yet re-echoing with the din of conflict.

And now look around you. There you see some mighty prince, his heart beating anxiously, his breath hesitant, struggling to put on a calm and collected air as he tries to deny to himself and to others what he nevertheless clearly sees is inescapable. And there you see another, his leathery old face furrowed with every vice, fishing out and bringing into play all those crafty little tricks which have already earned him many a little title and many a little medal; now a diplomatic smile spreads across his inscrutable countenance as he tries to calm down the snivelling Junkers and their swooning dames by the semi-official intimation that the highest authorities are already devoting their attention to this strange apparition, that couriers with Cabinet decrees have already been despatched in all directions, that the considered opinion of the wise statesman, Prince Metternich himself, is already on its way from London, that the competent security forces all around have been alerted, so that elegant society may look forward to the surprise of being able to inspect for themselves this notorious vagabond, Revolution – in chains, of course, in an iron cage – at the next Court ball. And there is yet a third, calculating the approach of the phenomenon, then running to the stock exchange to study and assess the rise and fall of the stocks, haggling and bargaining, trying to squeeze out the last ounce of speculative profit, until with one stroke his whole shabby business is blown to smithereens. And now again, see behind the dusty desk one of those rusted and furred-up cogs of our present-day bureaucracy, scratching his blunt old pens across the page with no thought in his mind but to add more and more to the ancient heap of the paper world-order. Between the piles of documents and contracts lie the hearts of living men, like dried plants, crumbling to dust in these modern torture-chambers. There there is immense activity, for the country-wide net is torn in several places and the

170

Große

Musik-Aufführung

am

Palmsonntage 1849.

1. **Ouverture von L. van Beethoven, Op. 124.**
2. **Cantate: Der büßende David, von Mozart.**
3. **IX. Symphonie mit Chören, von L. v. Beethoven.**

Dresden,
Druck der Königl. Hofbuchdruckerei von C. C. Meinhold und Söhne.

Programme of the concert given in Dresden on Palm Sunday, 1849, conducted by Carl Gottlieb Reissiger (1798–1859) and Wagner. Reissiger conducted Beethoven's overture *The Dedication of the House*, Op. 124, and Mozart's cantata *Davide Penitente*, while Wagner conducted Beethoven's Ninth Symphony. Dietrich Mack, Bayreuth.

surprised spiders are busily spinning new threads to repair the weak spots. No ray of light enters there, all is eternal night and darkness, and it is in night and darkness that the whole apparatus will disappear without trace. But from this side can be heard bright martial music, the swords and bayonets are gleaming, heavy cannons rattle past and the long columns of troops wind along shoulder-to-shoulder. The brave band of heroes have set forth to match arms with the Revolution. The general marches them right and left and places here the infantry, there the hussars and draws up his long ranks of soldiers and the shattering artillery; and the Revolution, head high in the clouds, approaches – and they cannot see it and wait for the foe; and it is already in their midst; and its tempestuous force seizes them and scatters their ranks and pulverizes their borrowed strength, and the general sits there still, studying the map and working out from which side the enemy might attack, and how strong he is and when he will come! And now the vision again changes: we see an anxious worried face, that of an honest and industrious citizen. He has worked and struggled his whole life long and faithfully served the common weal, as far as his strength allowed him; no tears, no injustice taints the little sheaf which he has fathered through his fruitful efforts, to support *him* in his weak old age and *his* children as they enter a hostile world. Certainly he felt the approach of the storm, certainly he realizes no power can resist it, but his heart bleeds as he looks back on his arduous existence, the sole fruit of which is now destined to be destroyed. We must not condemn him if he clutches anxiously at his little nest-egg and in his blind fervour vainly resists the impending change with all his strength. Harken, unfortunate!

171

Lift your eyes and look up to where thousands upon thousands are gathering on the hillsides to await the new sun, full of joyful expectation! Look at them, they are your brothers, your sisters, they are the host of all the poor, those wretches who have never yet known *anything* from life but *suffering*, who were strangers on this earth of joy; they are all longing for just *this* Revolution, which *you* are afraid of, to set them free from this world of despair, to create a new world of happiness for *everyone*! Look, there come thousands pouring from the factories; they have laboured and produced the finest cloths, but they themselves and their children are naked, they freeze and hunger for it is not to *them* that the fruits of their labour belong, they belong to the rich and mighty, who call the earth and its inhabitants their *own*. See how they come from the farms and villages; they have tilled the soil and made of it a garden of plenty, and their efforts have produced crops in abundance, enough to feed every man alive – and yet they are poor and hungry and naked, for it is not to them and the others who are in need that the earth's gifts belong, they belong to the rich and mighty, who call earth and its inhabitants their *own*. By the hundred thousand, by the million, they are all assembled on the heights and look out to the far horizon, where the gathering clouds announce the approach of the liberating Revolution, and all of them, who have nothing left to regret, whose very sons are stolen from them to be turned into devoted warders of their imprisoned father, whose daughters must walk the streets of our cities laden with shame, victims of the low desires of the rich and mighty, all of them with their pallid, care-worn faces, their weak and shivering limbs, all of them, who have *never* known happiness, they are gathered there on the heights and, trembling with excited expectation, they look out with fervent gaze upon the approaching phenomenon, and listen in silent rapture to the roar of the rising storm as it brings to their ears the greeting of the Revolution; 'I am the ever-rejuvenating, ever-creating life! Where I am not is death! I am the dream, the comfort, the hope of the oppressed! I destroy what is, and wherever I go new life springs from the dead rocks. I come to you to smash all the chains which crush you, to redeem you from the embrace of death and breathe young life into your veins. All that exists must pass away, that is the eternal law of nature, the rule of life, and I, the eternal destroyer, have come to fulfil the law and create the eternally youthful life. I will utterly annihilate the established order in which you live, for it springs from sin, its flower is misery and its fruit is crime; but the seed has ripened and I am the reaper. I will destroy every wrong which has power over men. I will destroy the domination of one over the other, of the dead over the living, of the material over the spiritual, I will shatter the power of the mighty, of the law and of property. Man's master shall be his *own* will, his *own* desire his only law, his *own* strength his only property, *for only the free man is holy and there is nought higher than he*. Let there be an end to the wrong that gives one man power over millions, which subjects millions to the will of one individual, to the evil which teaches that one has the power to give happiness to all others. Equals may not rule equals, equals have no higher power than equals, *and since all are equal I shall destroy all dominion of one over the other*.

An end to the wrong which gives death power over life, the past over the future. The law of the dead is their *own* law, it shares their lot and dies with them, it must not have power over life. *Life is its own law.* And because the the law is for the living and not for the dead, and because *you* are living and there is none who is over you, *then you are yourselves the law, your own free will is the only supreme law and I will destroy the power of death over life*.

Let there be an end to the injustice that makes man subject to his own works, to property. Man's highest possession is his creative power, that is the spring from which all happiness for ever arises and your greatest real pleasure lies not in *what is produced* but in the *act of production*, in the use of *your own power*. Man's works are lifeless and the living may not combine with the lifeless, may not subject itself to it. Let us then put an end to the evil which limits enjoyment, which constrains our free power, which creates properly outside man and makes him a slave of his own works.

Just look, you unfortunates, at those blessed fields which at present you roam through as slaves, as strangers. *Free* you shall be to wander, free from the yoke of the living, free from the chains of the dead. What Nature has created and man has planted and changed into a fruitful garden, belongs to all *mankind*, to *those in need* and none may come and say: 'It is to *me* alone that all this belongs, which men have created by their labour. I alone have a right to it and the others enjoy it only insofar as I choose and they pay me.' Let us destroy this lie along with the others; for what men's efforts have created, belongs to all men without constraint, like everything else upon the earth.

I will destroy the existing order of things which divides mankind into hostile nations, into strong and weak, into those with rights and those without, into rich and poor, for this order simply makes *wretches* of all. I will destroy the order of things which makes millions into slaves of the few, and these few into slaves of their own paper and their own wealth. I will destroy this order of things which divides work from enjoyment, which makes work a burden and enjoyment a vice, and renders *one* man miserable through want and *the other* miserable through excess. I will destroy this order of things which consumes men's strength in the service of the dominion of the dead, of lifeless matter which keeps half of mankind inactive or engaged in useless activity, which compels hundreds of thousands to devote the flower of their youth in busy indolence to the preservation of this damnable state of affairs as soldiers, officials, speculators and financiers, while the other half has to sustain the whole shameful edifice at the cost of the exhaustion of their powers and the sacrifice of any enjoyment of life. I will wipe from the face of the earth every trace of this crazy order of things, this compact of violence, lies, worry, hypocrisy, poverty, misery, suffering, tears, deceit and crime which fathers an occasional burst of impure lust, but almost never a ray of pure joy. Let there be an end to everything that oppresses you and makes you suffer, and from the ruins of this old world a *new* one shall arise, full of undreamed of happiness. Let there be no more hate, nor envy, nor ill-will, nor enmity among you; you shall see yourselves as *brothers* – *all* you who live in it – and be free to recognize the value of life, free in your desires, free in your actions, free in your pleasures. Therefore arise, peoples of the earth! Arise, you who lament and are oppressed and poor! And arise, too, all you others who seek in vain to disguise the inner desolation of your hearts with the idle pomp of your power and wealth! Arise, follow me all together, for I can make no distinction among those who follow me. From now on there will be but *two* races: those who follow me and those who resist. The former I shall lead to happiness the latter I shall crush underfoot, I am the sole *god*, whom all creatures recognize and who embraces all existence with life and happiness!'

And see, the hosts on the hillsides fall silent on their knees, they hark with dumb rapture, and as the sun-parched earth sucks up the cooling raindrops, so their hearts, scorched by misery, gulp down the draught of the thundering storm and new life courses through their veins. The storm rolls nearer and nearer, on its wings the Revolution; the re-awakened hearts open wide and the Revolution, victorious, enters into their minds, their bones, their flesh and fills them utterly. They jump up from the earth in divine rapture; no longer are they the poor, the starving, bowed down by misery, their proud figures arise, with the glow of enthusiasm transfiguring their faces, their eyes are alight with excitement and, with the heaven-shaking cry '*I am a man!*', the millions, the living Revolution, the man-become-god, burst forth into the valleys and the plains and proclaim to the whole world the new gospel of happiness!

Volksblätter, Dresden, 8 April 1849

Clara Schumann in her diary on the Dresden May Uprising, 1849:

On *Thursday the 3rd* we went to dinner at the Villa im Plauenschen Grunde and really abandoned ourselves to the magnificent countryside – what was going on back in the town, of course, we had no idea of. But we had scarcely been home for half an hour when the general alarm was sounded and the tocsin rang out from every steeple; soon we heard shooting, too. The king had refused to recognize the National Constitution [Reichsverfassung] until Prussia had done so, and they had cut the traces of his coach in which he had tried to escape, so forcing him to stay, and had tried to storm the arsenal, from which however shots had been fired on the people. The bitterness which this caused can be imagined. The night then passed fairly quietly but on *Friday the 4th*, when we went into town we found all the streets barricaded; on the barricades stood *Sensenmänner** and republicans, building the barricades up higher and higher; everywhere there reigned the most absolute lawlessness, the drains and the paving stones and cobbles were torn up and piled on to the barricades; at the Rathaus the democrats had met and were electing a Provisional Government (for the king had fled to König-stein castle during the night), which soon began issuing proclamations of all kinds, all relating to the struggle against the troops, who were stationed with cannons before the castle and in Neustadt. On our walk through the town we saw the dreadful sight of the fourteen corpses of

those who had been shot the day before, which lay on public view in a frightful state in the courtyard of the clinic. I could not forget this sight for a long time and only the greater turmoil that was to follow effaced the horrible impression. That day and the following night passed without fighting, the barricades rose to veritable fortresses, the tension was terrible, how was it all to end, and with what bloodshed!

Saturday the 5th, what a terrible morning! In our street a security patrol was formed and they wanted Robert for it; after I had twice denied he was there, they threatened to come and search for him, and we fled with Marie through the garden gate out on to the Bohemian Station. Here, amongst others, we met Oberländer who was about to go to the Königstein to try to persuade the king to give way. Here there were *Sensenmänner* who were watching to ensure that no one who was armed should leave. . . .

My fear the whole day through was awful, for the thunder of the cannons never ceased, and the children were in the town. I wanted to go to fetch them in the evening but it got too late, and then I could find no one to go with me so late. Robert could not come with me, for they had spread the word that the insurgents were calling on all able-bodied men in the neighbourhood and were forcing them to take part in the fighting. And so on

Monday the 7th I set out for the town at three in the morning accompanied by the estate manager's daughter. The people are holding out remarkably well, I should never have credited the Saxons with such courage. Reinforcements are reaching the town constantly and especially many men have come from the Erzgebirge. But the troops, too, are being reinforced constantly from Prussia, which has aroused the most intense bitterness among the people.

Tuesday the 8th passed indecisively. The struggle in the town continues unabated . . .

On *Wednesday the 9th* we could see clouds of smoke rising throughout the morning from the Räcknitz Heights and we supposed they were bombarding the city from there . . .

On *Thursday the 10th* we heard of the awful atrocities committed by the troops; they shot down every insurgent they could find, and our landlady told us later that her brother, who owns the *Goldner Hirsch* in the Scheffelgasse was made to stand and watch while the soldiers shot one after another twenty-six students they found in a room there. Then it is said they hurled men into the street by the dozen from the third and fourth floors. It is horrible to have to go through these things! This is how men have to fight for their little bit of freedom! When will the time come when all men have equal rights? How can it be that the nobility's belief that these men are different from us middle-class people can have become so ineradicably established over so many centuries! . . .

Soon my father came, but he had no wish to know about all the atrocities I had heard of. After he had gone Robert came: he had been unable to remain calm at what had

---

* Literally, 'scythe-men'; name given to poorly armed insurgents in the Polish uprisings of 1792 and 1848

happened outside. So we walked together through the main streets of the city to see where the worst battles had taken place. It is scarcely possible to give a picture of the devastation. You can see thousands of bullet holes in the houses, whole sections of walls broken down, the old opera house totally razed to the ground and the same with three fine houses in the Zwingerstrasse, and in the Kleine Brüdergasse, too; in short it is frightful to behold, and how must the houses look on the inside! The walls broken through so that the insurgents could keep in touch through several buildings. How many innocent victims died, hit in their rooms by stray shots etc. etc. St Mary's Church is full of prisoners, and there are already 500 of them. Kapellmeister Wagner is said to have played a part on the republican side, making speeches from the Rathaus, having barricades built to his instructions and much else besides! The streets are still mostly torn up, the pavements are still all over the place, only the barricades have been cleared. A state of siege has been declared in the city – it is swarming with Prussians – you can see them, lying about on straw, in the Old Market. It is a horrific but interesting picture, the streets now!

Berthold Litzmann, Clara Schumann, vol. 2, 3rd impression, Leipzig 1907, pp. 185–90

Hans von Bülow in a letter to his mother, Leipzig, May 1849:

Now, I know more of Wagner than you do. Rietz* told me at the Conservatoire here that Wagner had been active as Secretary to the provisional government; Meser,** whom I met yesterday at the Bookseller's Exchange, didn't exactly say he had been their secretary, but he was sure he had played a prominent part. Ritter's mother*** wrote to Meser today that he had gone away with his wife – where, they did not know at his home, or wouldn't say. A student heard him speaking to the people from a balcony – so the arch-traitor's operas – and *that's* his punishment – are banned for ever from the royal repertoire, and he himself is perhaps anything but out of danger.

Hans von Bülow, Briefe, ed. Marie v. Bülow, vol. 1, Leipzig 1895, p. 167

'Evidence against the sometime Kapellmeister Richard Wagner concerning his participation in the May Insurrection here in the year 1849', detailed by the Dresden Police:

1. The sometime Kapellmeister Wagner was intimately acquainted with the ringleaders of the insurrection, in particular with Bakunin, Heubner and Röckel.
2. Some time – say 6 weeks – before the outbreak of the insurrection various secret meetings took place at the lodgings of the law student Neumann, who lived in the so-called Menagerie-Garten; at that time Bakunin, who called himself Dr Schwarz, had taken rooms at Neumann's. The purpose of these meetings has not been established. But it is suspected that the same were connected with the uprising. It is even said that in

* Conductor at the Leipzig Stadttheater and composition teacher at the Conservatoire
** Publisher; published *Rienzi, Der fliegende Holländer* and *Tannhäuser*
*** Karl Ritter, composer and conductor, a friend of Wagner's; his mother, Julie Ritter, was Wagner's protectress

174

Soldaten!

Brüder! Die provisorische Regierung, welche nach der Flucht des Königs und der Minister in der Stadt Dresden niedergesetzt worden ist, ruft Euch zu, das Land gemeinschaftlich mit ihr zu schützen, dem Volke die Bruderhand zu reichen, und euch zur Verfügung der Landes- und Reichsverfassung zu stellen. Folgt dem Beispiele anderer braver Soldaten, vergeßt nicht, daß Ihr vereidete Staatsbürger seid, und daß Ihr für Aufrechthaltung der Rechte und Freiheiten des Volks zu wachen habt. Ihr seid erwählt, dem Volke zu zeigen, daß Ihr mit ihm geht, nicht gegen dasselbe seid.

Soldaten! Auf denn, haltet zu uns, die provisorische Regierung hat die Pflicht in der jetzigen Zeit die Gefahr des Vaterlandes abzuwenden, und braucht Eure Kräfte.

Die provisorische Regierung
Tzschirner. Heubner. Todt.

Public notices posted in Dresden during the uprising in May 1849, signed by the leaders of the Provisional Government of Saxony (Tzschirner, Heubner and Todt): above, an appeal to soldiers for their continued loyalty to their country following the flight of the king; opposite, a general order concerning supervision of watches at the barricades.

Neumann's lodgings there was a depot of arms and munitions. Wagner is accused of having taken part in these meetings.
3. Wagner is further accused of making his garden available for discussions of the arming of the populace. The following took part in these discussions: Röckel, the First Lieutenants Schreiber and Müller, Professor Semper and others.
4. The infamous brass-founder Oehme, one of the most deeply implicated participants in the insurrection, who is known to have attempted to set fire to the Prinzen-Palais, claims that Wagner and Röckel ordered a substantial number of hand-grenades from him before Easter 1849. These hand-grenades are supposed to have been destined for Prague and were sent to the despatch department of [the newspaper] the *Dresdner Zeitung*. However, they do not seem to have been sent to Prague for Oehme asserts that on 4 May 1849 Wagner instructed him to fill these same grenades, which were still lying in the despatch office of the *Dresdner Zeitung*.
5. Shortly before the outbreak of the insurrection Röckel had gone to Prague to work for a general uprising against established governments. When, during his absence, the insurrection broke out in Dresden Wagner informed Röckel of the fact and called for his immediate

return. The letter on this subject sent by Wagner to Röckel compromises the former in the extreme.

6. During the insurrection it is reported that

(a) on the day when the so-called 'provisional government' was elected, Wagner was present at the town-hall here and also invited Bakunin to go there;

(b) he 'held observation' from the Kreuzthurm [tower of the Kreuzkirche] and

(c) he accompanied a band of reinforcements from Zittau.

7. Moreover, on 9 May he is said to have met Heubner and Bakunin in Tharandt during the retreat of the insurgents and to have accompanied them to Freiberg. It seems as though during the uprising he was absent from Dresden for a while in order to raise support and reinforcements for the rebels in the surrounding country.

Lippert, pp. 17 ff.

Wagner describes his part in the Dresden Insurrection in a letter to the actor Eduard Devrient, Weimar, 17 May 1849:

As long as I was able to follow the Dresden rising it had my full and absolute sympathy, which I frankly proclaimed, admittedly not through any act – but in my opinions expressed to many individuals – never, though, to the masses (as a speaker for example!). I did not think much of the fables of the red republic, but under the banner of the 'German Constitution' (of which I will readily admit that it was not exactly for its sake that the masses let themselves

Barrikaden-Ordnung.

1) Den Oberbefehl über die Barrikaden hat der Oberkommandant der Dresdener Communalgarden Oberstleutnant Heinze. Stellvertreter ist Bataillonskommandant Vollsack.

2) Das Hauptquartier ist auf dem Altmarkte im Rathhause.

3) Für jede Barrikade übernehmen abwechselnd 3 Führer je 6 Stunden den Befehl und ernennen für jede Wache einen Unterführer, der die Namen der Wachenden aufschreibt.

4) Fällt nichts Außerordentliches vor, so bringt der Barrikadenführer nach Ablösung der 3. Wache diese Namenliste nebst dem Führerzettel aufs Hauptquartier.

5) Bei jeder Barrikade wird in dem am nächsten und passendsten Hause zu ebener Erde eine Wachtstube eingerichtet.

6) Gegen Vorzeigung des Führerzettels kann auf Rechnung des Oberkommando's an jede Barrikade das nöthige Bier, Brod, Pulver und Blei verabreicht werden.

7) Barrikadenführer sind an der Barrikade Nr.

für die 1. Wache von   Uhr bis   Uhr.
  „ „ 2.   „   „   „   „   „
  „ „ 3.   „   „   „   „   „

Dresden, am 5. Mai 1849.

Die provisorische Regierung von Sachsen.
Tzschirner. Heubner. Todt.

be shot!) I saw quite distinctly the very natural indignation of the citizens and the people against any ruler who calls in foreign troops to suppress public opinion, and also the quite local patriotic fury that it should be 'Prussians', to whom Saxony had already lost so much – who were now to occupy the remainder of the country. No thinking man will believe that the revolution was plotted, since otherwise at least the most important military targets would not have been abandoned to the troops from the very beginning. The assault on the arsenal was the impulsive act of an unarmed populace, which, after the ban on the parade of the citizens' militia, felt itself betrayed. I was full of suspense and followed all the public acts from close quarters, especially the constitution of the security committee at the town-hall; for I was confident that after the terrible events they would bring about a worthwhile concentration of the movement; I hoped that the greatest singlemindedness of both the authorities and the people would not only prevent further bloodshed but might also at last bring about a timely acquiescence on the part of the king. With this in view, my sole endeavour on the second day, by which time the town was already barricaded, was directed towards doing whatever I as an individual – without making public speeches – could do to prevent further conflict between the people and the military. I told two soldiers whom I met by the barracks next to the arsenal that if it should come to a further confrontation with the populace they had only to declare that they would be united with them to fight against foreign troops; at the barricades that I passed I spoke to individuals in the same way, pointing out that they should not provoke the troops, but simply ask them whether they would be with them against foreign troops. In fact they wrote this question on a poster and pinned it to the barricades, and it seemed to me crucial, above all else, by this or some other means, to unite the troops and the populace, not only in order to offer effective resistance to the Prussian invasion but especially also, by the same means, to keep the Dresden movement itself on the right original track. For at any rate a genuine alliance of the Saxon people with the Saxon army could only have occurred for the purpose of common resistance to the Prussian invasion, and on behalf of the German Constitution; and a resulting joint representation to the king of Saxony from his people and his troops could not have failed to produce the desired result of releasing the king from the oppressive Prussian influence and preserving the whole movement most effectively from any deviation in other directions. I therefore expressed my most earnest wish to one of the town councillors, whom I knew well from long acquaintance, that they should negotiate with the military governor with a view to including a number of army members on the Security Committee. The election of a provisional government still did not yet deter me, since the presence of Heubner and Todt in it guaranteed that the movement would not be allowed to lose sight of its true objectives and could hold meaningful negotiations with the king. I felt quite overjoyed when I heard that half the arsenal had been made available to the citizens' militia and I began to hope that the Prussian Cabinet conspiracy would be stopped by Saxony – perhaps even without bloodshed. But the third day, of course, dashed my hopes: the cease-fire was suspended, Prussian troops arrived and our own men *joined with them* to turn on the people. The resulting bitterness was unbounded, and although from then on I was no longer in immediate touch with the movement, I can assure you with absolute certainty that it was not the republic, red or blue, not Poland, not Russia that from then on inspired the most bitter and pitiless resistance in the struggles at the barricades, but simply the utterly subjective, personal fury of the citizens and the populace against the army, which was further aggravated by a particular hatred for the fusiliers sent from Leipzig, in whose corps an old personal feud against the citizens of Dresden had been inflamed, artificially enough, by their officers, for this corps had had to retreat before them back in 1830. I spent Saturday and Sunday as a peaceful observer of the struggle in the most objective position in the world – up in the tower of the Kreuzkirche – for, despite the pleas of my wife, I could not sit still at home. On Monday morning I again went to the town-hall to ask after the state of things, but the situation there was now very different: the force of circumstances and the need to handle the defence of the city in a thoroughly military manner had led to a hunt for strategists, for the commander of the militia seemed to be lacking in both competence and energy: a trained Polish officer had been recommended and was begged most urgently to prepare a plan of military defence. The claim that Poland had been involved from the beginning is untrue. I was now doubtful and unsure of my present subjective attitude to the movement and I left the town at 8 o'clock on Monday morning to take my wife, who had already packed, to one of my married sisters in Chemnitz. On the way we met numerous bands of rebels coming in from the furthest points of the state: this great interest, the courage and dedication which I found everywhere made an overwhelming impression on me: to their enquiries I replied with what I knew about the state of the fighting in Dresden, for them to hear the naked truth was enough to spur them into a hurried march. Towards evening I met the whole Chemnitz Communal Guard at Oederan: they surrounded our coach and demanded news of Dresden; when I told them what I knew some of them said they had different information, namely that Dresden had already fallen to the Prussians. They took me to the town-hall to get me to correct my statements there: and there I realized that I had been speaking to men who had been *forced* to march on Dresden and were now anxiously clutching at every piece of false information as an excuse to turn back for home without delay. My reports ruined their plans and they were disposed to arrest me on suspicion of being a deserter. I was able to avoid this only by promising to return to Dresden the following morning after accompanying my wife to Chemnitz; my word of honour was demanded and I felt it necessary not to refuse it. Moreover my concern for the relatives I had left behind and the desire to find out just how things stood made me want to go back to Dresden anyway. The mail-coach took me as far as the Feldschlösschen and there I learned that one could reach the town-hall in complete safety but not other parts of the city. When I got to the town-hall I had the opportunity of getting a clearer picture of the situation: the faint-hearted Todt and the coward Tzschirner had fled and the man on the centre-left, Heubner, was the only one to have remained with dignity, perseverance and

calm at his post. A moving incident gave me the chance to get to know Heubner a little better: a Communal Guardsman who was on the theatre staff came to me to ask me to intervene on behalf of young Fürstenau, who, suspected of having fired on the crowd from a window, had been captured by them and brought to prison. I immediately asked Heubner for an audience and tried to convince him that for various evident reasons I was personally convinced that the prisoner was innocent: Heubner told me not to worry and assured me of a satisfactory resolution of the matter. Having spent an hour in the town, and since I could not get through to my relations after all, I began to look around for an opportunity to get back to Chemnitz: but how was I to manage this at night and with no hope of getting a mail-coach or any transport? A man I knew from the University, who was now an adjutant on the general staff of the militia, was ordered to go to Freiberg as a courier as soon as possible to summon the Chemnitz Communal Guard to march here urgently; for this purpose he was provided with a mail-coach and horses and I made use of the opportunity to get away. On the next day I used the mail-coach going back empty from Freiberg to Tharand in order to return thus far again to find out something more definite about developments during the night: half-way along the road we suddenly encountered the completely orderly retreat of some 2,000 insurgents: out I get, find Heubner's coach and discover that the intention is to make Freiberg the seat of the provisional government. Outside Freiberg *Heubner* is met by a delegate of the Chemnitz Citizens' Militia, who invites him to establish the provisional government in Chemnitz: under a storm of pleas from wealthy Freiberg citizens, not to ruin their town, Heubner gives way, orders the insurgents after a short rest to march for Chemnitz and himself rides quickly ahead to get a few hours' sleep in a peaceful bed again at last. At the gates of Chemnitz he makes himself known – for it seemed to him both unnecessary and cowardly to conceal his identity – and lies down to sleep at the inn, along with several of his entourage. The rich industrialists of Chemnitz decide it would be a good thing to send the gendarmes to wake him take him to Altenburg and hand him over to the Prussian army.

Although I had had no more than a fleeting acquaintance with him, Heubner aroused in me the deepest personal interest: he was the most noble, reliable, honest – and unfortunate – hero of the revolution. My grief for him is great. Bakunin, with his terrible energy, was forced upon him under the pressure of events when all around him defected: although Bakunin's objectives went far beyond his, he could not turn him away at a time when energy and only energy was called for. But had Heubner been the pure and unmitigated revolutionary whose sole aim is victory at all costs – and this is the only successful revolutionary of the future – he would not have cared tuppence for the snivelling of the rich citizenry of Freiberg or Chemnitz, he would have been guided by the terrible logic of the revolution – he would not have fallen and the would not have been lost. But here I have realized that we are none of us revolutionaries, least of all I myself: we desire the revolution in order to be able to build something worthwhile on its foundation – and this serious intention makes us misunderstand it: the genuine, successful revolutionary can only wish to destroy and his only strength will be *hate*, not the *love* which is our guiding light.

I have sent this precise account ahead of me in order to acquaint you fully with my part in what happened. At the beginning I was in full sympathy with the uprising, full of bitterness the middle two days and full of excited suspense and curiosity the last two. But at no point was I active, either with weapons or with public speeches: and I never had any kind of official position in the provisional government. But it will not be hard to guess how base and vile the reaction may grow to be in Saxony under the protection of Prussian bayonets: I already felt unsafe at my relations' in Chemnitz and my meeting with the Citizens' Militia of that city was interpreted as high treason by that section of them who have now become very vociferous. Information from my relatives in Leipzig leads me to conclude that I am being denounced and defamed in Dresden. So for safety reasons alone I would not think of going back there now or for what, under present circumstances, is likely to be a long time to come. But there are other considerations, too, which now demand a decisive change in the course of my future life. You know the thorny nature of the artistic path I have embarked upon: I should not bother about the wounds, but I can no longer look with indifference upon the disintegration of my whole artistic nature. The despair at my official position, the crushing burdens which it imposes upon me, the worthlessness of every undertaking within the sphere of this official contract – have for years now been dragging me into a deep depression, which can only increase as time goes by. The only thing that really kept me alive was my artistic output – and that, after all was the very purpose of my existence: but this, too, the times and my circumstances have turned sour: I have had a new opera [*Lohengrin*] ready for two years: but nowhere do I find the encouragement that would make me want to reveal it to the public, and so for two years I have been dissipating my artistic powers without joy or relish. And so in the end I become a revolutionary – in thought if not in deed – and can find no pleasure in composing any more. The final catastrophe has at least brought me to myself in so far as I have become completely clear about this unhappy, shattered state of mind, and even before that I already had no further hope or longing other than to live out my life somewhere, with my poor long-suffering wife, in quiet seclusion, inactive, but also without guilt.

Sämtliche Briefe, vol. 2, pp. 660–67.

Text of the passport which was issued to Wagner in Zurich on 30 May 1849 for a journey to Paris:

Herr Richard Wagner of Leipzig, *compositeur de musique*
    Age: 36
    Height: 5 feet 5½ inches
    Hair: Brown
    Eyebrows: Brown
    Eyes: Blue
    Nose: Medium
    Destination: France
    Passport valid: for 1 year

Max Fehr, *Richard Wagners Schweizer Zeit*, Aarau and Leipzig (n.d.), vol. 1, p. 6

The Russian anarchist Michael Bakunin was interrogated on 19 September 1849. Of Wagner he said:

I immediately recognized Wagner as an impractical dreamer and although I spoke to him about politics amongst other things, I never committed myself to any joint action with him.

Lippert, p. 214

The German–American politician Carl Schurz (1829–1906) on his acquaintance with Wagner in 1849:

My most remarkable acquaintance in those days (the autumn of 1849) was that of Richard Wagner, who was also living in Zurich as a refugee as a consequence of his implication in the revolutionary events in Dresden. He had already created some of his most important works, but his greatness was only recognized by a small circle. He was by no means popular with those who shared his fate at that time. He was regarded as an extremely arrogant, domineering fellow whom nobody could be friends with and who treated his wife, a quite attractive, good-natured but not outstandingly intelligent woman, very meanly. Anyone who had prophesied his remarkable career to us at that time would have encountered little credence.

Carl Schurz, *Denkwürdigkeiten*, Berlin 1906, vol. 1, p. 253

While Wagner was living in exile in Switzerland his friend Franz Liszt worked for the performance and recognition of his works in Germany. On 28 August 1850 he conducted the première of *Lohengrin* in Weimar. He wrote essays on *Tannhäuser* (1849), *Lohengrin* (1850), *Rheingold* (1855) and *Der fliegende Holländer* (1854), and in 1853 he organized a Wagner-cycle in Weimar, with performances of *Der fliegende Holländer*, *Tannhäuser* and *Lohengrin*.

Franz Liszt in a letter to Wagner, written at the beginning of August 1850, on the preparations for the first performance of Lohengrin:

We are quite full of the *ethereal* sounds of your *Lohengrin* and I flatter myself that we shall succeed in putting it on as you intended. We are doing three or four hours of rehearsal a day and up to now we have got the solo parts and the quartet pretty well okay. Tomorrow I shall start the rehearsals with the individual wind instruments, of which we shall have the full complement required by the score. We have obtained a bass clarinet, . . . and the 'cellos, too, will be strengthened, . . . in short, rest assured that everything which is humanly possible in Weimar in this Year of Grace 1850 will be done for your *Lohengrin*, which in spite of all the nonsense that is talked, the false anxieties and the all-too-real incrustations, will be performed very respectably – I promise you – on the 28th of this month . . .

Briefwechsel zwischen Wagner und Liszt, Leipzig 1910, vol. 1, p. 313.

On the world première of Lohengrin, *1850:*

At last Wagner's opera *Lohengrin* has been produced in Weimar. The result, as was expected, was roughly the same as at the performances of *Rienzi* in Berlin and Königsberg, i.e. a gentle fiasco. Legationsrath* Dingelstedt, who had written a prologue to it, expresses himself very strongly about the lack of taste of Herr Franz Liszt (who promoted the performance very vigorously); Wagner reveals himself in this work (not to speak of his earlier ones) to be utterly *unmusical*; he has supplied us not with music but with noise – and such an infernal din, at that, that only a general cannonade on stage was missing from the thunder of hell itself. After this experience Herr Liszt will no doubt realize that the degraded taste of one individual is not enough to bring about a degradation of the taste of the whole public. In fact we are amazed that Herr Liszt could dare to present the raw product of a sham genius like Wagner to such a cultivated public; in the town where Goethe, Schiller, Wieland and Herder held sway for so long, only the élite of the present should be permitted to have their works staged.

Kleine Musikzeitung, Hamburg, [15] September 1850, p. 128

Franz Liszt on Lohengrin:

The music of this opera is characterized by such a predominant unity of conception and style that there is not a single melodic phrase, and even less a complete passage or ensemble, whose true sense and inner meaning are at all comprehensible if separated from the whole. Everything is interrelated, interlinked, interdependent; everything is most intimately interwoven with the story and is inseparable from it. In the music nothing is there by chance, nothing included for its own sake, no superfluous padding and so it would be difficult to form a proper judgment even of sizable excerpts of the composition; for everything in it is interlinked and interconnected like the meshes of a net, and everything is carefully calculated and logical and every harmonic progression is preceded or followed by a corresponding dramatic idea; utterly German in its premeditation and its systematic strictness, which enables us to say that this work is the most thoroughly thought-out of all inspirations. As it happens it is easy to explain why any episode listened to on its own is bound to lose its impact, if we simply think of the principle Wagner has employed to personify roles and ideas in the music. The repetition of five** themes, whose recurrences we have tried to follow, namely that of the introduction, the one which we hear at the pronouncement of the divine judgment, the one which appears with the arrival of Lohengrin and the one which accompanies the ominous threats of Ortrude, along with the less frequent but always justified repetition of the subsidiary motives, naturally makes it possible to follow the whole dramatic development and to feel all the excitement which is the inevitable result of such a new and definite, and, for all its constant twists, clear structure; but only if you are capable of appreciating all the complex nuances and all the implications concealed in the general layout of this beautiful monument.

* Honorary title (literally 'Embassy Counsellor')

** He lists only four, omitting the theme of Lohengrin's injunction to Elsa not to ask his name

There are men who, with the aid of a single idea, a single invention, an apprently insignificant discovery, can produce immense changes in the sphere to which these discoveries belong. But there are others who add nothing to the knowledge of their predecessors, no new facts, nor the introduction of hitherto unknown elements, but they still enlarge the scope of their intellectual world by seeing common, well-known things in an uncommon and hitherto unknown light. Wagner is a revolutionary of the latter kind; his system continues the tradition of Gluck through the importance he attaches to dramatic rhetoric; and the tradition of Weber through declamatory eloquence and a fine sense of orchestration. Wagner would certainly have written the dedication of *Alceste*, had Gluck not already done so. But he goes further than both Gluck and Weber in the practical application of their theories. Having mastered with unusual luck and the boldest intelligence all the musical improvements which have occurred since the deaths of these great men, and taking advantage of the wealth of beautiful new sounds which the new instruments can produce when used as they are by *Meyerbeer* and more expecially by *Berlioz*, he bends to his purpose all the techniques which we owe to progress made in recent times and now attempts by a more universal system than Gluck's and a more absolute principle than Weber's to secure the predominance of the dramatic idea, to which both had already subordinated the singers and the orchestra. If you have not read or heard Wagner's scores, and if you have not studied their intellectual subtlety and their scenic effectiveness, you will find it difficult to imagine adequately the result that he has achieved through the complete integration of these two sources – or rather these two torrents – of dramatic stimulus. He has succeeded in being at once an extraordinary symphonist and a great dramatist. By combining such rare and different qualities he is able to create an ensemble which you may like or dislike; but you will never be able to deny that from its colossal conception down to its tiniest detail it is logical and perfect in form. If Mme de Staël calls music the architecture of sounds let us be permitted to compare the structure of Wagner's magnificent edifices with an architectural order in which neither its supporters nor its detractors can change or remodel the slightest element without immediately robbing its style of its whole character. . . .

Right from his first operas, but especially in *Lohengrin*, Wagner has always mixed a different palette for each of his main characters. The more attentively you study this latest score, the more you realize what an interdependence he has created between his text and his orchestra. Not only has he personified in his melodies the feelings and passions which he has set in train, as we have already noted, but it was also his wish that their basic features should be underlined by a corresponding orchestral colouring, and as he creates rhythms and melodies to fit the character of the people he portrays, so also he chooses the right kinds of sound to go with them. Thus, for example, the motif which is lightly sketched in the first prelude: whether it is merely hinted at, as it is whenever the Holy Grail is mentioned, or finally fully developed, as in the narration in which Lohengrin at the end reveals his exalted secret – this motif is invariably entrusted to the violins. Elsa's motifs are almost exclusively accompanied

Announcement of the first Wagner cycle given at Weimar at the Court Theatre, February/March 1853, including performances of *Der fliegende Holländer*, *Tannhäuser* and *Lohengrin*.

by wind instruments, and this leads to the most magnificent contrasts whenever they follow a passage played by the brass. One is always particularly moved in the first scene, where the king's long narration, which is accompanied throughout by the dominant sounds of trumpets and trombones in the orchestra, is followed by a long silence and you then hear this soft and airy rustling sound developing, like the murmur of a wave created by a heavenly breath, convincing us of Elsa's shining innocence before she herself appears. The same orchestration appears like a refreshing dew to subdue the blazing passion of the duet between Friedrich and Ortrude as soon as Elsa appears on the balcony; and again it is employed for the bridal procession in the second act, characterizing this pious excitement, this orgy of innocence so powerfully that it makes this piece one of the most splendid, if not the most magnificent of the whole opera.

The problems involved in staging Wagner's operas properly, which arise from the deeply serious nature of their basic ideas and from their elevated style, as well as from the attention they demand from the audience, will unfortunately prevent them for a long time from achieving popularity. The seriousness of their conception and execution means that they lay no claim to that easy applause that we bestow upon short-lived works, nor to that spontaneous enthusiasm which greets the genius of a Rossini or a Meyerbeer when it bursts into sparkling fire or gives richly orchestrated expression to the whole gamut of human passions. Shall we then wait until the dust of time has covered Wagner's scores with a layer of dignified age, until the initiates have thumbed through them to discover the secret miracles of genius which they contain, and until our poets, with their easily stimulated admiration for the past, begin to wax enthusiastic over these heroes, who surpass our normal wretched conceptions a hundred-fold?

Franz Liszt, *Richard Wagners Lohengrin und Tannhäuser (German edition)*, Cologne 1852, pp. 76–83.

Friedrich Wilhelm IV of Prussia, to Franz Liszt, Charlotten-burg, 3 December 1851:

> To the Weimar Grand-Ducal Kapellmeister
> F. Liszt in Weimar

I have received with interest your essay on the latest musical creations of Kapellmeister Wagner of Dresden, a man whose talent makes him as admirable as his crime, alas, degrades him, and I thank you for it.

Briefe hervorragender Zeitgenossen an Franz Liszt, ed. La Mara, Leipzig 1904, vol. 3, p. 18.

Wagner in a letter to the producer Eduard Genast, Zurich, 23 September 1850, on cuts in Lohengrin:

My opera, as I am obliged to confess, suffers from the decided weakness of being too long, but do you really believe this would be the true reason if the opera should fail to reach a wider public? I can remember that wherever I have seen the *Huguenots* performed there were nothing but sleepy, yawning heads to be seen throughout the last act. But has this prevented the *Huguenots* from being performed year-in, year-out on every stage in the world? My own *Rienzi*, which, apart from its enormous length, had the additional fault of an overpoweringly loud orchestration, has always attracted the Dresden public *en masse*, whereas interest in my *Tannhäuser*, which is free of this weakness, has been maintained only through very special attention from above. And now, by shortening the performance time of *Lohengrin* by 10 or 12 minutes you hope to make it popular with the public who flock to see the *Huguenots* and *Rienzi* in droves, even though they are battered to sleep by them? My friend, those people who leave the performance after the second act of *Lohengrin* are not tired by the length, nor deafened by the din, they are victims – in direct proportion to their own seriousness – of the unexpected exertion to which they are subjected in trying to come to grips with a dramatic performance which directs itself not to a quarter or a half, but to the whole man. If you consider the matter thoroughly you will have to admit I am right. If you really want to educate this public, you must above all teach them strength, whip the cowardice and laziness from their philistine limbs and teach them to seek not amusement in the theatre but concentration. If you do not educate the public to put some effort into the enjoyment of art, then your friendly energy will obtain a wider audience for neither my works nor my aims. The Athenians used to sit watching performances of their trilogies from midday until late at night and they were surely as much men as our present public. But they participated in what they enjoyed.

This, most respected friend, is what I have to say on the matter in general. If I do not convince you then I must leave it to you to solve the problems relating to my work as you see fit. But please do not be upset if I express my conviction that your actions will at the most earn the acclaim of the honourable philistines of Weimar – but in no wise produce a wider acceptance of my opera. As to what that particular acclaim is worth to me – frankly not over-much.

But let me admit the basic cause of my resistance! I should have preferred not to know what cuts you are planning. For every one of them I could tell you, and I

imagine convince you, how sharply it strikes at my feeling of artistic honour. I ask you with what feelings, with what undermined enthusiasm, I shall soon be applying myself again to the composition of a musical drama if every time I come to work out the most deeply felt musical motifs, which after the most careful thought I consider to be essential, I am reminded of those passages in *Lohengrin* deemed dispensable by my best friends? . . .

Well, cut the work as much as you like: in view of this fault of excessive length, and above all since it has proved not only necessary but also possible to leave bits out – I'll renounce the opera entirely.

Eduard Genast, *Aus dem Tagebuch eines alten Schauspielers*, part 4, Leipzig 1866, pp. 139 ff.

───────────

Wagner lived in Zurich from 1849 to 1858. He had no regular income and was supported by friends. In three seminal essays – 'Art and the Revolution' (1849), 'The Work of Art of the Future' (1849) and 'Opera and Drama' (1851) – he explained the basis of his theory of art. **82 86, 84 87**

The (unprinted) title page to the manuscript of 'Art and the Revolution':

> I. Art and the revolution
> II. The artist of the future
> III. The art of the future

I. In the past the rich man lived by the principle that 'giving is more blessed than taking' – he enjoyed a happiness which unfortunately he withheld only from the poor. But the rich man of today says: 'taking is more blessed than giving'.

II. (man towards animals. (Butcher – hunter.)★ Unartistic lack of love for animals, which we see only as goods for industry. (riding = love of horses. – travel = steam.)

III. history of music: = Christian expression: 'where the word can get no further, music begins:' = Beethoven, 9th Symphony: proves the opposite: 'where music can go no further comes the word.' – (the word is higher than music.)

Richard Wagner, *Nachgelassene Schriften und Dichtungen*, Leipzig 1895, p. 135.

Wagner to his Dresden friend Theodor Uhlig, Zurich, December 1850:

I do you an injustice by writing to you just now, when I am rather jaded. I should really have preferred to give myself to you in a more lively state. I do not have to tell you that you make a great impression on me: but to reassure you about myself I will make the special point of telling you that the role which you allot me does not make me feel I deserve gentle ease: it inspires me to enthusiastic activity. Whenever you show someone the mirror of his desires, he always feels the more spurred on to acquire the skill to achieve those desires: and really – I believe I can only approach this achievement by seeking comrades in whose

★ Parenthesized thus in the original

company I can strive for that true art which one alone most certainly cannot reach. You cannot know what an unimaginable effort I am now making along these lines, in order to awaken a true understanding among all those who only half understand: in fact I want my enemies to understand, too – those who so far do not or will not understand anything: and yet in the last resort my greatest delight is that I myself am gradually coming to understand more and more. My book – which is now to be called 'Opera and Drama' – is not yet finished; it will be at least twice as thick as 'The Work of Art of the Future'; it will take me at least until the end of December to finish it, and certainly the whole of January for revisions and re-copying. I can tell you nothing about it in advance except the general plan:

I. Description of the essential nature of opera up to the present, with the conclusion: 'music is a procreative organism (Beethoven so to speak practised it for the birth of melody) – i.e. it is feminine.'

II. Description of the essential nature of drama from Shakespeare to the present day: conclusion, the poetic mind is a procreative organism, the poetic intention is the fertilizing seed which originates only in sexual excitement, and whose object is the fertilization of a female organism, which in turn must give birth to the seed which was conceived in love.'

III. (I am only just starting this part) 'Description of the act of birth of the poetic intention through the perfect language of music' – Oh, I wish I had told you nothing, for I see that I really haven't told you anything. But let me just add: I have spared no effort to be precise and detailed: which is why I decided right from the beginning to take my time and not to be rushed at any point. Let me also give you a diagram: I don't know whether to include it in the essay or not.

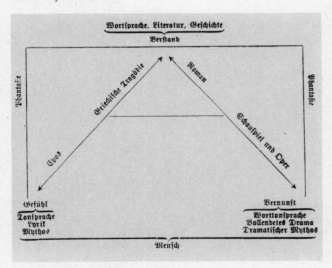

Schriften-Volksausgabe, vol. XVI, p. 93 ff.

Convinced that not history but myth must be the subject of musical drama, Wagner had in 1848 already written the text for a grand heroic opera, *Siegfrieds Tod* (*Siegfried's Death*). For this work, while he was in exile, he developed the Festival idea. He intended it as a protest against existing social and artistic conditions.

72

Letter from Wagner to the painter Ernst Benedikt Kietz, Paris, 14 September 1850:

But since I am alive, and with the best will in the world have no choice but to live now, I must after all do something which fits my make-up. I really do not intend to set Siegfried [*Siegfried's Death*] to music, only I am not disposed to leave its performance to chance in any old theatre: on the contrary I have conceived the boldest of projects, the realization of which would however require a sum not less than 10,000 thalers at the least. If I had that I would build here, just where I am, a theatre out of boards and planks to my own design, send for the most suitable singers and arrange whatever was needed for this one special case so that I could be certain of an outstanding performance of the opera. Then I would issue invitations to people everywhere who are interested in my works to make sure of a well-packed auditorium and – free of charge, of course – give three performances one after the other in the course of a week, after which the theatre would be dismantled and the affair concluded. This is the only sort of thing that can still appeal to me.

Burrell-Briefe, p. 415

Wagner to Theodor Uhlig, Zurich, 22 October 1850:

But these are of course exactly the arguments against which the real spirit of the revolution is aroused: and no metaphysical education is necessary to recognize them – what is needed is rather the elimination of this misleading science in favour of a perfectly simple natural response. But what then is the content of Socialism? Those who preach it have already lost touch with its meaning because they are too intent on organizing. Its sole object is: to render both superfluity and deprivation impossible. It is thus not necessary to teach the people anything, simply to tell them: You are right! And in fact they have been telling themselves this with increasing confidence since they have realized that their trust in *leaders* has led them only into misfortune. They have only to look at the nonsense of *politics*, to see what they can expect from this source, haven't they? If there was ever a historical period conducive to the lightning-quick correction of this misapprehension, it is that of our present-day reaction. Do you believe any man will still fight *for politics*? In fact you do believe this, for you say that you can conceive of a victory for the Revolution only through a new and indispensable alliance of the Constitutionals and the Democrats. I tell you: not a hand will be lifted for democracy, because any kind of political revolution has become impossible. No one needs any sort of revelation about politics: everyone *knows* our political conditions are dishonest: only the fact that the social question lies hidden at the back of it all gives them the cowardly courage to hold out. We no longer have any Movement except the utterly social one, but this has objectives quite different from any that our Socialists have ever dreamed of: everything else will remain weak and ineffectual until then. – Now, you ask me: 'All right, but where then are these men who will carry out this necessary revolt? I can see nothing but the most pitiful men around me, Philistines and cowards, and even in the lower regions I see only apathy and bovine obtuseness!'

My dear Uhlig, just think back to the day during the Dresden Rising when you met me on the Zwinger-promenade: with anxiety and apprehension you asked me whether I did not fear that a successful outcome must lead to mob-rule? – You had been horrified at the sight of precisely the men whom you now seem to be hunting for in vain. The fact that these men were still led by the nose by politics, that they stood so respectful before the higher political objectives which they saw embodied in their leaders, that they had not yet become and not yet done what they actually will become and will do, that they obeyed where they should have acted – it was this that reduced them to what they seemed to you, to louts who became drunk with political schnaps and bellowed through the streets – which they might perhaps have set fire to along with all the justiciary splendour of the fine city of Dresden, had they been allowed to act upon the anger in their hearts. I have seen these people again in Paris and Lyons and now know the future of the world. Up till now we have come across the expression of the enslavement of human nature only in *crime*, which repels and disgusts us: if robbers and murderers set fire to a house we rightly regard it as obnoxious and sickening: but what shall we feel when the mighty city of Paris is reduced to ashes, when the flames spread from city to city and we ourselves, with wild enthusiasm, finally set ablaze these uncleansable Augean stables to clear the polluted air? I assure you in full possession of my mental faculties and with an absolutely clear head that I now believe in no other revolution than that which begins with the burning-down of Paris: – we shall not fight another June battle there – for men have come to regard themselves as holy; but have realized that the filthy holes in which they are reduced to beasts are not. Does that shock you? Consider it honestly and carefully – you can come to no other conclusion! We shall need strong nerves and only real men will survive – i.e. those who have been made into men only through hardship and the most fearful terror. Whether something of lasting value will come out of it? Let us just see how we come round, after this fire-bath: I suppose I could picture it, I could even imagine some enthusiast here or there gathering together the living remnants of our old art and saying: who will help me perform a drama? Only those who are really keen would answer, for now there would be no more money to be had for it, and those who turned up would quickly rig up a wooden building and suddenly show everyone what art really is. At any rate everything will happen very quickly, for, you see, it is no longer a question of gradual progress: our redeemer will annihilate at a terrific pace all that stands in our way. – When? – That I do not know, for here nothing is being done, I only know that the next storm will surpass the earlier ones to just the same progressive degree as the February uprisings exceeded our expectations of 1847. There is only *one* more step to take and that is imperatively necessary.

R W A

Hans von Bülow – a pupil of Wagner's in Zurich – in a letter to his sister, St Gallen, 26 January 1851:

You, too, know of the love and admiration I have had for Wagner for a long time. I do not know whether you

182

understand it, but it is through this admiration, which also presupposes the understanding of his works, that I have really come to know myself. . . .

The fact that I am one of the very few to have recognized the greatest artistic phenomenon of our century – and perhaps of even greater historical importance – has aroused my ambition, self-confidence and desire to live. I realized I could become a spiritual partner of this man, his pupil, his apostle, and with this to strive after and this as my goal my life seemed worth living. I felt for him a full-blooded enthusiasm I had never felt for anything else.

Hans von Bülow, op. cit., vol. I, pp. 297–8

Siegfrieds Tod developed into a four-part work, the *Ring* tetralogy. One after the other he wrote *Der Junge Siegfried* (*The Young Siegfried*), *Die Walküre* (*The Valkyrie*) and *Das Rheingold* (*Rhinegold*). He published the complete *Ring* text in 1853 at his own expense, and read it aloud to invited guests in the Hotel Baur au Lac in Zurich in February of that year. On 1 November he began the composition sketch for *Das Rheingold*. This was his first major compositional work since *Lohengrin*.

103
93
100, 101

Wagner in a letter to August Röckel, Zurich, 24 August 1851, on the character of Siegfried; Röckel spent thirteen years in Waldheim prison for his part in the Dresden Rising:

I am now tired of theorizing: Liszt has inspired me to new creative work. And I have written a 'Young Siegfried', which, I may add, gave me great pleasure. My hero grew up wild in the forest, where he was brought up by a dwarf (the Nibelung 'Mime') who needs him to slay the giant dragon who guards the hoard. This Nibelung hoard is of immense significance: it is tainted with crimes of every kind. Now Siegfried is roughly the same young fellow who appears in the legend and sets out 'to learn fear' – which he can never do because his powerful natural instincts always show him everything as it really is. He slays the dragon and kills his foster-father, the dwarf, who is secretly trying to murder him for the sake of the hoard. Siegfried, longing for an end to his loneliness, now hears – the accidental tasting of the dragon's blood gives him this gift – the voice of a forest bird, who tells him of Brünhilde, who sleeps upon a rock surrounded by fire. Siegfried crosses through the fire and wakes Brünhilde – woman – to the passionate embrace of love. I cannot sketch in more for you here: perhaps I may be able to send you the book itself. Just one more thing, we had already touched upon it in our impassioned discussions: we cannot be what we can and must be until – woman is awakened.

Röckel-Briefe, pp. 7–8

Invitation to the reading of the Ring-*poem:*

I should like to extend to you a most hearty invitation to a reading of my recently completed dramatic poem 'The Ring of the Nibelung', the individual parts of which I propose to read aloud on four successive evenings (namely

Das Rheingold, page 7 of the finished score (Prelude), early 1854. Richard Wagner Archiv, Bayreuth.

the 16th, 17th, 18th and 19th of this month) at six o'clock, in the lower saloon of the annexe of the Hotel de Baur.

I should also be most pleased to welcome to the readings any lady or gentleman whom you may wish to bring along but who has not received an invitation, and whom you consider seriously interested in the subject.

Zurich, 12 February 1853.   Richard Wagner

Schriften-Volksausgabe. vol. 16, p. 21.

Wagner in a letter to August Röckel, Zurich, 25/26 January 1854, on the meaning of his Ring-tetralogy:

. . . We must learn to *die*, in fact to *die* in the most absolute sense of the word; the fear of the end is the source of all lovelessness and it arises only where love itself has already faded. How did it come about that mankind so lost touch with this bringer of the highest happiness to everything living that in the end everything they did, everything they undertook and established, was done solely out of fear for the end? My poem shows how. It shows nature in its undistorted truth, with all its opposites intact, which in their manifold and endless permutations also contain elements which are mutually exclusive and self-repelling. But the decisive source of the disaster is not that Alberich was repelled by the Rhinemaidens – which was perfectly natural for them; Alberich and his ring could not harm the gods if the latter were not already ripe for the disaster. So where is the nub of the catastrophe? Look at the first scene between Wodan and Fricka, which eventually leads to the scene in act 2 of *Die Walküre*. The rigid bond that unites them both, arising from love's involuntary mistake of perpetuating itself beyond the inescapable laws of change, of maintaining mutual dependence, this resistance to the eternal renewal and change of the objective world – lands both of them in the mutual torment of lovelessness. The course of the drama thus shows the necessity of accepting and giving way to the changeableness, the diversity, the multiplicity, the eternal newness of reality and of life. Wodan rises to the tragic height of *willing* his own downfall. This is everything that we have to learn from the history of mankind: to *will the inevitable* and to carry it out oneself. The product of this highest, self-destructive will is the *fearless*, ever-loving man, who is finally created: *Siegfried*. – That is all. In detail: the power of evil, the actual poison of love, is concentrated in the *gold*, which is stolen from nature and misused in the Nibelung's ring: the curse upon it is not redeemed until it is returned to nature, until the gold is once again delivered into the depths of the Rhine. This, too, Wodan does not learn until the very end, at the final goal of his tragic course: what *Loge* touchingly and repeatedly told him at the beginning Wodan most overlooked in his lust for power; at first he appreciates only the power of the curse – from Fafner's deed; it is not until the ring must destroy Siegfried, too, that he understands that only the return of the stolen gold will atone for the evil, and he therefore associates the terms of his own desired destruction with this atonement of the original wrong. *Experience* is everything. Siegfried alone (the male alone) is also not the complete 'man'; he is only one half, it is only with *Brünhilde* that he becomes the redeemer; *one* alone cannot

achieve everything; many are needed, and the suffering, self-sacrificing woman is the final true and knowing redeemer: for love is really 'the eternally feminine' itself. So much for the most general and dominant features: all the more precise individual themes are contained within them. . . .

After his separation from Brünhilde Wodan is no more than a departed spirit: in accordance with his highest intentions he can now only *accept* things, let things happen as they will; he can nowhere intervene decisively and that is why he has now become the Wanderer: look at him properly! he resembles *us* to a tee; he is the sum of the intelligence of the present, whereas Siegfried is the man of the future, willed and sought by us, but who cannot be made by us and who must create himself through *our destruction*. Like this – you must admit – Wodan is most interesting to us; whereas he would appear unworthy to us, he would be an underhand plotter, if he were to give advice which was *apparently* against Siegfried, but in reality for him and thus – and this is the point – for Wodan himself: that would be a deceit worthy of our political heroes but not worthy of my jovial self-annihilating god. Look how he faces Siegfried in the third act! Here, before his downfall, he is at last so involuntarily human that – despite his highest intentions – the old pride stirs again, stimulated, mark you, by – jealousy for Brünhilde; for she has become his most sensitive point. It is as though he does not simply wish to be pushed aside, but to fall, to be overcome: but this, too, is in no sense a calculated trick: in his quickly inflamed passion he fights to win – a victory which, as he says, could only make him the more wretched. In expressing the characters' motivation I felt I had to maintain an uncommonly delicate balance; naturally my hero cannot appear to be totally unconscious; rather I have tried to portray Siegfried as the most complete man I could conceive of, whose highest awareness is that all awareness can only be expressed in the utmost immediacy of life and action: to what immense pre-eminence I raise this awareness – *which may almost never be expressed* – you will realize from the scene with the Rhinemaidens. Here we discover that Siegfried is immeasurably knowing, for he knows the most important thing, that death is better than living in fear: he knows the ring, too, but scorns its power, for he has better things to do; he keeps it only as a symbol of the fact that he – never learned fear. You must admit it: the gods in all their glory must pale before this man! . . .

Let me tell you something more of *Brünhilde*. I am afraid you have misunderstood her, too, if you regard her refusal to surrender the ring to Wodan as hard and selfish. Did it not register that Brünhilde was severed from Wodan and all the gods because – of *love*, because while Wodan was all wrapped up in his scheming, she – only – loved? Since *Siegfried* completely re-awakened her she has no other knowledge than the knowledge of love. Now – the symbol of this love – after Siegfried has gone – is this *ring*: when Wodan demands it from her, all that comes to her mind is why she is separated from Wodan (because she acted out of love), and the only thing she now knows is that she has given up her immortality for the sake of love. But she knows that love is the only immortal thing: so Valhalla's splendour may fall in ruins, but the ring – (love) – she will not sacrifice. For goodness' sake, how wretched, mean and vulgar she would appear if the only reason for her refusing the ring was that she had found out (from Siegfried, for example) about its magic, its power? Surely you don't seriously suggest this magnificent woman's symbol of love is precisely this *accursed ring*, then that is just what I want you to feel, and to realize that this is the most awful, most tragic peak of the power of the Nibelung's curse: for then you will realize the real need for the whole last drama *Siegfrieds Tod*. This is just what we still have to go through to reach a full appreciation of the evil of gold.

Röckel-Briefe, pp. 35–41

Confidential report of the Viennese Police, 23 March 1854:

Strange rumours are again circulating about Richard Wagner. Not only does he live in Zurich in the most luxurious splendour, he also purchases the most valuable articles, like gold watches, etc. at fantastic prices. His apartment is fitted out with the most beautiful furniture, carpets, silk curtains and chandeliers, and this fills the simple Republicans with suspicious amazement and curiosity, so that it has been considered appropriate to ask around where this man, who came to Zurich so poor, gets it all from. He himself lets it be understood that he receives so much for performances of his operas in Germany. But according to the most searching investigations this is not true. The few theatres which are permitted to perform his works pay him nothing. And all his writings bring nothing in either, since he mostly has only 50–100 copies printed at his own expense. In Zurich not only does he receive nothing for his performances, on the contrary he has to make sacrifices to keep interest in them alive. It is therefore considered to be highly probable that he is secretly supported by some princely House in Germany, which however is all the more astonishing in that it is not only well known that he set fire to the whole theatrical stores during the Dresden Revolution, but also that even now he is still seeking by speeches and pamphlets to set in train a revolutionary movement through art, and to this end maintains contact with all the leading literary and artistic propagandists. Faith in his music of the future is fading significantly. One is becoming more and more convinced that his works have the advantage of splendid instrumentation but possess neither soul nor melody. What there is of the latter in his operas he is said to have stolen.

Lippert, pp. 45–6

Wagner on his situation in a letter to his brother-in-law Eduard Avenarius, Zurich, 2 September 1854:

Things will simply always be in a crazy state with me: if I were – really happy – then I should need almost no money at all: so I am always torn between an often quite eccentric desire for the comforts of life and – disgust with life, while as an artist and a man on the other hand I find myself more and more incapable of making the slightest concessions to the wage-earning world of today.

Familienbriefe, p. 215

From a letter by Wagner to Franz Liszt, December 1854, about Arthur Schopenhauer, whose philosophy he had discovered that autumn:

Apart from my – slow – progress with my music I have now devoted my time exclusively to a man, who – if only through his writings – has been a gift of heaven to me in my loneliness. This is *Arthur Schopenhauer*, the greatest philosopher since *Kant*, whose ideas – as he puts it – he has completed by thinking them through to their logical conclusion. The German academic world has – prudently – ignored him for forty years: but recently he was discovered – to Germany's shame – by an English critic. What charlatans are all the Hegels etc. compared with him! His central thought, the final denial of the will to live, is of frightful seriousness, but the only salvation. Of course this idea was not new to me and no one can think it at all in whom it did not already exist. But it was this philosopher who first showed it to me with such clarity. If I think back to the storms of my heart and the terrible cramp with which it clutched – against my will – at the hope of living, indeed when these storms even now still rise in tempestuous strength – now at last I have found a palliative, which alone helps me to sleep in sleepless nights; it is the deep and innermost yearning for death: total unconsciousness, absolute non-being, the extinction of all dreams – unique and final salvation!

It is marvellous that I am now constantly coming across your own ideas: though you express them differently, because you are religious, I still know you mean just the same thing. How deep you are! In your essay on the Dutchman you often struck me with lightning force. When I read Schopenhauer I was mostly with you: only you did not notice it. And so I am getting more and more mature: it is only to pass the time that I still play with art. How I try to entertain myself you can see from the enclosed page.

For the love of the most beautiful dream of my life, the young Siegfried, I suppose I shall have to get on and finish the Nibelung pieces: *Die Walküre* has claimed too much of me to deny myself this exhilaration; I have got as far as the second half of the last act. But it will be 1856 before I have finished the whole thing – and in 1858, the tenth year of my hegira, I can perform it – if I must. But since I have never in my life enjoyed the true happiness of love I will erect a monument to this most beautiful of all dreams, in which for once this *love* shall well and truly gorge itself from beginning to end: I have sketched a *Tristan und Isolde* in my head, the simplest but most full-blooded musical conception; with the 'black pennant' which flutters at the end I shall then cover myself up – to die.

Briefwechsel zwischen Wagner und Liszt, Leipzig 1910, vol. 2, pp. 42–3

———————

Wagner's circle of friends in Zurich included the writer Georg Herwegh and the Dresden architect Gottfried Semper, émigrés like Wagner, also Gottfried Keller and the Wesendoncks. Otto Wesendonck, partner in a New York silk company, supported Wagner and in 1857 put at his disposal a little house next to his villa on the Green Hill. Wagner occupied this 'refuge' for a year.

78
105
104
106

Gottfried Keller in a letter to Lina Duncker, Zurich, 13 January 1856:

Here in Zurich things have gone well so far, I have the best of company and see all sorts of people such as are not easily got together in Berlin. There is a Rhineland family by the name of Wesendonck here, too, originally from Düsseldorf, although they spent some time in New York. She is a very pretty woman called Mathilde Luckemeier, and this pair keep an elegant house, and are building a magnificent villa, too, near the town: they have received me kindly. Then there are fine supper-parties at the house of an elegant *Regierungsrat* [minister-councillor], where Richard Wagner, Semper, who built the museum and theatre, in Dresden, Vischer from Tübingen and several people from Zurich itself meet and where at two o'clock in the morning, after a fair old carousal, you get a cup of hot tea and a Havana cigar. Wagner himself from time to time serves a solid midday meal, at which some hearty drinking is done, so that where I thought I had got away from Berlin materialism I have simply jumped out of the fat into the fire.

Gottfried Kellers Briefe und Tagebücher 1830–1861, ed. Emil Ermatinger, Stuttgart and Berlin 1924, p. 393

Gottfried Keller in a letter to Hermann Hettner, Zurich, 16 April 1856:

I spend a lot of time with Richard Wagner, a genial and indeed a good man. If you get the opportunity to read his Nibelung trilogy, which he had printed for friends, do so. You will find in it some powerful poetry, ultra-Germanic, but purified by the spirit of ancient tragedy. . . That at least is the impression it made on me.

Gottfried Kellers Briefe . . ., op. cit., p. 407

Wagner's description to Julie Ritter, who gave him occasional financial assistance, of his move into the 'refuge on the Green Hill', from a letter written from Zurich, 6 May 1857:

My health, after which you enquire so sympathetically, of course always lets me down just when I want to let myself go. Happily I can thank my excellent doctor, Dr Vaillant, who treated me last summer in Mornex, for delivering me from an unpleasant attack of erysipelas and for a prescription designed to keep me well; but I was thoughtless enough while following his instructions – the only ones, I might add, to have any beneficial effect on me – to work incessantly and particularly hard, which finally left me in a state of great weakness and exhaustion. At the same time the torture I suffered from the musical racket of my countless neighbours became so unbearable, that I took a chance and gave notice to quit my apartment, with the idea of forcing myself to find quieter lodgings at any price. At this point my friend Wesendonck, whom you must also know, informed me that he had bought a superb little country cottage with a splendidly situated garden right next to his own, almost completed, magnificent country villa, with the sole object of letting it to me for life at a very low rent. Now that really gave me a kick; for it meant that my long-cherished yearning for a quiet country dwelling was fulfilled in the most perfect manner

186

conceivable. Well, the little house has been furnished and decorated most neatly and attractively and – I moved in a week ago.

Richard Wagners Briefe an Frau Julie Ritter, ed Siegmund von Hausegger, Munich 1920, pp. 118–9

In August 1857, after completing the orchestral sketch of the second act of *Siegfried*, Wagner interrupted his work on *Der Ring des Nibelungen*. The same month he wrote the prose sketch for *Tristan und Isolde*. In September he completed the libretto and by 6 August 1859 the whole score was completed. Otto Wesendonck's wife Mathilde was closely associated with Wagner's work. The intimacy which developed between her and Wagner was suspected by Minna Wagner. On 7 April 1858 she intercepted a secret letter from Wagner to Mathilde.

107

111, 112

99

Wagners 'Morning Confession' to Mathilde Wesendonck, 7 April 1858:

Mme Mathilde Wesendonck
          Just out of bed. –
Morning confession.
No, no! it is not De Sanctis that I hate, it is *myself*, for I am for ever surprising my heart in such weakness! – Shall I excuse myself with my ill-health and my consequent sensitiveness and irritability? Let us see how it goes. The day before yesterday at lunch-time an angel came to me, blessed me and revived me; that made me feel so well and happy that in the evening I felt badly in need of company and friends, to share with them my inner happiness; I know I should have been really kind and charming. Then I am told they did not dare give you my letter because De Sanctis was with you. Your husband was of the same opinion. I waited in vain and finally had the pleasure of the company of Herr von Marschall, who stayed the whole evening with us and with every word filled me with hatred for all the De Sanctis's of the world. He was lucky – he managed to keep her from me! And by what gifts? Simply by her patience. I could not blame him for being so serious about you; everyone who comes into contact with you takes it seriously! Look how seriously I take it! – enough to torture you! But why does she encourage this pedantic fetter? What's Italy to her? Well, it didn't take me long to find an answer to that. But the easier it was the more I was upset about the intruder; in my dream he got mixed up with Marschall and the two together coalesced into one figure who represented for me all the misery in the world. And so it went on the whole night through. Then in the morning I became reasonable again and was able to pray to my angel from the bottom of my heart; and this prayer is love! love! Love to rejoice the depths of my soul, the source of my salvation! Now came the day with its bad weather and the pleasure of your garden, which I had looked forward to, was denied me. And so my whole day was a struggle between ill-humour and longing for you; and when my heart most yearned for you, it was our long-winded pedant who was in the way, who kept you from me and I could only confess to myself that I hated him. Then, of course, I am sorry but I had to tell you; I couldn't help it. But it was pretty mean of me and I deserved to be punished for it. What is the punishment to be? Next Monday I shall come after tea and will be

really nice to De Sanctis all evening, and speak French, to please everyone.

What was that stupid argument about Goethe again yesterday? The fact that Goethe can be cooked up to accommodate the Philistines of the world depends admittedly in the last resort on a misunderstanding of the poet; but the fact that it *could* be done fills me with watchful suspicion towards him, and especially towards his interpreters and adapters. Now you know that yesterday again I accepted everything without demur, and especially your great delight in *Faust*; but in the end to keep hearing that *Faust* himself is the most significant human archetype ever created by a poet made me – (very foolishly!) – angry. I cannot leave my friends under an illusion on this point. Faust's despair of the world at the beginning is either based on knowledge of the world – in which case he is pitiful when he changes over and hurls himself with great energy into the world he despises; in my eyes this ranks him among those whose contempt for mankind still does not prevent them from spending their whole life in the sole object of deceiving men and making themselves admired by them; or alternatively – and this is more likely – Faust is just an academic with a wild imagination and has had no deep experience of the real world; in this case he is pathetically immature and we may well approve of his being sent out to learn about the world. But then it would surely be better if he really did learn what there is to learn – and that at the first – so suitable – opportunity, Gretchen's love. But goodness, how happy the author is once he has got him out of his deep spiritual involvement with this love, so that one bright morning he has forgotten the whole affair without a trace and can now sit back at his ease and have the real big world, the ancient world of art and the practical industrial world parade before him for the benefit of his oh, so objective observation. So for me this Faust simply represents a lost opportunity; and this opportunity was no less than the only hope of salvation and redemption. Of course the grey sinner himself feels this, too, in the end, and tries very visibly in a final tableau to catch up on what he has missed, pretty peripherally, after his death, when it no longer hurts; indeed it can only be most agreeable to him for the angel to clasp him to her breast and maybe even to awaken him to new life. Well, this I reckon is all very well and good and Goethe is still just as great a poet to me, for he always remains true and cannot be otherwise; and people may also call it objective, that is, when the subject never succeeds in absorbing the object, the world, in itself (which can only be achieved through the most active *com*passion), but rather simply sets the object before itself and becomes involved in it through contemplation, through observation, not through sympathy or charity (for through this he would himself become the world – and this subject-becomes-the-world is something for the saint, not for the Faust-author who has ended up as a model for Philistines); and finally what I always like about Goethe is that he always felt the dubiousness of what he did, that he found no comfort in the fact that he so strenuously kept this great compassion at arm's length – and, as I say, Goethe is like a gift of nature to me through which I may get to know the world as through few others. He did what he could, and – all honour to him! – but to call his wretched Faust the most noble type of man? This arises from the fact that the world

is seized by fear when it comes to the heart of the great problem of existence; how pleased people really are that Faust finally gives way and, since he really doesn't want to do without the world after all, decides to take it as it is. Yes, if only you knew that from here on he has only Mephistopheles left to guide him, and prepare yourself for eternal torture from the prince of darkness, since the fair redeemer, Gretchen the magnificent, painfully exalted, has turned her back on you. No doubt Goethe knew that; but you ought to know it, too!

What a load of nonsense I am writing! Is it the pleasure of talking to myself or the happiness of talking to you? Yes, to you! But if I look into your eyes I cannot speak another word, for then all is nought that I could say! Look, then everything is so incontestably true to me, then I am so sure of myself, when this wonderful seraphic eye rests upon me and I can lose myself in its gaze! Then there are no object and no subject; everything is then one and indivisible, deep immeasurable harmony! O, that is peace, and in this peace the highest, most perfect life! O fool, to try to win the world and peace from out there! Who in his blindness would not have known your eye, nor have found his soul within it! Only inside, on the inside, only in the depths is salvation to be found! Even to you I can speak and explain myself only if I do not see you, or – may not see you.

Be good to me and forgive me my childish behaviour yesterday: you were quite right to call it so!

The weather looks mild. Today I shall come to the garden, as soon as I see you; I hope to find you alone for a moment!

Take my whole soul as a morning greeting!

Burrell-Briefe, pp. 490 ff.

Minna Wagner in a letter to an unknown person, Dresden, 23 April, 1859, about Wagner's relationship with Mathilde Wesendonck:

Perhaps you will laugh, as I did, when my lord and husband wrote to me yesterday that he had been in Zurich last Sunday and Monday because Herr Wesendonck had urgently invited him to stay and had had him collected from the station in his coach. Herr W. having forbidden my husband ever to enter his house again, they had asked him this time to confound the gossips by his visit. The good fellow! But I am afraid this is like making out the bill without the landlord, for to confound the gossips my presence would be necessary, I should have had to establish a personal relationship with Mme W., from which may God for ever preserve me! I am utterly convinced that Herr Wesendonck would have not agreed to such a feeble idea if he had known what my own husband said to me when he called me to his room: 'Listen, we must separate, Frau Wesendonck, for whom I happen to have a passion, cannot bear our being together any more, she cannot stand you, she's jealous of you, and so on. (These are remarks that can only come from the coarsest of sensibilities.) On top of that Mme W. visited my husband in secret and vice versa, told my servant when he opened the door to her, not to tell me she was upstairs; I calmly let all this happen. It is after all so common for husbands to have affairs, why should I not put up with it from mine?

I was not jealous, after all. Only the indignities, these insults should have been spared me and my pitifully vain husband should have concealed it from me. I won't even mention the letter, which is still in my possession and which reveals an overt, tender love affair, but I cannot help regretting the all-too naive innocence of this good man.

Burrell-Briefe, p. 499

Mathilde Wesendonck in a letter to Wagner, 16 January 1862, on her relations with him:

I was reading Schopenhauer's biography and felt myself indescribably attracted by his personality, which has so much in common with yours. I was overcome by an old yearning to be able to gaze once into those inspired and beautiful eyes, into this deep mirror of nature, which is common to genius. Our personal relationship came back to me, I saw the whole rich world before me, which you opened up to my childish spirit, my eye fastened with delight on the marvellous edifice, my heart beat faster and faster with a sincere feeling of gratitude and I felt that none of it could ever be lost to me! As long as I breathe, I shall strive, and that I owe to you.

Wesendonck-Briefe, p. 347

Mathilde Wesendonck's reminiscences of Wagner's time in Zurich:

We made Richard Wagner's personal acquaintance in 1852 ... But it was only in 1853 that out relations became more cordial and intimate. It was then that he began to initiate me more closely into his projects. First he read the 'Three Opera-poems', which delighted me, then the introduction to them and gradually one after another of his prose writings.

Since I loved Beethoven he played me the sonatas; if there was a concert in the offing where he had to conduct a Beethoven symphony he was tireless in playing the various movements to me before and after the rehearsal until I really felt at home in them. He was pleased when I was able to follow him and when his enthusiasm set mine afire ...

In 1854 (from June 28 to December 27) he wrote and completed the sketches for *Die Walküre*. The short prelude bears the letters: G.S.M. [Gesegnet sei Mathilde – Blessed be Mathilde]!

About this time Wesendonck presented him with an American gold pen. They were still rare then, but also much, much better than those of today! With his gold pen he wrote the whole orchestral score of *Die Walküre* which, quite apart from its other incalculable value, is a real masterpiece of calligraphy. . . .

What he composed in the morning he used to come and play and check over on my grand piano. It was the hour between five and six o'clock; he referred to himself as 'the sandman'.

And then it would also happen that he was not satisfied with something and he tried to find another way of expressing it. That happened once while he was composing

the Valhalla motif. I said, 'Master, that is good!' But he replied: 'No, no, it must be better still.' For a while he walked impatiently up and down the salon, then finally ran out. The next afternoon he did not appear and he stayed away the next day and the next. Finally, he slips in quite quietly and unnoticed, sits down at the piano and plays the magnificent theme exactly as it had been before. 'Well?' – I ask. 'Yes, yes! You are right, I cannot make it any better!' . . .

The fine and spacious apartment in the Escherhäuser had become insufferable for him, owing to the many pianos in the neighbouring apartments. With a smith who lived opposite he had concluded an agreement according to which the smith was not allowed to hammer in the morning (Wagner's work-time) because Wagner was composing Siegfried's 'forging song'. Hence his longing for a home of his own, which was to be satisfied at last in April 1857. . . .

Richard Wagner loved his 'refuge', as he called his new home in the Enge, outside Zurich. He left it with pain and grief – left it of his own free will! Why? Idle question! It is from this period that we have the work *Tristan und Isolde*! 'The rest is silence and heads bowed in reverence.'

Allgemeine Musik-Zeitung, Berlin, 14 February 1896

The writer Malvida von Meysenbug on Wagner's marriage with Minna (Paris, 1860):

Unfortunately I became more and more deeply aware that my friend was not happy in his domestic relations. It had already become clear to me the previous winter that his wife was so little suited to him that she was not capable of lifting him above the many trials and difficulties of his material situation, not to alleviate them with soothing feminine charm and generosity. A man so dominated by his elemental spirit should from the beginning have had a high-minded and understanding woman at his side – a woman who understood how to mediate between the genius and the world by realizing that the two were bound to be eternally poles apart. Frau Wagner never realized this. She tried to mediate by demanding concessions towards the world from the genius, which the latter could not and must not make. From this total inability on her part to understand the nature of the genius and its consequences for his relations with the world there now arose almost daily conflict and torment in their life together, which, since they had no children, also lacked even this final mollifying and reconciling element. Even so, Frau Wagner was a good wife, and in the eyes of the world it was she who was the better and suffering half of the pair. I assessed the situation differently and felt boundless sympathy for Wagner, for whom love should have built the bridge across which he could reach other men, instead of which it merely made the bitter cup of life even more bitter. Actually I was on very good terms with Frau Wagner, she was friendly with me and confided in me and often came to weep on my shoulder. I did what I could then to make her understand her role in life better, but it was, of course, no use. She had not understood it in twenty-five years of marriage, and neither could she, for it was just not in her to do so.

Meysenbug, vol. 3, pp. 286–8

Hans von Bülow in a letter to the editor of the Neue Zeitschrift für Musik, *Franz Brendel, on* Tristan und Isolde, *August 1859:*

With the appearance of *Tristan und Isolde* the outward circumstances of the neo-German school enter a quite new phase. Since for the time being the *Nibelungs* are to remain locked in *Wagner's* desk-drawer, their place is taken by this single-evening opera. Here you have the realization of Wagner's theories, and in a quite unsuspected manner. No one expected music like this from Wagner. It follows straight on from late *Beethoven* – no analogies with *Weber* or *Gluck* any more. *Tristan* is to *Lohengrin* as *Fidelio* is to *Die Entführung aus dem Serail*, or as the C♯-minor quartet is to the F major, Op. 18, No. 1. I confess I have gone from one surprise of delight to another. A musician who will not believe in progress after this has no ears. On every page Wagner triumphs through his towering purely musical knowledge. You cannot over-estimate this architectural conception, this musical detail. In inspiration *Tristan* is W's most potent work. There is nothing so sublime as, for example, this second act. I have had remarkable experiences with various musicians who specifically do not belong to our party and to whom I have communicated excerpts. One, for example, was speechless with amazement: 'I should never have expected anything like this from W. – this is by far the most beautiful thing he has written – here he reaches the highest thoughts that the present is capable of thinking.' After *Tristan* there are only two parties – those who have learned something and those who have learned nothing. Anyone who is not converted by this opera has no music in his body. There are not all that many earlier scores with such rich, clear and original polyphony. You know me too well to think that I must have fallen into a state of neurotic adulation: you know that my heart first applies to my head for official permission to be enthusiastic. Well, in this case my head granted unconditional authority. Popular *Tristan und Isolde* can scarcely become, but no layman with any sort of poetic gift can fail to be gripped by the grandeur and power of the genius which are revealed in this work. Apart from all else: – I assure you, the opera is the summit of all music to date.

Neue Zeitschrift für Musik, Leipzig, 9 September 1859

'The art of transition': Wagner on the style of Tristan. *Letter to Mathilde Wesendonck, Paris, 29 October 1859:*

Of one characteristic which I have acquired through my art I am now becoming ever more clearly aware, for it has a decisive influence on my life as well. It is a fundamental element of my nature to change quickly and strongly between extremes of mood: the most extreme tensions in fact can scarcely avoid almost touching one another; it is this that even rescues life, often enough. At root true art, too, has no other theme than to show these highest moods in their most extreme relationship to one another: the only thing that can possibly matter in art, the crucial distinction, can of course only be derived from these extreme contrasts. But in art the actual application of these extremities can easily lead to a disastrous stylistic approach, which can utterly dissipate itself in snatching after super-ficial effects. This is what I saw happening to the most recent French school, with Victor Hugo at their head....

I now realize that the special fabric of my music (always, of course, most precisely related to the poetic conception), which my friends now regard as so new and so important, owes its construction above all to the highly sensitive feeling which directs me to interlink and interrelate every element of transition between the most extreme moods. I should now like to call my deepest and most subtle art the art of transition, for the whole fabric of my art is built up on such transitions: sharp and sudden changes I have come to dislike; they are often unavoidable and necessary, but even then they may not occur unless the atmosphere has been so carefully prepared for the sudden change that it seems inevitable. My greatest masterpiece of the art of the most subtle, most gradual transition is certainly the big scene of the second act of *Tristan und Isolde*. This scene begins with pulsating life at its most passionate – and ends with the most mystical, innermost longing for death. Those are the pillars: now, my child, just look how I have connected these pillars, how it leads across from one to the other! Now there you have the secret of my musical form, of which I am bold enough to assert that such a degree of consistency and clarity in a structure which embraces every detail has never before even been dreamed of. If you only knew to what extent that guiding principle has led me to musical ideas here – of rhythm, harmonic and melodic development – such as I could never hit on before, you would truly realize that even in the most specialized branches of art nothing worth while can be created unless it derives from such great principal motifs. – Well, that is art! But with me this art is very much related to life.

Wesendonck-Briefe, pp. 188–9

On 17 August 1858 Wagner left the 'refuge' and separated from his wife. He travelled to Venice, where he composed the second act of *Tristan* in the winter of 1858/59 in the Palazzo Giustiniani. Since his residence permit was not extended he returned to Switzerland in March. In the Hotel Schweizerhof in Lucerne the third act was composed. In the hope of having *Tannhäuser* performed in Paris, Wagner moved there in September 1859. He decided to prepare the ground with three concerts at the Théâtre des Italiens (25 January, 1 and 8 February 1860). These concerts won Wagner important supporters, including the poets Charles Baudelaire and Jules Champfleury, the painter Gustave Doré and the composers Charles Gounod and Camille Saint-Saëns. At the instigation of Princess Pauline Metternich, Napoleon III ordered the performance of *Tannhäuser* at the Grand Opera. Wagner revised the work and in order to satisfy the conventions of the Paris Opera he wrote in a ballet, the Venusberg Bacchanal. After 164 rehearsals the opera was produced on 13 March 1861. It ended in scandal. After three performances Wagner withdrew the work.

Hector Berlioz on the 1860 Wagner concerts in Paris – Zukunftsmusik *('Music of the Future'):*

He dared to make up the programme of his first evening entirely of orchestral and choral works or symphonies. That in itself was an act of defiance to the habits of our audiences who, under the pretext of enjoying variety, are always ready to demonstrate the most noisy enthusiasm for a pretty song well sung, a feeble cavatina well warbled, a neat pirouette on the E-string of a violin or a set of variations well piped on some wind instrument or other after they have given a respectful but frigid reception to some great work of genius. This is a public who regard kings and shepherds as equals even in their lifetime.

If a thing is worth doing it is worth doing boldly. Wagner has just proved it: his programme, devoid of any of the bonbons which lure children of all ages to musical galas, was nonetheless listened to with constant attention and a very lively interest.

He began with the overture to *The Flying Dutchman*, an opera in two acts which I saw in a performance in Dresden under the composer's own direction in 1841[*] and with Mme Schröder-Devrient in the main part. This piece made the same impression on me as it did just recently. It begins with a thunderous outburst in the orchestra which vividly calls to mind the howling of the gale, the cries of the sailors, the whistling of the rigging and the furious roar of the tempestuous sea. This opening is magnificent; it seizes the listener by the scruff of the neck and carries him away; but when the same compositional technique is relentlessly employed in what follows, tremolo giving way to more tremolo, chromatic scales leading to more chromatic scales, without a single ray of sunshine to light up these sombre, stormy clouds, with their heavy electric charge and their unremitting torrents of rain, without the slightest melodic figure to colour these black harmonies, the listener's attention slackens, becomes disheartened and finally evaporates. You can already see in this overture – whose development moreover strikes me as over-lengthy – the tendency of Wagner and his school to overlook the question of *receptivity*, to see only the poetic or dramatic idea that has to be expressed, without considering whether or not the composer can express it within the bounds of what is musically possible.

The overture to *The Flying Dutchman* is powerfully orchestrated, and at the beginning the composer has achieved an extraordinary effect with bare fifths. Presented like this, this harmonic device produces a strange and wild sonority which makes you shudder. . . .

The overture to *Tannhäuser* is the most popular of Wagner's orchestral works in Germany. Strength and grandeur are again the dominant features; but for me at least the composer's obstinate *idée fixe* in this work is decidedly wearisome. . . .

The excerpts from *Lohengrin* have more striking qualities and outshine the preceding works. It seems to me that there is more originality here than in *Tannhäuser*; the introduction, which takes the place of overture to this opera, is a most strikingly effective invention. You could describe it virtually like this: $<\ >$. In fact it is an immense slow crescendo which culminates in a climax of unparalleled strength and then works its way back to its starting-point in inverse progression and finishes in an almost inaudible harmonic whisper. I do not know what connection there may be between the form of this overture and the dramatic idea of the opera; but without concerning myself with this question, and taking the piece purely as a symphonic work in its own right, I find it admirable from every point of view. There is no theme at all, properly

* Correctly, 2 January 1843

speaking, it is true, but the harmonic development is itself melodic, spell-binding and one's interest does not flag for a moment, despite the slowness of both the crescendo and the diminuendo. Let us add that it is a miracle of instrumentation, in its gentle timbres as much as in its more brilliant colours, and that towards the end you can hear the bass rising diatonically, step by step while all the other parts are falling, which is a remarkably ingenious idea. There is moreover not a trace of harshness in this fine piece; it is as suave and harmonious as it is grand, powerful and resonant: as far as I am concerned it is a masterpiece. . . .

I have not yet mentioned the orchestral prelude to Wagner's latest opera *Tristan und Isolde*. It is strange that the composer played it at the same concert as the introduction to *Lohengrin*, for he has followed the same scheme in both. Once again it is a slow piece, beginning pianissimo, rising gradually to fortissimo and then subsiding into the quiet of the opening, with no other theme than a sort of chromatic moan, but full of dissonances, whose cruelty is further accentuated by long appoggiaturas which completely replace the true harmony-note.

I have read and re-read this strange score; I have listened to it with both the most profound attention and an acute desire to make sense of it; well, I must confess that I have not yet the slightest idea of what the composer intended. . . .

Let us now examine the theories which are reputedly those of his school, which is today generally known as the school of the music of the future, because it is supposed to be in direct conflict with the musical taste of the present time, but certain on the other hand to coincide perfectly with that of a future age. . . .

If the school of the future says this:

'Music today, in the flower of its youth, is emancipated, free; it does as it wishes.

Many old rules are no longer valid; they were made by inaccurate observers or by routine minds for other routine minds.

New aspirations of the mind, of the heart and of the sense of hearing call for new experiments, and in certain cases even the breaking of the old rules.

Various forms are just too worn-out to be admissible any longer.

In any case, *everything is good*, or *everything is bad* according to how you use it and why.

When united with drama, or only even with the snug word, music must always maintain a direct relationship with the sentiment expressed by the word, with the character of the person singing, often even with the accentuation and vocal inflections which one feels must be the most natural in the spoken language.

Operas must not be written for singers; on the contrary, singers must be trained for operas.

Works written solely to show off the talents of individual virtuosos are bound to be second-rate compositions of little worth.

The performers are only more or less intelligent instruments, whose task is to illuminate the form and inner meaning of the works; their tyranny is over.

The maestro remains the master; it is for him to command.

Sound and sonority are secondary to the idea.

Announcement of the concert given by Wagner at the Théâtre des Italiens, Paris, on 25 January 1860; this concert, the first of three, included items from *Der fliegende Holländer*, *Tannhäuser*, *Tristan und Isolde* and *Lohengrin*. Richard Wagner Archiv, Bayreuth.

Long, fast coloraturas, vocal ornaments and trills, excessive rubato cannot be reconciled with the expression of most serious, noble or profound sentiments.

It is consequently nonsense to write for a *Kyrie eleison* (the most humble prayer of the Catholic Church) music which sounds like the din of a crowd of drunkards at a night-club.

It is perhaps no less nonsensical to use the same music for a pagan invocation of Baal or the prayer to Jehovah of the children of Israel.

It is even more odious to take an idealistic creature, the daughter of the greatest of poets, an angel of purity and love, and make her sing like a prostitute, etc. etc.'

....

If such a musical code of the school of the future, we too are of this school, we belong to it body and soul, with the deepest conviction and the warmest sympathy.

But so does everyone; everyone today professes this doctrine, in whole or in part, more or less openly. Is there a great master anywhere who does not write *what he wants to*? And who believes in the infallibility of academic rules, other than a few timid fellows who would be afraid of the shadow of their own nose, if they had one? . . .

So in this sense we all belong to the school of the future.

But if they come with the following:

'We must do the opposite of what the rules say.

We are tired of melody; we are tired of melodic ideas; we are tired of arias, duos, trios, pieces in which the theme is systematically developed; we are tired of harmony based on consonances, as well as simply prepared and resolved dissonances, and natural, skilfully handled modulation.

You only need to consider the idea and pay not the least attention to feeling.

We must despise that rascal, the ear, treat it brutally to subdue it: it is not music's job to please it. It must get used to everything, to series of rising or falling diminished sevenths resembling a mass of snakes writhing and hissing as they tear at each other; to triple dissonances, unprepared and unresolved; to inner parts forced to run together although they do not fit one another either harmonically or rhythmically so that one constantly buffets the other; to actrocious modulations which introduce a new key in one corner of the orchestra before the old one has died away in the other.

No regard must be had to the art of singing, and neither its character nor its requirements are to be considered.

In an opera one must limit oneself to following the

pattern of the words, even if it means using the most unsingable, most ridiculous and ugliest intervals.

No distinction is to be drawn between music destined to be read by a musician sitting quietly at his music-stand and that which must be sung by heart, on stage, by an artist obliged at the same time to consider his own dramatic action and that of the other actors.

Never worry about the capabilities of performers.

If singers experience as much difficulty in memorizing a part, intellectually and vocally, as they would in learning by heart a page of Sanskrit or in swallowing a handful of nutshells – that is their problem; they are paid for their work: they are slaves.

Macbeth's witches are right: "fair is foul and foul is fair." '

If this is their religion, very new indeed, I am a very long way from being a convert; I never have been, am not and never will be one.

Hector Berlioz, 'Concerts de Richard Wagner: La Musique de l'Avenir', *A Travers Chants*, Paris 1862, pp. 293–302

Letter from Wagner to Hector Berlioz, Paris, February 1860:

Dear Berlioz,

When our common fate brought us into close contact in London five years ago, I reckoned I had one advantage over you, the advantage of being able to understand and appreciate your works completely, whereas mine would always remain foreign and incomprehensible to you in one fundamental respect. By that I mean mainly the instrumental nature of your works, for experience has taught me how perfectly orchestral works may be performed, given propitious circumstances, while dramatic musical works, the moment they leave the traditional framework of the really frivolous operatic genre, can at best be given only very inadequately by our opera companies. But in concentrating on this point I almost overlooked the principal obstacle to the understanding of my aims which you face, namely your lack of knowledge of the German language, which is so intimately bound up with my dramatic conceptions. . . .

Through your latest article devoted to my concerts however – which for me contained so much that was flattering and appreciative, you have presented me with another advantage, which I should now like to make use of, in order briefly to enlighten both yourself and the public, to whose attention you quite seriously drew the question of a 'musique de l'avenir', about the nature of this strange phenomenon. Since you, too, seem to be under the impression that this is the title of some 'school' of which I am the Master, I am obliged to conclude that you, too, are one of those people who really see no reason to doubt the fact that somehow or other I have taken it upon myself to advance certain theories which may be split into two groups; the first – those you are prepared to accept – being distinguished by long-established and uncontested universal validity, whereas the second group, against which you feel moved to protest, contains utter nonsense. You do not express very definitely whether it is only the foolish vanity of wanting to give out something long accepted as something new, which you are inclined

192

to credit me with, or whether I am guilty of the wrong-headed madness of wanting to uphold something totally nonsensical. In view of your friendly disposition towards me, I cannot but believe that you would be happy to be relieved of this doubt at the earliest opportunity. Therefore understand that it was not I who invented 'musique de l'avenir' but a German music critic, Herr Professor Bischoff of Cologne, a friend of Ferdinand Hiller's, who again will be known to you as a friend of Rossini's. The immediate cause of the invention of this crazy expression seems to have been a misunderstanding, as daft as it was malicious, of an essay I wrote and which I published ten years ago, under the title 'The Work of Art of the Future'. I wrote this essay at a time when certain distressing events in my life had kept me from the exercise of my art for a long period, and when after many and various experiences I had been able to concentrate my mind on a detailed investigation of problems of art and life which until then had puzzled and bemused me. I had lived through the Revolution and realized in what incredible contempt it held our public art and its institutions, so that in the event of a total victory, particularly of the social Revolution, the complete destruction of those institutions seemed probable. I considered the reasons for this contempt and to my astonishment came to the same conclusions that for example, lead you, dear Berlioz, to expatiate at every opportunity with energy and bitterness on the spirit of those public institutions; namely the awareness that these institutions, that is principally the theatres and in particular the opera-house, in their relations with the public, pursue policies which have not the least thing in common with true art and genuine artists, and only use the latter as a front to give an air of respectability to the satisfaction of, at root, no more than the most frivolous inclinations of the public of large cities. I then asked myself what must be the position of art vis-à-vis the public if it is to inspire the latter with an inviolable reverence for it, and, in order not to develop the answer to this question completely in a vacuum, I took as my starting-point the position which art once enjoyed in the public life of the Greeks. This, of course, immediately led me to the very *work of art* which has always been regarded as the most perfect, namely *drama*, because here the highest and deepest artistic intentions can be expressed most clearly and in the most universally comprehensible manner. If . . . once 30,000 Greeks could follow with intense interest the performance of tragedies like those of Aeschylus, I wondered what means they could have employed to bring about such extraordinary effects, and I realized that the means lay in the unification of all the arts in the only true and great work of art. My aim thus became to demonstrate the possibility of a work of art in which the highest and deepest sentiments, that the human spirit is capable of conceiving, could be communicated in a readily comprehensible manner to minds receptive only to the simplest of purely human sympathies and to communicate them moreover so definitely and convincingly that no critical reflection would be needed for their absorption. This work I called: the work of art of the future.

Judge for yourself, dear Berlioz, how I must feel ten years later to find this silliest of all misinterpretations – of an idea which may be wrong but which is at least not superficial – this catchword of a 'musique de l'avenir' thrown in my face, not only from the pen of obscure scribblers, from the rabble of half or completely mad buffoons, from the prattle of the for ever parrot-like dull masses, but also from so serious a man, such an uncommonly gifted artist, so honest a critic and deeply valued friend as yourself, and in conjunction moreover with assumptions which, if I really did have any part in propounding the theories you outline, would immediately rank me among the silliest of madmen. Please believe me, since my book will no doubt remain unknown to you, that music itself and musical grammar are not even discussed in it, so that the question of nonsense or folly therein does not arise; in view of the scope of my project and since I am no musicologist I clearly had to leave such details to others. But personally I heartily regret having published the ideas I sketched out at that tine, for if an artist is to be so misunderstood even by other artists, as has just now again been the case, if even the most cultivated critic is so utterly the victim of the prejudices of the half-educated dilettante that he sees and hears things in a work of art which are simply not there, and on the other hand fails to notice what is quintessential to its nature – what hope has the philosopher of art of being understood by the public other than in the same sort of way as my essay was understood by Professor Bischoff in Cologne?

Schriften-Erstausgabe, vol. 7, pp. 115–9

The poet Charles Baudelaire to Richard Wagner, Paris, 17 February 1860:

When I first went to the [Théâtre des] Italiens to hear your works I was ill-disposed towards you, even, I confess, strongly prejudiced; but that was excusable; I have so often been taken in; I have heard so much music by charlatans with grand pretensions. I was immediately won over by you. What I felt is indescribable, and if you will deign not to laugh, I shall try to translate it for you. At first I felt I already knew this music, but later, as I thought it over, I realized where this mirage came from: it seemed to me that this was my music, and I recognized it the way every man recognizes what he is destined to love. For anyone but a man of culture this phrase would be immensely fatuous, especially written by someone who, like myself, *knows nothing of music* and whose whole education is limited to having heard (with great pleasure, it is true) a few beautiful pieces by Weber and Beethoven.

Then what struck me above all was the grandeur. It represents what is great, and its aims are great. Throughout your works I found the solemnity of great sounds, of the great aspects of Nature, and the solemnity of great human passions. You immediately feel carried away, under a spell. One of the strangest pieces and one which gave me a new musical sensation is the one which is intended to portray a feeling of religious ecstasy. The effect produced by the Entry of the Guests and the Bridal Procession is immense. I felt all the majesty of horizons far wider than ours. And another thing: I often experienced quite a strange feeling, the pride and enjoyment of understanding, of being engulfed, overcome, a really voluptuous sensual pleasure, like rising into the air or being rocked on the sea. And at the same time the music sometimes breathed the arrogance of life. In general these deep harmonies reminded me of those stimulants which accelerate the pulse of the imagination. Finally, I also felt, and I beg you not to laugh, things which are probably derived from my own turn of mind and my many preoccupations. There is everywhere something elevated and elevating, something reaching out beyond, something excessive, something superlative. For example, to use a comparison borrowed from painting, I imagine before my eyes a vast expanse of sombre red. If this red represents passion, I can see it gradually changing through every shade of red and pink to the white heat of the furnace. It would seem difficult, indeed impossible, to achieve any greater intensity; and yet: a final rocket appears to trace an even whiter streak across the white that was its background. This would be, if you like, the final cry of the paroxysm of the soul.

I did start to write some thoughts on the excerpts from *Tannhäuser* and *Lohengrin* that we heard; but I realized it is impossible to say everything.

So I could continue this letter for ever. If you have been able to read this, I thank you. I should only like to add a few words more. Since the day I heard your music I keep saying to myself, especially in bad moments: *if only I could at least hear some Wagner this evening.* Without doubt there are other men like me. All in all you must have been satisfied with the audiences – their instinct goes much deeper than the inadequate knowledge of the journalists. Why do you not give a few more concerts with additional new pieces? You have given us a foretaste of new pleasures; have you the right to deny us the rest? – Once again, Sir I thank you; in difficult moments you have brought me back into touch with myself and with greatness.

Ch. Baudelaire

I am not adding my address because you might think I had something to ask of you.

Correspondance Générale de Charles Baudelaire, Paris 1963, vol. 13, pp. 32–5

Wagner in a letter to Mathilde Wesendonck, Paris, 10 April 1860, on the Tannhäuser *bacchanal:*

For the time being I must work up a good mood to – write a grand ballet. What do you say to that? Do you despair of me? Well, you will be sorry one day when you hear it. For the moment I'll say only this: not a note, not a word of *Tannhäuser* will be altered. But a 'ballet' is indispensable and this ballet must appear in the second act because the season-ticket holders of the Opera never arrive until rather late, I was told, after consuming their hearty dinners. Well at that I declared that I did not need to be dictated to by the Jockey Club and would withdraw my work. But now I will help them out of the problem: the opera doesn't need to begin until eight and then I will add a really worth-while version of the unholy Venusberg.

This court of Lady Venus was obviously the weak section of my work: at the time I had no good ballet company and I got by with just a few rough brush-strokes, and thereby did a lot of damage: for it made this Venusberg completely flat and undistinguished, with the result that the important background was lost, against which the later tragedy must build up. All the later, so decisive reminiscences and reminders, which are supposed to fill us with great horror (because it is only through this that the action makes sense) lost almost all their effect and significance: we had no sense of fear and constant anxiety. But I now also realize that at the time I wrote *Tannhäuser* I was not yet in a position to create what is needed here: a far greater technical mastery was necessary and I only now possess this: it is only now that I have written Isolde's final transfiguration that I have become capable not only of finding the right solution to the end of the *Flying Dutchman* overture, but also – the horror of this Venusberg. You see, you become all-powerful once the world is nothing but play. Of course I must think out everything myself in order to be able to set down every last nuance for the choreographer; but one thing is certain: only the dance itself can put the score across: but what a dance! People will be astounded when they see what I have concocted. I have not yet had time to write anything down: these few notes here are my first attempt. Do not be surprised that I do it in a letter to Elisabeth.

Venus and *Tannhäuser* remain as the original stage directions specify: only, at their feet lie the three *Graces*, in an elegant embracing pose. A whole tightly entangled mass of childish limbs surrounds their couch: these are sleeping cupids, who have tumbled on top of one another like children playing and have fallen asleep.

All around on the ledges of the grotto loving couples are reclining at their ease. Only in the middle are there nymphs dancing, teased by fauns, from whom they are trying to escape. This group intensifies its movement: the fauns become more importunate, the flirting flight of the nymphs summons the men from the reclining couples to protect them. Jealousy of the abandoned women: increasing impertinence of the fauns. Tumult. The Graces rise and step in to demand restraint and elegance: they too are teased but the fauns are chased off by the youths; the Graces reconcile the couples – Sirens are heard. – Then you hear a distant roar. The fauns, to get their revenge, have called in the Bacchantes. The wild throng comes storming in, the Graces having resumed their places in front of Venus. The whooping procession brings with it all kinds of strange beasts: from amongst these they select a black ram which is carefully checked to make sure it has no white in its fleece: it is then dragged amidst jubilation to a waterfall; a priest fells it and makes sacrifice with horrific gestures.

Suddenly the crowd goes wild with excitement as the Nordic Strömkarl (whom you know about) rises from the swirling water with his great, strange fiddle. Now he strikes up a dance tune and you can imagine everything I have to invent to give this dance the right character; more and more mythological characters fill the stage. All the animals which are sacred to the gods. Finally centaurs, who tumble about amid the wild swirling mass. The Graces are at their wits' end as to how to stop the tumult. They cast themselves desperately into the riot; in vain! They look around to Venus for help; with a wave of her hand the latter then wakens the cupids, who let loose upon the rioters an ever growing shower of arrows; their quivers are constantly being refilled. Now everyone begins to form clearly into pairs; wounded by the arrows they fall into one another's arms: everyone is seized by a wild longing. The mass of flying arrows have hit even the Graces. They can no longer control themselves.

Fauns and Bacchantes storm off in pairs: the Graces are

carried off on the backs of the centaurs; they all reel towards the back: the pairs lie down together: the cupids have run off chasing the wild band, still shooting their arrows. Signs of exhaustion. Mists gather, The Sirens can be heard further and further off. Everything is covered in darkness. Silence.

At last – Tannhäuser wakes from his dream with a start. Something like that. What do you think of it? It's fun to be able to use my Strömkarl with the eleventh variation. It explains, too, why Venus has come north with her Court: it was only there that she could find the fiddler who should play to the ancient gods. I like the black ram too. But I could do that bit differently, too. The maenads would have to come frolicking on, carrying the murdered *Orpheus*: they would throw his head into the waterfall – and then the Strömkarl would appear. The only thing is that this would not be so easy to follow without words. What do you think?

Wesendonck-Briefe, pp. 223–26

Minna Wagner in a letter to the painter Ernst Benedikt Kietz on the rehearsals for the Paris performance of Tannhäuser, 123–129
1 February 1861:

Yesterday evening I went along to a rehearsal which pleased me greatly. Had you been with me I should have enjoyed it twice as much, and how I should have liked to point out to you all the beauties of the music. It is a great, noble, original work! I cannot but believe that it will appeal to the superficial French – the open-minded unprejudiced public, that is. The press is another matter, they simply horrify me – and to suborn the rabble as Meyerbeer would – well, we haven't got the money and it would be rather beneath Richard's dignity. This much is certain, that the performers are gradually beginning to realize what it's all about, the orchestra are already enthusiastic too and applauded wildly yesterday evening – and they are already playing quite respectably. The singers are really good, some of them unsurpassable and truly enjoying it.

Burrell-Briefe, p. 508

From the memoirs of the authoress, Malvida von Meysenbug, concerning Wagner's time in Paris 1860–61:

Meanwhile the *Tannhäuser* rehearsals were progressing 123–129 and Wagner invited me to go to the first full orchestral rehearsal. There were only a few privileged guests present in the great Opera House, the only ladies being Wagner's wife and myself. And so for the first time I heard this music complete from the orchestra, which had for so long been the object of my longing and I was moved by it as by something sacred, touched by it as by the breath of truth. Everything went splendidly, too, and after the magnificent sextet in which the Minnesänger greet their rediscovered friend Tannhäuser the orchestra rose to their feet as a man and burst into enthusiastic cheering for Wagner. It was one o'clock in the morning when the rehearsal finished. Wagner was happy and excited because everything seemed to promise such a splendid outcome. . . .

Tannhäuser, page 11 of the Venusberg Bacchanal, specially written in 1860/61 for the Paris production of this opera; there were only three performances, the first on 13 March 1861. Richard Wagner Archiv, Bayreuth.

However, shortly after this fine rehearsal the chances of a brilliant success began to fade. The kill-joy hobgoblins, who so love to upset any ideal moment in our life, were at work and on all sides the clouds of discontent, envy and iniquity gathered. Political speculators were dissatisfied that it was Princess Metternich who had first brought about the introduction of this work which was so foreign to the French temperament. The press were dissatisfied because, unlike Meyerbeer and others, Wagner did not give *dîners fins* for the critics to suborn their taste in advance. The claque, who were usually actually engaged by every composer, had been utterly disdained by Wagner and were thus fuming with rage. The orchestra, too, split into parties, and especially the rather incompetent conductor had become very hostile. We, his friends and supporters, deeply lamented the fact that Wagner had from the very beginning refused to conduct the work himself, which we all longed for him to do. But finally – and this was the main thing – it was the young Parisian lions, the gentlemen of the Jockey Club, who were outraged that there was to be no ballet in the usual form and at the usual time, i.e. in the second act. It was notorious that the ladies of the ballet had their income supplemented by these gentlemen, who went to the opera after dinner not to hear music but to see that most unnatural and horrible monstrosity of modern art, the ballet, at the end of which they repaired behind the stage to pursue more closely their intercourse with the prancing nymphs. What did these upper-class rakes care about the performance of a chaste work of art which celebrates the triumph of saintly love over the intoxication of the senses? Indeed not only did they not care about it, they were bound to hate and condemn it before they had even heard it. For it was God's judgment on their inner baseness, their boundless depravity. It was thus they who were at the root of the principal plot to ruin the performance. They were mean enough to buy little whistles in advance, with which to express their artistic judgment. . . .

Then came the day of the performance. I shared a box with ladies of my acquaintance and Czermak. The overture and the first act passed without incident, and although the arrangement of the ghoulish mythological reel in the Venusberg came nowhere near Wagner's concept of it, and although the three Graces appeared in pink ballet dresses, even so I breathed more easily and hoped our fears would prove groundless. But at the transformation scene, that overwhelmingly poetical change from the unbridled bacchanal below to the pure morning peace of the Thuringian valley and the sounds of the shepherd's pipe and his song, the long prepared onslaught suddenly broke loose and the music was interrupted by an almighty burst of whistling and noise. Naturally the opposition did not remain inactive, that is, Wagner's supporters and that part of the audience who wanted to hear first and form their own opinion. Since they were numerically superior they had their way, too, and the performance continued. The singers were not intimidated and did their best. However, it was not long before the noise began again. So, too, did the protests of the majority, who won every time, so that the work was played right through to the end. But, of course, it had been so cruelly interrupted and mutilated that even the most sympathetic spectators had no opportunity of forming a proper idea of the work as a whole.

Next day I went to the Wagners'. I found him manfully calm, so much so that even the most violent newspapers admitted, in the battle which simultaneously erupted in the press, that he had borne himself with the utmost dignity in the face of the uproar during the performance. From the outset he proposed to withdraw the score and render a further performance impossible. He had rightly concluded that with this audience at the Paris Grand Opera a genuine success was out of the question. But all we close friends around him held the opposite view and voted for a repeat, since we felt sure the work must succeed. In our impassioned agitation we failed to see that this was now quite impossible.

And so the second performance approached. The hostile party had prepared themselves even more determinedly, but so also had the supporters. The battle was even more embittered than the first time.

Wagner was now even more inclined to prevent any further scandal, but all the rest of us called for a third performance. This was to take place on a non-subscription day and we now firmly hoped the trouble-makers would stay away and only people who really wanted to hear the work would come. But Wagner had decided nevertheless not to go himself so as to spare himself unnecessary agitation . . . The trouble-makers had come in even greater numbers to finish the job, and indeed were there right from the beginning, which was not at all their custom. The singers behaved really heroically, they often had to stop for fifteen minutes at a time and longer, to let the storm subside in the audience. But they stood calmly there, gazed steadfastly into the audience and as soon as the noise stopped they started singing again. This time, too, they completed the performance, although the ferocious tumult naturally quite spoiled any enjoyment of the individual performances and the fine scenic effects. . .

Meysenbug, vol. 3, pp. 290–8

After vain efforts to have *Tristan und Isolde* premièred at Karlsruhe, Wagner tried to produce the work at the Vienna Court Opera. Numerous rehearsals took place into the winter of 1863/64 but they did not succeed in overcoming the difficulties of the score. The performance never took place.

Wagner's view of his situation, in a letter to his wife Minna, Vienna, 19 October 1861:

But now, my dear good wife, help me to endure my *misery*! Take a good look at my position and recognize that, with all the dreadful worries and anxieties which threaten to overwhelm me, it is very wrong of you to conjure up even more troublesome and useless torments for yourself and for me in the way you are doing – however good your intentions. Consider the situation that I'm in! As yet not one of my efforts to get a permanent appointment has had the least success: an ordinary post as a Kapellmeister would be the death of me. My older operas are being put on all over the place, but with my new works I am having insuperable difficulties. With my new works I am far, far in advance of my time, and of what is within

Announcement of the second performance of *Tannhäuser*, on 18 March 1861, at the Imperial Opera House, Paris. Bibliothèque Nationale, Paris.

the capabilities of our theatres. Karlsruhe has already done *Tristan* no good: my enemies are gleefully spreading the word that 'it's my best score, but it's unperformable'. I arrive in Vienna. Ander★ is ill; eventually it emerges that it won't really be possible to count on him for the whole of this winter. This misfortune provides yet another opportunity to brand the opera unperformable. The new tenor, Morini, whose début I am looking forward to, has first of all got to learn all his parts again in German: if he's to be of any use in the repertory, it will be difficult to release him for two months in the middle of the winter season for a new opera. I have got to get used to the idea that I probably can't expect a performance before the autumn of next year. In the circumstances the management, too, is quite unable to make a decision: it's difficult for me to demand a large fee, but I'm not going to undersell myself either. It also proved impossible for me to hold new rehearsals for *Tannhäuser* and *Lohengrin* here, and so to draw attention to my abilities as a conductor (which would have been an easy path to obtaining a post as director of music). So that at the moment I can do nothing, nothing for myself in Vienna. Are things different anywhere else?

Nobody is asking for me. I have got to start again, completely from scratch. There is no demand for my art, and the times as a whole are very bad for the interests of art.

Richard Wagner an Minna Wagner, 3rd ed., Berlin and Leipzig 1908, vol. 2, p. 218f.

Minna Wagner on her situation, in a letter to an unknown friend, 15 December 1861:

The 24th of last month was our so-called silver wedding day, which I spent very sadly (solo). If I could expunge these 25 years of my life, then perhaps I might be cheerful again too. But I mustn't sin, I must be thankful that I've managed to keep body and soul together. Anyway, on the 25th anniversary of my wedding, my husband sent me a gold bracelet and made his congé for a whole year. After that, he said, we might perhaps see each other in Munich or the Rhineland, but for the time being I ought to settle where I am, but I haven't even had a permit to do so from the authorities here. They make things difficult for me, as the wife of one of the people involved in '49, even for a short stay. That's what it's like in the kingdom of Saxony! I am staying here until next April, and where I shall turn my steps then, the gods alone know. *This is all thanks to the Tristans!* You've perhaps already heard more directly about *Tristan* coming to grief in Vienna. *Ander* has lost his voice, bar a few ruins. So Isolde will have to possess her soul in patience until the right hero is found for her. They really are a much too enamoured and odious couple.

Wilhelm Tappert, 'Minna Wagner, geb. Planer'; *Die Musik*, Berlin 1902. p. 1408

Wagner justifies the need for a theatre of his own, in a letter to Hans von Bülow, Paris, 17 December 1861:

A single look at the present-day theatre has shown me once again that there is only one thing which will enable my art to take root and not to vanish, totally misunderstood,

into thin air. I need a theatre such as I alone can build. It is *not possible* that my works should establish themselves in the same theatres where simultaneously the operatic nonsense of our time – and that includes the classics – is put on, and where everything, the presentation, the whole approach and the desired effect, is basically in direct opposition to what I desire for myself and for my works. Put the Court theatres in Vienna and Berlin at my disposal, make me the master of everything I need; I simply can't imagine it happening, and – suppose as a result of insane efforts we managed to produce something worth while for once, the whole thing would collapse like a house of cards the very next day, as soon as *Le Prophète*, or even *The Magic Flute*, or even *Fidelio* itself was put on again. I cannot allow 'opera' to be anywhere in the vicinity when my music-drama is being planted. So more than ever it is clear to me: I need a theatre all my own, which *I* in my turn can then bar to others. There are only three cities in which I *can* have it: Paris – Vienna – Berlin. Only the largest cities will provide a big enough audience for this speciality (as it must be regarded to begin with). Since I can't become a Frenchman now, I'm left with the two German capitals. Although Vienna is very musical, I think Berlin, even as you depicted it recently, is the more important and the more worth pursuing.

Richard Wagner, *Briefe an Hans von Bülow*, Jena 1916, p. 170f.

Wagner had known of his amnesty since July 1860. It allowed him to return to Germany, Saxony alone still being barred to him. In Mainz, on 5 February 1862, at the house of his new publisher Franz Schott, he gave a reading of the poem of 'The Mastersingers of Nuremberg', which he had completed on 25 January in Paris. Still in February, he moved into a new apartment in Biebrich, very close to Schott, and began the composition of *Die Meistersinger* in March. Wagner hoped to finish the work quickly, in order to overcome his financial difficulties.

Wendelin Weissheimer, composer, Kapellmeister and friend of Wagner, recalls an evening at Wagner's home in Biebrich in July 1862:

One evening, when we were once again gathered around Wagner, and he was in a very communicative mood, he began to talk about the works he was planning once *Die Meistersinger* and the 'Nibelung' were completed, and he disclosed his ideas for *Parsifal* at length; even at that time his conception was already very detailed. Then he went on to talk about an Indian subject that fascinated him; but he said that he thought it would hardly come to anything, for he always had the premonition that *Parsifal* would be his last work. He had obviously talked himself into a certain state of emotion. Tears were to be seen on Frau Bülow's face – there was a pause. I slipped out on to the balcony, and Hans von Bülow★ quietly followed me, whispering to me the prophetic words: 'However slight the hope, and however faint the prospect of realizing his

---

★ The singer who was to have taken the part of Tristan

★ Hans von Bülow, with his wife Cosima (*née* Liszt), visited Wagner at Biebrich in July 1862 in order to study *Tristan und Isolde*

198

plans – *you will see, he will achieve his goal and will bring Parsifal, too, to fruition.*'

Wendelin Weissheimer, *Erlebnisse mit Richard Wagner, Franz Liszt und vielen anderen Zeitgenossen*, 2nd ed., Stuttgart and Leipzig 1898, p. 126

Ten years after the private printing of the poem of the *Ring*, Wagner published a new edition of the text of the Nibelung tetralogy in 1863. In the foreword written specially for the new edition he explained the idea of the Stage Festival and how it might be realized.

From Wagner's Preface to the published text of his Stage Festival, Der Ring des Nibelungen (The Ring of the Nibelung):

My close friends, to whom I showed the poem of my Stage Festival a long time ago, have also long been aware of how I envisage a complete musico-dramatic performance of it could be presented. Since I still cherish the idea and have not yet learned to doubt the real success of the venture, once adequate material support has enabled it to be put into effect, let me, with the publication of the poem, communicate my plan to a wider circle.

My principal concern has been how best to achieve such a performance free from the influences of the routine repertory of our existing theatres. This consideration rules out any but the smaller cities of Germany; one in a favourable situation with the facilities to receive exceptional guests must be sought, and indeed one where there would be no clash with an existing theatre of any great size nor a confrontation with the usual theatre-going public of a large city and its habits. Here we would build a temporary theatre, as simple as possible, perhaps just of wood, and with no other consideration in mind but the suitability of its interior for the artistic purpose; I have discussed a feasible plan, with an amphitheatrical auditorium and the great advantage of a concealed orchestra, with an experienced and imaginative architect. Thither we would then summon outstanding dramatic singers selected from the companies of the German opera houses; they would assemble in early spring, let us say, in order to rehearse the several parts of my stage work without the distraction of any other kind of artistic activity. I have in mind perhaps three performances in all, the invitation to attend which would be extended to the German public as a whole, making the performances available, as is the case already with our great music festivals, not to an audience from one town only, but to all friends of art, near and far. A complete performance, in high summer, of the dramatic poem published here would consist of *Das Rheingold* on one evening, and of the three principal pieces, *Die Walküre*, *Siegfried* and *Götterdämmerung* [*Twilight of the Gods*], on the three succeeding evenings.

The advantages that these conditions would bestow on the performance itself, as the first consideration, seem to me to be as follows. (From a practical artistic point of view I see no other way in which a truly successful performance would even be *possible*.) With the utter stylelessness of German opera and the almost grotesque incorrectness of its performances, any hope of finding the artistic forces ready to meet a higher challenge in the existing company of one of our major theatres is out of the question; the author who has it in mind to put a seriously meant higher challenge to the benighted public realm of art will find nothing to build his hopes on but the genuine talent of some *individual* singers, not trained in any school or in any style of performance, and these he will find are few and far between – for this kind of talent is at best rare among the Germans – and left entirely to their own devices. Thus what no one theatre can offer, might, with luck, be attainable only by uniting dispersed forces, brought together at a particular spot for a particular time. These artists would benefit in our theatre first of all from having only one challenge to meet for a period of time; they would grasp the character of the work all the more speedily and surely for not being interrupted in their study of it by the distractions of their normal work in an opera house. The success of this concentration of their gifts on One style and One challenge simply cannot be rated highly enough, if one considers how little success could be expected in normal circumstances, e.g. when a singer who performed in a badly translated recent Italian opera the evening before, has to rehearse Wotan or Siegfried the very next day. This method would moreover have the practical outcome of needing relatively far less time to be spent in rehearsals than would be possible in the context of the ordinary repertory routine: and that in turn would greatly benefit the continuity of study. . . .

To crown the impression of a performance prepared with this degree of care, I would in particular lay great value on the orchestra's being invisible, which could be achieved by architectural means if the auditorium were constructed in the form of an amphitheatre. The importance of this provision will be clear to everyone who attends performances of opera in our theatres, with the intention of receiving the true impact of a dramatic work of art, and, thanks to the inescapable sight of the mechanical actions of the players and the conductor, is made an involuntary observer of technical procedures which should be hidden from him with almost as much care as the ropes, pulleys, struts and boards of the sets, the sight of which from the wings is well known to destroy all illusion. Anyone who has ever experienced how transfigured and pure the sound of an orchestra can be, when it is heard through an acoustic sound-wall, purged of every trace of the non-musical sounds which the instrumentalists cannot avoid making in producing their notes, and who then is able to realize the advantages for the singer of standing virtually directly in front of the hearer, needs only to deduce how much more easily comprehensible the enunciation will be, to appreciate to the full the likely success of my acoustic and architectural proposals. But those provisions could only be made in the case I have outlined, of a specially constructed, temporary theatre.

A performance in these conditions would not only be a success in itself, but would also, I am convinced, be equally striking in its effect on the audience. Accustomed until now, as a member of the regular opera-going public in a town, to seek mindless distraction in the highly questionable displays of this ambiguous art form, and to reject, with the demand for something better, what does not perform that service, the person who attended one of our festival performances would suddenly be placed in a totally novel relationship to what is offered. Clearly and distinctly instructed as to what it could expect in this theatre on this occasion, our audience would consist of the public invited from near and far, who would have travelled to the hospitable town where the performance was due to take place for the precise purpose of experiencing the performance. . . .

Two courses suggest themselves to me.

An association of wealthy art-loving men and women, formed initially to furnish the money necessary for a first performance of my work. But when I consider how mean the Germans usually are in such matters, I cannot find the courage to entertain any hope of success from an appeal of that kind.

It would on the other hand be very easy for a German prince: he would not need to make extra provision for it in his budget, but could simply use the sum he had hitherto set aside to spend on maintaining the worst of his public artistic institutions, the one which reveals, and continues to lower yet further, the standards of German appreciation of music: his opera house. . . .

But after I had shown him the quite extraordinary influence he would be able to bring to bear upon the morality of an art form that hitherto has degraded us, after I had demonstrated the magnitude of the creation of an intrinsically German kind it would be in his hands to promote, he would set aside from his annual budget only the amount normally spent on supporting the opera in his capital, and assign it to festival performances of the kind that I have specified, to be given annually if the sum were sufficient, or every two or three years if funds needed to accumulate. By this act he would found an institution which would assuredly earn him an incalculable influence on German artistic taste, on the development of the German artistic genius, on the formation of a true, not an illusory, national spirit, and which would bestow eternal renown on his name.

Is such a prince to be found?

'In the beginning was the Deed.'*

While awaiting that deed, the author feels himself compelled to consider beginning with the 'Word', quite literally the word, without music, without sound even, just the word as it is transmitted in print, and has decided to offer his poem, as such, to the public at large. If, in doing so, I contradict my earlier wishes to present only the completed whole, of which the music and stage performance are essential parts, I willingly confess that I am at last exhausted by patience and waiting. I do *not* hope, any longer, to live to see my Stage Festival performed; I may hardly hope to find the leisure and the inclination to complete its musical composition. Thus it really is just a dramatic poem, a literary product, that I offer to the reading public. It is not very likely that I shall see it make an impression even there, for it does not really have a market. The literary man will push it aside as the text of an opera, of interest only to the musician; the musician will do the same because he will not see how this text can

be set to music. The public that has taken up my case with such enthusiasm demands the 'Deed'.

And that, alas, does not lie in my power!

Schriften-Erstausgabe, vol. 6, pp. 385–9, 393 ff.

Between December 1862 and December 1863 Wagner conducted numerous concerts in Vienna, Prague, Budapest, St Petersburg, Moscow, Karlsruhe, Löwenberg and Breslau. These concerts included the first performances of excerpts from *Der Ring des Nibelungen*. While the three held in Vienna (26 December 1862, 1 January and 11 January 1863) ended with a deficit, the St Petersburg and Moscow series (March – April 1863) brought in large profits. On 12 May 1863 Wagner moved into new lodgings in Penzing, a suburb of Vienna. The lavish furnishings led to new financial difficulties. Threatened with arrest for debt in the spring of 1864, Wagner fled from Vienna. The author Eliza Wille, who had known Wagner since 1852, gave him temporary refuge at Mariafeld, her country house on Lake Zurich.

The playwright Friedrich Hebbel on Wagner's concerts in Vienna, 1863:

The hero of the hour is Richard Wagner, who has been entertaining us with excerpts from his uncompleted operas in concerts conducted by himself. Nevertheless, he does not by any means command unanimous or even great applause, however vociferous they are in the Theater an der Wien, where the experiment is taking place, or however often they call him back to take another bow. His adherents, mostly personal pupils, call the 'Ride of the Valkyries' music of blood and iron, which leaves Handel and Gluck, Mozart and Beethoven at the post. His opponents declare that he has rediscovered the trumpets of Jericho and that it is to be regretted that he did not arrive in Vienna a little earlier: the city council would have saved a considerable amount of money, for the ramparts would certainly have fallen down of their own accord. The impartial public, which undoubtedly has the first say in musical matters in Germany, is less extreme in its judgment. It recognizes that the 'Ride of the Valkyries' is a highly characterful piece of music, which cannot fail to make an impact in any company, but it also observes that the piece debases the material means in a way that far exceeds Spontini. Personally I do not dare to pronounce whether the music grips the soul more than it shakes the spinal cord. The opera to which the 'Ride' belongs will offer an astonishing spectacle to the eye, far more than any by Meyerbeer, which is rather surprising in view of Wagner's harsh strictures on the composer of *Le Prophète* for not having scorned the effects of skating and sunrises. But what are skating and sunrises compared with the theatrical effects that the programme of Wagner's piece promises! All the same, the 'Ride of the Valkyries' is an excellent overture to the Vienna Carnival. It whistles, hisses, rings, roars and storms as if the moment has come when even stones will be given sounds and voices, and one only wonders that the last beat does not blow composer, theatre, audience and all sky-high.

Friedrich Hebbel Säkularausgabe 1813–1913, Berlin [n.d.], vol. 10, p. 317f.

---

* 'Im Anfang war die That'; this phrase occurs in Goethe's *Faust*, Part I – spoken by Faust shortly before the first entrance of Mephistopheles – and is an adaptation of St John's Gospel I, 1: 'In the beginning was the Word . . .'

From an article 'Richard Wagner in St Petersburg' by the critic Alexander Nikolayevich Serov:

The very title of this article, *confirming* an event currently taking place, is bound to arouse the attention of that sector of the public that is interested in music. Large numbers of those, even, who have no great concern for music, and who only go to the Italian opera because it is regarded as the right thing to do, but who steer well clear of Beethoven, for instance, will know that somewhere or other in the world there is musical 'reformer' called Wagner, who has stirred up every kind of rumour and controversy in educated and musical circles in Germany and whose *Tannhäuser* was booed off the stage in Paris. But those who follow events in music and literature probably also know that Wagner has been regarded as a musician of importance ever since his five-act opera *Cola Rienzi*, an extremely effective work in the style of Spontini and Meyerbeer, was performed in Dresden in 1842. . . .

The profundity of its ideas and its formal complexity mean that Wagner's music can never reckon on the popularity that the operas of Verdi and Flotow enjoy, but nowadays, both in Berlin and in Dresden, Prague,

Programme of a concert given by Wagner in Prague, 8 February 1863; he conducted his *Faust Overture* and excerpts from *Die Meistersinger*, *Tristan und Isolde*, *Die Walküre* and *Tannhäuser*. Dietrich Mack, Bayreuth.

Page 5 from the 'explanatory programme note for the performance of music by Richard Wagner', for the concert given by him in Vienna on 26 December 1862; this page deals with the Ride of the Valkyries and Siegmund's love song in *Die Walküre*.

Pest and everywhere where *Rienzi*, *Lohengrin* or *Der fliegende Holländer* are played, they bring *full houses*, while those theatres which do not yet present Wagner's operas, or which, in conservative obduracy (as in Munich), *have not yet made up their minds* to do so, are now the rare exceptions. . . .

It must not be forgotten that Wagner, whose literary significance puts him on a par with the foremost writers and thinkers of our age, has from the first composed his operas only to texts written *by himself*, all of which are distinguished by passages of great beauty, even judged from a purely literary viewpoint.

In order, however, to see the total artistic personality in its true light, in its diametrical opposition to the picture of a poetaster, which has been put about by Wagner's enemies in Paris (and even in Germany), it is necessary to understand that the literary side of his achievement, the reworking of the material garnered in his immensely wide reading, goes hand in hand with the purely musical side; this applies equally to the creative as to all the technical aspects, in mastering which alone others take a lifetime and then believe themselves *justified* in ignoring history, literature and every other intellectual sphere, and in never looking up from their music desks.

In his command of all the mysteries of counterpoint and orchestration, in which he is often superior to Meyerbeer, for instance, and as a *conductor*, Wagner's only equals are the two leading *virtuosi* in this field, Hector Berlioz and Franz Liszt (without exception, there is no other *chef d'orchestre* who can be named in the company of these three).

Several times Wagner had to conduct symphonies by Beethoven, including even the *Ninth*, at a time when he had no opportunity to look at the score beforehand, but he knows all Beethoven's symphonies *by heart*, as well as he knows his own music, so that he was able to conduct even the *Ninth Symphony*, in rehearsal and before the public, *without the score, from memory*. He conducts in a highly individual manner, and certainly *does not beat time* in the diligent way our workaday conductors do; he merely shapes *the light and shade and the character* of the music. It is obvious that *without* such nuances, *without* such disclosure of its character, the performance of any piece of music is only a series of more or less beautiful sounds, and fails to plumb the composer's intention, and it is equally obvious that, since instrumental music depends so directly for truthful expression upon the conductor, he must possess a full and complete *understanding of the meaning and the intention* of the work. To expect an ordinary workaday musician, who directs an orchestra because of his contract or other *circumstances*, or because of misplaced *self-esteem*, to have a *true* understanding of Beethoven's symphonies, in which all he sees are *notes* and *chords*, is as absurd as it would be to expect a barely literate journeyman tailor . . . to give a discerning reading of poems by Pushkin or Lermontov. . . .

Alexander N. Serov, *Aufsätze zur Musikgeschichte*, German translation by Felix Loesch, Berlin 1955, pp. 327–330

The Viennese conductor Heinrich Esser, who was to have directed the first performance of Tristan und Isolde, *which was, however, cancelled after numerous rehearsals, gives his opinion of Wagner in a letter to the publisher Franz Schott, Vienna, 28 March 1863:*

After reading what you have to say about him, it strikes me that Wagner cannot be in full possession of his faculties. If he starts a new love affair in every town he happens to visit, that's his business, and nothing to do with me. Perhaps his tender heart is incapable of resisting the eccentric, enthusiastic ladies who throw themselves at him, and with all my heart I wish him joy in the soft embraces of so many gentle arms. But after the loss he made on his concerts here, which a Viennese friend is said to have covered for him, to use the thousand gulden that he told me he had made in Prague to buy a plot of land in Biebrich, and to start building a really magnificent house with the money he earned in St Petersburg, while he's got nothing to live on, that seems to me to verge on imprudence – to use a temperate expression.

It seems utterly ridiculous to me that he is offended at you for engraving other things besides the works of Wagner. Indeed I can't believe that that is the real reason why he has taken offence. It strikes me as far more likely that he is ignoring you because he has realized that there is no more money to be extorted from you. Wagner has

202

the fatal habit of honouring people with his friendship for just so long as he believes that they can be useful to him, and of dropping them the minute the lemon has been squeezed dry. Indeed, I find it extremely foolish of him to commit such a *faux pas* towards you, who can, after all, be very useful to him.

Edgar Istel, 'Richard Wagner im Lichte eines zeitgenössischen Briefwechsels', *Die Musik*, Berlin 1902, p. 1371

Heinrich Esser on Wagner's financial situation, in a letter to Franz Schott, Vienna, 10 May 1863:

A week ago today, as I told you in my last letter, I received a written invitation from Richard Wagner to a dinner-party, which duly took place. There were only a few of us: Dr Standhartner, chief medical officer at the General Hospital and a great admirer of the famous composer, our first violinist Hellmesberger and my poor self. The dinner left nothing to be desired. . . .

Of course Wagner talked a great deal about his Russian triumphs and showed us several presents given him by members of the orchestras in St Petersburg and Moscow, a silver drinking-horn and a gold tobacco-box. Apart from the gifts, his pecuniary success in Russia must have been considerable, because Wagner left here in a very dejected mood and is now in quite high spirits, and I am very much inclined to suppose that the dejection and the elation are very precisely associated and attuned to the state of his means of existence or his purse.

One of the local papers has been saying that Richard Wagner brought back 25,000 francs with him from St Petersburg, which strikes me as an overstatement, but he may very well have a sum of 7 to 8,000 gulden at his disposal now, and I would like to hope that this will be enough to keep him out of difficulties for two years and allow him the leisure to finish his 'Hans Sachs' [*Die Meistersinger*]. But Wagner is just like a child when he has money in his pocket, and it doesn't seem to enter his head that it won't last for ever. Add to this his claim that he can't work at all unless his rooms are luxurious, and unless he has the sole, personal use of a large garden, in short, unless he is living like a lord.

Edgar Istel, op. cit., p. 1372 f.

Wagner to his Mainz friend Mathilde Maier, Vienna, 4 January 1863:

When I ask myself very seriously what will become of me, I can see only one hope of salvation. I need a home: – not a place, but a person. I shall be 50 next May. I cannot marry as long as my wife is alive: to get a divorce from her now, in the present condition of her health (a dilation of the heart in an advanced state), when the lightest of blows would end her life, I cannot give her what might be that fatal blow. On the other hand she will endure everything as long as she has her legal title. Behold! This is the situation, this is the sorry pass that is destroying me! I need a female being who, in spite of everything and everyone, will have the resolution to be to me what a wife can be in these miserable circumstances – must be, I say, if I am to thrive. Perhaps I am being blinded by my excessive self-esteem,

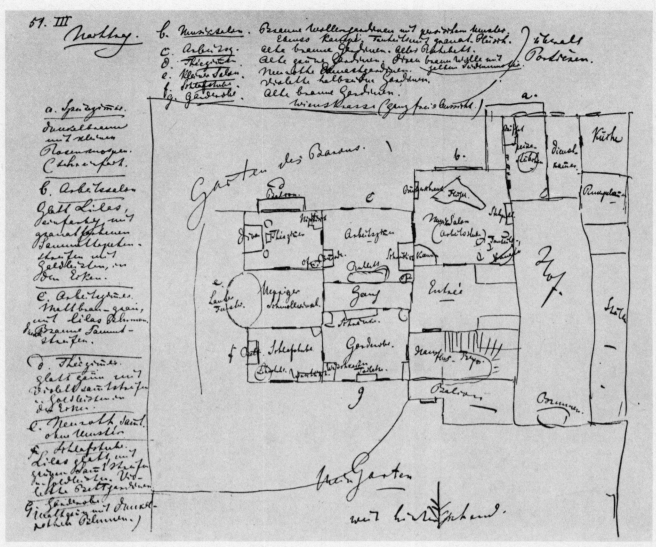

Plan of Wagner's apartments in Penzing, Vienna, drawn by the composer, from a letter to Mathilde Maier, 25 May 1863. See *Briefe an Mathilde Maier*, 2nd ed., Leipzig 1930, p. 99.

Key to the plan of the Penzing apartments:

a) Dining room.
Dark brown with little rosebuds (very simple).
b) Work salon.
Glossy lilac, with garnet-coloured velvet drapes with gold edges in the corners.
c) Work room.
Matt brown-grey, with lilac flowers. Dark brown velvet drapes.
d) Tea room.
Glossy green with violet drapes and gold borders in the corners.
e) Scarlet velvet, unpatterned.
f) Bedroom.
Glossy lilac with green velvet drapes and gold borders.
g) Dressing room.
Matt green with dark red flowers.

Postscript
b) Music salon.
Brown wool curtains with a Persian pattern. Ditto sofa. Armchairs with garnet plush.
c) Work room.
Old brown curtains. Old daybed.
d) Tea room.
Old green curtains. Divan brown wool with yellow silk pattern.
e) Small salon.
Scarlet damask curtains.
f) Bedroom.
Violet half-silk curtains.
g) Dressing room.
Old brown curtains.
Portières everywhere

when I go so far as to suppose that a woman with the resolution to devote herself to me in such inauspicious circumstances would abandon all human relationships that have no useful place in the life and work of a person like me. It wouldn't even be necessary to reassure her that in other countries and in others social circles the situation she was entering would be regarded as in no way improper, she would have to understand instead that her position was far superior to all the customs and usages round about her. That's the sort of thing I say to myself! God! How many are there to whom it wouldn't be possible to say it? But that cannot comfort me. It only increases my longing: there is no other escape: every other leaves the gaping void wide open. Not the Rhine, not Biebrich, not here, not there! – I want a loving woman at my side, and let be a daughter at the same time! And then I think: somewhere there must be a woman who would love you enough for that. Yes, but how would you take care of her? And now I've found the answer to that, too.

Richard Wagner an Mathilde Maier, ed. by Hans Scholz, Leipzig 1930, p. 49 f.

The writer Eliza Wille recalls Wagner's stay in her house, Mariafeld, in March and April 1864:

I can still see him sitting in the armchair that stands now, as it did then, beside my window, and listening impatiently as I spoke to him one evening of the magnificence of the future that quite certainly lay before him. The sun had just gone down in glory, earth and sky were bathed in a radiant glow.

Wagner said: 'What's the use of your talking about the future, when my manuscripts are shut up in the cupboard? Who is going to stage the work that I, only I, with the aid of *benevolent* spirits, can give substance to, so that the whole world can know that this is how it is, *this* is how the master envisaged his work?'

In his excitement he was walking up and down the room. Suddenly he stopped in front of me and said: 'I am a different kind of organism, my nerves are hypersensitive, I must have beauty, splendour and light! The world owes me what I need! I cannot live the miserable life of a town organist, like your Master Bach! Is it such a shocking request, if I think I deserve the little bit of luxury I like? I, who have so much enjoyment to give the world and thousands of people!'

Saying this, he raised his head as if in defiance. Then he sat down in the chair by the window again and stared in front of himself. What did he care for the magnificent view and the peace of Nature? It was not all joy while Wagner was staying at Mariafeld.

Wille-Briefe, p. 64

On 3 May 1864 Wagner received a summons to Munich from Ludwig II, who had succeeded to the throne of Bavaria on 10 March. The very next day the king and Wagner met for the first time in the Residenz (palace) in Munich. The legendary friendship of the king and the composer lasted a lifetime, in spite of all the intrigues and misunderstandings. The king settled all Wagner's debts and supported him with great generosity. All told, Wagner received 500,000 marks. He gave the king several manuscripts: seven scores and five texts. Later the king supported the Bayreuth Festival undertaking to the tune of 400,000 marks, which Wagner's heirs repaid with royalties. On 7 October 1864 the king officially commissioned Wagner to complete *Der Ring des Nibelungen*. It was intended that Gottfried Semper should build a large Festival Theatre in Munich specially for its performance. That plan came to nothing.

The first letters exchanged between Wagner and Ludwig II:

Dear and gracious King!
I send you these tears of the most heavenly emotion, to tell you that now the miracles of poesy have dawned upon my sorry, love-starved life as a divine reality! And that life, all the poetry and music of which it is yet capable, now belongs to you, my gracious young king: dispose of it as of your own!

In the utmost ecstasy, faithful and true

Stuttgart   Your subject
3 May 1864.   Richard Wagner.

Honoured Sir!
I have instructed Counsellor Pfistermeister to discuss suitable lodgings with you. Rest assured that I will do everything in my power to compensate you for your past suffering. I want to lift the menial burdens of everyday life from your shoulders for ever, I want to enable you to enjoy the peace for which you long, so that you will be able to unfurl the mighty pinions of your genius undisturbed in the pure ether of your rapturous art!

Unknowingly, you were the *sole source of my joys* from my earliest boyhood, my friend who spoke to my heart as *no other* could, my best mentor and teacher.

I will repay you to the best of my ability! – O, how I have looked forward to the time when I would be able to do so! – I hardly dared to nourish the hope of being in a position to prove my love to you so soon.

With the most heartfelt greetings,

                                              Your friend, Ludwig,
5 May 1864   King of Bavaria

Königsbriefe, vol. I, p. II

Wagner describes his first meeting with the king, in a letter to Eliza Wille, Munich, 4 May 1864:

Dearest Friend!
I should be the most ungrateful of men if I did not tell you at once of my immeasurable good fortune!

You know that the young king of Bavaria sent for me. Today I was taken to him. He is so handsome, so great in spirit and in soul, so glorious that, alas, I fear that his life will evanesce in this mean world like a fleeting dream of godhood. He loves me with the intensity and fire of first love: he knows everything about me and all my works, and understands me like my own soul. He wants me to stay near him always, to work, to rest, to have my works performed; he wants to give me everything I shall need for that purpose; I must finish the 'Nibelungen' and he will have it performed as I want. I shall be completely my own master, not a court Kapellmeister, nothing but myself and his friend. And he understands everything seriously and perfectly, as if we two, you and I were talking to each

204

other. All my troubles shall be taken from me, I shall have whatever I need – as long as I stay with him.

What do you have to say about that? What can you say? Was there ever anything like it? Can it be anything but a dream?

You can imagine my rapture!

A thousand heartfelt greetings! My happiness is so great that I am crushed by it. You simply cannot conceive the spell his eyes cast: if only he lives; it is an unheard-of miracle!

My heartfelt friendship to Wille and the boys!
Always gratefully yours,
Richard Wagner

Do not spread any of this!
Nothing to the newspapers! It is all a secret and must remain so.

Wille-Briefe, p. 75

Ludwig II describes his first meeting with Wagner to his cousin, later his fiancée, Duchess Sophie Charlotte of Bavaria:

If only you could have witnessed how his thanks shamed me, when I gave him my hand with the assurance that his great Nibelungen work would not only be completed but performed as he wished it to be, that I would faithfully see to it. At that he bowed deep over my hand and seemed moved by what was after all so natural, for he stayed in that position for a long time, without saying a word. I had the sensation that we had exchanged roles. I bent over him and drew him to my heart with a feeling as though I were silently taking the oath of fealty: to remain true to him for ever.

Königsbriefe, vol. 1, p. xxxv

The painter Friedrich Pecht comments in his memoirs on the friendship of Wagner and Ludwig II:

The young king's hero-worship of the composer was at first almost childlike, his attitude to him in everything was as an adviser and a friend, while Wagner in turn outwardly showed him the most paternal tenderness, but at the same time he already imagined himself joint ruler of the whole kingdom of Bavaria. I also got to read many of the letters and notes the king sent Wagner, which even then impressed me less by their intellectual content than by their ecstasy of expression. It was only too likely that continued association with the artist, who was inspired but in a state of incredible excitement, could do nothing to moderate the king's transports, the more so because of the master's pronounced inclination to despise the whole human race, with very few exceptions, and to treat it as mere material for exploitation by the elect. Wagner's influence on the young king was certainly not a good one, if only because it encouraged his tendency to cocoon himself in a world of dreams and fantasies. The composer himself was only too ready to believe that the world existed solely in order to listen to Wagner's music and to despise everything else. Egoism of this order is perhaps natural in a genius, but it was the last thing to wield a beneficial influence on a character like the king's, whose own egoism could only be fed by it. Since, additionally, Wagner had a heap of debts and extravagant requirements, he was obliged to make excessive demands on the king's exchequer, and this in itself was enough to earn him the silent hostility of all the Court officials.

Friedrich Pecht, *Aus meiner Zeit*, Munich 1894, vol. 2, p. 134 f.

Wagner to Ludwig II, Starnberg, 26 September 1864:

It is to Your Majesty's favour, as completely unexpected as it is undeserved, that I owe my removal to a new, hopeful situation in life. May I take this opportunity of disclosing to my gracious protector the resolves which were bound to come to maturity in such benign circumstances, and then address to Your Majesty a truly humble request that arises from them?

With my powers at their zenith, I am in my fifty-second year: if I may be permitted to expect to crown my achievements at this moment in time, I must nevertheless not delay in addressing my powers to the task.

It is possible that I might gain more advantage from the relative ease of performance of other works, but I have resolved to place them all on one side for the time being, so as to be able to devote myself exclusively and without delay to completing the composition of my great Nibelung work.

To do so will also, I believe, be in accordance with the exalted wishes of my gracious protector, and his enthusiasm for what is highest, and it is in this belief that I beseech Your Majesty most graciously to grant me the formal commission for the completion of my tetralogy *Der Ring des Nibelungen*, together with the appropriate preparation and eventual performance of the work in Munich. Your Majesty would be pleased to allow me suitable lodgings in Munich to pursue this purpose, and the means to live freely and independently for the time that it will take, without the need to seek any other livelihood.

The loftier intuition of Your Majesty may be pleased to attribute to this work the great and far-reaching national significance, to which I drew attention when I published the poem; to give me a definite commission to complete it would, in my own opinion, though not all will share it, announce to all the world, clearly and unmistakably, a noble, unique purpose, a work whose performance would be detrimental to none and would bring honour to the fatherland; my position, which is so greatly envied, would be explained and there would be no need to conceal its full beauty any longer; and it would be as easy as could be wished for Your Majesty graciously to bestow on me the favours that are still necessary to me to attain the complete peace my work demands.

Königsbriefe, vol. 1, p. 25

Wagner to Ludwig II, Munich, 6 November 1864:

There is a secret that can only be revealed to my exalted, gracious friend in the hour of my death: then he will understand fully what must seem obscure at present – that he alone is the creator and author of everything that the world will from now on attribute to my name. The only true reason I have for living is the miraculous love that showers down upon me from the heart of my royal friend –

as if from the bosom of God – and nourishes the new seeds of life in me! Last All Soul's Day, I felt as if I was decking my own grave with the joyous flowers of this love. Truly, I – am no more! I have experienced and suffered too much; this dispersal of myself, with life and the ever more alien considerations of life constantly tugging me away from my own inner self, was in the end too deep and too disturbing. If I now at last gather myself together again – and only the magic power of your love and enthusiasm could make it possible – it is as if I was doing it on the grave of my past, to begin a new, second life! And the sole creator of this life is my gracious friend, the saviour who leads me to a new religion, which deep within me is bearing a second, new life – the life that will not know death!

I dedicate the convalescent's first signs of returning strength to my royal friend in these weak lines. I have reason to hope that the painful crisis that broke out in an old, chronic ailment will have made the ailment itself less troublesome that it has been, for some time to come; so that I regard it as a good omen to have some reassurance about my health at the very moment of completing the move into my last refuge. Soon, very soon indeed, I shall be at work again, new-born, and shall not abandon it again until it is finished. The place at which I shall resume composition, after putting the finishing touches to some existing passages, is sublime! It is the most exalted scene of the most tragic of my heroes: Wotan, that is, the all-powerful Life-will, has resolved to sacrifice himself; greater now in renunciation than he ever was in desiring, he now feels himself to be all-powerful and cries out to the primeval wisdom of the earth, to Erda the Nature-mother, who once taught him to fear his end, that no terrors can bind him any longer, since, with the same will that he once desired life alone, he now wills his end. His end? He knows what Erda's primeval wisdom does not know: that he lives on in *Siegfried*. Wotan lives on in Siegfried as the artist lives on in his work: the freer the work to live for and by itself, the less trace it bears of the creating artist, so that the artist himself is forgotten in the work, – the more perfect is the artist's satisfaction: thus, in a certain higher sense, his oblivion, his disappearance, his death – is the life of the work. This is the mood in which I now return to complete my work: I will – in order to live eternally – let myself be destroyed by my Siegfried! O beautiful death!

With what holy dedication I shall now awaken *Brünnhilde* from her long sleep! She slept while Siegfried grew up to young manhood. How significant this all now necessarily seems to me! The last music I wrote was the Woodbird telling Siegfried that he would be able to wake Brünnhilde if he had not learned fear: he ran laughing after the bird, who fluttered away ahead of him, to show him the way to the enchanted rock. That way – gracious, royal friend – was long and arduous for me. I believed that I should never reach the rock. But, if I am Wotan, I have succeeded through Siegfried: it is he who wakes the maiden, the most precious thing in the world. My work will live – it does live! . . .

At this juncture I can only take very unreliable, general notes on the basis of what our singers have managed to achieve in the ordinary operatic repertory: the important question is the extent to which they are *educable* – and on

206

that I cannot form an opinion until I have been able to test them. It is with real longing that I look forward to the chance to do so, now that *Der fliegende Holländer* is at last to be performed. I hope that that will not be long now: it will be the beginning. It is of the utmost importance that my royal patron should succeed in his heroic efforts to win *Schnorr* to sing exclusively for us. When, as I hope, this gifted and amiable artist visits us in the near future, we must take all the necessary steps to ensure that he will be free to do so. In winning him we shall gain so much that I shall be able to proceed to present my exalted friend with exemplary performances of *Lohengrin* and *Tannhäuser*, and of *Tristan und Isolde*.

Königsbriefe, vol. 1, p. 20 ff.

Ludwig II to Wagner, Hohenschwangau, 26 November 1864:

I have decided to have a large masonry theatre built, so that the performance of *Der Ring des Nibelungen* shall be perfect; this incomparable work must be given a worthy place for its presentation; may your efforts in regard to capable dramatic singers be crowned with glorious success! – I expect to discuss the details of this theatre with you in person; in short, your injunction in the preface to the poem of *Der Ring des Nibelungen* shall be fulfilled; I cry aloud: 'In the beginning let there be the *deed*!'

Königsbriefe, vol. 1, p. 39

The architect Gottfried Semper explains the principles of the Festival Theatre intended to be built in Munich according to Wagner's conceptions:

The nucleus of the building, around which everything else will be arranged in an ancillary role, is the large auditorium with the stage. The construction of both of these differs in some important respects from traditional theatres.

The architect was governed by the following specifications:

1. Complete separation of the ideal world on the stage from the reality represented by the audience.

2. In accordance with this separation, the orchestra to be unseen, perceptible only to the ear.

Of these two, the latter is particularly important in its consequences for the construction of the auditorium, and indeed of the whole building. For the only way to conceal the orchestra from every member of the audience, without placing it so low beneath the floor of the auditorium and the stage as to impair or even disrupt altogether the indispensable interrelationship between the performance on the stage and the performance of the orchestra, is to model the auditorium on the ancient Greek and Roman pattern with rows of seats rising step by step (*cavea*), and to abandon altogether the modern convention of vertical tiers of boxes.

It is thus not an antiquarian fancy that dictates this form of auditorium, but first and foremost the necessity of satisfying the client's requirements. It has, however, much to recommend it from acoustic, as well as optical, considerations, inasmuch as it enables all the different elements of dramatic presentation to make their effects that much more easily, in particular to be equally effective for every seat in the theatre.

Lowering the position of the orchestra simultaneously fulfils the important subsidiary purpose of separating the *cavea* from the stage, as requested.

It creates between the two what may be called a neutral space, whose boundaries in every direction, upwards, downwards and sideways, are visible to the spectator, so that the eye can no longer measure the true distance of the stage surround rising on the far side of the neutral space, for lack of points of reference, especially if the eye is further deceived as to the distance by appropriate use of perspective and optical illusion.

Manfred Semper, *Das Münchener Festspielhaus, Gottfried Semper und Richard Wagner*, Hamburg 1906, p. 107 f.

———

Wagner resumed work on the *Ring* late in 1864; he sketched musical themes for Act 3 of *Siegfried*, and the orchestration of Act 2 occupied him until 2 December 1865. At the same time he was preparing the first performance of *Tristan und Isolde*, with the intensive support of Hans von Bülow, whom King Ludwig had engaged at Wagner's request. The first performance took place on 10 June 1865 under Bülow's direction. Ludwig Schnorr von Carolsfeld, whose interpretation of Tristan was outstandingly faithful to Wagner's intentions, died unexpectedly a few weeks after the final performance of the run.

Meanwhile an intimate relationship had developed between Wagner and Bülow's wife Cosima (daughter of Franz Liszt), and on 10 April 1865 their first child, Isolde, was born in Munich. Bülow, who had at first been ignorant of the liaison, subsequently tolerated it and eventually (1869) also agreed to a divorce. Wagner's and Cosima's second daughter, Eva, was born on 17 February 1867, and Wagner's only son, Siegfried, on 6 June 1869.

The composer Peter Cornelius on Wagner, in a letter to Josef Standhartner, a mutual friend in Vienna, Munich, 24 January 1865:

My relationship with Wagner is not socially tenable, and it's driving me into my grave. Wagner does not know, and would not believe, *how exhausting he is – in this incessant fever*, this slow languishing since the 'accursed drink'. For example! We called on Frau von Bülow recently. Wagner at once picks up Schack's *Firdusi* and reads us several poems about Rustum and Sohrab. Meanwhile Bülow concludes his statutory hour – it lasts barely 12 minutes – and we plunge straight into *Tristan und Isolde* – the whole of the first act is sung to us. Meanwhile tea is served – we have drunk barely half a cup by the time Wagner is deep into telling us the story of his *Parzifal* – and that lasts the whole evening until we all leave. Now just imagine poor little Heintz, a really talented pupil of Bülow's from Berlin. She hears *Tristan* for the first time (a girl of 16 or 17) – then the story of Parzifal – then Bülow gives her *Die Meistersinger* and *Tristan* to take away with her, and she sits up till 3 or 4 in the morning, reading the texts one after the other; fortunately for her, there are 14 pages missing from *Die Meistersinger*, so that makes her task a little easier. And that's not what happens *once* in a while, it's what nearly always happens. Our great friend has to talk about *himself*, he has to sing and read from his *own* works, or he is unhappy. That's why he always wants to be surrounded by a small, intimate circle, because he can't have what he wants with other people.

From the moment when I dine with him – 2 o'clock in the afternoon – I cannot hope to get away, except on very exceptional occasions, and the situation is killing me. And it is *impossible* for me to tell him so. It would be unjust, cruel – he doesn't understand – doesn't suspect, how being with him on such terms is draining the marrow from my soul, how badly I need solitude, and above all freedom.

Of course we are grateful when he sings to us from *Siegfried*. But when he gives us the whole of the Flying Dutchman's great scene with the same unction!

On that at any rate we agree!

The Bülows agree with me, too, on the whole business. They are excellent people! Cosima is a rare creature, the true child of Liszt, a dear woman; full of goodness and understanding; she has not only wit but humour as well. Wagner, too, thinks very highly of them both – and knows what good friends he has in them.

Peter Cornelius, *Ausgewählte Briefe*, vol. 2, Leipzig 1905, p. 25 f.

From Wagner's invitation to his Viennese friend, Friedrich Uhl, to attend the first performance of Tristan, *Munich, 18 April 1865:*

The first performances of *Tristan und Isolde*, of which it is certain as may be that there will be three, will be exceptional and exemplary in every way. Above all the two uncommonly difficult principal roles are to be played by my dear friends Ludwig and Malvina *Schnorr von Carolsfeld*, who have been engaged specially; with them there is my old comrade-in-arms in the battle of art, Anton *Mitterwurzer*, as Kurvenal, incomparably staunch and true. As far as circumstances have permitted, trouble has been taken and no expense spared to get the best available singers for the other parts: every member of the cast is sincerely well-disposed towards me. So as not to be disturbed by daily performances in the [Court and National] theatre, I have been given the exclusive use of the intimate theatre in the royal palace [Residenztheater]; and there every care is being taken to reach a performance of insight, clarity and deep understanding in accordance with my wishes. The superb Court orchestra, the exemplary creation of Franz Lachner, is at our disposal almost every day for rehearsals; concerned only with the highest standards of artistic refinement and correctness in delivery, the large number of rehearsals give us all the leisure and time we need to achieve them without strain. Since the production as a whole benefits if I am in a position to supervise it at all points, I have my dear friend *Hans von Bülow* to conduct the orchestra – the very man who once accomplished the impossible, making a piano reduction of this score that can actually be played, although nobody yet understands how he contrived to do so. He knows this score, which still completely mystifies so many musicians, so well that he has every least little bit of it by heart, and has absorbed every last nuance of my intentions. With him, a second self, at my side, I can attend to every detail of the musical performance and of the staging in the tranquil, relaxed, artistic atmosphere which only the sympathetic collaboration of artists who are also true friends can evoke. The care that is being lavished on the preparation of beautiful sets and extremely fine artistic costumes is such that you would think it was not a theatrical production that was at stake, but a monumental exhibition.

And so, as if transported from the desert of the usual theatrical bazaar to the refreshing oasis of a delightful artistic studio, we are preparing a dramatic performance which, purely as such, must be a landmark in the experience of all those who attend it.

These performances, perhaps only three in number – as I mentioned – for the moment, are to be regarded as festivals, to which I can invite the friends of my art from near and far: they will therefore be far removed from the atmosphere of ordinary theatrical performances and will depart from the normal relationship obtaining between theatre and public in our time. My gracious patron wishes that these epoch-making performances shall not be offered to common curiosity, but solely to those who have a more serious interest in my art; I am empowered, therefore, to extend an invitation to every distant region where there are hearts won over by my work.

The performances will probably take place in the *second half of May*, and as soon as the dates are known with reasonable certitude, they will be announced in good time in the newspapers with the widest circulations. We assume that anyone who is prepared to travel to Munich specially for this purpose, will not wish to combine the journey with any other superficial end, but will be demonstrating his serious interest in the success of a significant and noble artistic undertaking; anyone who, with this understanding, makes his interest known to the management of the Court and National Theatre in Munich, can be assured of a place being reserved for him in the theatre for the performance of his choice. The same invitation, in purpose and expression, will be sent to both foreign and native friends of my art.

In the event of sneers that these measures appear to be designed to ensure particularly well-disposed audiences, whom it will not take any very great art to please, we shall calmly reply that on this occasion we are not concerned with the extraordinary modern theatrical game of chance, of pleasing or not pleasing an audience, but solely with whether the artistic challenges that I have set in this work can be met, how they are to be met, and whether it is worth the trouble of meeting them. And that last question does not, of course, mean whether productions of this kind could make a lot of money (for that is what is understood by success or failure in the present-day theatre), but simply whether works of the kind in question, in exemplary performances, are able to impress a cultivated human mind in the way that it is hoped they will; in other words, what is at stake is the solution of purely artistic problems, which requires the participation only of people who have been prepared and qualified to attend the performance by a serious interest. If we have found the right solution to the problem the question will take on a wider application, and how we are to allow the general population to have a share in the heights and the profundities of art, to what extent we are prepared to help them to that share, will also emerge in their turn; even so, for the moment we do not believe that we can entertain any immediate hopes of the normal theatre-going public in its present state.

Schriften-Volksausgabe, vol. 16, pp. 39 ff.

Ludwig II to Wagner, written immediately after the first performance of Tristan und Isolde, *10 June 1865:*

Only One! – Hallowed One!

What rapture! – *Perfect*. Overwhelmed by delight! – . . . To drown . . . sink down – unconscious – highest bliss. – *Divine* work! –

Eternally
true – till death and beyond! –

Königsbriefe, vol. I, p. 105

From the Munich newspaper, Der Volksbote, *15 June 1865:*

Munich, 14 June. The crafty attempt to lay the blame for the objections to Richard Wagner's *Tristan und Isolde* and everything connected with it at the door of the 'Ultramontanes', which is actually said to have succeeded in certain quarters, is as naive as it is malicious, in fact it is *ridiculous*. And the claim that the applause the work received from an immense claque, following blatant manœuvres such as Munich has never before witnessed, was the spontaneous appreciation of an *unbiased audience*, is every bit as ridiculous.

A review of the first performance of Tristan und Isolde:

What is veiled by a mysterious nimbus in the hysterical Senta . . . is paraded openly in the new musical drama *Tristan und Isolde*: not to mince words, it is *the glorification of sensual pleasure*, tricked out with every titillating device, it is unremitting *materialism*, according to which human beings have no higher destiny than, after living the life of turtle doves, 'to vanish in sweet odours like a breath'! In the service of this end, music has been enslaved to the word; the most ideal of the Muses has been made to grind the colours for indecent paintings!

The most indecent thing of all, in our view, is the very act of transferring the poem of *Tristan und Isolde* to the modern stage. What Wagner presents here is not the life of the heroic Nordic sagas, which might edify and strengthen the German spirit; instead he shows us heroism at the instant of its ruin at the hands of sensuality; he pays homage to a point of view that was surely discredited long ago, the sly Frenchified outlook of Gottfried von Strassburg, the adversary of Wolfram von Eschenbach, in that he makes *sensuality itself* the true subject of his drama.

Allgemeine Musikalische Zeitung, Leipzig, 5 July 1865

Wagner's recollections of Ludwig Schnorr von Carolsfeld:

Even now, writing after an interval of three years, it is truly impossible for me to express what *Schnorr* accomplished in the part of Tristan, culminating in the third act of my drama, perhaps for the simple reason that it was beyond the sphere of comparisons. Completely at a loss as to how I can give even an approximate idea of his achievement, I think that the only way that I can give permanent form to what was so dreadfully transient a miracle of musico-mimetic art is to recommend all true friends of my work and of me, now and in the future, to look first of all at the score of the third act. To begin with they need only study the instrumental writing, follow the musical themes from the beginning of the act to Tristan's death, restlessly entering, developing, joining, parting, then mingling afresh, growing, diminishing, finally contending, embracing, almost consuming each other; then let them consider that these themes, whose expressive significance required the most sophisticated harmonization and the most independently impelled orchestral presentation, are the expression of an emotional state veering between the utmost ecstasy of desire and the most profound yearning for death, such as until then no purely symphonic writing had been able to encompass, and which even now could be represented only by instrumental combinations of a richness such as purely instrumental composers had hardly yet felt the need to employ. Now recall that, in the context of the opera, the relationship of this immense orchestra to the monologue pouring from the singer lying up there on the stage, is no more than that of an accompaniment to a 'solo piece', and then form your own conclusions as to the impact of Schnorr's achievement, if I may call on everyone who genuinely listened to those Munich performances to bear witness that from the first bar to the last all attention and interest were directed towards, riveted on the singer alone, and that there was not a single moment, not a single word of the text that was met with inattention or distraction, rather that the orchestra completely disappeared beside him, or – more accurately – appeared to be subsumed in his delivery. But indeed, anyone who has made a close study of this act, will know all he needs to know of the unforgettable greatness of my friend's artistic triumph, if I say that even after the dress rehearsal it was to this act that unprejudiced hearers ascribed the most popular impact and for which they predicted the most general success.

For myself, as I attended each of the performances of *Tristan*, an initial sensation of respectful wonder at my friend's heroic deed grew into genuine dread. Finally it appeared blasphemous even to think that this deed might become part of the regular operatic repertory, to be repeated on demand, and during the fourth performance, after Tristan's curse in love, I felt compelled to declare emphatically to those around me that this must be the last performance of *Tristan*; I would not permit any others.

Schriften-Erstausgabe, vol. 8, p. 232 ff.

———————

Wagner wrote the first prose sketch of *Parsifal* between 27 and 30 August 1865, and sent the king a fair copy.

Ludwig II to Wagner, Hohenschwangau, 5 September 1865:

My Only One! My godlike Friend!
At last I have a moment to myself, at last I am free to thank my beloved friend from the bottom of my soul for the sketch of 'Parcival'; the fire of enthusiasm fills me; every day that passes my love glows more ardently for the only one I love in this world, the one who is my

highest joy, my comfort, my trust, my all! O Parcival, when will you be born? I worship this highest love, this immersion, this surrender of self in the anguished suffering of a fellow man! The tale grips me so strongly! Truly, this art is holy, is the purest, most sublime religion. –

Königsbriefe, vol. 1, p. 169

———————

At Ludwig II's request, Wagner began to dictate his autobiography, *Mein Leben* ('My Life'), to Cosima von Bülow on 17 July 1865. Constantly interrupted, the dictation was not completed until 1880. Wagner published it in four parts in a private, limited edition. He presented the first volume to the king at Christmas 1870.

The first page of Wagner's autobiography, Mein Leben, *which he began in Munich on 17 July 1865 at Ludwig II's request (see also illustrations overleaf):*

Born on 22 May 1813 in Leipzig, on the second floor of the Red and White Lion, on Brühl street, I was baptized *Wilhelm Richard* in the Thomaskirche two days later. My father *Friedrich Wagner*, who was Police Registrar in Leipzig, with the expectation of promotion to Director of Police, at the time of my birth, died in October of the same year in the epidemic of typhoid fever to which he succumbed as a result of overwork during the disturbances caused by the war and the Battle of Leipzig. I later learned of his father's position in life; though he was among Leipzig's less well-off citizens, being the toll-collector at the Ranstädter Gate, he distinguished himself from others in his sphere in that he gave his sons a higher education, one – my father *Friedrich* – studying jurisprudence, the other – the younger son, *Adolph* – theology. My uncle was later to exercize a not unimportant influence on my development; we shall encounter him again at a decisive phase in the narrative of my youth.

———————

The relationship between the king and Wagner aroused the resentment of conservative circles in the government and at Court. The tensions which eventually led to a confrontation between Wagner and the Cabinet Secretary Franz von Pfistermeister reached a climax in the last months of 1865. The king finally had no alternative but to tell Wagner to leave Bavaria.

The Austrian ambassador, Count Blome, in a report on the current situation in Munich, May 1865:

There are regrettably a host of rumours in general circulation which do little to arouse confidence in the new government. The hero-worship which the king shows for Richard Wagner has made the worst impression of all on the public. I pass over the 80,000 gulden that His Majesty has already offered up to the whims of this artist, as being of little consequence, likewise the various scandals which have accompanied the preparations for the première of his opera *Tristan und Isolde*, and which have filled all the newspapers for weeks. But what comment can one make on the reports that Wagner is showing people letters from the king, in which he is addressed as 'Du' and praised in the most extravagant terms? That musicians were summoned to the king's bedside during His Majesty's illness, while urgent affairs of state were ignored and no minister could obtain an audience? That Wagner was invited to Schloss Berg two days ago on his birthday, was received by the king with a bouquet of flowers, and the servants received extraordinary gratuities to mark the joyful occasion? . . .

Richard Wagner is now generally referred to as 'Lolus',[*] and King Ludwig I is reported to have said to someone yesterday: 'Very sad, my grandson's aberration.'

Ludwig II von Bayern Augenzeugenberichten, ed. by Rupert Hacker, 2nd ed., Düsseldorf 1966, p. 84 f.

Friedrich Pecht on the king's attitude to Wagner:

If the king had spent ten times as much on a pretty mistress, it would have seemed perfectly natural, not only to the upright philistine, but to the Court circle as well, but on a great artist – that was quite intolerable! Then, of course, there were certain people who had no difficulty in exacerbating the turmoil caused by the allegations that the king was governed by his favourite. But in sober fact this was never the case. It very soon emerged that although the king loved to have Wagner with him from time to time, he was not the least inclined to permit himself to be unreasonably influenced by him, or by anyone else. . . . I soon had abundant proof of how little truth there was in the poetic saying that the artist was walking hand in hand with the king, or that he ever might do so. . . . Although he was young and as beautiful as an Antinous,[**] and therefore idolized by the ladies, the king was already affected by that revulsion for his loyal subjects and their more or less adoring stares that caused him, as is well known, to have the plays and operas that he loved performed for him on his own. One day it so happened that he had ordered a private performance of *Tristan und Isolde*. Wagner wanted to give Frau von Bülow and myself the opportunity of attending a performance in such unusual circumstances, so, after consultation with the king's confidant, the Cabinet Secretary, Counsellor von Pfistermeister, he placed Frau Cosima, my wife and myself in the box immediately beneath the king's, where he would not be able to see us at all. In the total dark and ghostly stillness of the auditorium, the immensity of which one could only sense, the performance made an impact of almost demonic force, especially as Wagner himself was conducting. But since there was none of that interrelationship between artists and audience, which is so necessary to the former, the impression was eery rather than elevating. After the second act the king left his box, to go to supper. Since he was expected to return very soon, the conductor and orchestra, as well as the singers, had to wait where they were, in order to be able to start again as soon as he did return. But in fact a whole hour passed, and then another – in short, it was a stultifyingly long wait until His Majesty

Am 22. Mai 1813 in Leipzig auf dem Brühl im ›roth und weissen Löwen‹, zwei Treppen hoch, geboren, wurde ich zwei Tage darauf in der Thomaskirche mit dem Namen *Wilhelm Richard* getauft. Mein Vater *Friedrich Wagner*, zur Zeit meiner Geburt Polizeiactuarius in Leipzig, mit der Anwartschaft auf die Stelle des Polizeidirectors daselbst, starb im October des Jahres meiner Geburt in Folge grosser Anstrengungen, welche ihm die überhäuften polizeilichen Geschäfte während der kriegerischen Unruhen und der Schlacht bei Leipzig zuzogen, durch Ansteckung des damals epidemisch gewordenen Nervenfiebers. Ueber die Lebensverhältnisse seines Vaters vernahm ich späterhin, dass dieser in dürftiger bürgerlicher Sphäre als Thoreinnehmer am Ranstädter Thore, sich dadurch vor seinen Standesgenossen auszeichnete, dass er seinen beiden Söhnen eine gelehrte Erziehung gab, indem er den einen — meinen Vater *Friedrich* — Jurisprudenz, den andern, jüngern — *Adolph* — Theologie studiren liess. Mein Oheim gewann später einen nicht unbedeutenden Einfluss auf meine Entwickelung; wir werden ihm in einer entscheidenden Phase meiner Jugendgeschichte wieder begegnen. Ueber mei-

1

was pleased to return to hear the third act. This total lack of consideration for his alleged bosom friend and for some few dozen artists was then not even mitigated by an apology, and left me in no doubt as to the true nature of 'walking hand in hand'.

Friedrich Pecht, *Aus meiner Zeit*, Munich 1894, vol. 2, p. 135 ff.

Peter Cornelius on Wagner's influence over Ludwig II, in a letter to his fiancée, Munich, 15 November 1865:

There was nothing on at Wagner's on Sunday, because – he was with the king and apparently *still is*. A military band was ordered out to play Wagner a little serenade. Now they will be discussing everything most thoroughly, *perhaps*, or perhaps not, if the two are in the mood for rhapsodizing. Another possibility is that Wagner has seized the opportunity to discuss his position, the conservatory, etc. Something I have never told you before is that Wagner is also playing politics with the king, and has become a kind of Marquis Posa.[*] The king is supposed to have asked what his views were on German affairs, and ever since Wagner has been sending him regular letters expounding his opinions. . . .

It's bound to lead to trouble, an artist getting any real influence in the running of the State. But – nobody must say so! The circumstances are really quite extraordinary. Things are looking so bad everywhere in Germany – Bavaria is the most important of the Central States – it's

---

* The nickname Lolus is an allusion to Lola Montez, whose affair with Ludwig I had led to his abdication in 1848
** Young favourite of the Roman Emperor Hadrian in the 2nd century A D, who was deified by the latter following his death by drowning in A D 130

* Character in Verdi's *Don Carlos*

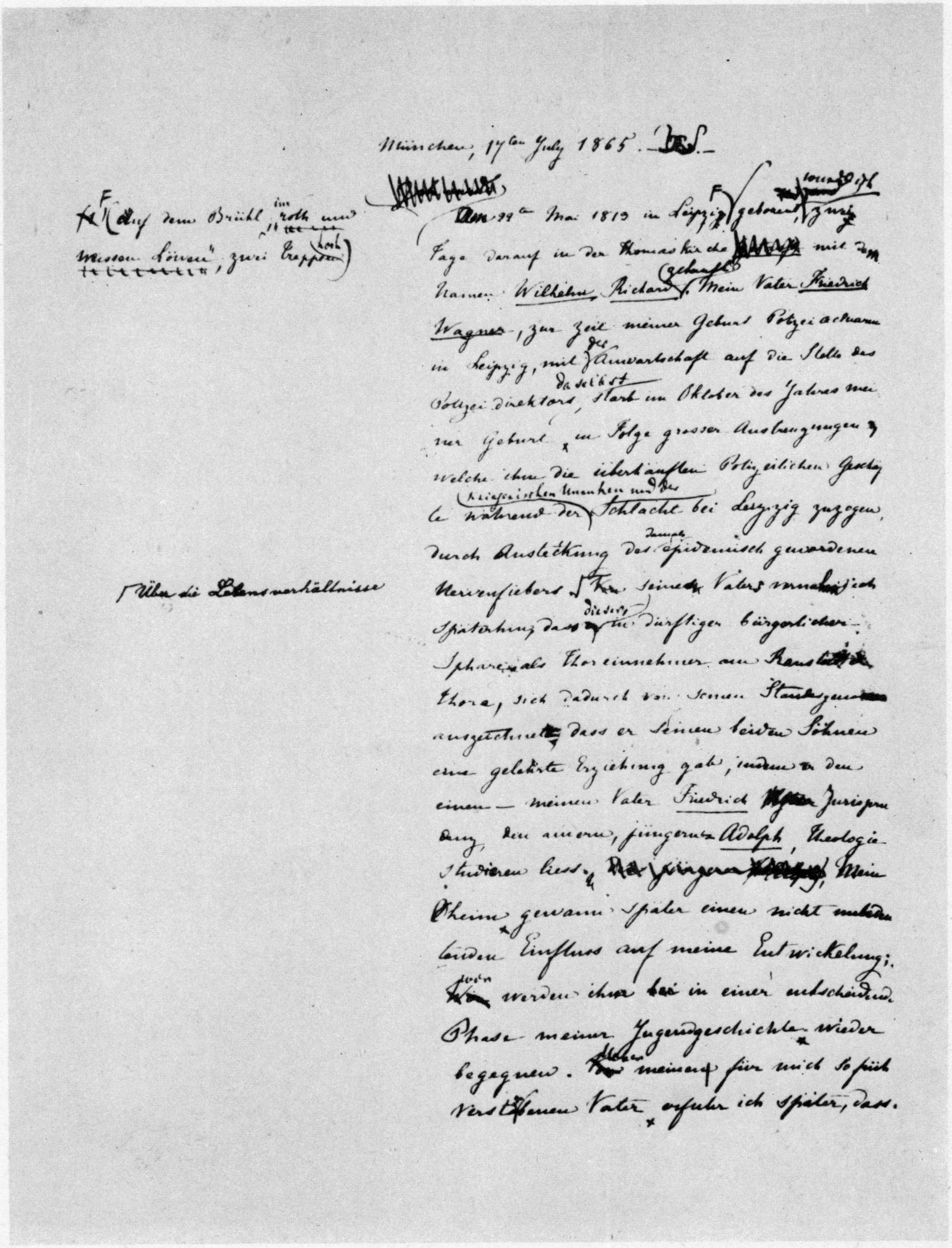

München, 17ten July 1865.

Über die Lebensverhältnisse

Auf dem Brühl "roth und weissen Löwen" zwei Treppen

Am 22ten Mai 1813 in Leipzig geboren, zwei Tage darauf in der Thomaskirche mit dem Namen Wilhelm Richard getauft. Mein Vater Friedrich Wagner, zur Zeit meiner Geburt Polizei actuar in Leipzig, mit Anwartschaft auf die Stelle des Polizeidirektors daselbst, starb im Oktober des Jahres meiner Geburt, in Folge grosser Anstrengungen, welche ihm die überhäuften polizeilichen Geschäfte während der Schlacht bei Leipzig zugezogen, durch Ansteckung des epidemisch gewordenen Nervenfiebers. Seines Vaters, eines dürftigen bürgerlichen Sphäre als Thoreinnehmer am Ranstädter Thore, sich dadurch von seinem Stande auszeichnete, dass er seinen beiden Söhnen eine gelehrte Erziehung gab, indem er den einen — meinen Vater Friedrich Jurisprudenz, den andern, jüngeren Adolph, Theologie studieren liess. Mein Oheim gewann später einen nicht minder bedeutenden Einfluss auf meine Entwickelung; wir werden ihm in einer entscheidenden Phase meiner Jugendgeschichte wieder begegnen. Meinen für mich so früh verstorbenen Vater erfuhr ich später, dass.

Page 1 of Wagner's *Mein Leben* as written out by Cosima von Bülow and, opposite, as printed in the first edition; Wagner began dictating his autobiography in 1865 at Ludwig II's request (see p. 209). Richard Wagner Archiv, Bayreuth.

(see p. 209)

just possible that someone like Wagner, an inspired, protean spirit, who broadly speaking always pursues a single, noble ideal, could provide the impulse needed to start a favourable development. But as long as it remains impossible to look more deeply into the circumstances and form one's own opinion, outward appearances continue to be ominous, dangerous, and the old proverb comes to mind: 'Shoemaker, stick to your last' – perhaps it would be more appropriate in this case, in view of *Die Meistersinger*, which Wagner has started for Schott, to say: 'Poet, stick to your shoemaker!'

Peter Cornelius, op. cit., vol. 2, p. 295 f.

An anonymous article published in the Munich newspaper Neueste Nachrichten, *29 November 1865, attacking the Cabinet Secretariat, especially the Cabinet Secretary himself, Franz von Pfistermeister. It is assumed that Wagner himself had a hand in this article, which was intended to procure Pfistermeister's dismissal by the king:*

You have asked me to tell you about *Wagner's position here* and his circumstances. . . .

When the king sent for Wagner eighteen months ago, his sole purpose was to give a man who had been homeless for so long a permanent refuge and the leisure to do his work. Wagner told the king frankly that a quiet little house with a garden, and means enough to release him from the need to work solely to earn money, would satisfy all his wants. The agreeable establishment Wagner was consequently able to set up for himself ought not to have stirred up any real unpleasantnesses for him, were it not that the envy, which even favours of that order arouse only too easily, was deliberately brought into play when it emerged that it was in the personal interest of the members of the Cabinet to remove Wagner quickly and forcibly from Munich, as his supposed undue influence over the king seemed to be more than certain gentlemen would stand for. . . .

Nobody sees more plainly than Wagner that his artistic innovations are only realizable if the condition of German art in general begins to flourish more than at present. . . .

He therefore believed that it was his duty to let his voice be heard, speaking reassuringly and instructively, and did so in a report to the king on a proposed German College of Music to be founded in Munich: not a single critical voice of any significance was raised when this report was published. But from that time hence it became evident that there was a much more widespread conspiracy, whose obvious goal was to make it impossible for Wagner to remain in Munich, by fabricating and accumulating annoyances of every kind. Since there was no objection they could make to Wagner's well-reasoned assessment of our artistic situation, they simply took the course of calumniating him in the eyes of the general public, in order that the success of their calumny should in turn alarm the king. . . .

These people, whom I do not need to name, because they are now the objects of a general feeling of scorn and indignation in Bavaria, see it as not merely useful but as positively their last hope of salvation, if they spread rumours on every side, flattering the interests of every

party, representing the king's unshakable friendship for Wagner as pernicious. . . .

I dare to assure you that the removal of two or three people, who do not enjoy the least respect among the people of Bavaria, would rid the king and the people of Bavaria at one stroke of these tiresome disturbances.

The Bavarian Minister of State, Ludwig Freiherr von der Pfordten (one of the King of Saxony's ministers during Wagner's Dresden period), gives his view of the situation in a letter to Ludwig II, 1 December 1865:

As far as Rich. Wagner is concerned, feelings here are running very high, especially since the article in No. 333 of the *Neueste Nachrichten*, which obviously originated with Wagner himself and which has the unprecedented effrontery to refer to Your Majesty's 'unshakable friendship' and demands the removal of those closest to Your Highness. That the rumours include some exaggerations and inaccuracies, your humble servant does not doubt. But there are incontrovertible facts, such as Wagner's stay at Hohenschwangau, the requisitioning of quite extraordinary sums from the Treasury, most recently 40,000 florins by Frau von Bülow, and Wagner's unparalleled presumption and undisguised meddling in other than artistic spheres. . . .

Your Majesty stands at a fateful crossroads and has to choose between the love and honour of your faithful people and the 'friendship' of Richard Wagner. This man has dared to assert that the members of Your Majesty's Cabinet, men who have proved their loyalty, do not enjoy the least respect among the people of Bavaria, yet it is rather he himself who is despised by every class of the people among whom the throne must seek, and among whom alone it will find, its support. He is despised, not for the democratic views he airs, which the democrats themselves disparage, but for his ingratitude and betrayal of patrons and friends, for his wanton and dissolute self-indulgence and squandering, for the shameless way he exploits the undeserved favour he has received from Your Majesty.

This is the view, not only of the nobility and the clergy, but also of the respectable middle class and the workers who laboriously earn their bread by the sweat of their brows, while arrogant foreigners luxuriate in the proceeds of royal generosity and show their gratitude by slandering and mocking the Bavarian people and their affairs.

Your humble servant is far from misunderstanding or underestimating Your Majesty's enthusiasm for art and poetry. But he cannot divorce himself from the general conviction that that enthusiasm is being exploited and misused in an unparalleled fashion by one who is unworthy of your favour. Your humble servant also feels compelled to emphasize that while the cultivation of the arts and of ideals is a noble cause to flower from a healthy body politic and one becoming to a prince, *it is not the primary and certainly not the only objective, especially in times like the present, when the very existence of states and thrones is under serious threat from many quarters, and when, therefore, there is a far greater need for action in the real world than for dreaming in the ideal world.*

Sebastian Röckl, 'Von der Pfordten und Richard Wagner', *Süddeutsche Monatshefte*, Munich April 1928, p. 539f.

'Richard Wagner's position in Bavaria', article in the Neuer Bayerischer Kurier, *2 December 1865:*

Really, we ought to be heartily grateful to Hr. Richard Wagner in certain respects for the article in the *Neueste Nachrichten* in which he expatiates on his position here. The people of Bavaria will now be fully enlightened about the cry that has suddenly been raised against the king's Cabinet Secretariat. *Any doubt* that there may have been as to the *author* of that cry, or to what its *purpose* may have been, is now *impossible*: Hr. R. *Wagner himself* has shed all the illumination we could possibly need on the subject.

The man is absolutely right when he says the whole affair *is inspired by the basest self-interest*. There can be absolutely no remaining doubt about that: *but foul motives of personal advantage hold sway only on his side! Money*, a lot of *money* and ever more *money* is what he wants. This man went to the barricades in Dresden, repaying the great favours he had received from noble King Friedrich August II of Saxony by placing himself at the head of the band of arsonists who set fire to that same king's palace on 7 May 1849 and tried to blow it up! He needs money, a lot of money, this man who sheltered his intimate friend, Hr. Eckart, an *active* participant in the abominable murder and mutilation of the elderly Minister of War, Latour, in Vienna in 1848. Then this subtly calculating man remembers the old German proverb: he who sits in the middle of a reed bed and doesn't cut himself pipes is a fool. 'There's money in the Bavarian Civil List,' he thinks, 'I'm very close to that now, that's where I must lay my hands on the money I need.' True, he assures us that, when the king sent for him eighteen months ago, he asked for nothing except 'a quiet little house with a garden and means enough to release him from the need solely to earn money': that would be enough to 'satisfy all his wants'. How modest and self-denying it sounds! And how sad that it is not the whole truth. Hr. R. Wagner is pleased to say nothing about the 23,000 florins that had to be paid to his creditors in Vienna before he could come here. Wisely, he does not say a word, either, about the debts he has repeatedly incurred here, in spite of an enormous income, and which have been settled by our youthful monarch's generosity. And equally he does not think it worth the trouble even to mention the 40,000 florins drawn only recently from the royal Treasury! And we are assured that he is far from being satisfied yet, that his appetite only grows as he eats!

Ludwig II informs his Minister of State, Ludwig von der Pfordten, of Wagner's banishment, 7 December 1865:

My dear Minister of State,
My decision is made. – R. Wagner must leave Bavaria. I will show my beloved people that their trust, their love are worth more to me than anything else. – You will know that it was not altogether easy for me; but I have overcome; – –

I wish to see you here after 11 o'clock. –
Cordial greetings from
Your sincere friend and King,
Ludwig.
(Wagner's departure will also, I confidently expect, see the end of the scandalous calumnies against myself.)

Sebastian Röckl, 'Von der Pfordten und Richard Wagner', *Süddeutsche Monatshefte*, Munich, April 1928, p. 541

Report in the newspaper Der Volksbote *on the mood in Munich at the prospect of Wagner's departure:*

Munich, 9 December. The news that Richard Wagner has been ordered to leave Bavaria ran through the city the day before yesterday *like wildfire*, which is enough in itself to show the extent and the depth of the agitation that the man has aroused by his behaviour. Expressions of the liveliest satisfaction have been voiced everywhere, by no means *schadenfreude*, as claimed in an Augsburg newspaper, but a patriotic joy, which only increases as gradually more and more is learned of how, in spite of all the previous denials, Wagner has tried to exploit our youthful monarch's favour, even going so far as attempting to influence him in matters of state.

Der Volksbote, Munich, 10 December 1865

Peter Cornelius describes Wagner's enforced departure from Munich, 10 December 1865:

We went to the station at 5 o'clock in the morning, and had to wait rather a long time for Wagner. At last the carriage arrived. Wagner looked like a ghost; pale, distraught, his long lank hair looking quite grey. We accompanied him to the train, Franz and Pohl were travelling with him.* Wagner had a last, urgent conversation with Cosima, of which Heinrich made out in particular the word 'silence'. Cosima had broken down completely. When his carriage disappeared beyond the pillars, it was like the fading of a vision.

Diary extract of 11 December 1865, Peter Cornelius, op. cit., vol. 2, p. 318

Wagner went to Switzerland and rented a house near Geneva, where he resumed the composition of *Die Meistersinger*. On 15 April 1866 he moved into Triebschen, a country house near Lucerne, where he lived until 1872. The rent was paid by Ludwig II, who visited Wagner on 22 May 1866, his 53rd birthday.

153–155
162

Ludwig II to Wagner, in a telegram, 15 May 1866:

Ever-increasing longing for the Dear One. The horizon grows ever darker,** the crude sunlight of peaceful day torments unspeakably. I beg my friend for a speedy answer to the following questions: If the Dear One so wishes and wills, I will joyfully renounce the crown and its barren splendour, come to him, never to part from him again. And when he sits at the mysterious loom, weaving his wondrous works, be it my care to shield him from the world, the thief of peace and calm; for I must repeat: I cannot endure any longer to remain separate and *alone*. But to be united and with him, withdrawn from earthly existence, is the only means of preserving me from despair and death. This is not a passing impulse, it is the dreadfully painful truth! I long for your answer.

Ludwig

Königsbriefe, vol. 2, p. 34f.

---

* Wagner left accompanied by his servant (Franz) and his dog (Pohl); besides Cornelius, Wagner's disciple Heinrich Porges, chorus master and writer on music, was also present to see him off
** The king was alarmed by the political developments, which were to lead to the outbreak of war (between Austria and Bavaria on the one side and Prussia on the other) on 14 June

The liberal publicist Julius Fröbel had been acquainted with Wagner since the Dresden uprising and was recommended by him in 1865 to be the editor of a newspaper propagating Ludwig II's political and cultural policies; nothing came of the plan, however. Fröbel characterizes Wagner's art in his memoirs:

If Richard Wagner did not actually go so far as to found a new religion, in which the theatre would have taken the place of a church, he at least succeeded in creating in his adherents a sectarianism which, like all such phenomena, I found objectionable and repellent. When I was in Paris in the spring of 1869, I heard Emile Ollivier, who had been married to the sister of Frau von Bülow, as she then was, and so eventually became Wagner's brother-in-law, refer to him, in conversation with me and others, while expressing the highest admiration for his works, as a 'musical Cagliostro'. For myself, while recognizing the grandeur of his conceptions and experiencing in isolated places the powerful effect of his realizations of them, the only judgment I could pass on him on that occasion was that he possessed all the failings as well as all the virtues of an arch-romantic, though that did not prevent me from regarding him as a man of genius and a great artist. But I have become steadily more convinced that the *confusing of epic style with dramatic style*, the associated matching of the music to the most detailed shifts of thought, the so-called infinite melody and the need to employ immense forces to produce artistic effects, which is another concomitant of the epic concept, are four mistakes, each of which on its own is capable of a detrimental effect on a *dramatic*-musical work, but which combined will ruin completely all but the works of an artist possessed of great abilities.

Julius Fröbel, *Ein Lebenslauf*, vol. 2, Stuttgart 1891, p. 487

Memorandum of a visit from Wagner, by the Bavarian Minister Prince Chlodwig zu Hohenlohe-Schillingsfürst, dated 12 March 1867:

After Wagner had asked to see me the day before yesterday and had later excused himself on the grounds of illness, I wrote to him today, asking him to see me this evening. He arrived at 6.30. At first he was rather strained, spoke of general matters and apologized for coming to see me when he really had no right to do so. I put him more at his ease by remarking that we had two things in common, we were hated by the same party and united in our devotion to the king. Thereupon he became more communicative, talked of the way the king had been treated and tormented, so that he had twice written to him threatening to abdicate, and told me, under protestations of not wishing to boast of it, that *he* had recommended me to the king as minister; then he came to Bavaria's role as a German state, uniting in its population the adroitness of the Franks with the imagination of the Swabians and the earthy vigour of the Bavarians, that the king was just the man to rule this state and embody the German ideal, then began to talk about his art, about his experiences here, about his plans for the foundation of a school of art, about the obstacles that had been placed in his way, and at last about the Cabinet. Among other things he said that it was imperative that I should remain at the Ministry. Whereupon I replied that it did not depend on me. I could not guarantee that the king's confidence in

me would not be undermined by someone, and could be all the less sure because the king followed the tradition of the royal house in not communicating with me directly but only through the Cabinet. He then said that that could not continue, whereupon I pointed out to him that it was very dangerous to throw down the gauntlet to the Cabinet, as he knew better than anyone.

Denkwürdigkeiten des Fürsten Chlodwig zu Hohenlohe-Schillingsfürst, vol. 1, Stuttgart and Leipzig 1906, p. 211

———————

On 24 October 1867, at Triebschen, Wagner completed the score of *Die Meistersinger*. He himself directed the rehearsals of the work at the Hofoper in Munich, with Hans von Bülow conducting. The first performance took place in the presence of the king on 21 June 1868, and was a great success.

A newspaper article describing a rehearsal of Die Meistersinger:

Bülow raps with his baton: 'Gentlemen, if you please, let us begin,' he calls in his thin, hoarse voice to the orchestra, which has been augmented by various brass players and numbers ninety. The music begins, Bülow uses his whole body to indicate the nuances he wants and puts such ferocious energy into each gesture that one begins to tremble for the violinists and the lamps within his reach.

The other man who arrived with Bülow stands on the stage. It is Richard *Wagner*, with the bird-like features that all Germany knows. In a state of continuous excitement that makes one nervous, he accompanies every note sung with a corresponding gesture that the singers imitate as closely as they can; only someone who has seen the composer toiling and gesticulating in this way can have any idea of the multitude of nuances that he wants to be conveyed. Almost every step, every movement of a hand, every opening door, is 'musically illustrated', and there is in *Die Meistersinger*, in particular, such a quantity of music illustrative of the singers' mime that we would regard it as miraculous if a production of the opera that was not rehearsed under the composer's supervision managed to introduce all the actions intended to accompany this music. Only when Fräulein Mallinger is singing does Wagner suspend his instructions, listens with visible pleasure, trots to and fro with one hand in his trouser pocket, sits down on the chair beside the prompter's box, gives pleased, approving nods and smiles all over his face. But if something in the orchestral playing displeases him, which happens rather often, he leaps up as if bitten by a snake, clapping his hands, Bülow stops and raps his baton, and Wagner calls to the players: '*Piano*, gentlemen, *piano*! That must be soft, soft, soft, as if it's coming to us from another world.' And the orchestra starts again. 'More *piano*!' Wagner shouts, and makes the appropriate gesture with his hands. 'So, so, so – good, good, good – beautiful!' And it goes on like that all evening.

Neue Freie Presse, Vienna, 21 June 1868

Eduard Hanslick, 'Richard Wagner's *Mastersingers of Nuremberg*', *June 1868:*

The first performance of Wagner's latest opera took place yesterday, before a large, if not quite a capacity audience, and lasted from 6 to 11 in the evening. To state that the gala performance was a wild success is really superfluous: that was a foregone conclusion, with the presence of the composer's friends and admirers assembled from the four corners of the earth, and with the king himself, the most enthusiastic of patrons, at their head. In any case the audience's appetite had long been whetted by hints of the splendours of the spectacle, and powerfully orchestrated articles in the press, by the composer himself, had successfully engendered a receptive mood. . . .

The young, slender monarch, with his idealistic looks, heard the opera from beginning to end, to all appearances alone in the large Court box. But when persistent cries arose for Richard Wagner, as well as for the singers, at the end of the second act, the composer came forward from the obscurity behind His Majesty to take his bow from the front of the royal box. This affectionate greeting, which was repeated in exactly the same form at the end of the third act, rather surprised the strangers in the audience, some of whom expected that the king would be the next to be called for.

As a theatrical experience, *Die Meistersinger* is well worth seeing, the musical presentation excellent, the scenic incomparable. Dazzling scenes of colour and splendour, ensembles full of life and character unfold before the spectator's eyes, hardly allowing him the leisure to weigh how much and how little of these effects is actually of musical origin. Anyone who is told the plot of *Die Meistersinger*, which takes only a few words, will be left wondering how it can give rise to an opera of greater length than *Le Prophète* or *Les Huguenots*. The violent stretching and tugging of a skinny little plot, which has to mark time without sub-plot or intrigue to create tension, and hardly provides enough material for a modest, two-act *Singspiel*, is the biggest practical fault of *Die Meistersinger*. . . .

Wagner has remained completely loyal in *Die Meistersinger* to his musical principle, which was already dominant in *Lohengrin* and saturated *Tristan und Isolde* with the strictest consistency. It always creates a good impression when an artist holds fast, seriously and with unshakable conviction, to the principles which he regards once and for all as the right ones, and only true ones. This kind of consistency is not to be deflected by any objections, and it gives *Die Meistersinger*, too, a sureness and a certitude that impress at every turn. Wagner knows exactly what he wants; every note of the score bespeaks conscious intention, nothing is there by chance, and this means that it also lacks those happy accidents which bestow the crowning charm on the creations of artistic imagination and of nature alike. We must respect the consistency with which Wagner clings to his characteristic principle; but not even *Die Meistersinger* has converted us to the principle itself: the conscious dissolution of all fixed forms in a formless, intoxicating sea of sound, the replacement of self-sufficient, articulated melodies by shapelessly vague melodizing. We might as well use Wagner's own oblique phrase, 'infinite melody', as the technical term for it, since everyone already knows what it stands for. 'Infinite melody' dominates *Die Meistersinger* as it does *Tristan*, which means that it musically undermines both. A little motif starts off, but before it becomes a proper melody it is shaped into a theme, that is, it is turned round, bent, raised

or lowered by incessant modulation and enharmonic shifts, continued by Rosalias, then broken up and abbreviated again, repeated or imitated by first one instrument, then another. Anxiously avoiding every concluding cadence, ever renewing itself from itself, this form without bone or muscle flows on indefinitely. Scanning one large section of this kind of writing after another, one receives the same impression each time of the uniformity of the whole, while the details are continuously and nervously agitated. The few places where there is a lyrical *point d'appui*, a song-form provided by the text (Walther's songs, the shoemaking song), are the only opportunities the singing has to shape itself, for a while at least, into real self-sufficient melodies. But as long as the drama itself is proceeding, in the monologues, the dialogues and the big ensembles, the melodic thread is held, not by the voices, but by the orchestra, which spins it off, as 'infinite' and as uniform in texture as the product of a cotton-mill. This melody-spinning orchestral accompaniment constitutes the really coherent and self-sufficient compositional structure of *Die Meistersinger*, the vocal line accommodates itself to the accompaniment, weaving in its own phrases, half declamatory, half singing. . . .

The chorus and orchestra of the Munich Opera emerged the victors from the musical battle of *Die Meistersinger*, it is a considerable achievement in itself that the unprecedentedly difficult ensembles do not fall apart. The chief credit for that, as for the accuracy of the whole performance, is due to Herr von Bülow, the conductor. Bülow's whole energy and agility, his astonishing memory and his enthusiastic devotion to Wagner are indispensable factors in the result. Richard Wagner himself, who directed the rehearsals on the stage and supervised the production down to the last detail, has once again proved himself a born operatic producer, and brilliantly vindicates his reputation for genius in the field of *mise-en-scène*. Nor must we forget the calm and sensitive hand which has guided the reins of Phaëton's chariot in Munich, the unseen hand of Baron von Perfall, the amiable, cultivated artist and Intendant. He hopes to give four more performances of *Die Meistersinger* with the original cast, and then to be able to replace the guest-artists partly by local singers, partly by new engagements.

The Munich production of *Die Meistersinger* will be acknowledged by every music lover as an interesting artistic experience, though not one of those whose genuine beauty remains with us, to enrich and illuminate our lives. We do not find this opera to be a work of profound originality, or of enduring truth and beauty, but an interesting experiment, which owes the striking impression it makes to the dogged energy with which it has been carried out and to the undeniable novelty, not indeed of its invention, but of the method of its invention. The work that has been presented to us is not the creation of a true musical genius, but that of an ingenious intellect, a chameleon amalgam, half-poet and half-musician, who has used his very individual talent, which is wanting in the main thing but dazzling in the subsidiaries, to create a new system which is mistaken in its basic premisses and unlovely and unmusical in its consequent realization. In a word, we number *Die Meistersinger* among the interesting cases of musical deviation or sickness. If such cases were accepted as normal it would mean the end of art, but as long as they are understood to be special cases their influence can be more significant and more persistent than that of a dozen of the mundane operas of the host of healthy composers, whom to call half-talents is to honour too much by half.

Neue Freie Presse, Vienna, 24, 25, 26 June 1868

---

178 Wagner made the acquaintance of Friedrich Nietzsche (1844–1900) on 8 November 1868, in the house of his brother-in-law Hermann Brockhaus. Nietzsche, who was appointed *professor extraordinarius* in Classical Philology at the University of Basle in February 1869, visited Wagner at Triebschen no less than 23 times between then and April 1872. The powerful impression that Wagner's personality and work made upon him inspired Nietzsche to write *Die Geburt der Tragödie aus dem Geist der Musik* ('The Birth of Tragedy from the Spirit of Music'; 1872) and *Richard Wagner in Bayreuth* (1876). The admiration was mutual but was later to give way first to a more critical attitude, then to repudiation.

Friedrich Nietzsche on his visits to Triebschen, in a letter to his mother, June 1869:

But what is very important is that I have the friend and neighbour I so much wanted, in Lucerne – not near enough, but at least not too far to prevent me seizing every free day as an opportunity to meet him. This friend is *Richard Wagner*, who is as great and singular a man as he is an artist. I have already spent many happy days with him and the brilliant Frau *von Bülow* (*Liszt*'s daughter): last Saturday and Sunday for instance. *Wagner's* villa is on the shores of the Vierwaldstätter see, at the foot of the Pilatus, in a setting of enchanting solitude, surrounded by the lake and mountains, and as you can imagine, it is superbly furnished and decorated: we spend our time together there in the most animated conversation, the most agreeable of family circles, and quite removed from the usual social triviality. This is a great find for me....

Friedrich Nietzsche, *Werk und Briefe* (Historische-kritische Gesamtausgabe): Letters, vol. 2, Munich 1938, p. 326 f.

Friedrich Nietzsche to his friend Erwin Rohde, 17 August 1869:

... Instead I will tell you more about my Jupiter, R. *Wagner*, in whose company I have the chance to breathe deeply from time to time, thereby refreshing myself more than the whole band of my colleagues could possibly imagine. The man has not yet been awarded any orders, and has just received his first honour, the honorary 166 membership of the Berlin Academy of Arts. A rich, fruitful, awe-inspiring life, quite out of the common run and unknown among average mortals! And so he stands alone, firmly rooted in his own strength, with his gaze steadfastly directed above and beyond everything that is ephemeral, in the very finest sense not of his time. He gave me a manuscript recently, 'On the State and Religion', intended as a memorandum for the young king of Bavaria: I would like to be a king, if it meant receiving advice of such loftiness of spirit, so far removed from temporal considerations, of such nobility and *Schopenhauerian* seriousness.

Incidentally, I sent him recently a few passages from your letters, for Frau *von Bülow*, who had asked to see them several times. The time before last that I was with them, actually during the night I spent there, a little boy was born, whom they gave the name '*Siegfried*'. And the last time I was there, Wagner had just finished the composition of his *Siegfried*, and was exulting in his powers.

Friedrich Nietzsche, op. cit., p. 353 f.

Minna Wagner died in Dresden on 25 January 1866. From May onwards, Cosima von Bülow and her children lived with Wagner at Triebschen almost permanently. In June 1869 Cosima asked her husband for a divorce, which was granted on 18 July 1870. Wagner and Cosima were married on 25 August in Lucerne. 176

Wagner on the divorce of Cosima from Hans von Bülow, in a letter to Marie von Muchanoff-Kalergis, Lucerne, 24 August 1869:

It's about Cosima's divorce from Hans von B. Bülow is now fully cognizant that it is imperative. . . .

C. realized the necessity of an absolute divorce from B. in July last year, when I told her that it would be quite impossible for me ever to return to Munich, and that I had made an unshakable resolution to that effect. That I would be driven to some such decision was first made clear by the conclusion to be drawn from the observations I repeatedly made of the impossibility of fruitful artistic activity in Munich, for, after my exertions in the preparation and performance of *Die Meistersinger*, accompanied as they were by the most consuming anger at the miserable trials I met at every turn, the plain conclusion was that it would be fatal to my health and crippling to all further productivity. But the other, equally important factor in my decision was the conclusion I drew from the trial year, on which I had insisted for that very reason, that a continuing friendly existence within the context of C. and B.'s marital relationship was quite impossible. There was no longer any use in denying that the situation was inexorably exhausting and undermining the spiritual and physical health of all those involved. The incredible aspersions cast earlier on this marital relationship by the Jesuit cabal, which had now sprung to life again and was seizing every opportunity which offered the slightest hope that vilification of that kind would prove a hindrance, had – quite apart from all other internal reasons – turned this marriage into a relationship intolerable to every person of delicate feelings. The only hope was to escape from a misery that was destroying everything noble. When I communicated the decision I had made, based on all these considerations, to C., during her visit to me last summer, she at once agreed with me. She did not share the opinion of me that so many of my friends were happy to have formed, to their own relief, namely that I was a man who was past helping. She knew what would help me once and for all, and knew how it might be achieved, and did not hesitate for a moment to offer me that help in the possession of herself. In declaring that the sole purpose of all my future striving shall be to retain possession of her, I may not, and I will not invoke the unparalleled happiness, the immeasurable blessing that she bestowed on me in so doing; for even a man of my sort would lay himself open to reproach if he brought suffering upon others for the sake of his own highest happiness. Instead I invoke an emotion that all hold sacred, I invoke as my lode-star the preservation of an incomparably solicitous mother for the sake of her children, whose welfare she alone can ensure: the knowledge that this duty has been laid upon me makes me ruthless towards everything and anything that might hinder me from discharging it.

Königsbriefe, vol. 5, p. 93 ff.

168–170 Against Wagner's wishes, Ludwig II ordered *Das Rheingold* to be staged in Munich. The conductor Hans Richter and the singer Franz Betz demonstrated their loyalty to Wagner by refusing to take part. The work was performed for the first time on 22 September 1869 under the musical direction of Franz Wüllner. 171, 172 The following year the king insisted on *Die Walküre* being performed (26 June 1870), also against Wagner's wishes.

Ludwig II to Court Counsellor von Düfflipp, Schloss Berg, 30 August 1869:

The way *Wagner* and the theatrical rabble are behaving is truly criminal and quite shameless; it amounts to open defiance of my orders and I cannot suffer it. *Richter* may on no account conduct again and is to be dismissed forthwith; that's final. The people in the theatre are to obey my orders and not *Wagner's* whims. Several newspapers have insinuated that I have called off the performance, as I foresaw: it is very easy to spread false rumours, and it is my wish that you should announce the true position at once and summon every resource necessary to enable the performance to take place; for if *Wagner's* loathsome intrigues were to succeed, the whole mob would grow more impudent and shameless, and would finally become uncontrollable; the evil must therefore be eradicated, root and branch. – *Richter* must go, and *Betz* and the others must be brought to heel. I have never experienced such effrontery in my life.

Königsbriefe, vol. 5, p. 101

Wagner to the conductor Franz Wüllner, September 1869:

Keep your hands off my score! Take my advice, Sir, or the devil take you! Go and beat time for choral societies and glee clubs, or if you must have opera scores at all costs, get hold of the ones your friend Perfall* has written! And tell that fine gentleman, if he doesn't frankly admit to the king that he is incapable of putting on my work, I will light him a blaze which all the gutter journalists he pays with what sticks to his fingers from the *Rheingold* budget will be unable to blow out. You gentlemen are going to have to take a lot of lessons from a man like me, before you realize that you have no understanding of anything.

Königsbriefe, vol. 4, p. 201 f.

---

* Intendant (manager) of the Court Opera, and himself a composer

---

Review of the first performance of Die Walküre:

A drama of this kind ought to proceed in simple, sculpturally rounded tableaux. In order to make its point, in order merely to hold the attention even, it ought to be based on morally elevating motives, not on the most dubious aspects of sexual behaviour, not on weakness of character, infidelity and perjury on the part of gods and men alike.... We will say no more about the straining for mystical obscurity displayed by the text, than the instrumentalists and singers, called upon at every turn to perform impossible and unsuitable figures, say of their distress. We will not find fault with the outrageous demands and dangerous situations that Wagner imposes on performers and instruments and décors, but . . . we will summarize the overall impression made by *Die Walküre* as follows: in the first act the voices manage to hold their own with the orchestra, which in the second act they can do only in places, whereas in the principal scene of the third act, the Ride of the Valkyries, it is barely possible to hear isolated shrieks from the singers through the tumult of the orchestra. The first act, though for the most part wearyingly long-winded, has unity, and its finale glows with wonderfully sensuous colour; the second act drags, being broken into segments which only occasionally spring to life; the third act begins so deafeningly that total stupor would be ensured even if the rest were less long-winded than it is. The overall effect the music makes is not agreeable; it is permeated by what I can only call pagan sensuality, a straining for frivolous naturalism, which swiftly suppresses all the surges of nobler feeling that occasionally arise, and produced nothing in the end but a dull enervation.

Süddeutsche Presse, Munich, 28 June 1870

Extract from the review, by the writer Gustav Freytag, of Wagner's Das Judentum in der Musik *('Jewry in Music')* 85 *which was published in book form in 1869, having first appeared in 1850 in the* Neue Zeitschrift für Musik:

We have no intention of examining the question as to whether Jewish composers and virtuosi, who have followed the trend of the times in exactly the same way as Christians, have been more of a blessing or a curse to modern music. For we non-Jews have lost the right to accuse our Jewish artists of bias, in music as in other spheres, and indeed we rather fear that Herr Wagner himself has displayed the characteristics and weaknesses, for which Jewish artists are not uncommonly criticized, in his own works and in a highly pronounced degree, although he drapes them in slightly different colours from his predecessors. By the terms of his own booklet, he is the biggest Jew of all. The straining for effect, the pretentious and calculated striving to produce results uncontrolled by a reliable artistic taste, the lack of the ability to express a musical sensation purely and fully in the appropriate melodic and harmonic language, excessive, nervous restlessness, delight in the exotic and the recherché, the effort to disguise the occasional lapses in his musical invention by ingenuity and extraneous artistic means, even the considerable talent for sophisticated stage-management of effects, and finally, at the back of everything, in place of the sure, strong mind of an artist, in which form takes shape effortlessly alongside content, we find the ill-bred pretension of an opinionated dilettante, making ambitious sallies beyond the frontiers of his own art and contradicting the laws of beauty because, among other reasons, he is incapable of following them; an adventurous spirit, which seeks its satisfaction in immensities, careless of whether his works will be the ruin of singers, orchestras and the whole beautiful organism of musical drama. Weaknesses and serious blemishes of this kind are to be found everywhere in his works, as well as passages of truly beautiful, sometimes truly ravishing invention. This attribute of his talent, remarkable and momentous as it is, in its effect on music in our time, seems to us to be precisely what he would characterize as a typically Jewish trait. But as Herr Wagner will certainly not share the opinion that he is himself part of 'Jewry in music', we too have assuredly lost all right to speak of the limitations of Jewish musicians. And that's what strikes us as funny about this prolonged storm in a teacup.

'Der Streit über das Judentum in der Musik', in *Die Grenzboten* XXVIII, Leipzig 1869, p. 336

know, and none better, the pain undervaluation causes a great artist. Wagner, to his good fortune, is so unashamedly arrogant that criticism does not touch his heart – assuming he has a heart, which I doubt.

Zeitschrift für Musik, Mainz 1950, p. 428

With his plans for Munich thwarted, Wagner began to look for another place to hold his festivals. Reports from various sources, and an article in an encyclopedia, drew his attention to Bayreuth, in March 1870. The hope that it would be possible to stage the *Ring* in Galli Bibiena's baroque opera house there was quickly dispelled. But the town's size and position suited Wagner's requirements, and the town council, led by the mayor, Theodor Muncker, and the banker Friedrich Feustel, welcomed his proposals. On 12 May 1871, in Leipzig, his birthplace, Wagner officially announced the first Bayreuth Festival.

185
186

Wagner to Ludwig II, Lucerne, 1 March 1871:

What are those works to me now? If they were once pale, trembling wraiths, longing for release, how can they be anything more than bloodstained, grimacing ghouls? . . .

So what is to become of me now? What is to become of my work? Enthusiasm for it always revives in me when you praise it, and say that it is the greatest thing ever produced by a human spirit. – One thing is certain: things cannot remain as they are. I must have a definite prospect that my requirements as to the only way that my work can be performed properly will be met, if I am to regain the courage and the energies to complete it. This is what I have been pondering, with great suffering, and what, since you so graciously wish it, I will now retail to you.

You have been gracious enough to appeal to me not to keep myself quite so distant from my friends, not to show my face so seldom. It gives me such joy to feel that I can regard this loving appeal as the advance expression of your consent to a plan which has been determined, after mature reflection, by anxiety for the life of my great work. – The Royal Academy of Arts in Berlin has done me the unsolicited honour of making me one of its members; I am expected to express my thanks for this distinction, the first of its kind that has been shown me in Germany, and I intend to fulfil this obligation by giving a lecture on 'The Destiny of Opera' at a public session of the Academy. I have decided to communicate my proposals for the performance of my great Stage Festival as part of this lecture, which should give me a chance to gauge the possibilities of arousing active interest in furthering my enterprise. There are already various significant indications that the response will not be unfavourable. My purpose in doing this is – if things work out favourably – to summon a German national undertaking into existence, the direction of which must, of course, be placed entirely in my hands alone. I have already specified, in my preface to the text, the only form the enterprise can possibly take, if it is to be successful. Should my appeal be effective, I shall, I hope, have occasioned you, my sublime friend, a great relief, if you yourself still retain your earlier predilection for the idea to which I now hold faster than ever. For of course you know, my gracious King, that I would never entertain

180–183 The Franco-German War 1870–71 ended with the defeat of France. In January 1871 Wagner sent his poem *An das deutsche Heer vor Paris* ('To the German army outside Paris') to Otto von Bismarck. With the coronation of Wilhelm I of Prussia as German Emperor at Versailles on 18 January, the German Empire was proclaimed.

Translation of Bismarck's letter to Wagner, Versailles, 21 February 1871:

Sir

I thank you for having dedicated a poem to the German army and for sending me the text of it. Greatly honoured as I feel, that you address this poem to me alone, as I learn, it would give me equal pleasure to see it published.

You, too, have overcome the resistance of the Parisians after a long struggle, with your works, in which I have always had the keenest interest, although at time inclining towards the opposition party; it is my belief and my hope that many more victories will be granted them, at home and abroad.

Please accept the assurance of my most profound respect
von Bismarck

RWA

Georges Bizet on Wagner, in a letter to his mother-in-law, Paris, 29 May 1871:

I am no friend of Wagner's, and have only a moderately high opinion of him; but I cannot forget the immeasurable pleasures that I owe to his genius and innovation. His music has an indescribable allure. It is rapture, tenderness, love itself! – If I were to play it to you for a week you would be swept off your feet by it! . . . The Germans, who are easily our equals in music, alas, have realized that Wagner is one of their strongest props. The German spirit of the nineteenth century is embodied in that man. You

Versailles 21 Februar 1871

Hochgeehrter Herr

Ich danke Ihnen, daß Sie dem deutschen Heere ein Gedicht gewidmet, und daß Sie mir dasselbe haben überweisen lassen. So sehr ich mich [illegible] fühle, daß Sie dieses vaterländische Gedicht, wie mir gesagt wird, für mich allein bestimmen, so sehr würde ich mich freuen es veröffentlicht zu sehen.

Auch Ihre Werke, denen ich von jeher meine [illegible], wenn auch zuweilen mit Neigung zur Opposition gemischter [illegible] zugewandt [illegible], noch fortan [illegible] den Widerstand der [illegible] zu überwinden, und ich glaube und wünsche, daß dieselben noch viele Tage, [illegible] beschieden sein werden.

Genehmigen Sie die Versicherung meiner ausgezeichneten Hochachtung.

v. Bismarck

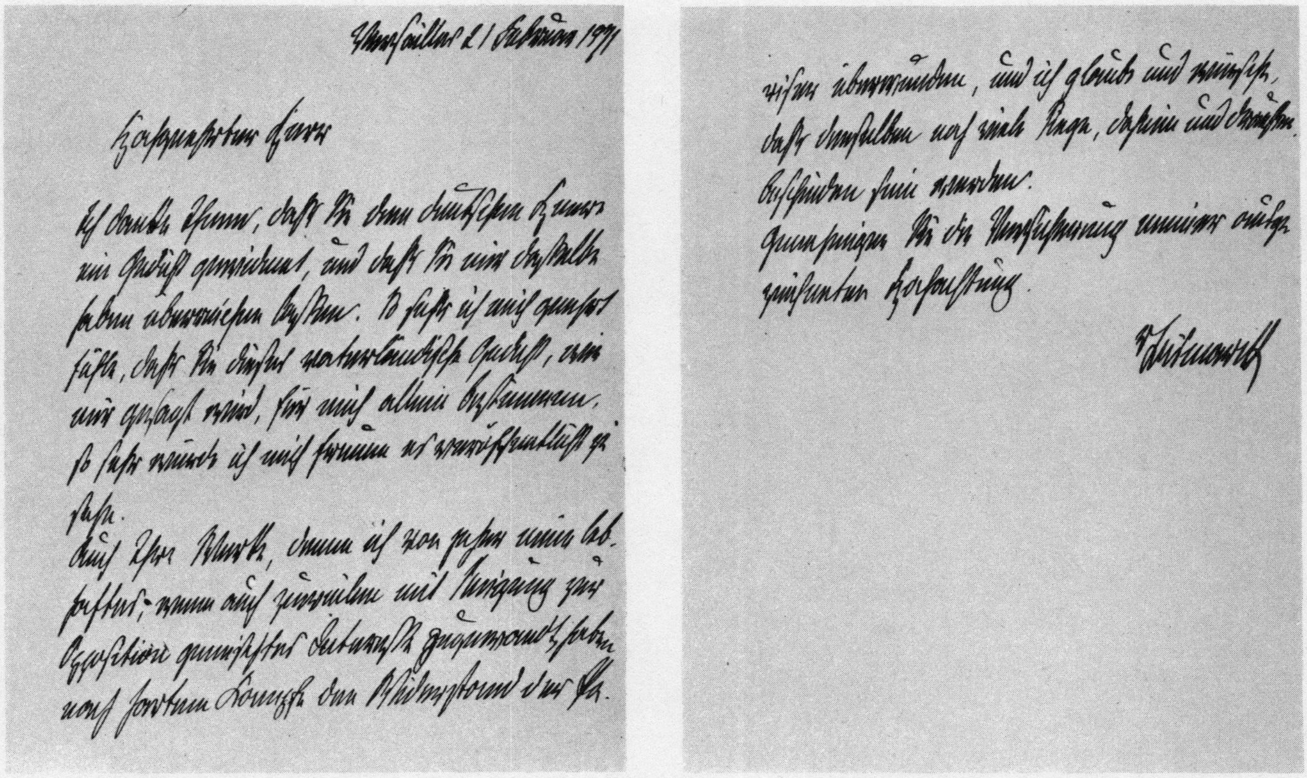

Letter to Wagner from the Imperial Chancellor, Otto von Bismarck. Versailles, 21 February 1871 (for translation see opposite). Richard Wagner Archiv, Bayreuth.

the thought of any enterprise, particularly this one, if the noblest and finest part of it did not fall to you, any more than I would ever believe myself capable of conceiving anything more of any importance without my unshakable faith in your sublime friendship and generosity.

I have in fact already chosen the spot which shall be the scene of our great artistic deed; and to tell the truth, the discovery of it has given my plan the first solid footing. The place I have in mind [Bayreuth] corresponds in every respect to the stipulations I made in that preface; it lies in Bavaria, and thus has my sublime friend as its prince.

Königsbriefe, vol. 2, p. 318 ff.

The announcement of the Festival:

The Stage Festival *Der Ring des Nibelungen* will be performed complete, under my personal supervision, on three consecutive evenings, and will be repeated twice, in the two weeks immediately following. The place designated for the performances is Bayreuth, the date, one of the summer months of 1873. A theatre will be built especially for the performances, the interior construction of which will be in exact accordance with my particular requirements, while its durability and exterior appearance will depend on the means placed at my disposal. I envisage that the building of the theatre, and the installation of the special equipment necessary for the performance of my Stage Festival, will occupy the period from the autumn of this year, 1871, to the spring of 1873. Then the outstanding singers and musicians whom I shall have selected by that date will assemble in Bayreuth, to devote two months to rehearsing the parts of the festival work.

Fifteen hundred comfortable seats will be available for those patrons and benefactors of my undertaking, who, through the medium of a Society of Friends, in whose hands I lay this part alone of the necessary arrangements, will have contributed the financial means appropriate to the execution of my project. These Friends will have the title and the rights of *Patrons of the Stage Festival in Bayreuth*, while the realization of the undertaking itself will be entrusted to my experience and skills and to my endeavours alone. The real property proceeding from this common undertaking shall be regarded as being at my disposal and destined to whatever uses in the future as shall seem to me most appropriate to the purpose and the ideal nature of the undertaking.

I leave the details of the action to be taken in respect of raising the necessary financial means entirely in the hands of the close friends who have expressed the wish to take this burden upon themselves, and whose endeavours I salute gratefully as encouraging proof of energy and zeal in the service of German art and, in equal measure, of unanimous confidence in myself.

12 May 1871 — Richard Wagner

Schriften-Volksausgabe, vol. 16, p. 131 f.

Ludwig II to Wagner, Hochkopf, 26 May 1871:

The gods have inspired your plans for performing the Nibelungen work in Bayreuth; I cannot believe that the performance could take place as early as next year, heavenly though it would be, when I think of the many difficulties there are to be overcome, the erection of the temporary theatre, the large number of rehearsals necessary, etc., etc. O, if only I were wrong! – The melancholia that always seizes hold of me in the detestable city, in the thick of the political drudgery that is now so unrewarding, has given way to a feeling of optimism and elation, thanks to your wonderful letter and to this visit to my beloved mountains, far removed from the world with which I was, and still am, always inwardly at war, and to which I shall never be reconciled. – But we understand each other, that is the main thing, we will remain true to each other; true till death.

Königsbriefe, vol. 2, p. 324

Heinrich Esser outlines the discrepancies between the proposed arrangements for the performances of the Ring *at Bayreuth and the provisions he would consider essential, in a letter to Franz Schott, 28 December 1871:*

Wagner is travelling around, conducting concerts to raise money for his project, and let us assume that he really will manage to get the 300,000 thalers he wants. Now I'm not very good at arithmetic, but Wagner is no good at it at all, while you at least are better at it than the two of us put together. I simply do not understand what has given Wagner the idea that 300,000 thalers, which is an extremely modest sum for the sort of undertaking he has in mind, will be enough to cover the enormous expenditure he will face. Building his ideal theatre, the stage machinery needed for *Der Ring des Nibelungen*, the highly complicated lighting installations, the sets etc., are already gobbling up a very significant portion of his funds, especially when you think of the kind of labour he's going to have to employ over a long period to do the installation. We're drawing close to the time now when all this is supposed to have been completed, and when work should start on the actual musical preparation. Of course, the soloists can study their parts at home and learn them by heart in advance, since there aren't any ensembles, but they must be on the spot several weeks beforehand, to rehearse together. There's no need for a male-voice chorus, but I suppose a women's chorus will have to be got together and put up in Bayreuth for at least six weeks to two months, like the soloists, at the composer's expense. Then there's the orchestra, which will need no end of rehearsals, and of course provision will have to be made for understudies. The minimum number of full-dress rehearsals he will need for four such operas will be 20 to 24, and you can work out for yourself from these quick jottings, the mass of personnel, time and work that will have to be paid for, before Wagner finally reaches his goal of the first performance. All the money available will have been spent, and there will be no takings, because everything will already have been paid in advance. Will he find a generous prince again, to restore financial order? Of course, I don't know if there is any foundation for all these doubts of mine – but I am positive of one thing at

220

least, that if Wagner doesn't have an honest man at his elbow to help him look after the financial arrangements, I have very little faith in the success of the grand undertaking.

Edgar Istel, op. cit., p. 1864

Wagner gives his reasons for the choice of Bayreuth for the Festival in a letter to Friedrich Feustel, Lucerne, 1 November 1871:

The town ought not to be a capital city with a permanent theatre, nor one of the more popular large spas, which would attract precisely the sort of public I least want, especially in summer; it ought to be somewhere near the centre of Germany, and it ought to be in Bavaria since I am also thinking of a permanent residence for myself, and if I am to continue to enjoy the great favours that the king of Bavaria has shown me, I think it is only proper that it should be in Bavaria.

Bayreuther Briefe, p. 14 f.

Wagner on the finances of the Festival undertaking, in a letter to Friedrich Feustel, Lucerne, 12 April 1872:

I am in complete agreement with your general principles in respect of the allocation of the financial resources we require. In more detail, the priorities are as follows:

1. The theatre building itself to be *provisional* only; I would be quite content for it to be completely of wood, like the pavilions put up for gymnastics events and choral festivals; it should be no more solid than is necessary to prevent it falling down. So economize on it – economize, no ornamentation. This building should be merely the silhouette of our idea, and we offer it as such to the *nation to build* in monumental permanence.

2. Stage machinery and sets. Everything required for the ideal, inner work of art – absolutely *perfect. No* economies here: everything to be as if it will have to last a long time, nothing provisional. –

3. Singers and musicians are receiving only their expenses from me, no '*payment*'. Anyone who will not come to me for the honour and out of enthusiasm can stay at home. Much use a singer who only came for one of their insane '*fees*' would be to me! A creature of that sort would never measure up to my artistic standards. These, my dear friend, are *my* miracles, which I shall show the world here: how to collect the right people to meet this great challenge, and my friends must have faith in me. It's a different matter, of course, when the usual Court theatre Intendant is dealing with such people: they are at once possessed by the devil that *I* know how to control. I need about 20 soloists; these will not cost me more than 30,000 thalers for the two months, or else–I should be wasting my time with them anyway. 100 musicians at 50 thalers a months, 10,000 thalers altogether at the outside. I *guarantee* this – for this is *my* empire.

Bayreuther Briefe, p. 78 f.

In 'Das Bühnenfestspielhaus zu Bayreuth' (1873), Wagner describes the ceremonial laying of the foundation stone of the

The time now seemed ripe to embark on the necessary preparations for carrying out my undertaking. Quietly and unnoticed, I was considering my eventual choice, *Bayreuth*, for the purpose as early as the spring of 1871; the idea I entertained of using the famous Margraves' Opera House was abandoned as soon as I became cognizant of its interior construction; but the character and the position of the hospitable town itself were what I had been seeking, so I made a return visit there in the wintry late autumn of the same year, but this time in order to make a direct approach to the civic authorities. I do not need to reiterate here the profound gratitude that I owe those worthy and much-respected men, whose welcome and co-operation in my bold undertaking have far exceeded my hopes, providing the soil in which my own life is to flourish from now on. I was given an incomparably beautiful and extensive site, not far from the town itself, on which to build my theatre. After I had agreed on its structure with a man of proven ingenuity and invention, and with distinguished professional experience in the interior layout of theatres, we were able to entrust the more detailed design and execution of the provisional building to an architect who was also experienced in theatre construction; and in spite of the great difficulties which arose in organizing the whole, unusual project, we made progress enough to be able to invite our friends and patrons to the ceremony of laying the foundation stone on 22 May 1872.

187, 188   I then hit on the idea of offering the patrons who came for the ceremony as accomplished a performance as possible of our *Beethoven's* great Ninth Symphony, as a form of artistic recompense for their trouble in making the journey. A simple invitation to the best orchestras, choruses and famous individual artists sufficed to procure a body of performers of such quality as can hardly ever before have been assembled for such a purpose. One could not help but look on this first success as a highly encouraging omen for the later success of the great theatrical performances themselves. It induced so excellent a humour in all participants that even the inclemency of the weather, which marred the actual laying of the stone, was unable to suppress the mood of cheerful excitement. The stone enclosed a capsule in which we had placed a message from the noble protector who has made my best work and creativity possible, a number of relevant documents and, additionally, a verse composed by myself:

> Hier schliess' ich ein Geheimniss ein,
> da ruh' es viele hundert Jahr':
> so lange es verwahrt der Stein,
> macht es der Welt sich offenbar.

('May the secret that I bury here rest undisturbed for many a century; as long as the stone covers it, it will continue to declare itself to the whole world.')

I made the following speech to the assembled gathering:

'My friends and honoured patrons!
Thanks to you, I stand today in a position such as surely no artist before me has ever occupied. You believe in my promise to found a national theatre for the German people, and you are giving me the means to construct a prototype of that theatre for them to see. For the time being, that purpose shall be served by the provisional building whose foundation stone we are laying today. When we meet here again, you will be greeted by the sight of that building, and you will be able to read at once in its unique characteristics the history of the idea it embodies. You will see an outer casing executed in the meanest materials, which will remind you at best of the wooden pavilions which used to be knocked up hastily on occasion in German towns, for choral festivals and similar gatherings, and dismantled again immediately after the event. But as soon as you enter this building you will begin to realize which of its features are intended to be more durable. Inside, too, you will at first be aware of the poverty of the materials, the complete lack of decoration; you will perhaps be surprised to notice the absence even of that minimal ornamentation usually found in those wooden pavilions. But instead you will find expressed in the proportions and the arrangement of the auditorium and the seats an idea, the comprehension of which will at once place you in a new relationship to the drama you will have come to see, and different from any that you have previously experienced in our theatres. Should this first impression be already pure and perfect, the subsequent mysterious entry of the music will prepare you for the unveiling and visible presentation of scenes such as you might imagine had come from an ideal world of dreams, which will reveal to you the complete reality of the most intelligent deception of a noble art. There will be nothing "provisional" here, to engage you with mere hints; the most up-to-date artistic resources will be used to offer you scenic and mimetic perfection.'

. . . Coming now to an exposition of the plan according to which the Festival theatre is now being built in Bayreuth, I believe I can best start by referring again to my conviction that the technical 'hearth' of the music, the orchestra, must be concealed from view; for this *one* essential priority was the source from which the whole shape of the auditorium of our neo-European theatre gradually emerged.

Readers of my earlier publications on the subject will already be familiar with my views on the concealment of the orchestra, and even if their own experience did not already bear me out, I hope that subsequent attendance at a performance of an opera in today's conditions will have convinced them that I am right to condemn the annoyance and distraction caused by the constant and inescapable visibility of the technical apparatus necessary to the production of sound. In my essay on Beethoven I have explained how, ultimately, through the force with which the whole sensory system is tuned to another pitch during overwhelming performances of great works of music, the evil I deplore can be rendered unobtrusive, in that one's sight can be neutralized, as it were. But when it is a question of a theatrical performance, the sight must be accurately tuned and alert to perceive the scene, and that can only be achieved if it is completely impossible to see anything of the reality that may intervene, such as the technical apparatus used to create the stage-set itself.

Accordingly the orchestra had to be placed, without being covered, at a depth such that the spectator would look directly over the top of it to the stage; it followed inevitably that the only way to place the seats was in rows climbing in regular steps to an ultimate height determined solely by one's ability to obtain a clear view of the stage from it. Our whole system of tiers of boxes was thus ruled out, because from their height, beginning as they do immediately beside the proscenium, a view into the orchestra could not be prevented. And so the arrangements of our seating took on the character of the amphitheatre of ancient Greece; except that there could be no question of the amphitheatre's extending itself so far round on both sides as to form a semi-circle or even greater segment, because while the spectators in the Greek theatre directed their gaze on the chorus in the *orchestra* that was thus almost entirely surrounded, the object of the spectators' vision in our theatre is the stage, merely a shallow projection to the Greeks, but used by us in its full depth.

Consequently we had to subject ourselves totally to the laws of perspective, which permitted the rows of seats to be widened steadily as they climbed, so long as they continued to face the stage directly. With that proviso, the *proscenium* governed all other aspects of construction; the actual frame of the stage necessarily became the fundamental constant from which all else proceeded. My stipulation that the orchestra should be concealed at once suggested to the genius of the famous architect, with whom I was fortunate enough to deliberate in the first instance, the proper function of the void thus created between the proscenium arch and the seats of the audience: we called it the 'mystic abyss', because it served to separate the real from the ideal, and the master enclosed it to the front by a second, wider proscenium arch, the effect of which in relation to the smaller proscenium arch behind it, he was sure, would create the miraculous illusion that the scene looks further back than it actually is, miraculous because the spectator has the impression that what is happening on the stage is remote, and yet can see it with perfect clarity because really it is close; and that creates the further illusion that the figures on the stage are of enlarged, superhuman stature.

The result of this arrangement ought to suffice in itself to give an idea of the incomparable effect of the relationship so created between the spectator and the scene on the stage. As soon as he has taken his seat, the spectator finds himself quite truly in a '*theatron*', that is, in a room which is made for no other purpose than for him to look into, specifically, in the direction indicated by his position. There is nothing clearly perceptible between himself and the stage tableau, but merely a distance, suspended as it were between the two proscenium arches by architectonic means, which holds the stage remote from him and gives it the unapproachability of a vision in a dream, while the music rising ghost-like from the 'mystic abyss', like the vapours rising beneath the seat of Pythia from the holy womb of Gaia, transports him into that visionary rapture in which the scene spread before him now becomes the truest image of life itself. . . .

It was specifically the means made available to us that governed our decision to include nothing in our building that was not strictly functional or necessary to achieving our objective: but the function and the objective consisted solely in creating the proper relationship between the auditorium and a stage planned on the largest scale to accommodate scenery perfect in every way.

Richard Wagner, *Das Bühnenfestspielhaus zu Bayreuth. Nebst einem Berichte über die Grundsteinlegung desselben*, Leipzig 1873, pp. 8–11, 15f., 21–4, 26

Wagner sent the preceding text, accompanied by the following letter, to Otto von Bismarck on 26 June 1873. His hopes of gaining the German Imperial Chancellor's interest and patronage for the Festival undertaking proved illusory. Bismarck did not even trouble to answer his letter.

Letter from Wagner to Bismarck, 26 June 1873:

Most honoured Prince! Your Serene Highness would perhaps obtain the clearest explanation of why I considered it essential at least to attempt to bring the contents of my pamphlet to your attention, by reading its final pages. No one will understand more readily than I if Your Highness is unable to do me even that small honour; but some might think it a regrettable omission on my part if I allowed apprehension to deter me from leaving unexplored any proper path whereby I may acquaint the great restorer of German hopes with the cultural idea that inspires me, and that I feel myself compelled to express in terms the nation will understand, devoting the greatest exertions of which I am capable to the task. Since I am forced to acknowledge that any further attempt to engage Your Serene Highness's attention by persuasive means would be both improper and futile, then I wish that these lines will at the very least excuse any annoyance my missive may have caused. Nevertheless I am confident that even in your eyes it will seem allowable for me to express my anxiety at the thought that an enterprise such as mine should be put into execution without the participation of the only truly beneficial and ennobling authority, whose approval is necessarily of the profoundest importance to me. If such were to be the case, however, I would have to console myself with the fate that befell the renascence of the German spirit through the agency of our great poets of the second half of the last century, which the true hero of the renascence, Frederick the Great, persistently regarded with cold antipathy.

With the expression of my boundless respect, Your Serene Highness's most sincere admirer, Richard Wagner

Richard Wagner an Freunde und Zeitgenossen, 2nd ed., Berlin and Leipzig 1909, p. 560f.

———

Wagner had first made the acquaintance of the Austrian composer Anton Bruckner in Munich in 1865. Bruckner visited Bayreuth early in September 1873 and asked Wagner to accept the dedication of one of his symphonies. He also attended the Festivals in 1876 and 1882.

Anton Bruckner on the dedication of his Symphony No. 3 in D minor, in a letter to Hans von Wolzogen, written in 1891:

[undated]

My Lord Baron!
It was about the beginning of Sept. '73 (Crown Prince Frederick was in Bayreuth at the time) when I asked the master if I might show him my No. 2 in *C minor* and No. 3 in *D minor*. The Thrice-blessed refused because of lack of time (the theatre was being built) and said he couldn't look at the scores now, since even the 'Nibelungen' had had to be laid on one side. When I replied: 'Master I have no right to rob you of even $\frac{1}{4}$ of an hour, and I only thought

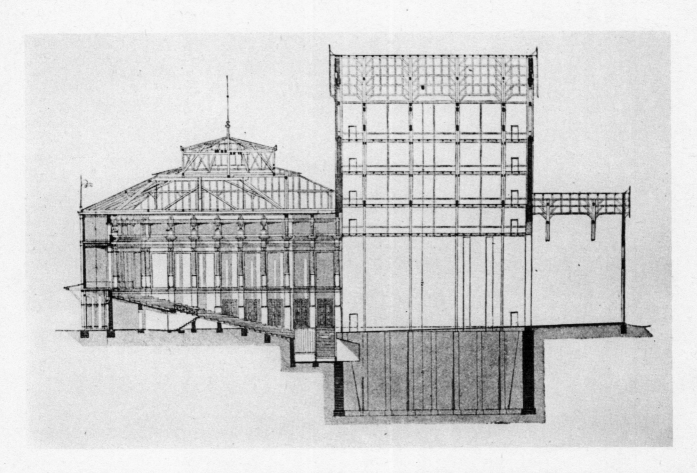

Drawings, showing section and view of auditorium of the Bayreuth Festival Theatre, appended to 'Das Bühnenfestspielhaus zu Bayreuth', Leipzig 1873. Cf. pp. 220ff.

that with the master's powerful perception, a single glance at the themes would suffice for the master to know the substance of it.' Thereupon the master said, slapping me on the shoulder, 'Come on then', went with me into the salon and looked at the 2nd [Symphony]. 'Very good', he said, but he seemed to find it rather tame, . . . and picked up No. 3 (*D minor*), and exclaiming 'let's see, let's see – well – ah! – ', he went through the whole of section 7 (the exalted one singled out the trumpet part and then said: 'Leave this work here with me, I will take a closer look at it after dinner' (it was 12 o'clock). I thought to myself, 'Shall I make my request?', when Wagner asked me what was on my mind. Very shyly, my heart pounding, I then said to my dearly beloved master: 'Master! I have something in my heart, that I do not trust myself to say!' The master said: 'Out with it! You know how much I like you.' Thereupon I made my request, but only in the event of the master's not disapproving, since I did not want to profane his thrice-famous name. The master said: 'This evening, at 5 o'clock, you are invited to Wahnfried,* I shall be there, and after I've had the chance to look at the *D minor* symphony properly, we'll talk about *this matter* again.' I had been up to the theatre site immediately before I went to Wahnfried at 5 o'clock. When I arrived the master of masters hurried towards me with open arms, hugged me and said: 'My dear friend, the dedication is quite all right. The work gives me *uncommonly great pleasure.*' For $2\frac{1}{2}$ hours I was fortunate enough to sit beside the master, while he talked about musical affairs in Vienna, offered me beer, took me out in the garden and showed me his *grave*!!! Then I had, or rather was permitted, blissfully happy, to accompany the master into his house. The next day he sent good wishes for a pleasant journey – adding, 'to where the trumpet introduces the theme'. In Vienna and in Bayreuth he often asked if the symphony had already been performed; '*perform it, perform it.*' In '82, already sick, the master took me by the hand and said: 'Rely upon it, I myself will perform the symphony and all your works.' I said: 'O Master!', whereupon the master replied: 'Have you been to *Parsifal* yet? Do you like it?' Since he had hold of my hand, I went down on my knees, pressing his noble hand to my lips and kissing it, and said: 'O Master, I worship you!!!' Then the master said: 'Gently now, Bruckner, good *night*!!!' This was the last thing the master ever said to me. The next day the master sent me one more threatening message, from where he sat behind me during *Parsifal*, because I was applauding so strenuously.

My lord baron, please take great care of this! My most precious bequest!!! – until I arrive up there!!!

My lord baron,

My stomach!!!   Your most grateful A. Bruckner

Anton Bruckner, *Gesammelte Briefe, Neue Folge*, ed. Max Auer, Regensburg 1924, p. 166 ff.

It was intended to finance the Festival undertaking by selling a thousand Patrons' subscriptions at 300 thalers each. Fewer were sold than expected, and work was in danger of coming to a

* Bruckner was mistaken about the date; Wagner did not occupy Wahnfried until 28 April 1874

halt in the autumn of 1873. For this reason a meeting of Patrons was called in Bayreuth on 31 October 1873. At Wagner's request, Friedrich Nietzsche composed his 'Mahnruf an die Deutschen' ('Exhortation to the Germans'), which, as Nietzsche said in a letter to his friend Gersdorff, the meeting 'politely but firmly' rejected.

Nietzsche's 'Mahnruf an die Deutschen', October 1873:

In France, or England, or Italy, or even in one of our smaller neighbours, if a man who, in the teeth of all public opinion and authority, had presented the nation's theatres with five works written in a uniquely great, powerful and thoroughly national style, which were then in constant demand from one end of the country to the other and cheered everywhere to the echo – if such a man cried: 'Our existing theatres are alien to the spirit of the nation, as public art they are a disgrace! Help me to build something worthy of the national spirit!', would not everyone come to his aid, if only out of a sense of self-respect? Of course! And here the spur would be not only a sense of respect, not only the blind fear of acquiring a bad reputation, but the chance that you would all have of uniting with each other, of learning and knowing together, of rejoicing together from the bottom of your hearts, when you resolved to help in the common cause. All your sciences are generously supplied by you with costly experimental laboratories; and will you stand idly by, when there is an opportunity to build a laboratory for the questing, experimenting spirit of German art? . . .

We believe that wherever Richard Wagner has aroused, and continues to arouse, indignation, the reaction hides a great and fruitful problem of our culture; but when, as so often, the indignation results only in critical conceit and ridicule, and so rarely in thoughtful reconsideration, it tends to inspire in us the shaming suspicion that perhaps the 'Race of Thinkers' has already exhausted its capacity for thought, and has replaced thought by conceit. What a tangle of mistaken notions there is in circulation, how often we have had to contradict the notion that what took place in Bayreuth in May 1872 had something to do with building a new theatre, and to explain that no existing theatre is capable of fulfilling the purpose of that undertaking; what pains one must take to open the eyes of those intentionally or unintentionally blind to the fact that the word 'Bayreuth' is important to more than a limited number of people, a claque with particular musical tastes: that it is important to the nation as a whole: that it is a clarion call, sounding far beyond the frontiers of Germany alone, inviting the serious and active involvement of all those who have at heart the cause of ennobling and purifying drama, and who have understood Schiller's marvellous intuition that tragedy may one day emerge from opera in a nobler shape. Whoever has not yet forgotten how to think – even if, again, it is only due to his sense of self-respect – must acknowledge and approve the *moral* implications of an artistic undertaking which is supported to such an extent by the readiness for sacrifice and the selfless enthusiasm of all involved, that man must see that the undertaking is hallowed by their earnest avowal of a lofty and severe opinion of art and of their hopes, specifically, that German music and its transfiguring effect on popular drama will prove to be the most important agent in encouraging an original, German way of life. Let us confess to an even loftier and more general belief: the German nation will only appear honourable and redemptive in the eyes of other nations when it has shown both that it is to be feared and that *it wishes this fear to be forgotten in the exercise of its loftiest and noblest artistic and cultural powers.*

We believe it our duty to recall the Germans to a sense of their obligations at this time, when we must appeal to them to summon all their strength in support of a great artistic enterprise, born of German genius. We expect to hear a joyful, sympathetic response from wherever the fires of serious thought still glow in our tumultuous age: the German universities, academies and schools of art, in particular, will not let us call out in vain, but will promise the support we ask, whether individually or corporately; and those political representatives of German interests in the imperial and provincial parliaments, too, have good cause to consider that, now more than ever, the people need the purification and dedication that the sublime enchantment and dread of genuine German art alone can give them, if the powerfully excited urgings of political and national passions, and the headlong pursuit of happiness and pleasure, whose traits are inscribed on the physiognomy of our life, are not to compel our descendants to admit that we Germans began to lose ourselves at the moment when we had at last found ourselves.

[Postscript addressed to Wagner:]
Here is my draft, dear master. I really wanted to read it aloud to you myself, with full dramatic expression, but it seems better that it should reach you as quickly as possible. If it more or less measures up to its intentions (to enrage the evil and, through that anger, to unite and inspire the good) then I think it is important that there should be no delay in translating it into French, Italian, and probably English as well, for obvious reasons. As for the *signatories,* I think it would be better if these are not representatives of the subscribing Patrons, but rather a fairly small body, *selected by us,* of men from a wide range of classes and callings (nobles, civil servants, politicians, clergy, academics, businessmen, artists). Each one will have to be sent a copy of this appeal and asked if he is willing to put his signature to it. I will bring with me enough copies for that purpose. As soon as we have their replies, the definitive version must be printed as quickly as possible. A short note on the practical, business aspect will have to be appended to the text, below the rule and the names; we can discuss all that on Friday. I shall arrive on Thursday afternoon.

Yours in faith and love, F.N.

RWA

On 28 April 1874 Wagner and his family moved into their new house, Wahnfried. Prior to that they had lived in the Hotel Fantaisie at Donndorf, outside Bayreuth, and on the Dammallee. Wahnfried, partly paid for by a gift of 25,000 thalers from Ludwig II, and erected by the Bayreuth master-builder Carl Wölfel, became one of the foremost artists' houses of the nineteenth century.

Wagner on Wahnfried, in a letter to Ludwig II, Bayreuth, 25 May 1874:

My house is finished: thanks to your generosity! I had to give it a name and sought one in vain for a long time; at last I have thought of one, and I am having it inscribed in the following verse:

Hier wo mein Wähnen Frieden fand
Wahnfried
sei dieses Haus von mir benannt!

('Let this house be called "Peace after madness", because here my longings found peace.')

In the middle of the open space in front of the house, there is a circular piece of grass enclosed by a hedge; and in the middle of that I have had a granite plinth erected, which as yet bears nothing. But I have already contacted Master Zumbusch, and have come to an understanding with him about a bronze cast of the bust of the hero of my life, to whom I first paid homage ten years ago, as the gracious protector to whom I owe my existence. It shall be the youthful god, as the sculptor captured him then, when he called me in the darkness; but he shall soar up, double life-size, from among the rose bushes in front of the house; I think it will then be easy to understand the inscription above the door. And whoever then enters the house will learn from the marbles in the hall, the frieze with the Nibelung Ring, what else there is to know about the hallowed associations that the bronze head outside has for 'Wahnfried'.

Königsbriefe, vol. 3, p. 35

Susanne Weinart, a governess in the Wagner household 1875–6, describes Wagner's study in Wahnfried in her diary:

It is a large room overlooking the garden. The floor is covered with a carpet patterned in black and dark red, and a second carpet, in brighter, matt colours is laid on top of that. The walls are papered in red and lined with bookshelves, on which expensively bound volumes are arrayed in the most orderly fashion. From the earliest origins of German literature to the present day, the works of native and foreign *coryphaei,* the antagonists in every field of human knowledge, stand peacably next to each other.... Opposite the desk there is a valuable grand piano. Otherwise the room is filled with luxurious furniture in unforced order, or inspired disorder. Here, in a cosy corner, an armchair covered in yellow satin. There, a carmine-red *causeuse,* with soft upholstery that one positively sinks into; facing the fireplace we espy a charming little sofa covered with gaily patterned silk damask, before it a small oval table bearing a cloth that hangs down very low, in sky-blue satin with a woven flower pattern in silver; throughout the room there are scattered small tables, pouffes and chairs in a variety of shapes, a richly gilded flower-stand laden with beautiful exotic plants, and hanging over everything, suspended from the ceiling, a magnificent chandelier, whose radiance lends a homely glow to the colourful clutter in the evenings.

Burrell-Briefe, p. 569 f.

196, 197

In a letter of 19 September 1874, Ludwig II asked Wagner to describe his day-to-day life in Bayreuth, and to report on the progress of the preparations for the festival.

Wagner to Ludwig II, Bayreuth, 1 October 1874:

... My principal assistant and adviser in the whole practical side of the production has from the first been *Carl Brandt* of Darmstadt, a scene-builder of genius; he helped me find the architect to carry out the extremely difficult structure, but he was always at a loss to find the right man to recommend as a scene-designer, since what we wanted were truly artistic innovations in a new style, not merely the usual style of stage sets, however competently executed. I came upon the right man by chance. The painter *Joseph Hoffmann* designed and painted two lots of sets for the opening of the new opera house in Vienna, for *The Magic Flute* and *Der Freischütz* (which were generally acknowledged to be excellent), although he had never worked in the theatre before, and he completely withdrew from it again afterwards. At the beginning of last year I invited him to sketch designs for every part of my work, which he completed and showed me by the autumn. Not I alone, but everyone who saw them – including the leading cognoscenti in Vienna – was delighted in the highest degree by his work: the most difficult challenge of all, the appearance of Valhalla in *Das Rheingold*, we had to wonder at as a truly inspired stroke of genius. However, this artist has no workshop and no assistants of the sort he would need for building sets; since he would have had to set everything up from scratch, we came to an arrangement with him, that the sets should be built and painted, under his supervision, by the *Brückner* brothers, painters to the Court Theatre in Coburg, for whom Brandt furnished excellent references. . . .

I have accordingly drawn up the following programme, which must be strictly adhered to, for the musical and dramatic preparation of the performance. The singers that I shall have selected before this year, 1874, is out, will have to come to Bayreuth next year for the whole of July and August, to spend the first month studying their parts at the piano, and the second month rehearsing on the stage, with the major part of the scenery already set up, so that they will already know their roles well enough to be able to proceed immediately, in the following year, to the so-called dress rehearsals. I cannot engage any singer who is unable to commit himself to me unconditionally both for the two months indicated in 1875 and for the three months of June, July and August 1876. For in 1876 we shall begin immediately with the full rehearsals for all four evenings at once; spending the first two months rehearsing the company with the orchestra, the machinery and the lighting every day, I envisage that we shall progress well enough for me to go ahead with the three projected complete performances in August. They will take place in the second, third and fourth weeks of the month, beginning with *Das Rheingold* on a Saturday in each case, and the three principal works on the days immediately following. Each performance will begin at 4 o'clock in the afternoon: the second act will follow at 6 o'clock and the third at 8 o'clock, allowing a substantial interval between each of the acts, which will be the opportunity for the audience to walk in the gardens surrounding the theatre,

226

and to take refreshments in the open air amid delightful surroundings, so that when the trumpets sound from the upper storey of the theatre to recall them to the auditorium, they will be fully refreshed and as receptive as they were at the beginning of the first act. I think, too, that the sunset before the last act will induce a particularly elevated mood.
Königsbriefe, vol. 3, p. 40 ff.

In the same letter to the king, Wagner describes the sgraffito 196
on the façade of Wahnfried:

In fact my wife had the excellent idea of having a 'scrafito' executed by a friend of ours, a young history painter, *Krausse* of Weimar, who has truly mastered that art form. It is to be a monumental representation of the 'Art Work of the Future'. The central figure is Germanic Myth; since we wanted the figures to have characteristic physiognomies, this one has been given the head of the late *Ludwig Schnorr*; Wotan's ravens are flying down to him from each side, and he is relating the tidings they bring him to two female figures, one representing Classical Tragedy, a portrait of Schröder-Devrient, and the other Music, with the head and figure of Cosima; a small boy, armed like Siegfried and with the head of my son, holds her by the hand and looks up at his mother, Music, with bold delight. I believe it will be wonderfully successful.
Königsbriefe, vol. 3, p. 49 f.

In March and in May 1875 Wagner gave five concerts in Vienna, 199, 204
to raise funds for the Festival Theatre. The Austrian painter Hans Makart held one of his famous studio parties on 3 March in Wagner's honour.

Wagner to Hans Makart, Bayreuth, 31 March 1875:

Most honoured Sir and Friend,
What must you think of me, still labouring under the charge of ingratitude, ever since the incomparable evening party that you arranged for me in your wonderful studio? Of course I had no idea at the time that I would not have a single opportunity of seeing you again while I was in Vienna. But there really was no opportunity, and now I have no other choice but to press your hand in thanks for your great kindness, very late and by letter. Now that, too, gives me great pain and I would certainly have misgivings, were I not sure that I can rely on your magnanimity, your outstanding characteristic both as an artist and as a man, which will certainly lead you to forgive me, or at least not to attribute my fault to indifference.

It was a wonderful evening, for the success of your hospitality was such that it was really possible to delude oneself that one was somewhere else altogether, in an altogether different age, among people altogether different from those whom we seem always to meet nowadays. It is with the readiest and the most cordial gratitude that I now greet you from afar with the greatest regard as

    Your most indebted and devoted Richard Wagner
RWA

I.
Grosses scenisches Vorspiel.
II.
Siegfried's Tod.
III.
Schlussscene des letzten Actes.

Orchester der k. k. Hofoper.

Gesang: Frau Friedrich-Materna, k. k. Hofopernsängerin, Herr F. Glatz.

Preise der Plätze:

Cercle-Sitze	fl. 20
Im Parterre 5. bis 17. Reihe, in der 1. Reihe der Logen und der 1. Galerie	fl. 10
Im Parterre 18. bis 30. Reihe, in der 2. Reihe der Logen und der Orgelgalerie 1. Reihe	fl. 8
Logensitze in der 3. Reihe, 1. Galerie Mitte 2. bis 7. Reihe und Divansitze	fl. 5
1. Galerie Seite 2. und 3. Reihe und Orgelgalerie 2. und 3. Reihe	fl. 3
2. Galerie	fl. 3
Eintritt	fl. 1

Der Billetenverkauf findet ausschließlich in der Kanzlei der Gesellschaft der Musikfreunde täglich zwischen 9 bis 12 und 3 bis 5 Uhr statt.

Den Stiftern und Gründern wird das Vorbezugsrecht auf ihre Sitze vom 11. bis 15. Februar Mittags vorbehalten. Vormerkungen auf Sitzplätze werden in der Gesellschafts-Kanzlei gegen Erlag des bezüglichen Betrages angenommen, woselbst auch vom 16. Februar angefangen die Ausgabe der vorgemerkten Billets stattfindet.

Die Vormerkungen werden am 15. Februar Mittags geschlossen und tritt der Einzelverkauf ein.

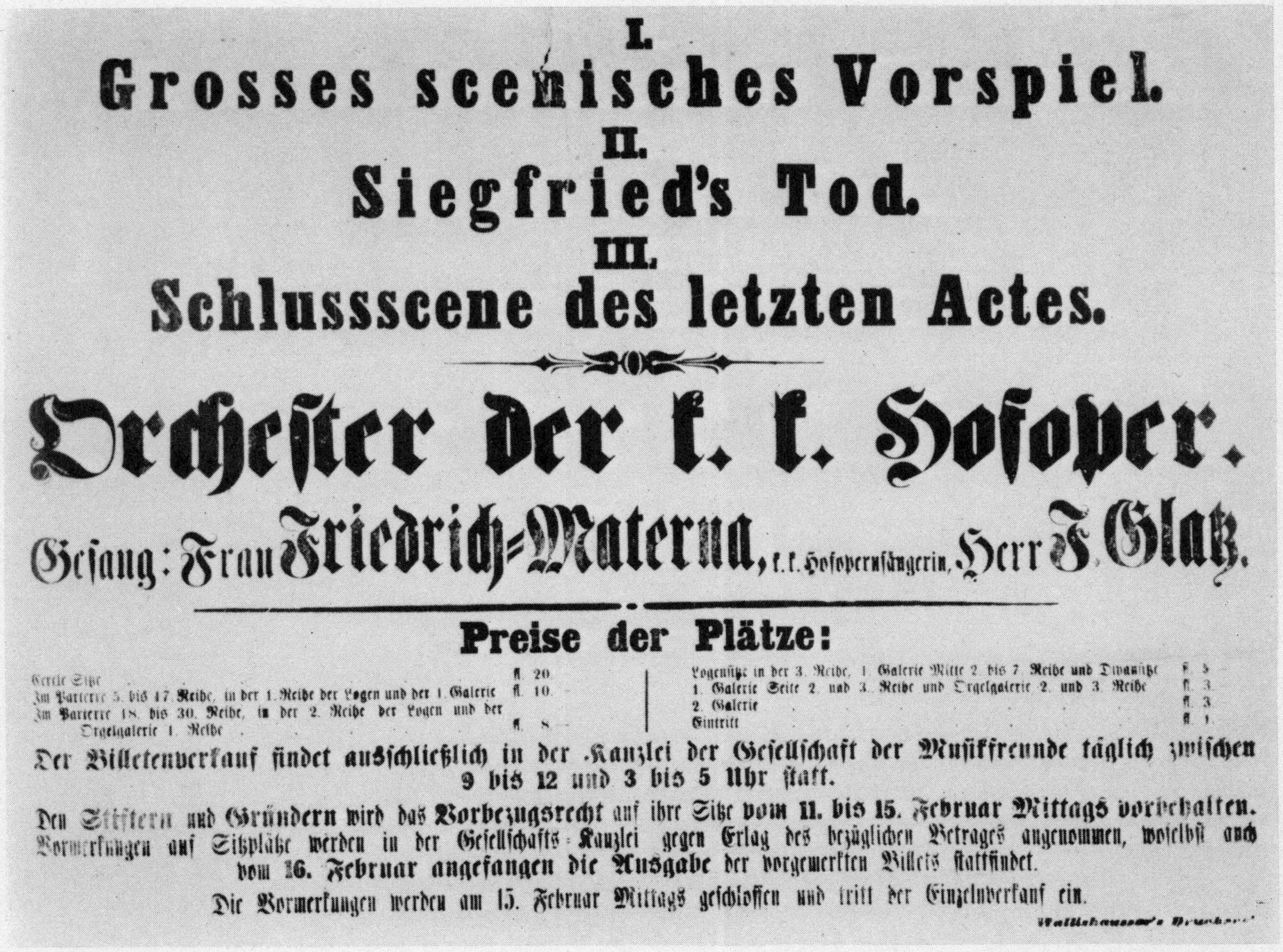

Announcement of Wagner's concert in Vienna; 1 March 1875 (see also overleaf). The programme, which consisted of excerpts from *Siegfrieds Tod*, was played by the orchestra of the Royal Court Opera House with the singers Amalie Materna and F. Glatz; it included the Grand Prelude, the death of Siegfried from Act III and the closing scene of the opera. Gesellschaft der Musikfreunde, Vienna.

Preliminary rehearsals took place in Bayreuth in the summer of
209 1875. The interior of the theatre was ready except for the seating and gas lighting, and the sets were not yet completely finished. Wagner rehearsed with the soloists at the piano and on the stage from 1 July to 31 July, followed by rehearsals with the orchestra, under the direction of Hans Richter, from 1 to 12 August, with the sets on stage for some sessions. Adolph
207 von Menzel made a drawing of Wagner at the table where he sat during the rehearsals. Great enthusiasm. Erwin Rohde wrote to Nietzsche that Wagner made a remarkably lively and 'elastic' impression. Franz Liszt was one of many friends who came to watch.

Franz Liszt to the historian Carl Hillebrand, Bayreuth, 2 August 1875:

The newspapers will be keeping you *au courant* with the wonders of the Wagner theatre here in Bayreuth. The performances of the tetralogy *Der Ring des Nibelungen* (announced for August '76) will be the pinnacle of dramatic art, both as a whole and in its separate components of poetry, music, mimetic art, scene design and stage presentation, united with a mastery unprecedented in this century.

There is not merely a chance, it is a certainty that it will be a great success, a *succès fou*, in view of the sublimity of the work itself and in view of the enthusiasm which it already arouses in the large number of artists entrusted with its interpretation. In spite of the difficulties of Wagner's outstanding new style, learning and rehearsing the work are a delight to the singers and to the orchestral players.

Franz Liszts Briefe, ed. La Mara, vol. 2, Leipzig 1893, p. 224f. (original French)

The sculptor Gustav Adolph Kietz's recollections of the preliminary rehearsals in 1875:

Wagner arrived outside the theatre just before five o'clock. As he entered with his family, he was greeted with a rendering of '*Vollendet das ewige Werk*' and, when that was over, with three hearty cheers.

Wagner was deeply moved, went into the orchestra pit and spoke warmly to the musicians, while we all listened with the greatest attention. Among other things he said: 'There will no doubt be widely differing opinions

hilde auf: Siegfried in den Waffen der Walküre, welche ihm, da er auf neue Thaten auszieht, auch ihr Ross übergibt. Feurige Gelöbnisse; Treueschwäre: heldenhafter Abschied. — Siegfried führt sein Ross den Felsenabhang hinab: jauchzend ruft ihm Brünnhilde nach, bis jener ihrem Auge plötzlich, wie hinter einem Felsenvorsprung, entschwindet, und sie nur noch seinen Hornruf aus der Tiefe vernimmt: dann erblickt sie ihn aber wieder, wie er in weiterer Ferne rüstig von dannen zieht: überwältigt winkt sie ihm noch einmal zu. Durch das den Felsen umgebende Feuer, dessen Flammen mit hellem Getöne ihn lustig zu umtanzen scheinen, zieht Jener nun, rüstig sein Horn blasend, weiter davon, bis er an den Rhein gelangt, wo die Rheintöchter ihn, als ihren Helden und Erlöser, zur ferneren Fahrt in Willkommen nehmen. Sie geleiten ihn dorthin, wo nun, am Hofe der Gibichungen, durch Hagen, den Erben des Nibelungenringes, sich sein Schicksal erfüllen soll. —

II.

Siegfried's Tod.

(Dieses Bruchstück des dritten Aktes beginnt bei dem Auffliegen der Raben Wotan's, am Schlusse der Erzählung Siegfried's von seinem ersten Abenteuer mit Brünnhilde. Das Orchester begleitet den, hier nur als pantomimisch dargestellt zu denkenden Vorgang, welchen der scenische Text mit Folgendem giebt.)

Zwei Raben fliegen aus einem Busche auf, kreisen über Siegfried und fliegen davon. Siegfried fährt auf, und blickt, Hagen den Rücken wendend, den Raben nach. Hagen stösst seinen Speer in Siegfried's Rücken. Siegfried schwingt mit beiden Händen seinen Schild hoch empor, Hagen damit zu zerschmettern: die Kraft verlässt ihn, der Schild entsinkt seiner Hand; er selbst stürzt krachend über ihm zusammen. Hagen, auf den zu Boden Gestreckten weisend, bedeutet, dass er nur einen Meineid gerächt habe; worauf er sich ruhig zur Seite abwendet, und langsam über die Höhe davon schreitet. Gunther beugt sich, schmerzlich ergriffen, zu Siegfried's Seite nieder. Die Mannen umstehen theilnahmvoll den Sterbenden. Da schlägt Siegfried noch einmal die Augen glanzvoll auf, und beginnt mit feierlicher Stimme:

3

„Brünnhilde —
heilige Braut —
wach' auf! öff'ne dein Auge! —
Wer verschloss dich
wieder in Schlaf? —
Wer band dich in Schlummer so bang? —
Der Wecker kam;
er küsst dich wach,
und aber der Braut
bricht er die Bande: —
da lacht ihm Brünnhilde's Lust! —
Ach, dieses Auge,
ewig nun offen! —
Ach, dieses Athem's
wonniges Wehen! —
Süsses Vergehen —
seliges Grauen —:
Brünnhild bietet mir — Gruss!"

Er stirbt. — Lange Stille der tiefsten Erschütterung. — Die Mannen erheben dann die Leiche auf den Schild, und geleiten sie in feierlichem Trauerzuge über die Felshöhe langsam von dannen. Diesen letzteren scenischen Vorgang begleitet das Orchester in der Weise eines Trauerchores, welcher zugleich die Herkunft, die Herrlichkeit, sowie das Schicksal des als göttlich gepriesenen Helden feiert und beklagt.

III.

Schluss-Scene des letzten Aktes.

(Auch dieses Bruchstück beginnt mitten in einer heftigen Handlung. Hagen hat, im Streit um den Nibelungenring, soeben Gunther erschlagen, und greift nun, mit dem Rufe: „her den Ring!", nach des todten Siegfried's Hand, welche sich ballt und drohend emporrichtet. Allgemeines Entsetzen und lauter Aufschrei, während dessen Brünnhilde, vom Hintergrunde her, fest und feierlich dem Vordergrunde zuschreitet.)

(Above) Pages 2 and 3 from the programme note for Wagner's concert in Vienna, 1 March 1875. See also preceding page.

Zum Richard Wagner-Konzert.

Der Erfolg war außerordentlich — dies schicken wir voraus. Wie ungleich großartiger würde sich derselbe aber erst gestaltet haben, wenn die Instrumentenmacher gleichen Schritt mit den Ideen des Meisters zu halten verstünden! Denn Eines steht fest: Richard Wagner braucht auch neue Klänge; Klänge, die sich dem jetzt in Gebrauch befindlichen Material nicht entlocken lassen. Es bleibt daher nichts übrig, als daß Kikeriki wieder seine Erfinderhose anzieht.

Nehmen wir beispielsweise an, man hätte ihm diese Monstre-Harfe zur Verfügung gestellt! Wie ganz anders wäre stellenweise die Wirkung gewesen!

Eine Katze, deren Bauch man mit dem Fiedelbogen streicht, müßte in der Instrumentation von Klageliedern eben so gut zu verwenden sein.

Das rapide Geklirre, womit Wagner gerne den Zusammenbruch irgend einer Seele ausdrückt, wäre durch das Ausleeren von Glasscherben gewiß ganz gut zu imitiren,

Gewisse schrille Töne, wie sie Richard Wagner in seinen Schöpfungen braucht, ließen sich doch so leicht mittelst schartiger Messer alten Porzellantellern entlocken.

wie der empfindliche Jagdhund, welcher den Ton einer Kindertrompete nicht verträgt, und daher mit seinem Jammer bis in's hohe C hinaufgeht.

während endlich gewisse Aufschreie und temperamentvolle Quirlschlaute sicherlich auf obige Weise zu Stande gebracht werden könnten.

Cartoons published in *Kikeriki* on the occasion of Wagner's concert in Vienna, 1 March 1875. Gesellschaft der Musikfreunde, Vienna.

about our great undertaking, but I believe that everyone participating in it will be convinced that it is a work of art of great significance, not an imposture.'

Then he went across the gangplank on to the stage, to his little table close to the orchestra pit. On the table was the heavy score leaning against a box, on which the oil-lamp stood.

Hans Richter was conducting. Wagner followed in the score, but was so excited that all the time he was moving not only his arms but his legs as well. Master Menzel managed to capture him in a crayon drawing in a very characteristic attitude, in spite of the darkness in the auditorium. I was extremely alarmed by the improvised desk; it would have been so easy for one of Wagner's lively gestures to send the table, box and lamp flying and set the whole place on fire! During a break I went to find Brand[t] and asked him to have the table screwed to the floor before the music resumed, so that the lamp could not be knocked over. He had it done at once and I was then able to abandon myself to the enjoyment of the music without anxiety.

Kietz, op. cit., p. 216f.

Wagner on the planned performances of the Ring *in 1876, Bayreuth 1875:*

The Stage Festival *Der Ring des Nibelungen*

will now definitely be performed in the summer of the year 1876 in the theatre specially built in Bayreuth. The three performances of the complete work promised to the patrons of my undertaking will take place on the following dates:

First performance:

Sunday,	13 August:	Das Rheingold
Monday,	14	,,	Die Walküre
Tuesday,	15	,,	Siegfried
Wednesday,	16	,,	Götterdämmerung

Second performance:

Sunday,	20 August:	Das Rheingold
Monday,	21	,,	Die Walküre
Tuesday,	22	,,	Siegfried
Wednesday,	23	,,	Götterdämmerung

Third performance:

Sunday,	27 August:	Das Rheingold
Monday,	28	,,	Die Walküre
Tuesday,	29	,,	Siegfried
Wednesday,	30	,,	Götterdämmerung

My warrant for making this definite announcement lies principally in the devotion and self-sacrificing zeal of the outstanding artists I have engaged, whose co-operation and punctilious observation of every obligation enabled this year's preliminary rehearsals to achieve an unprecedentedly high standard. If I now feel that my sole and true support is the sincere participation of my fellow artists, who have placed their noblest abilities at my disposal without honorarium, indeed for the most part without any compensation for real sacrifices, so I also believe that I may confidently look forward to such collaboration from

outside as my undertaking, eschewing as it does every form of profit, must claim if it is to be carried out in a business-like way. For I believe that there will be another success, for which I shall be able to thank the zeal, above all praise and free of every trace of self-interest, of my fellow artists: the German public's mistrust of an undertaking that could only be carried out with sacrifices on the part of everyone concerned in it, a mistrust incessantly and often shamelessly aroused and nourished in other quarters, will vanish.

Consequently I issue my invitation to assist this undertaking yet again; true to my original idea, I expect this assistance to take the form only of subscription to the patronage scheme, according to the published conditions, reiterated below; I remain steadfast in my intention of allowing impoverished artists and friends of art completely free entry to the performances, whilst the merely curious, who have rendered no assistance to the undertaking, will find that, however high the sums they may offer for admission to this performance or that, the Festival Theatre will remain barred to them.

Bayreuth, 28 August 1875   Richard Wagner

Schriften-Volksausgabe, vol. 16, p. 153f.

Extract from a newspaper article before the first Bayreuth Festival, 1876:

Richard Wagner's bold new building rises above the old seat of the margravate, just below the Bürgerreuth [hill]. The site is a substantial gift from the civic authorities. Anyone who visited the spot to observe the beginnings and further progress of the work could not help but be impressed. The building's dimensions are in fact astonishing, even at first glance. If you consider that the south front is 178 feet wide, while the building measures 236 feet at its widest point and the depth from the south front to the furthest extremity of the backstage area is also 236 feet, that the roof of the southern part, containing the auditorium, rises to a height of 82 feet, and that of the northern part, comprising the stage and backstage areas, to 120 feet, then even the most widely travelled student of theatrical architecture will abandon the hunt for parallels between the Wagner theatre and others in Germany. As for the interior, it leaves the beholder at a loss as to which is the more breathtaking, the grandeur of the dimensions or the originality of the overall architectonic conception. One particularly significant innovation, which has been under discussion for years now, is the concealment of the orchestra from the audience. While the idea may not be new by any means – Goethe, in *Wilhelm Meister*, already touched on the advantages of hearing instrumental music without needing to see it played – nevertheless the value of actually putting it into practice is not diminished for the idea's having been mocked, like Columbus's egg. Wagner explains his views on the subject at some length in the preface to *Der Ring des Nibelungen*; if his intention is to relieve the spectator of the inescapable sight of the mechanical actions of the players and the conductor with as much care as the ropes, pulleys, struts and boards of the sets are hidden, then the advent of the concealed orchestra, provided that there are no acoustic disadvantages outweighing the optical benefits, can only be hailed with delight. And where, in fact, is the orchestra, the technical 'hearth' of the music, located in the Bayreuth theatre? It is in a large niche, partly underneath the front part of the stage, in such a position that the niche is open towards the auditorium, and throws the sound waves out into it. The seats for the audience are placed in rows which climb in regular steps to a final height determined solely by the ability still to obtain a clear view of the stage from it. The whole system of tiers of boxes, found in most theatres, is thus ruled out, because from their levels, beginning as they do immediately beside the proscenium, a view into the orchestra could not be prevented. The auditorium climbs gradually, in 31 rows increasing from 32 to 64 seats each, after the model of the Greek amphitheatre. All in all it extends 112 feet in breadth, 106 feet in depth and 54 feet in height; it contains 2,000 seats. The stalls, comprising 1,500 seats, are reserved for the patrons, who have paid 300 thalers for the privilege of attending the whole Festival. In addition to the patrons, Wagner expects the presence of royalty. Boxes behind the stalls have been provided for this eventuality, and it is hoped to accommodate their highnesses in various ancient castles in the vicinity of Bayreuth. Higher still above the stalls there are 300 seats for artists, representatives of the press, and relatives of all those involved in the performances; Wagner is issuing a free ticket to each of these last, to dispose of as they please. With the inclusion of the 52-foot-wide offstage area, the total width of the stage is 95 feet, its depth is 126 feet, and the height from the floor below the stage to the roof above the grid is 135 feet. The space above the grid is twice the height of the stage, and the 36-foot-high space below the stage is likewise capable of receiving the sets all in one piece, so that they can disappear at once, without having to be rolled up. The building also incorporates some very practical measures against the risk of fire. Ground water collects in the depths of the foundations, on the one hand ensuring that the building is dry and on the other hand providing a reservoir, water from which is pumped by a steam engine into iron tanks below the roof, and from there numerous pipes lead to every corner of the building. The original design of the theatre was by Gottfried Semper; it was modified to suit the particular conditions of the site by the Leipzig architect, Otto Brückwald.

It is probably safe to say that rarely have so many outstanding talents united to work together on a major building as here in Bayreuth; the technical intelligence is working in complete agreement with the artistic intention; whatever has been pronounced theoretically and practically excellent in the widest variety of fields is here being realized. . . .

Illustrirte Zeitung, Leipzig, 29 April 1876

A letter written by Friedrich Nietzsche to greet Wagner on his birthday, 22 May 1876:

On a day such as your birthday, most highly honoured of men, only utterances of the most personal kind have any right to be heard; for everyone has experienced, thanks to you, something that affects him alone, in his heart of hearts. Experiences of that nature cannot be added together, and the expression of birthday greetings on behalf

Letter written by Friedrich Nietzsche on the occasion of Wagner's birthday, 22 May 1876 (for translation see text).

of a large number of people would be worth less today than the shyest word from an individual. It is almost exactly seven years since I paid my first visit to you at Triebschen, and I do not know what else I can say on the occasion of your birthday than that I too, since then, have celebrated my own spiritual birthday in May every year. For ever since then you have lived and moved incessantly in me like a new drop of blood that was certainly not in me before. This element, that had its origin in you, drives me, shames me, encourages me, spurs me on and has left me no peace, so that I could almost wish to berate you for this eternal agitation, were I not absolutely sure that this very unrest ceaselessly urges me on to be freer and better than I was. And so I must be most profoundly thankful to him who roused it in me; and the most shining hopes that I have for the events of this summer are that *many* will similarly be placed in the same state of unrest by you and your work, and thus receive a share of the greatness of your being and your life. My only wish for your happiness today is that that will happen (what other happiness is there, that one could wish you?). Receive the wish kindly, from the mouth of

Your truly devoted

Basle 1876   Friedrich Nietzsche
RWA

—————————

das aus Ihnen seinen Ursprung
hat, treibt, beschämt, ermuthigt, sta-
chelt mich und hat mir keine Ruhe
mehr gelassen, so dass ich beinahe
Lust haben könnte, Ihnen wegen
dieser ewigen Beunruhigung zu zürnen,
wenn ich nicht ganz bestimmt fühlte,
dass diese Unruhe mich gerade zum
Freier- und Besserwerden unaufhör-
lich antreibt. So muss ich dem,
welcher sie erregte, mit dem aller-
tiefsten Gefühle des Dankes dank-
bar sein; und meine schönsten Hoff-
nungen, die ich auf die Ereignisse
dieses Sommers setze, sind die, dass
Viele in einer ähnlichen Weise durch
Sie und Ihr Werk in jene Unruhe
versetzt werden und dadurch an der
Grösse Ihres Wesens und Lebens-
ganges einen Antheil bekommen.
Dass dies geschehen möge, das ist
heute mein einziger Glückwunsch
für Sie (wo gäbe es sonst das
Glück, das man Ihnen wünschen
könnte?) Nehmen Sie ihn freund-
lich an aus dem Munde
Ihres wahrhaft getreuen

Friedrich Nietzsche.

Basel 1876.

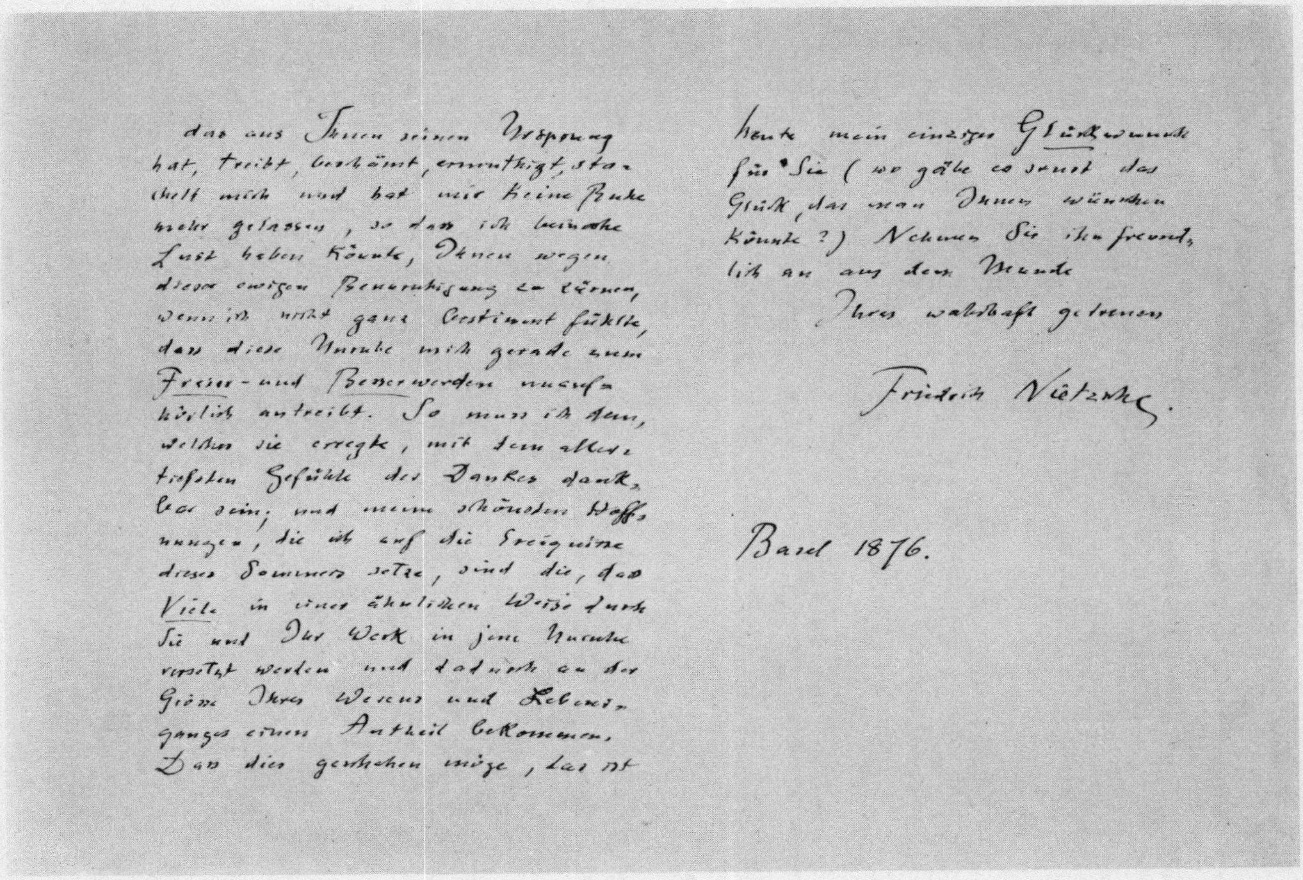

As early as 6 November 1872, Wagner wrote to Heinrich Porges asking him to follow the rehearsals with the utmost care and write down all his remarks, however closely related to a particular context, on the comprehension and the performance of the *Ring*, and thus 'publish a fixed tradition'.

Heinrich Porges writes in the introduction to 'Die Bühnenproben zu den Bayreuther Festspielen des Jahres 1876' (Rehearsals for the Bayreuth Festival of 1876):

'A *permanent institution* promoting the development of a classical tradition of *stylistic purity in the performance of original German works of music and music drama'* is what we have to create. Only if we achieve this aim, and what is more, do so within not too long a period will we be able to say that the performance of *Der Ring des Nibelungen* in 1876 had the result that was truly intended of it. For that undertaking was not simply a matter of presenting a new work of art to the public, its principal purpose was to allow the work to appear in its authentic form, to give an example of the only correct style for the performance of music drama, such as is still virtually unknown in our modern theatres. The erection of the Festival Theatre in Bayreuth and the performances of the *Ring* that then took place in it proved that the will to create the ideal drama was alive in at least a segment of the nation as a whole–and that that will could become deed. Here, for the first time, members of the public entered into the only proper relationship with art, not passively inactive, as audiences usually are, while artistic creations are presented to them, but playing a part themselves in calling the works into being. That general struggle to give birth to the work of art, however, is directly acted out by artistic fellowship. But fellowship of that kind is only created when a substantial number of individual artists awake to the realization that the power of divine creativity has gathered in one particular person to a pitch of irresistible force, and recognize further that their appointed task is to translate the ideal form, hovering as a mere possibility before the spirit of that genius, into the reality of outward, perceptible existence. And in turn that individual artist, whose inmost being has felt the breath of the divine spirit, will be governed by no other wish than to give to his fellow artists that which filled him with such blissful delight in solitary hours and through them to give it to the whole world; for he can complete his work in no other way than by yielding it up entirely.

This is the remarkable process that unfolded in the rehearsals for the first German stage festival. The rehearsals were of crucial significance for the development of the new dramatico-musical art that has to be founded, but before I go on to describe them with the greatest possible fidelity, I will attempt to define in general terms the unique character of the personal intervention of the work's creator in these rehearsals. A group of artists, knit into an organic whole, had been assembled to embark on the kind of freely creative activity normally obtained only by individuals working alone. In order to achieve that artistic freedom, the first requirement was that the members of the whole subordinated themselves unconditionally to the creator of the work and attained to that wonderful capacity of *self-yielding* which Wagner characterizes with such profound insight in his masterly essay *Über Schauspieler und Sänger* ['On Actors and Singers', 1872] as the real root of all histrionic talent, even of all artistic productive ability. Now our master himself possesses this truly daemonic gift of transforming himself into all possible shapes to such a degree that, Proteus-like, in a flash, he can assume any identity at will, place himself in any conceivable situation; and he gave such an astonishing demonstration of this gift during the stage rehearsals for the *Ring* that I can find no more accurate way of describing what he did than to say that he stood before us as if he were the one *collective actor* of the whole drama. This personal gift of influencing the theatrical presentation, of bringing it to life by direct example, is also indicative of Wagner's close and interior affinity to the genius of Shakespeare. It is particularly important to note that his principle of the style of dramatic presentation is essentially the same as Shakespeare's. For all the instruction that the master gave to the artists, everything he required of them in the way of mime and gesture, stance, accentuation of the words, derived from that basic principle, which he himself has defined as the dominant principle in Shakespeare's works, namely that of '*mimetic and dramatic naturalness*'. It would be a mistake, however, to suppose that this one insight exhausts the unique essence of the dramatico-musical style we sought. As I have already explained in my study of *Der Ring des Nibelungen*, the special character of the work's style consists of the perfect organic union of a lofty, stylized art, aiming at direct embodiment of the ideal, with an art rooted in the soil of truth to nature. If, as has just been indicated, Wagner illustrated the latter principle in the rehearsals in the most immediate and personal manner, literally embodied it in every movement, facial expression, sound and word, at the same time it should not be forgotten that he was confronted with the whole multiform complex of the dramatico-musical apparatus which it was his overriding purpose to imbue with inner life, to transform into a living organism. The reason why he needed such a wealth of aids from every field of art is that he had given himself the task of generating a faithful image of living reality from the most uncompromising, the most characteristic sphere of art. Only by employing every artistic means known to man is it possible to create a collective effect which bears simultaneously the features of ideality and of truth to nature. And that goal is not fully reached until, at the moment of living interaction, the total effect of all the artistic means working together in unity forces us to forget their presence completely, so that we are gripped solely by the action unfolding before us. For the objective here is neither a purely formalist artistic performance, polite in its forms and inwardly cold, nor, equally, over-stimulation and stupefaction of the senses;

instead, it would be the highest triumph of the spirit, if the spirit proved capable of mastering and conquering all the sensual and daemonic vital forces that have been brought to life.

Wagner's most important action has been to release us from the witches' brew of modern opera, which had become a true pandemonium, and to have created a genuinely German dramatico-musical art. . . . Performing *Der Ring des Nibelungen* was a means of reaching the goal of fusing the realism of Shakespearean tragedy with the idealism of classical tragedy, of achieving the organic union of a lofty, stylized art, aiming at direct embodiment of the ideal, with an art rooted in the soil of truth to nature. *An ideal naturalness and an ideality which has become entirely nature*: that was the end to which the master sought to guide the performers.

Bayreuther Blätter, May 1880, pp. 141–4

210–226

In 1876, after nine weeks of rehearsals under Wagner's direction, from 3 June onwards, the first Bayreuth Festival began on 13 August, at 7 o'clock, with a performance of *Das Rheingold*. The *Ring* cycle was given three times in all, ending on 30 August. The German Emperor, Wilhelm I, was present, but not Ludwig II of Bavaria, who went straight back to Hohenschwangau after attending the final dress rehearsals. Wagner's 'Last Request', in the form of a placard on the doors of the theatre, concerned the clarity and truth to life of the acting.

208

The Berlin critic, Isidor Kastan, on the audience and the atmosphere in the Bayreuth Festival Theatre in 1876:

It was probably about half-past six when the auditorium began to fill. Anyone who had read the detailed accounts of the interior, which had been spread everywhere for months on end, was hardly able to avoid a sensation of bitter disappointment. Not that we did not think the appearance of the room agreeable, with its rather abruptly raked rows of seats, and the lines of Corinthian pillars framing the actual stalls. It was just that after the exaggerated descriptions, one had expected to be astonished in some way. And that was certainly not the case. To translate the roar of the enthusiasts into sober language, it must be said that we find ourselves in an auditorium constructed and furnished in a manner perfectly suitable to its purpose, which contains, like most theatres, good seats and bad seats, and which, again like most theatres, is really rather warm. Now let us look about us at the other members of the audience. But we must hurry, for the minutes are numbered and on the stroke of seven an almost total darkness will descend upon the room. Our imperial capital has sent a relatively large contingent of spectators and notabilities of all kinds. All the Music-of-the-Future Amazons, Valkyries in mufti one might say, are present and correct. Frau Marie von Schleinitz seems to be afloat on a sea of ecstasy, while her husband, His Excellency the Minister, may perhaps regard the matter a trifle more coolly. Nay, we even gain the impression that a trace of sarcasm plays on his lips. Countess Dankelmann looks about her, no less confident of victory. Right in the centre of the auditorium, a group of women of really imposing beauty has assembled.

Our eyes are involuntarily drawn to the delicate form and lovely face of *our* Countess Dönhoff. Not far from her, we espy the proud, statuesque Hildegard von Usedom, a truly classical, Junoesque apparition. Over there our glance chances on a lady who evidently would prefer not to be seen. It is *Marie Seebach*. Niemann, our *Heldentenor*, and his dainty wife, Frau Hedwig Raabe, wave to us, as dear friends from our home town on the green banks of the Spree. But the authentic air of Berlin hangs over one corner, where Dohm, Scholtz, Lindau, Ehrlich and others have made their rendezvous. To think, on that truly god-forsaken spot, puns are being bandied about here in Bayreuth, in the presence of the 'Master'! It is monstrous. There, a group of artists and their lovely artists' wives, Paul Meyerheim, Hans Makart, Angeli, Anton von Werner, gnarled Menzel, and not far from them, Boden-stedt – they all lend the whole a kind of aroma, the piqu-ancy of which cannot be expressed in words. Among all these people, the most interesting head, the cynosure of all eyes, is – *Franz Liszt*. The extraordinary mixture of worldly elegance and priestly demeanour, the flowing grey locks and the venerable black coat of clerical cut, give his evergreen genius a uniquely attractive charm. But we are abruptly torn from these musings by a strange signal-motif. All heads turn to the Royal Box. The emperor has just entered the theatre. Emperor Wilhelm in civilian clothes is certainly an unfamiliar sight to us Berliners and probably to most Germans. We really cannot imagine him in anything other than a general's uniform. In fact several seconds passed before the crowd recognized the emperor. But then a storm of applause broke out, suddenly filling the great room like a hurricane. 'Long live Kaiser Wilhelm', again and again – it seemed as though the cheers would never cease. The emperor stepped forward to the parapet of the box and bowed to the gathering in all directions, smiling delightedly. As a conscientious chronic-ler I must not omit to report that the springs at Bad Gastein have truly rejuvenated our emperor. By the youthfulness of his appearance, by the firmness of his movements, Emperor Wilhelm makes a mockery of his great age. He has become the avowed darling of the ladies in these two days; and wherever he goes one hears exclamations like 'God! what a handsome man!' and 'I could throw myself into his arms!'

Berliner Tageblatt, 16 August 1876

Eduard Hanslick on the production of the Ring *at Bayreuth, 1876:*

Never before has an opera had such an accumulation of scenic miracles to offer. Feats that have previously been thought impossible or, more correctly, that have never before entered anyone's head, follow one upon the other without pause: the Rhine maidens swimming in the depths of the river, the gods strolling across a rainbow, the transformations of Alberich into a giant serpent and then into a toad, the fire-breathing, singing dragon, the magic fire, the gods' fiery downfall etc. With them the poet has presented the composer with a full range of opportunities to display his most dazzling accomplishment, that of painting in sound. But is it right that the highest ambition of a dramatic composer should be to provide a musical accompaniment to a series of magical effects produced by machines? A declared supporter of Wagner's, Karl Lemcke, in a thoroughly favourable review of the *Ring*, deplores the deleterious influence of these 'tricks remini-scent of Bosco's Hall of Magic', which will simply lead to a '*cult of legerdemain*'. In fact, Wagner's *Ring* comes closest, in point of theatrical genre, to magic plays and '*féeries*'. The decidedly material effects deployed in it stand in a curious contradiction to the pure ideality which Wagner boasts for his work. Wagner strives at every point to make the strongest impression on the senses, using every kind of means.

Musikalische Stationen, Berlin 1880, p. 247 f.

The critic Wilhelm Mohr on the Ring *at Bayreuth in 1876:*

This much, I think, is certain: a work that has attracted the attention of the whole cultivated world, as Wagner's Stage Festival has, cannot be the work of an insignificant artist. Is it not therefore worthwhile at least to attempt to sum it up in clear and unadorned language, and to set out the artistic significance of the new work, or, what amounts to the same thing, its historical position in the evolution of art? . . .

If Wagner were a native of France or Italy, I am con-vinced that the critics in that country, if for no other reason than simple patriotism, would have treated the artist with more respect and would not have provided such a lamentable example of incapacity and opinionated embarrassment. At all events the unrestrained, uncritical enthusiasts stand incomparably higher in my moral estimation than those canny critics who do not hesitate to lay an artistic force of such magnitude as a burnt offering on the altar of their personal vanity.

I thank God that I, at least, have no reason to fear that forthright surrender to an artist who teaches me things that I did not know before will tarnish the halo of my critical reputation. And so if I am to answer the above question in the light of my forthright conviction, the only thing I can say is that, as things were and as they are now, Wagner has *won* the battle. His work has won it, even if his artistic theories may not all have proved valid in practice. He has won, even though the theatre building was an idea that was half unsuccessful and at least three-quarters unnecessary, he has won, even if people perspire at Bay-reuth as much as they do in the Berlin opera house, he has won, and would still have won if there had been twice as many gutta-percha dragons, artificial bears, realistic rams and similar shoddy pantomime magic. He is the victor, even though his 'Work of Art of the Future' has been laid low and emerges as an exaggeration or perhaps a prema-ture idea. . . .

He has won the battle, and curiously enough he has done so in the one area where he was not trying to win it, and where, conversely, his victory was most obstinately contested: in the *musical* area. He has not enhanced his reputation as a poet, the old dramatic cunning has certainly nothing to offer that we have not already seen in *Lohengrin* and *Tannhäuser*, the new scenic miracles are actually at odds with – not merely the capabilities of modern stage machinery or stage technicians – but, far worse, the very nature of art itself. But the victory has gone to Wagner the *musician*. With an inventive power that sometimes seems to pour forth whole rivers of gleaming gold, with thematic ideas of striking character and greatest purport, with totally new roles for harmony, rhythm, dynamics and, though to a lesser extent, melody, with the completely individual and strongly marked physiognomy and identity of everything he produces, such as has never before existed. . . . *Because of* his principles, *incidentally to* his principles, and *in spite of* his principles, he has created beauty, burgeoning life, musico-dramatic organisms of a new, previously unknown kind. The old form has not been smashed to pieces in this new beauty, but has undergone the same transformation as the sword Nothung, it has been filed down, melted, recast and forged, to emerge resplendent.

Wilhelm Mohr, *Richard Wagner und das Kunstwerk der Zukunft im Lichte der Baireuther Aufführung betrachtet*, Cologne 1876, pp. 63, 65–8

Extracts from correspondence between the aesthetician Conrad Fiedler and the sculptor Adolf von Hildebrand, on the performances of the Ring *at Bayreuth, 1876:*

Crostewitz, 27 August 76
My dear Hildebrand!
. . . I don't need to tell you that I have little time for the whole business of Germanic gods and Nibelungs, for poetic theatre or the crude effects of scenic trickery; but even in reading the text I was amazed to discover, lurking behind all the forced and strangely unpoetic surface, a potency in the original grasp of certain events in nature and human existence that one rarely comes across today; the superhuman element in the poem, which only too often acts as a deterrent, is not always hollow exaggeration of the straightforward, but frequently the still rather rough but powerful expression of a passionately heightened, spontaneous experience of the events. This is discernible only here and there in the text; but when one hears the music, it is impossible to deceive oneself any longer; for even if the music has no independent existence, as in opera (the 'Nibelungs' simply cannot be called operas at all), neither is it merely a carefully calculated illustration of the words and actions; rather it has grown directly out of the same necessity that enforced expression in the words and in the dramatic action. In Wagner something often struggles successfully for expression, which would be served neither by words nor by music alone, but demands combined expression if it is to be even half adequately realized. Of course if he were a better poet, he would be able to express more of the fullness of life in words; but one must concede that there is a resounding side to the world for the musical sensibility, and that life appears incomplete, one-sided if the musical side remains hidden. It seems obvious to me that the point of departure for his efforts and his creativity lies in his sense of a discrepancy between the power and richness of life, struggling in him for formal expression, and the means of expression that have existed until now; he found the means he needed in music drama, and that is its artistic justification. In the Bayreuth performances it certainly struck me at many points that through the medium of the music Wagner was stirring up depths of the sensations, situations and events depicted on the stage, which would otherwise, without the music, have been incapable of realization. From this point of view one naturally comes to judge Wagner's music by a quite different criterion from other music, and while I would never agree that his is the only music, let alone that what he has created is at last the true art that mankind has always sought, as he and his adherents claim, I still believe that he has found an individual and valid form of artistic expression to meet a genuine, original need. . . . You will find little objective or reliable comment in the newspapers; the hacks always settle on the trivia and forget, or fail to understand, the important things; even if there is only a single spark of true art in Wagner's music dramas, then that alone is valuable enough to make everything else irrelevant, and the arguments and recriminations about Wagner's pretensions, about his adherents' excessive fanaticism, about isolated excrescences in the works, about certain inadequacies in the performances etc., are simply nauseating.

Florence, 5 September 76
Dearest Fiedler! What you had to say about the performances was very interesting, even if I couldn't really follow it. Since I haven't shared the experience, I shall have to go by your impressions. I don't understand the great difference from other operas. . . . Every opera needs both media, drama and music, and if Wagner delves more deeply and seriously into life for his texts, characters and situations than was the case with earlier operas, there still remains the question as to whether that really makes so much difference. The main difference lies in the music, I suppose, and that strikes me as far less clear, far less significant artistically than in the work of earlier composers. But we can't argue about that in a letter. I am unable to see the new side of life which you say Wagner has discovered and in which you place so much hope, for the element in which you see it has always been the preserve of musicians. You know that I ascribe his mysterious effect to the chaotic and indefinite in his music. And it is my opinion that it will not be able to generate any new form, if his subjectivity remains unaltered. His subjectivity, his nature must be of an original kind, apparently daemonic, and that is why it is not yet very artistic, and if he has to give it vent, I don't know whether the outcome will be works of art of any significance. When Beethoven or Michelangelo, or Goethe in the second part of *Faust*, create a daemonic effect and express that aspect of the world, they do it through the force of their creative power, through the loftiness of the abstract expression which acts purely as an overwhelming force, isolated from an ordinary, naturalistic context. Wagner's artistic heights do not convince me in that way. Of course it would be unjust to deny him all artistic competence or intention, but it seems to me at the moment that his true centre lies somewhere quite other than in art. The public today have no notion of the formal clarity of the creative arts, they have no feeling or understanding for their nature, and they gain far more excitement from the brutal means employed in new works; I put very little trust in their artistic instinct. . . .

Crostewitz, 20 September 76
Dearest Hildebrand! . . . It would be a curious procedure to deny artistic ability to the present generation by overlooking the one individual in whom an important artistic talent may be at work. All the same I admit that the real point at

issue is whether the forces at work in Wagner are essentially artistic ones; if they are not, then his works have only the appearance of importance, and their success and their effectiveness rest on a grandiose delusion, a possibility that I by no means rule out. Unfortunately I know too little about music to form my own opinion as to whether the accusation of formlessness which is made against Wagner is fully justified or not; there are at all events a large number of musicians who do not concede it, and people like Michelangelo and Beethoven were also accused of formlessness. It's a curious thing about form, it's nothing permanent, nothing distinct and tangible; it is forever recreating itself in new shapes, as soon as there is a need to express a content that has never before been expressed. Once an independent new form has come into being by this means, it gains new life for a time, but then it gradually becomes a mode in the hands of those who have mastered it. Our entire artistic production consists almost exclusively of modes of expression, empty clichés. Any truly new production, shaped by its content, will always be an act of revolution against that state of affairs, and will appear at first to be formless. Also it will sometimes happen that the person whose independent individuality places him outside the bounds of accepted, existing forms, forms that he cannot use, will not be equipped with adequate talent to achieve a finished, self-sufficient means of formal expression; even in a case like that it must be admitted that the struggle to find a self-sufficient form is an artistic activity. And I cannot deny that quite often during the performances at Bayreuth I had the impression of just such a struggle going on. You say that you cannot see the difference between Wagner's works and earlier works that I insist exists; of course the difference is not a matter of the essence of the music, which is and must always remain the same: basically Wagner, if he is a great musician, and all the great musicians who will come after him, will not be able to do anything other than what all great musicians before him have done. He has not invented music, much as his adherents would like us to believe it. The difference is only that for him music does not have an independent existence, detached from the phenomena and events of nature and of life. . . . In Wagner the dramatic action and the music are not separate components, rather, it is only in the music that the dramatic action comes into being at all. The music is never independent of the action but, so to speak, never lets the action go, and is never let go by it, so that the expression of the action grows steadily more intense. As for what you say about the effect of Wagner's music, that it does not derive from its artistic qualities, that is quite true for a very large section of the public; but it is no proof that Wagner's works do not possess artistic qualities.

Adolf von Hildebrands Briefwechsel mit Conrad Fiedler, ed. Günther Jachmann, Dresden 1927, pp. 65–7, 69–75

From the essay on Bayreuth and the Ring *by the French composer and friend of Wagner, Camille Saint-Saëns:*

There are other differences besides the layout of auditorium and orchestra between the theatre at Bayreuth and familiar opera houses. The skill of the transition from auditorium and stage is such that one is totally unaware of an apron stage. Its disappearance is the more effective because the singers almost never approach it. but normally remain in line with the second lot of flats, where they are strongly lit from the apron and the proscenium. In the complete darkness of the auditorium, attention is thus concentrated upon them. There is no prompter's box; he stands in the wings or behind the scenery on the stage as occasion demands. Steam plays a large part in the scenic effects: puffs of white steam simulate clouds, and under red lighting it turns into the glow of fire.

The concealed orchestra is undoubtedly a gain, one that ought to be employed everywhere in future, and probably will be as soon as the way has been found to make the final improvements required.

There is a great waste of musical art at Bayreuth. A lot of interesting details are lost in the huge orchestra pit, the gigantic chasm which guards the stage like Fafner. But there can be no doubt of the gain in scenic illusion.

On the occasion of the first performance of the *Ring*, Richard Wagner made a speech, the essence of which was: France has a national art, Italy has a national art, Germans have only to desire one, and your country too will at last have a national art. It was not to everybody's taste. Even his admirers admitted that his rudeness is as great as his talent, and paid no attention to such utterances. If I had revealed in public the remarks he made about a certain exalted personage it would probably have led to a diplomatic incident.

In any case he denied that it ever entered his head to offend France. Why ever should he want to? – –

Nobody knows the answer to that, not even he. It is simply absurd to represent him as the national enemy of our country. He was only the enemy of those who were inimical to his music. They may be right, but it is certainly not right that they should represent the author of the works at which they jeer as a thoroughgoing monster.

Wagner-mania is a pardonable aberration, Wagner-phobia is a child's fear of bogeymen.

Die Musik, Berlin 1902, p. 883 f.

The Berlin critic Gustav Engel on Wagner as a 'German' musician:

Wagner has three qualities as a musician which redound to the credit of the German nation. The works of his later style show that he knows how to avoid triviality. That may not seem very much to some people, but it is in fact a great deal in an artist's later period. He has forged a distinctive personal character, a completely individual style for himself, and we are never plagued by the sensation of travelling along a path already worn smooth by frequent use, of having to listen once more to something we have already heard a hundred times before. This is a German quality, for a German endeavours to possess a personality. Secondly: Wagner is concerned with absolute truth of expression; rhetoric and meaningless phrase-making are nothing to him. This is a characteristic that at the time of the Reformation already distinguished the German from the Italian. It was lost for a time during the Enlightenment, but was never completely suppressed. Even Meyerbeer, who was half French, was true to it. Thirdly: Wagner always strives for profundity, for exhaustive exposition. The difficult nature of his sound combinations and the excessive expansion of certain dramatic and musical processes are both facets of that quality. To be as fair as possible in the face of the often appalling *longueurs* of one of Wagner's music dramas, we must remember one important thing: that his deliberate intention is to overthrow the kind of swift-moving entertainment that is based on nothing more than a request for diversion, reflecting a merely frivolous view of art. He demands a serious, collected attitude in his listeners, a kind of reverence for art – and he is right to do so, only he goes too far. . . .

And that is why I say: Wagner's fundamental Germanness is un-German; he is representative of only one thread in the life of the nation, the obstinate, German-at-all-costs side: the striving for depth without clarity, for truth without beauty, absolute subjectivity without any objective restraints. In a word: Wagner's work has about it something Gothic, barbarian – in the sense which Goethe used to give the words – and we must try to rid ourselves of this kind of Gothicism and barbarianism.

Vossische Zeitung, Berlin, 9 September 1876

The Berlin critic Karl Frenzel on the audiences at Bayreuth in 1876:

Who did you see at Bayreuth? If we may be permitted to leave on one side the presence of the German emperor and some other royal persons who, squeezed together in the hot, cramped royal circle of the Wagner theatre, did not present anything like the splendid, dazzling spectacle that is to be seen at a gala performance in the opera house in Berlin, then the assembled company of other 'patrons, subscribers and friends' was not very remarkable. I have before me four lists which, with a few exceptions, include the names of all the people who attended the first series of the Festival performances. None of our own great statesmen and generals was present; Austria was represented by Count Andrassy; Herr von Keudell and Herr von Radowitz were the most prominent members of our diplomatic corps. There are three parliamentarians on the list: Franz Duncker, Marquardsen, Cornelius Heyl. But one looks in vain for a Bennigsen or a Forckenbeck, a Stauffenberg of a Völk, a Lasker or a Richter at this 'Conclusion of the History of the World'. Not a single member of the Centre – fond though they are of painting the modern Twilight of the Gods, the revolution, in the fiery clouds, just like Wagner – thought it worth the trouble to go to Bayreuth to see the end of the world *en miniature*. The Socialists, understandably, could not raise any enthusiasm for an art form which demanded, as the first and only condition of its enjoyment, a third share in a subscription voucher costing 300 Reichsmarks. Things were different, they say, and I echo them, in violet-wreathed Athens, where the citizen could hear and see the *Eumenides* of Aeschylus and *The Knights* of Aristophanes for nothing! But if the men who work in the hard world of facts were absent, was perhaps the representation of artistic interests all the more impressive for it? There were musicians in plenty, headed by Franz Liszt: singers, instrumentalists, conductors, composers, dilettanti of noble and not so noble birth: to name a few: Stockhausen, Kapellmeister Eckert,

236

Professor Stern, Minnie Hauck, Marianne Brandt, Kapellmeister Damrosch, Franz Servais, Herr and Frau von Bronsart, Louis Brassin, Kapellmeister Dessoff, Franz Krolop, Eduard Lassen, Kapellmeister Levi, Nikolaus Rubinstein, Dr Gunz, Herr Director Jauner, Kapellmeister Alois Schmidt from Schwerin, Wilhelm Taubert; worthy artists, excellent in their way, but, as they would themselves no doubt be the first to admit, not of a standing to allow us to overlook the absence of Joachim, Brahms or Anton Rubinstein. The failure of both Verdi and Gounod to appear is no mystery to the Wagnerians, who are confident that they would have shrivelled, pierced to the core by the sense of theit own nothingness. But since Richard Wagner is in any case as great a poet as he is a composer, did writers perhaps compensate for the absent composers? Alas! Neither Karl Gutzkow nor Berthold Auerbach was to be seen, neither Gustav Freytag nor Victor Scheffel, not Emanuel Geibel, not Paul Heyse, not Spielhagen, who would have found events and characters in plenty for a contemporary novel. So far as I can tell, there were three German writers who were in Bayreuth of their own free will: Friedrich von Bodenstedt, Ernst Dohm and the Ritter von Mosenthal; all the other writers there had been compelled to make the pilgrimage out of harsh duty. The visual arts were the most impressively represented: seated at that table were Hans Makart and Heinrich Angeli from Vienna, Adolf Menzel, Anton von Werner, Karl Becker and Paul Meyerheim from Berlin, Franz Lenbach from Munich, Schauss from Weimar. The stage sent none of its heroes but some leading ladies came: Frau Marie Seebach from Dresden, Fräulein Clara Ziegler from Munich, Mesdames Marie Kessler and Clara Meyer from Berlin – I will be generous and include Frau Hedwig Niemann in the list as an enthusiastic Wagnerian, rather than as a loyal wife. The two greatest German character actors among the disciples, sombre Joseph Lewinsky and tempestuous Richard Kahle, watched Wagner's Doomsday with very different emotions. The jury-box presented the most remarkable spectacle of all. Never have so many clever, critical and, if you like, malicious faces assembled to report to their readers on, to express myself in parliamentary language, a flop. The press has, from the first. been forced by the public interest to devote a degree of attention to the Wagner theatre undertaking that was out of all proportion to its significance. To list only the well known names, Vienna sent Ludwig Speidel, Eduard Hanslick, Professor Schelle, David Spitzer, Wilhelm Singer and Hugo Wittmann; Berlin sent Paul Lindau, Gustav Engel, Ehlert, Professor Ehrlich, Ludwig Pietsch and Hans Herrig. There was Hermann Schmid, the respected novelist, from Munich, and Karl Hillebrand from Florence; French literature was represented by Albert Wolf, Catulle Mendès and Edouard Schuré. What an expenditure of intellect and hard work to pronounce judgment – not on a work of art, the text of which has been familiar to the well-read for more than a decade, while two of its parts are in the permanent repertory of the Munich opera – but on the official opening of a theatre building which, with the single exception of its sunken, covered orchestra pit, proved to be deficient in every respect! Besides these 'knights of the intellect', or rather, to the fore of them, there was the aristocracy by birth. Much mention has already been made of the aristocratic ladies

1876.

Verzeichniß

sämmtlicher bei den Bayreuther Bühnen-Festspielen

(Ring des Nibelungen von Rich. Wagner)

mitwirkenden Personen.

(Separat-Abdruck aus dem Bayreuther Plakat-Anzeiger.)

Sänger:

Name.	Ort.	Rolle.	Wohnung.
Betz	Berlin	Wotan / Wanderer	Villa Landgraf, nächst dem Wagner-Theater.
Eilers	Coburg	Fasolt / Donner	Maurermeister Popp, Dürschnitz 284.
Gura	Leipzig	Donner / Gunther	Priv. Schnaufer, Dürschnitz 263.
Herlich	Berlin	Froh	Apotheker Wiedemann, Jägerstraße 666.
Hill	Schwerin	Alberich	Frau Regimentsarzts-Wittwe Seitz, Bürgerreutherstr. 672.
Niemann	Berlin	Siegmund	Hôtel Fantaisie.
Riering	Darmstadt	Hunding	Buchbinder Senfft, Priestergasse 380.
v. Reichenberg	Stettin	Fafner	Hôtel Sonne, Rennweg.
Schlosser	München	Mime	Kfm. Barth, Markt 12.
Gustav Siehr	Wiesbaden	Hagen	Ed. Stützer, Ludwigsstr. 348.
Unger	Bayreuth	Siegfried	Ed. Stützer, Ludwigsstr. 348.
Vogel	München	Loge	Hôtel Sonne.
Bürger	Coburg	*Führer der Mannen*	Priv. Hille, Rennweg 284.
Eilers	Berlin		Siehe oben.
Herlich	Berlin		Siehe oben.
Koch	Breslau		Priv. Dörnhöffer, Jägerstr. 602.
Riering	Darmstadt		Siehe oben.
v. Reichenberg	Stettin		Siehe oben.
Weiß	Straßburg		Kaufmann Herold, Maxstr. 5.
Baum	Hamburg		Hauptmann Lindhammer, Ludwigsstraße 318.
Bruckner	Wien		Maler Kummer, Schrollengasse 333.
Brozegg	Wiesbaden		Kfm. Moritz Harburger, Canzleistraße 1.6.
Ebers	Wien		Kreisbaurath Hauser, Markt 19.
Friemel	Berlin		Flaschner Hoffmann, breite Gasse 364.
Haag	Wien		Wagner Griebhammer, Rennweg 285.
Hoffmann	München		Wildprethändler Hertmann, Spitalgasse 470.
Hobbach	Wien		Schreiner Enes, Kreuz 582½.
Kineky			Metzgermstr. Morg, Moritzhöfen 407.
Koschat	München	*Mannen*	Prem.-Lieut. Meyer, Jägerstr. 638.
Martini	Hannover		Kreisbaurath Frank, Bauhof (Schrollengasse)
Moritz			
Reisinger	München		Conditor Eibinger, Breite Gasse 366.
Salomen	Dessau		Riemermstr. Winterling, Markt 97.
Schuberth	Wien		Pfarrer Nägelsbach, Priestergasse 449.
Sommer			Schreiner Enes, Kreuz 582½.
Thülecke	Berlin		Priv. Trips, Rennweg 239.
Veith	München		Lehrer Künzel, altes Schulhaus (Münzgasse).
Vogel	Berlin		Conditor Eibinger, Breite Gasse 366.
Winter			Druckereibesitzer Pöhl, Rennweg 244.
Wirsing	München		Consistorial-Rath Kraußold, Dammallee 440½.
Weingärtner	Wien		Metzgermstr. Morg, Moritzhöfen 407.

Sängerinnen:

Name.	Ort.	Rolle.	Wohnort.
Frl. Ammann	Wien	Siegrune	Hôtel Sonne, Rennweg.
Frau v. Sadler-Grün	Coburg	Fricka / Norne	Schreinermeister Stelzner, Dammallee 441¾.
Frl. Haupt	Cassel	Freia / Gerhilde	Eduard Stützer, Ludwigsstr. 348.
Frau Jaïde	Darmstadt	Erda / Waltraute	Schreinermeister Schultheiß, Rennweg 247.
Frl. Lammert	Berlin	Floßhilde / Roßweiße	Frau Pfarrerswittwe Frohwein, Jägerstraße 639.
" Lilli Lehmann	"	Woglinde / Helmwige	Apotheker Wiedemann, Jägerstr. 666.
" Maria Lehmann	"	Wellgunde / Ortlinde	Frau Pfarrerswittwe Frohwein, Jägerstraße 639.
Frau Materna	Wien	Brünnhilde	Hôtel Sonne, Rennweg.
" Reicher-Kindermann	München	Grimgerde	
Frl. Scheiffzky	"	Sieglinde / Norne	Conditor Friedmann, Ludwigsstraße 307.
Frau Jachmann-Wagner	Berlin	Schwertleite / Norne	Fr. Feustel, Jägerstraße 664.
Frl. Weckerlin	München	Gutrune	Priv. Schnaufer, Dürschnitz 263.
" Aumüller	Wien	*Normen*	Schuhmachermeister Baer, Ochsengasse 136.
" Eisenschütz	"		Spinnmstr. Nützel, St. Georgen
" Först	Weimar		Freifrau von Großschädel, Friedrichstraße 436.
" Hochberger	Wien		Kassier Schoberth, b. d. Stadtkirche 150.
" Ida Kalmann	Berlin		
" Meta Kalmann	"		Alb. Dietz, St. Georgen.
" Kirschstein	"		
" Krauß	Wien		Frau Post-Konducteurs-Wittwe Köhler, Maximiliansstr. 42.
" Vogelhuber	Wien		Frl. Karf, St. Georgen 23b.
Frau Weiglin	Neustrelitz		Heinr. Wendler, Ludwigsstr. 360.

Orchesterleitung:

K. K. Hof-Kapellmeister Hans Richter aus Wien, bei k. Schloßverwalter Bram, neues Schloß.

Musikalische Assistenz:

Capellmeister Anton Seidl,
„ Franz Fischer, } bei Priv. Say, Dürschnitz 267.
„ Demetrius Lallas, bei Oberförster Gränzer, Louisenburg.
„ Felix Mottel,
„ Herm. Zimmer, } Hôtel Sonne.

Clavierbegleitung:

Concertmeister Joseph Rubinstein, bei Schönfärbereibesitzer Samelson, Ziegelgasse 209.

Scenische Leitung:

Obermaschinenmeister: Karl Brandt aus Darmstadt, Wagnertheater.

Decoration:

Joseph Hofmann
Gebr. Brückner } bei Aufseher Simon, Neuerweg 699.

Costüme:

Professor Emil Döpler aus Berlin, Wagnertheater.

Choreographie:

Balletmeister Richard Fricke aus Dessau, bei Carl Gießel Opernstraße 162.

Gaseinrichtung:

Gebr. Staudt aus Frankfurt a. M., Wagnertheater.

List of performers appearing in the *Ring* cycle at the first Bayreuth Festival, 1876.

from Berlin, Vienna and St Petersburg, who form the real moving force of Wagnerianism, cinctured like Valkyries, ogling and smiling, playing the role appropriate to them. Behind them came their cavaliers, willingly or unwillingly following the banner of the prophet; bringing up the rear, a chorus of enthusiasts, thirsting for vengeance. Everyone knows the story of the Patriarch Cyrillus, who always walked through the streets of Alexandria accompanied by monks armed with cudgels. Here, too, every third word of this rearguard was Hit!: a call to naked force. In this respect, the exclamation of one Wagnerian the day after the last performance was extraordinarily apt: 'Thank God!' he cheerfully called to a lady, 'no one was stabbed or beaten to death.' That was typical of the society in which, despite all the lovely and well-bred ladies, one moved in Bayreuth – and this society, conspicuously lacking all but a very few of the great names of Germany, is what they had the impudence to call the flower of the German nation!

Karl Frenzel, *Berliner Dramaturgie*, vol. 2, Hanover 1877, pp. 199–203

Peter Tchaikovsky on Bayreuth, 1876:

. . . a small, unimportant town, where a few thousand people assembled. The *service* is very bad. We had booked a room in advance, our room is very nice, but on the first day I had the greatest difficulty in getting luncheon, and I owed my breakfast yesterday morning to a stroke of luck.

Allgemeine Musik-Zeitung, Berlin, 23 March 1906

The Berlin critic Paul Lindau on the sale of Wagneriana on the fringes of the Bayreuth Festival in 1876:

It was predictable that industry would take advantage of the Wagnerian cult. I have already added a 'Nibelungen' cap and a Wagner cravat to my wardrobe. The only striking thing about the Nibelung cap is its tasteless shape; at first glance there is nothing to distinguish the Wagner cravat from other cravats, but if you lovingly take hold of this cravat and look at it more closely, you perceive a black silk thread under the strip securing the ends; if you pull the thread the central section of the tie unfurls and there in the middle, in a medallion frame stitched in silk, is a photograph of the Lenbach portrait of Wagner. Thus the enthusiasts can wear the master round their necks at all times, without the profane being aware of it. There is also a Siegfried hat. The sparkling hocks served in the Wagner restaurant bear the names 'Rheingold' and 'Richard Wagner'.

Nüchterne Brief aus Bayreuth, Breslau and Leipzig 1876; from the 10th ed. 1880, p. 24 f.

There are numerous testimonies to Wagner's dissatisfaction with the artistic outcome of the first Festival. 'Next year' he wanted to do everything differently, more accurately. There was, however, a deficit of 148,000 marks. The nation and the audiences, to say nothing of the press, had in Wagner's eyes failed him. For the first time the idea of a Foundation was mentioned, which Wagner hoped would give him financial independence.

238

Wagner to Ludwig II, Sorrento, 21 October 1876:

What we have suffered from, so far, has been insufficient finances: that was the root cause of all the hindrances and delays which made it impossible for me to have everything ready in time to make checks and improvements – which were absolutely indispensable. It is a state of affairs that can be transformed in the future, because the essentials now exist: once the whole of the costs of the structure and the initial staging have been covered, the costs of maintenance and future use will cover themselves. We would in fact, as I calculated, have completely met all our expenses already, if the detestable newspapers had not upset all our calculations with their base defamations. . . . Suggestions and aspersions like that must in future be kept away from my works and my endeavours, if I am to retain any desire or strength for them! And that is why I have come to the following conclusions: the annual stage festivals in Bayreuth must remain an absolutely free foundation, with the sole objective of serving as the model for the establishment and development of an original, German, musico-dramatic art. To that end it is necessary that the theatre itself should now be relieved of any of the outstanding debts pertaining to costs of materials, and should be guaranteed in perpetuity against financial loss with, please note, the irrevocable proviso that the undertaking itself is never exploited for financial gain, and in particular that its director never claims any compensation for his labours. – Now I shall be able to see where the 'German Empire' stands on this – for I could hardly turn again to those who have been my patrons up till now, except, at the outside, with a request to contribute towards the outstanding costs, which, as it is, would probably meet with a sluggish enough response. As I see it, there are two ways of laying the matter before the 'Empire': either the proposal can be moved in the Reichstag by one of the deputies, among whom, however, I know of none who seems fit for the task; or the proposal can be introduced by the Imperial Chancellery, for which I would have to approach the emperor, from whom likewise I cannot really expect any deep understanding of the matter. A third course would be for the King of Bavaria, as guardian and protector of the interests of higher German culture, to instruct his representative to introduce the proposal in the Federal Council, and to take it to the Reichstag from there. The proposal might be worded something like this:

'The Imperial Government takes possession of the Festival Theatre in Bayreuth with all its appurtenances, against defrayment of all the costs still outstanding incurred in setting up and equipping the theatre, and transfers it, as a property of the nation, to the town council of Bayreuth, to be administered by it, with the injunction and the obligation to organize annual performances, as intended by the theatre's founder and in accordance with directions and statutes to be laid down by him, after the model of those instituted by me [*sic*] in 1876. The annual costs will be met by the sale of 1,000 seats for each performance, and additionally by the annual grant of the sum of 100,000 marks by the nation; this grant will give the nation the right to allocate the remaining 5 to 600 seats free to indigent German nationals, whereby the whole institution will best assume a 'national' character in its external constitution as well as its artistic purpose. Associations should be formed in all the German states, to recommend suitable recipients of free tickets, while additionally the winners of first prizes to academies of music and dramatic art and at grammar schools should from the first be recommended for the award of free tickets for the performances by State governments.

Königsbriefe, vol. 3, pp. 95 ff.

From an address to delegates of the Bayreuth Patrons' Association, made by Wagner on 15 September 1877:

. . . We are in a terrible position. Help from the Reichstag is out of the question. There is not *one* single person in the Reichstag who understands what is at stake for us. Bismarck would say in all probability, if we asked for assistance: 'Wagner has had enough; a lot of princes, the emperor himself was there at his performances; what else does the man want?' We will get no support from that quarter. We cannot count on any assistance of that sort to remove the deficit from our shoulders.

What can be done? All kinds of strange views have been forthcoming from people who have exaggerated everything. My friends have been unable to give any help. In order to settle the most pressing debts I had to borrow capital of 32,000 marks at 5 per cent interest. The London concerts, from which I was promised a substantial profit, sufficed only to provide a reasonable breathing-space. . . . The management of the Munich Court theatre, too, has made me an offer of good will to cover the deficit. I have been given to understand that it would be a token of gratitude for assigning my works to the management of that theatre, because they recognize that they could expect substantial takings from performances of them in Munich during the summer. His Majesty the King of Bavaria already owns the performance rights in any case, and it was only by a magnanimous concession on his part that I was permitted to perform my work for the first time here in Bayreuth. But now he wishes to claim his right. I hope that the favourable attitude that the management of his Court theatre has shown me will go so far as to relieve me of the deficit of last year's Festival if I allow the complete *Ring* to be performed in Munich. One condition of that, however, would be that they would be able to use our sets and everything else pertaining to the production. We have no proprietary rights in these things. The king once gave me 200,000 marks to cover the whole cost of building the the scenery. It is true that a great deal of it could not be used in any other theatre, and the king's selfless generosity will surely allow us to keep that. But the movable sets, machines and properties belong to his Majesty, according to the agreement made between the Court Secretariat and ourselves, which lays down that everything remains the property of the Treasury until we have repaid our debt. Since I have no earthly prospect of meeting the deficit, I shall have to consent to the use of the materials in question by the Munich theatre. I still have all sorts of expenses to defray for the sets as well.

Thus it was with considerable misgivings that I considered repeating last year's performances in Bayreuth. But even in more favourable conditions it would have been difficult for me to resolve on their repetition. For under the pressure of the circumstances then prevailing, and also because no one believed that our performances would actually be ready to take place in time, many of the people involved neglected to do their work properly. Some things were done carelessly, some things inadequately prepared. There was negligence of all kinds, on my part, too. Last year's performances did not measure up to my ideal. If it is to be reached in the future, I must be given a breathing-space, I must be relieved of the most oppressive burdens, so that my exhausted strength may be revived. . . .

You know the goal of all my efforts, of our entire Bayreuth undertaking: a style and an art of a kind that cannot be cultivated in the wretched theatres of the present day. . . .

I have had the idea of founding a school here for training singers, players and conductors in the correct performance of musico-dramatic works of the truly German style, and I will take the liberty of explaining to you briefly the form I envisage it will take. To begin with the school is planned for a period of six years, from 1 January 1878 to 30 September 1883.

Reported by Franz Muncker, Richard Wagner Jahrbuch, vol. 1, ed. Joseph Kürschner, Stuttgart 1886, pp. 205–8

On 24 September 1878 Friedrich Feustel presented the final accounts of the first Festival of 1876; the sum for the artists corresponds to Wagner's own direct contribution:

The overall figure is:

Building, fittings, costumes, etc. cost	M. 1,095,052·10
The artists received	177,823·99
Total outgoings	M. 1,272,876·09

The money was found as follows:

Patronage scheme	M. 724,775·32
Voluntary contributions	233,912· 1
Treasury	216,152·44
Management of the Hoftheater	95,000·—
Interest	5,096·32
	M. 1,274,936· 9

so that on 1 September we had a balance of M. 2,060.—

Königsbriefe, vol. 3, p. xxvii

Wagner had made the first prose outline of *Parsifal* in April 1857; he wrote the poem twenty years later and he began the composition of the music in September 1877. After his wearing experiences with the *Ring* in 1876, he resumed work with considerable hesitation. His letters to the French writer Judith Gautier-Mendès, whom he had known since the Paris performances of *Tannhäuser* in 1861, contain some valuable information about the genesis of the new work.

From Wagner's letters to Judith Gautier:

[undated]

Beloved soul! Cry and protest no more! Your embraces live in my memory as the most entrancing ecstasy, the greatest cause of pride in my whole existence. They are a last gift of the gods, who would not allow me to succumb to the chagrin of the lies spread about the *Nibelungen* performances. But why recall that wretched business! I do not cry out, but in my best moments I am aware of so sweet, so salutary a longing, the longing to embrace you once more and never lose your heavenly love. You are mine, aren't you?

[undated]

. . . All this in aid of mornings free for *Parsifal*.

The name is Arabian. The old troubadours no longer understood it. 'Parsi-fal' means: 'parsi', think of the Parsees, the fire-worshippers, 'pure'; 'fal' means 'foolish'. In an elevated sense it means a man who is untutored but possessed of genius ('fellow' in English appears to be related to this Oriental root). You will perceive (rather, you will learn, forgive me!) why this naive man bore an Arabian name like that!

Farewell, my dearest, my 'dolcissima amica'.

27 November 1877

. . . The last melody? Think of it as an *Albumblatt*. But you will see, in the second act, Klingsor's enchantresses, the flowers from his magic garden (tropical), they blossom in the spring and live until the autumn, so as to twine gracefully and naively about the champions of the Grail in the form of young girls. They caress Parsifal, stroke his cheeks, his chin, like children at play. Perhaps you will sing, to this melody, 'Come, come! Youthful hero, handsome boy', etc. You will see it soon enough and you will like it.

But if you do not! And even if you do not want me to, I will kiss you just the same! O, I have a pretty little thing, and its name is Judith.

4 December 1877

. . . '*Ein furchtbar schönes Weib!*' A woman, that is, of a beauty (why not of two beauties) that inspires terror. But '*furchtbar*' sounds funny in this context – 'frightfully beautiful'! '*Unheimliche Schönheit*' – I rejected that. What's uncanny or weird about beauty? By '*furchtbar schön*' I mean something like '*terrifiant*' in French. But that won't do: you use the word '*terrifié*', which means exactly the opposite. So much for logic! Perhaps there's too much logic, when language is a product of nature and totally irrational, whereas an academy is highly rational, logical and everything else you care to mention, but it is not creative, it merely arranges and defines conventions.

[undated]

. . . The 'Araby dialect' in which 'fal' is supposed to mean fool or uncouth was my invention. I wanted to ascribe the word to some dialect or other because it suits me! I didn't mean 'Let us look' seriously. But I am re-reading Görres, he must be quite sure of his case. He probably didn't know Arabic, but he will have had it from an Orientalist. Anyway, it doesn't worry me. What do I care about the real meaning of Arabic words, and I fancy that there will not be an excessive number of Orientalists among my future audiences!

Gautier-Briefe, pp. 145, 149, 158 f. 162, 175 f. (originals French)

During the last three years of his life Wagner spent three lengthy periods in Italy with his family. He finished the score of *Parsifal* in Palermo.

240, 239

Siegfried Wagner on his visits to Italy with his parents:

Our frequent visits to Italy had a decisive influence on my whole development. Sick of the everlasting grey skies of Germany – I can remember my father shaking his clenched fists at the clouds and shouting 'Those damned potato sacks!' – he packed up and took us all across the Alps, with the kind help of King Ludwig II, so as to forget his worries and struggles for a time at least, and to enjoy the sunshine, the visual arts and the light-hearted life of the people. Apart from assistance from the king, the journey was made possible by the payment for the *Festmarsch*, which had just arrived and was very lavish for that date. After the artistic success, on the whole, but financial fiasco of the first Festival in 1876, our journey took us via Verona, Venice and Bologna to Rome and Naples. That was when my passion for architecture was kindled. I rushed like one possessed from church to church, from palazzo to palazzo, and my first attempts to reproduce my impressions with paper and pencil were decidedly crude to begin with, but gradually became quite passable, so that while my parents smiled they were really pleased to see the talent that was developing, to everyone's surprise.

Siegfried Wagner, *Erinnerungen*, Stuttgart 1923, p. 7 f.

Auguste Renoir on the visit he paid Wagner in Palermo early in 1882, in a letter to a friend in Paris, Naples, January 1882:

238

. . . Mademoiselle Wagner tells me that her mother isn't here, but her father will be with me directly, and then she runs away. I hear muffled steps approaching across the thick carpets. It is the master, in his velvet gown with wide sleeves faced with black satin. He is very handsome and kind and shakes my hand, invites me to sit down again and then we launch into the craziest conversation, interspersed with 'hi' and 'oh', half in French, half in German, with guttural periods.

'I am very happy – Ah! Oh!', and a guttural noise, 'You have come from Paris.' 'No, I have come from Naples,' and I tell him about the loss of my letter, which makes him laugh a lot. We talk about every conceivable subject. When I say 'we', I must explain that all I managed to say was 'Dear master', 'Of course, dear master'. Then I stood up to take my leave. Whereupon he took my hands and pushed me back into my chair. 'Wait a little longer, my wife is coming – and the good Lascoux, how is he?' I tell him that I haven't seen him, that I've been in Italy a long time and he doesn't even know I'm here. 'Ah! Oh! But you won't fail to visit him. Ah! Ah!', followed by a German guttural. We talk about *Tannhäuser* at the Opéra, in short, it goes on at least three-quarters of an hour. . . . We spoke about impressionism in music. What a lot of rubbish I must have talked! Towards the end I was burning with embarrassment, I felt quite giddy and red as a turkey cock. In short, once a shy man gets started he goes too far. All the same, I know he was very pleased with me, though quite why I don't know. He detests German Jews, including Wolff. He asked me if *Les Diaments de la Couronne* was still popular in France. I found something ill to say about Meyerbeer. In short, I had time enough for every imaginable *sottise*! Then he suddenly said to Joukovsky: 'If I feel all right around midday, I can sit for you until my lunch. You know, you must make allowances, but I will do what I can, if it doesn't last long, it won't be my fault. Monsieur Renoir, ask Monsieur Joukovsky if he minds if you do my portrait as well, providing it doesn't disturb him.' Joukovsky says: 'But how could it? *Cher Maître*, that's exactly what I wanted to ask you to do', etc., etc., 'How do you want to do it?' I replied, '*En face*'. He says to me: 'That's very good, I will stand with my back to you, since my composition is already complete.' Then Wagner says to him: 'You will paint me with your back to France, and Monsieur Renoir will do me from the other side. Ah! Ah! Oh!...'

I was there at noon the next day. You know the rest. He was very cheerful, I very nervous, and sorry that I was not Ingres. In short, I believe that I made good use of my time: thirty-five minutes is not long, but if I had stopped sooner it would have been very good, as my sitter lost some of his cheerfulness towards the end and became stiff. I responded to these changes too faithfully. Well, you will see.

At the end Wagner wanted to see it. He said: 'Ah! Ah! I look like a Protestant minister.' Which is perfectly true. In short, I was very glad that I didn't make too much of a fiasco of it. At least it's some sort of souvenir of that marvellous head.

Best wishes   Renoir.

I will not read my letter through again, otherwise I shall tear it up – and that would be the fifteenth. If I have forgotten anything I will tell you when we see each other.

He said several times that the French read the critics too much. 'The critics! Ah! Ah!', and a roar of laughter. 'The German Jews! But, Monsieur Renoir, I know that there are decent people in France, whom I don't lump together with the German Jews.' Unfortunately I can't reproduce the frank good humour the master showed throughout the whole conversation.

Martin Geck, *Die Bildnisse Richard Wagners*, Munich 1970, p. 54 f.

Italy gave Wagner some of his major ideas for the sets of *Parsifal*. The Russian artist Paul von Joukovsky (1845–1912), whom Wagner had known since his visit to the Villa Angri in January 1880, painted a lot of sketches for the Grail Temple and for Klingsor's enchanted garden, inspired by Siena Cathedral and the Palazzo Rufolo in Ravello. Wagner returned to Bayreuth on 1 May 1882. After scenic and musical preparations, the rehearsals for *Parsifal* began on 2 July. There were seven days for each of the acts. There were alternating casts and two conductors, Hermann Levi and Franz Fischer. The first performance of *Parsifal* took place on 26 July 1882; there were sixteen altogether.

244, 243
242

247

245–255

Franz Liszt to Hans von Wolzogen, Bayreuth, 27 July 1882:
Honoured Freiherr,
During and after yesterday's performance of Wagner's *Parsifal*, the general feeling was that there is nothing that can be said about this miraculous work.

Silence is surely the only possible response to so deeply moving a work; the solemn beat of its pendulum is from the sublime to the most sublime.
Most sincerely,
F. Liszt

Franz Liszts Briefe, ed. La Mara, vol. 2, Leipzig 1893, p. 329

From Wagner's report to Ludwig II on the first performance of Parsifal *in 1882, in a letter of 8 September 1882:*
What can I tell you of these festive days in Bayreuth that I could regard as worthy of a report to you, the noble sufferer? The work was a success – that I must say to the honour of the executants. The most deeply moving thing for me was the wonderful zeal of all the participants – from the first to the last: it is not the first time that I have had cause for joy at such enthusiasm, but this time it seemed even more intense than ever before. Often, arriving fatigued and weary for one of the performances, which followed close upon each other's heels, I attempted to commiserate with my singers or players on the unremitting strain, but every time they replied in the highest of spirits, assuring me that the only grounds they had for commiseration was the prospect of the end of the Festival and their return to the ordinary theatrical and musical round. Many of them were genuinely inconsolable at the end: Fräulein Malten, who had had to leave us on 15 August, came back specially from Dresden for the last performance, in which Frau Materna sang, so as to be able to attend the performance as a member of the audience at least. All of them assured me that they had won from their managements the condition that for the time being after their return they would have to appear only in works by me. Theatre directors, amazed at the uncommonly accurate performance, asked me who had produced it all, to which I jokingly replied that anarchy was the order of the day in my theatre, and everybody did what they wanted; but since everybody wanted the same as I wanted, everything was always in accordance with my intentions. And in fact that, and that alone, is the sober truth.

As for what the individual singers accomplished in meeting the great and completely new challenges, I was sorry that I was too exhausted by the preceding rehearsals to be able, in my resulting very poor state of health, to rehearse them again after each of the performances. Such subsequent rehearsals would have been useful for correcting points of detail, and no one was *more* ready to take part in them than my singers themselves: they asked me to hold them, and I had to refuse. But even the few emendations that I seriously undertook, primarily with Kundry and Parsifal for the long crucial scene in the second act, were rewarded handsomely: visitors to the Festival who had attended the first performances and then returned for the last were amazed by the advances they saw. It was a good thing that the two performers of the part of Kundry (Frau Materna and Fräulein Malten) and the two singers of Parsifal (Herr Winkelmann and Herr Gudehus) were all fairly well matched to each other; only Materna and Winkelmann had the advantage over the other two of being able to stay here the whole time and thus they could run through their parts more often. Scaria as Gurnemanz set Siehr, who is outstanding in any other company, an unenviable task; Siehr is perhaps the more accurate vocally and musically, and certainly extremely dignified in his playing of the part, but Scaria's performance was transfused by a certain naive genius, which won him all hearts. The scene with Klingsor's enchanted flowers was quite unsurpassable, probably the most masterly example of scenic-cum-musical production that I have ever seen: it had all depended on assembling six 'principal' sopranos with equally light, high voices, and in addition finding twenty-four young chorus leaders with equally good voices and attractive appearances. Thanks to the zeal of worthy Kapellmeister Levi, which I cannot praise highly enough, we were completely successful in this: five Court theatres sent us singers who at home sing Elisabeth, Elsa, Sieglinde, even Brünnhilde (Fräulein André from Brunswick). There is no describing the appealing eagerness of these ladies; worthy Porges took a notable share in coaching them, too. If I have to specify a major difficulty in the prospect of mounting a performance of *Parsifal* in Munich for my noble benefactor, then I admit it lies in the impossibility of seeing this scene equally well performed, unless we succeed in assembling the same cast for it again.

The costumes taxed our wits, especially as the Flower Maidens, designed very sketchily by Joukovsky, had to be rethought almost entirely from scratch when it came to making them: we succeeded in giving them the most perfect naivety; they really were flowers, just like the giant flowers in the garden itself: the finishing touch consisted simply of their breaking off some of those flowers and popping them on their heads like children, which created an effect so charming as to defy description. The sets were more successful than anything I have ever previously experienced: with these the Brückner brothers have attained the full dignity of artists. The only weakness was that the late *Brandt* made an incomprehensible error in calculating the time needed for the transformation: it required twice as much music as I had allowed for it; since the only thing to be done was to repeat the music, the whole process assumed a tedious length which was completely contrary to the magical character I had intended. We have already decided that the scenery for the first transformation will be reduced by half in future performances, while the second (in the third act), which we did not use at all this time, will merely be hinted at and then lead at once to the gates in the cliffs, swathed in darkness until that moment, which will then open to lead directly into the Grail Temple.

Königsbriefe, vol. 3, p. 247 ff.

Wagner's statement, thanking the citizens of Bayreuth:

I should like to express publicly the heartfelt thanks, already frequently and gladly expressed to them in person, that I owe to those of my amiable fellow-citizens, their young men and their lovely daughters, whose assistance, as willing as it was creditably skilled, made so gratifying a contribution to the success of a noble realization of the scenic action in the performances of *Parsifal*. The success of their assistance has shown the way in which the citizens of Bayreuth can participate in presenting a work of art for the world to see; to be able to take the benefits of such

participation into account seems to me not the least valuable outcome of the Festival that we have just celebrated.

3 September 1882   Richard Wagner

Bayreuther Tagblatt, 5 September 1882

The conductor Felix Weingartner's memories of the production of Parsifal *in 1882:*

The auditorium grows completely dark. A breathless hush falls. Like a voice from another world, the first expansive theme of the prelude begins. This impression is unlike anything else, and is ineradicable. I have heard *Parsifal* at Bayreuth in later performances which were the most bitter disappointment to me, but the solemnity of this beginning was always the same. The inspiration, the instrumentation, the acoustic and, in a negative sense, the optical impression work together here in a unique manner that is impossible anywhere else.

The curtains part fairly slowly and a setting of grave beauty unfurls before the eyes: Gurnemanz is roused by the distant trombone fanfare. The glorious figure of Emil Scaria stands before us and his wonderful voice awakens the pages. This performance is given with the same cast as at the première and is a triumph not only for Bayreuth but also for Vienna, for almost all the principals are artists of the Viennese Court Opera: Materna, Reichmann, Winkelmann, Scaria. Only the black magician Klingsor is played by the magnificent Hill from Schwerin, the famous Alberich of the Nibelung cycle, and the voice of Titurel, resonating like a mighty admonition from sunken worlds, is sung by Kindermann from Munich, the father of Frau Reicher-Kindermann. The conductor is Hermann Levi, originally banned by Wagner because he is a Jew. King Ludwig would have refused to allow the Munich orchestra to take part if Wagner had persisted in his ban. Members of the audience who were not blindly partisan could judge the full magnitude of Levi's achievement only later, when he no longer conducted.

When Gurnemanz started to lead Parsifal to the Grail Castle, I suddenly felt slightly giddy. What was happening? It seemed to me that the theatre and the whole audience were beginning to move. The scene had started to change by means of moving the backcloth. The illusion was perfect. One did not walk, one was carried. '*Zum Raum wird hier die Zeit*' ['Here time becomes space']. Corresponding scenery unrolled on two or three columns facing each other on either side of the stage, until the last cliff moved aside and the magnificently proportioned interior of the Grail Castle stood before us. Light flooded over the majestic scene precisely on the C-major chord. An imcomparable effect was achieved by the simplest means. . . .

The transformation of Klingsor's tower, sinking in an instant, into the enchanted garden, which appears with equal suddenness, is astonishing. A few years later, when I attended several rehearsals and performances of *Parsifal* at the theatre, I had the opportunity to study and to admire the functional simplicity of this extraordinarily effective transformation machinery. I have seen the curtain fall at this point in performances in present-day theatres. How much we have lost in many respects, in spite of our

1882.
XXVII. Jahrgang.

№ 246.

Dienſtag
den 5 September

Bayreuther Tagblatt.

Oberfränkiſche Volkszeitung.

(Die Verantwortlichkeit für Inſerate trägt deren Einſender.)

Erſcheint täglich.
Alle kgl. Poſtan-
ſtalten u. Land-
poſtboten liefern
das Tagblatt
vierteljährlich
für 1 M. 60 Pfg.
Preis für den
2. und 3 Monat
des Quartals
55 Pfg.
per Monat.

Abonnements
für Bayreuth
1 Mark 40 Pfg.
vierteljährlich, bei
freier Zuſtellung
in's Haus 1 Mark
60 Pfg. Preis für
den 2. u. 3 Monat
des Quartals
48 Pfg.
Preis der einzelnen
Nummer 10 Pfg.

Bei Anfragen von Auswärts iſt Franco-Marke für die Rückantwort beizufügen.

Denjenigen meiner freundlichen Mitbürger, ſowie den jungen Männern und artigen Töchtern, welche durch eben ſo willige als würdevoll geſchickte Mitwirkung zu dem Gelingen einer edlen Aus- führung der ſceniſchen Actionen in den Vorſtellungen des „Parſifal" ſo höchſt erfreulich beitrugen, ſage ich, wie dies bereits perſönlich immer gern geſchah, hiemit auch vor aller Oeffentlichkeit meinen herzlichen Dank. Wir ſind durch ſolche geglückte Mitwirkung auf die Pfade einer ſchönen Antheil- nehmung der Bayreuther Bürgerſchaft auch an dem der Welt vorzuführenden Kunſtwerke ſelbſt ge- rathen, deren förderliche Bedeutung in Erwägung ziehen zu dürfen mir als ein nicht werthloſer Er- folg der erlebten Feſtſpiele erſcheint.

3. September 1882.

Richard Wagner.

Wagner's public announcement in the *Bayreuther Tagblatt*, 5 September 1882, expressing his 'heartfelt thanks to fellow citizens', to whose collaboration he felt the success of the first performances of *Parsifal* at the Festival was due.

vaunted progress! Our whole scenic apparatus is clumsy and overladen, two-dimensional in spite of all its di- mensions and completely without imagination when it tries to be simple. We must set to, to introduce some healthy reforms which on the one hand will not prevent the audience's imagination from participating creatively, but on the other hand will not bore them, either, with spurious sobriety.

The Flower Maidens rush in from all sides and encircle Parsifal. Their costumes are tasteless, quite incomprehen- sibly tasteless, but their singing is beyond all praise, sublime. Heinrich Porges, the 'Flower Father' as he is generally called, coached them, and thereby ensured a more handsome memorial for his name than by his activities as a critic in Munich. At the exquisite diminuendo '*Wir welken und sterben dahinnen*', a warm, heartfelt 'Bravo! Bravo!' is heard from one of the boxes. It was the voice of Wagner himself. I had already been told that he expressed his approval at this point in every performance. I heard the cry at both the later performances that I went to that year. Rarely have I felt so acutely the vacuum death creates in our earthly life as at performances of *Parsifal* that I attended at Bayreuth in later years, when there was a blank silence at that point.

The great scene between Kundry and Parsifal makes a very strong impression indeed. The close of this act, the collapse of Klingsor's enchanted castle and the laying waste of the flower garden, is another masterpiece of the art of production. Wagner's opponents had claimed that

Parsifal was simply a copy of his earlier works and this scene just a love duet like the earlier ones. There could be no more foolish assertion. Wagner never repeated himself, either in this or in any other work. It is only small spirits that follow recipes.

After this act I thought that the climax had already been reached, but the third act rose to a yet greater height. I was too young that first year to grasp the full significance of this act. The agent of the powerful impression that I received was Scaria, whose performance can only be called sublime; in my experience, it has never been sur- passed since. This Gurnemanz was a giant in stature, a warrior who you could see had once borne arms, and yet a child in his tenderness and inwardness. I can still hear the soft break in his voice at the words in which he tells of the death of his old leader, Titurel: '*Er starb, ein Mensch wie alle.*' But Wagner himself surpassed in this act everything he had done before. Here, in this act, he came to the threshold that lies between time and eternity.

Felix Weingartner, *Lebenserinnerungen*, Vienna, Leipzig 1923, pp. 165–9

Hermann Levi describes the final performance of Parsifal *on 29 August, in a letter to his father, 31 August 1882:*

The final performance was magnificent. During the transformation music the master came into the pit, wriggled up to my desk, took the baton from my hand

and conducted the performance to the end. I remained at his side because I was afraid that he might make a mistake, but my fears were quite groundless – he conducted with the assurance of one who had been nothing but a conductor all his life. At the end of the work the audience burst into applause that defies all description. But the master did not show himself, but stayed with us musicians, making bad jokes, and when the noise in the audience showed no sign of abating after ten minutes, I shouted 'Quiet! Quiet!' at the top of my voice. They heard it above, and really did quieten down, and then the master, still at the conductor's desk, began to talk, first to me and the orchestra, then the curtain was raised, the whole cast, chorus and technical personnel had assembled on the stage, and the master spoke with a warmth that reduced everyone to tears – it was an unforgettable moment!

RWG

Franz Liszt to Hans von Wolzogen, Venice, 24 November 1882:

It goes without saying that Wagner ought to reign and govern, as legitimate monarch, until his Bayreuth project has reached its complete and final realization: model performances of all his works, under his aegis and direction, in Bayreuth.

The achievement of this goal demands the support of all who claim a part in the art and culture, born of our history and civilization, in the years that remain of the nineteenth century.

Franz Liszts Briefe, ed. La Mara, vol. 2, Leipzig 1893, p. 339

In September 1882 Wagner and his family went to Italy again. His last residence was the Palazzo Vendramin-Calergi in Venice. He conducted his early C-major symphony, the parts of which had recently been rediscovered, at the Teatro la Fenice on 24 December 1882.

Siegfried Wagner on his father's conducting of the Symphony in C major at the Teatro la Fenice:

The best thing that happened, however was the performance of his early symphony in honour of my mother's birthday. It was the third time that I had the chance of seeing him conduct. Some years before, also on my mother's birthday, it had been Beethoven's A-major symphony and movements from the F-major, which he conducted in Wahnfried with the Meiningen orchestra. His method of conducting, which his pupils, like Hans von Bülow, Klindworth, Richter and later, indirectly, Mottl, Muck and Nikisch, strove with some success to emulate, was distinguished by its plastic simplicity and great clarity. . . . My father used his eyes above all else, and repeatedly referred to them as the most important means of communicating the conductor's wishes. Consequently his passion was more restrained in its external manifestations; it revealed itself to those who went up to him at the

244

end in his very heavy perspiration. The sight always remained an aesthetic one for the audience, without any of the exaggerated gesticulation which is so popular nowadays and creates the impression that the ultimate object of the music is the conductor, and the work being performed is incidental. It was his eyes that electrified.

Siegfried Wagner, op. cit., p. 32 ff.

From Ludwig II's last letter to Wagner, Hohenschwangau, 26 November 1882:

I am delighted by your plan to mount worthy, exemplary productions of all your glorious works at Bayreuth in the course of the next few years, after '84. As you will remember, we already spoke of doing so in the 'Nibelungen' year. Of course my orchestra will be at your disposal, my adored friend, as often as you need it. And now to the performances of *Parcifal*. In the 'Nibelungen' year I decided to attend the first, epoch-making performances in Bayreuth itself, and did so in fact, and then was able to enjoy the wonderful trilogy in Munich as well (without the shrieks of the public, without needing to parade myself in the streets), and it was my intention to do the same in the case of *Parcifal*. Unfortunately when the 'Parcifal' year came, which is still with us, indeed, my illness made it impossible for me to attend the first performances of the work I had yearned to see, which was a great pity; ever since then I have been looking forward instead to hearing the sublime work for the first time in Munich in the coming spring (which would have been so appropriate a season: the re-awakening of nature after the frozen sleep of winter), just as you yourself, dearly beloved friend, earlier suggested to me. Now it seems, delicately as you allow it to emerge, that the idea is no longer quite acceptable to you! It really is a shame! . . .

I would be so glad to have news of your son Siegfried again. Is he growing and flourishing? Is your idea of educating him according to *Wilhelm Meister* proving a success? It is my sincere hope that the Italian climate will suit him better this winter than last year. Please convey the most cordial greetings on my behalf to my revered friend, your wife, and to the children. In the deepest love and never faltering loyalty to the majestic light that I wish may yet shine for a long, long time, a sun to replenish and quicken the world with its celestial rays,

Your truest friend and most enthusiastic admirer,

Ludwig

Königsbriefe, vol. 3, p. 254 f.

From Wagner's last letter to King Ludwig II, Venice, 10 January 1883:

The prime impossibility is adapting the *Parsifal* sets for use in Munich before the major alterations, and rebuilding in some cases, which can finally be tried out only in the Festival Theatre in Bayreuth, after I too have inspected them very thoroughly. For the time being, both the backcloths used for the transformations are in pieces, waiting to be remade, and cannot possibly be used. The alterations necessitating this could not be deferred, once I had made up my mind to establish the definitive production of this work, my farewell to the world, at Bayreuth. Since my noble friend has devoted his kind attention to my essay 'On the Stage Dedication Festival at Bayreuth', I have reason to hope that my explanation of this matter has not remained unapproved. But if my all-gracious lord remains unwilling to bestow the transfiguring favour of his presence on the Festival performances themselves on any account, yet, as we must certainly not forgo that presence, perhaps three or more performances could be staged for my noble benefactor after the public performances were over, with the same cast, under my personal supervision, and in the fullest realization of my artistic intentions. Since Munich is again the scene this year of one of those wretched 'international' or 'world' exhibitions, which demand a little opera as a sideshow, and therefore the time in which I can have the use of the Court orchestra and chorus, placed at my disposal once again by your boundless generosity, is rather short, I shall have to make haste if the number of performances that I believe necessary for the success of my undertaking are to be accomplished by about 15 August, so as to have perhaps another week in which the company can remain together in order to give the private performances for my adored lord. But it is quite essential that those performances take place in Bayreuth itself, because it would be utterly impossible to install the uncommonly complicated technical staff and performance material in Munich quickly enough for my singers' leave not to be exhausted before we were ready. Furthermore, since the management of the Court Theatre is now clamouring agonizingly for opera to put on during the exhibition, it would doubtless hardly be in accordance with my noble benefactor's wishes that private performances, from which the public were totally excluded, should take place in Munich at that particular time.

After weighing all this well – and unwell, too in sleepless nights – I have come to the conclusion that I may dare a last, humble assault on the heart of my royal lord and friend, that heart which has been more than gracious to me in the past, to beseech him to allow the work, that after all I wrote for him alone, to be performed for him in the conditions in which alone I can guarantee its proper effect, whereas every departure from them cannot fail to cause me fatal distress. What am I saying? Perhaps I am pronouncing the sentence of death on myself and the whole of my work for art: for I must fear that even he, whom I call the lord of my life, may very well choose to regard all my views and all my pleading as worthless. Yet I know what I am asking: it is the purpose for which that lord extended his protection to my life when it was in ruins. Let him then crown his work, as he raised me up in his grace: let him permit me to pay him homage in deepest gratitude, to lay the work that is my farewell to life at his feet exactly as I want it to be. I have suffered so much in order to be able to do so! . . .

While I thus leave it to time to shape the eventual effect of my work, I can rejoice in the splendid hopes that my son awakens and nurtures in me. Until now it was almost exclusively architecture that engaged his attention, but now music too is beginning to cast its powerful spell on him: he is showing the keenest interest in the study of harmony; but the theatre too, the plays which he loves to go to at the Teatro Goldoni here, interest him to the extent that he has already written several tragedies, which he intends to perform with his young friends in Bayreuth.

He has a good mother! He is on excellent terms with his sisters, who all love him very much, and all of them, mother, son and daughters, hold their father fortunate in the love of his glorious protector, his noble benefactor, the king that God sent to him!

And so today, once more, the circle of my existence closes with the thought of the grace, in the noble enjoyment of which I shall end my days as my adored lord and friend's

eternally own:

Richard Wagner

Königsbriefe, vol. 3, p. 257ff.

————————

On 13 February 1883 Wagner died of heart failure in Venice. The grief-stricken Cosima, who was at his side when he died, remained beside the body for a whole day before being persuaded by the family doctor to come away. The cast for the death-mask by the Italian sculptor Augusto Benvenuti was taken on 14 February, before arrangements were made for transporting the composer's remains first by gondola, and then overland to Bayreuth, where the funeral – attended by thousands – took place on 18 February. Wagner was buried near his old home, Wahnfried.

262

The painter Paul von Joukovsky to Franz Liszt, Bayreuth, 261
20 February 1883:

Honoured Master, I do not know whether you have been able to obtain a precise account of Wagner's end. I am fully aware that I ought to have let you have one long ago, if I had been fit for anything; but it has been as if I were paralysed. Today is the first time that I feel any alleviation of the numbness in my heart. Wagner got up on the morning of 13 February, saying to his valet, 'I must go carefully today.' In spite of that he had coffee with his wife and began to work on his new essay on 'Male and Female'. He stayed in his room until midday. At two o'clock he sent us word that he had his usual cramps, and we should go to table without waiting for him. We were in high spirits as usual. In the middle of the meal [the maid] Betty came to tell Frau Wagner that he was asking her to come at once. The children and I waited in the salon for their parents until four o'clock. Doctor Keppler had already arrived at three, which had set our minds completely at rest. But around four we began to worry again, for we were all supposed to be going out with Wagner, to visit Walkoff's house. Suddenly we heard cries of despair and we were brought the truth. He died in his wife's arms, he fell asleep without pain; for he died of heart failure caused by the strain imposed by his usual cramps. By the time the doctor came it was too late. Frau Wagner remained with him throughout the whole of the first day and the following night. At two o'clock on Wednesday the doctor managed to get her into another room. I am not in a fit state to describe to you the days in Venice during which we were torn this way and that between our sorrow and the profound fear that we might lose your daughter as well.

Briefe hervorragender Zeitgenossen an Franz Liszt, vol. 3, p. 398f. (original French)

Siegfried Wagner recalls the day of his father's death, 13 February 1883:

One event, concerning my mother, on the day of my father's death has remained vividly in my memory. Although she was a superlative pianist – Séghers, their music master, had said of the sisters: '*Blandine sera une excellente musicienne, Cosima une grande artiste*' – I had never heard her play; she was so busy ministering to my father in every way that she had had to neglect the instrument entirely. But on that 13 February I sat in the salon, practising the piano. My mother came in. She sat down at the grand piano and began to play. When I asked what she was playing, she replied, with a completely transported expression, 'Schubert's *Lob der Tränen*'. A few minutes later the chambermaid brought the news that my father had been taken ill. I shall never forget the way my mother rushed to the door. It expressed the force of a passionate anguish; she ran into the half-open door so hard that it almost split. When I watched her at Festival rehearsals in later years, acting parts like Kundry, Isolde, Sieglinde, Brünnhilde, I was often reminded of that moment in Venice; she acted then with a classical greatness such as I have only once seen on the stage: in the portrayal of Othello by Salvini, then already seventy-seven years old.

Siegfried Wagner, op. cit., p. 35 f.

EXTRACTS FROM COSIMA'S DIARIES

Cosima Wagner, still Cosima von Bülow to begin with, kept a diary from 1868 onwards. It supplements Wagner's own autobiographical writings, which only cover the years up to 1864 (in the case of *Mein Leben*) and 1868 (in the *Annals*).

1877

1 December. In the evening Acts 3 and 4 of *Henry VI* part 3; R. thinks Edward's wooing of Lady Grey a masterpiece of dramatic virtuosity, for all its naivety, we must constantly admire the playwright's ability, he express what others do not say. R. said, historical plays are something quite alien to him, but if he had ever written his Barbarossa, he would have done it in the light rhyming couplets of the period, so as to introduce a popular element. But we have come too far from things like that; Shakespeare still had a tradition to link him to his origins.

2 December. R. told me: 'I shall still write *Parsifal* for my wife, but I wouldn't say it's a sign of faith in the German spirit any longer.' After Act 4 of *Henry VI* he said, 'I will write funeral music for the fallen after all, but it won't end with an apotheosis, you can rely on that.'

18 December. In the evening two of the preludes from the *Well-tempered Clavier*, played by R., utterly absorbing for us. Of the E flat minor he said, 'That shaped my handwriting. It's incredible how much of the musical repertory has passed over me without making any impression, but *that* made me what I am. It is immortal, and nobody has ever done anything like it again!'

21 December. Some artists in Vienna are planning a Germanic parade, and have asked Richard in the most extravagant terms to write music for it! There is a very strange gap between this kind of admiration and what really satisfies R! . . .
R. has won his rhythmic battle and told me, as he left his work, 'I have composed a philosophical maxim today: "*Hier wird der Raum zur Zeit*" [Here space becomes time; cf. p. 242].'

28 December. R. is working on the Grail March, he has cut out the crystal bells; he looked at Father's *Glocken von Strassburg*, to see whether he is committing plagiarism.

1878

4 January. He told me that when he had had arguments with his mother as a child, he had shown a compulsion to confess.

When I went down to see him, he said: 'You've just come at a baritone bit, a difficult baritone bit!' *Divina Commedia* again this evening. For all his admiration for the poet, R. feels a strong aversion to the object of the poet's fantasy.

5 January. I don't know how the conversation came round to the Venetians. R. said: 'Superb statesmen, quite heartless as human beings, just as there is nothing that can be more implacably opposed to what we call religion than the state!'

7 January. 'What wells up from the soul cannot be called work,' R. said, à propos of his progress on *Parsifal*.

10 January. Correcting the proofs of the *Idyll*, R. said, 173, 174 'It is my favourite composition!'

11 January. R. worked. Towards midday he told me he feels so well that he wants to compose *Die Sieger* straightaway after *Parsifal*, so as to prolong this condition.

12 January. Around noon, R. played me what he has composed so far of Amfortas's lament; the phrase '*Nach Ihm*' occupied him the whole morning, he said. Talking about it at lunch, he said: 'I sit there, look at your picture, shriek, rave, yes, I'm insane when I'm composing, it's an incessant frenzy.'

13 January. This evening he said he would have to rewrite everything he did this morning. He had tried to modulate, and the mechanical transposition had been impossible for him! 'A fine musician I am', he said, laughing; only when he is writing without stopping to reflect is everything at his command, but when he has to think about how to bring a theme into another key, he gets confused.

18 January. R. was working and told me later he has never composed anything as 'fantastic' as this, it is getting greater all the time!

19 February. 'Who is Titurel?' he asked me. I thought hard. – 'Wotan', he said; 'In renouncing the world he gains redemption, the greatest treasure is entrusted to him and now he stands guard over it, martial, godly.' What a fine thought! I said it ought to be possible to recognize Wotan's name in Titurel's; he said: 'Titurel, little Titus, Titus the emblem of royal dignity and power, Wotan the god-king.'

20 February. Talking of the oboe, R. said: 'It is the naive, tragic instrument.'

247

22 February. R. spoke of a symphony that he wants to dedicate to Fidi★, he had had another idea for a theme today, it would be as friendly and cheerful as the boy himself.

23 February. After dinner R. reverted to the subject of Mozart and especially *The Magic Flute*; some of the things in it, he said, make up a whole chapter in the history of art; Sarastro introduces a dignity that is warm and sincere instead of merely conventional. There are certain things by Mozart that will never, ever be surpassed.

26 February. R. was longing for some music and took up Haydn's Bear Symphony for the pleasure of the last movement. Then he showed friend Seidl the Andante of Haydn's G major symphony and told him it was one of the most beautiful things ever written; and what a marvellous sound! Pursuing the subject of music, he said that there are certain things in music that precisely satisfy the longing for it; the Adagio of the Ninth is one, it can go on as long as it likes, it's like a Sabbath, complete rest, it relaxes the whole body! But a lot of other things are what he calls 'cold music', e.g. Beethoven's B flat major, you have to be in the right mood for it. The Scherzo is splendid, but in the Adagio he always feels like saying: 'I *know* that already', and the theme of the first movement means nothing to him. The F major, on the other hand, never fails to impress him.

2 March. I told him I knew why I loved God and was grateful to him; R.: 'Yes, not the God who made the world, but the one who takes us from it.'
Comparison of Alberich and Klingsor. R. told me that he used to feel complete sympathy with Alberich, who represents the yearning of ugliness for beauty. In Alberich the naivety of the non-Christian world, in Klingsor the curious phenomenon which Christianity brought into the world: he does not believe in goodness, just like the Jesuits, and that is his strength – but also his downfall; there is always *one* individual at any one time throughout the ages.

7 March. Some music in the evening, the prelude to the third act of *Die Meistersinger*, 'I was the lonely man then,' said Richard; 'I do not need that solace any more.'

14 March. In the evening we looked at the prelude to *Parsifal*, friend Seidl played it, and R. had a great deal to say about the tempo, which Seidl had taken too slowly, or rather, *wrongly*; R. said tempo ought not to be marked at all, every piece has its own way of being played; of course there are pitfalls where the tempo has to be observed with immense precision and strictness, but you have to know which they are, you have to learn it from the master, and that was why he had wanted to found a school: 'where I should have died of rage every day', he added.

15 March. After dinner R. said he was frightened by the prospect of the big scene between Kundry and Parsifal; he had already done several scenes of the same kind, the Venus scene, for example; Mozart had done a scene like the

★ Pet name for Siegfried

248

apparition of the Commendatore only once, and it was inconceivable that he would ever have written another like it.

25 March. Yesterday evening R. said 'I was so looking forward to my Flower Maidens, and now it's just as difficult as the rest!' He asked how I thought they ought to be costumed when they first come on. R. thinks they should be wearing 'something like flower tendrils, and then they adorn themselves with petals'.

31 March. R. said to me, 'Do you know how Kundry calls Parsifal's name?' He sang me the insistently tender call. 'It's the first time the name is pronounced, and that is how his mother called him! Only music is capable of that.'

30 May. Recently R. told me: 'Herzeleide dies very simply, she fades and dies like a branch on a tree.' He said there are some things where he wants to hear the orchestra right away, he would like to set some passages in full score directly, it would help him, the same way as he wrote out the *Rheingold* prelude; he really needs to hear the horns in certain places.

3 June. R. sent me an urgent message, it's started! The scene between Kundry and Parsifal, up to his cry of 'Amfortas'! Inexpressibly exciting: 'A moment of daemonic surrender' is how R. describes the bars which accompany Kundry's kiss and in which the motif of amorous yearning coils like poison, devastating in its effect.

15 June. Richard was rejoicing that he did not introduce what happens in church into *Parsifal*, but let everything be contained in the benediction of the Grail.

6 July. R. turned to the Socialists, whom Feustel had described as easily suppressed. Certainly they are for the time being, he said, but they would always come up again; they shouldn't have been allowed to get a voice in the Reichstag, the questions they ask should have been looked at, their principles should have been investigated and the trouble attacked at the source. But everyone is stupid, and the Socialists themselves are crude and stupid, 'for they, too, eventually want to take control of the State in order to institute totally impossible conditions'.

8 September. R. is bemoaning his task (the great scene: Parsifal and Kundry, Act 2). The 'duet' in *Die Walküre* was pure joy by comparison, he says, and in *Tristan* there is at least the bliss of the anguish of longing, but here there is only the wild anguish of love.

23 September. Coming to *Parsifal* he said: 'Oh, my heart sinks at the thought of everything to do with costumes and make-up, when I think that characters like Kundry are going to be personified on a stage, it immediately puts me in mind of those dreadful artists' balls, and now I've created the invisible orchestra, I'd like to invent invisible acting too!'

28 September. This evening the third act of *Tristan*, played by R.! I was musing aloud that he should have created this miracle in a hotel, with no one to look after

him or watch over him, when he said: 'Yes, people have no idea of the remoteness of all experience, all reality, when these things are in motion, or of how long youth continues to flow in one; in fact I was tempted even then, out of sheer revulsion with everything, to throw the whole thing in the "mire", and I did throw it down and didn't want to work any more; but when the German emperor cries "How much in love Wagner must have been", it's simply ridiculous, and now, they say, of course I'm writing *Parsifal* because of my relationship with the Christian church, and of course you are Kundry! I felt the need to let myself rage in music, just as if I had written a symphony.'

11 October. R. spoke of the orchestral writing in *Parsifal*, and said he felt that in the 'Nibelung' he didn't have the singers to match the orchestra, sometimes the demands he had made, the cothurnus he had put on their foot, were more than they could manage, so that they could no more dominate the orchestra than could a single instrument, a clarinet for example; e.g. Materna in the scene with Waltraute. I remarked that the balance in the last scene, above all, had seemed wonderful; he replied: 'I'm talking about the passionate scenes; I haven't got the singers capable of singing them.'

Before supper R. showed me that he had finished the second act.

17 October. R. said to me yesterday that he would like best of all to write symphonies, light-hearted amiable ones, in which he would not even attempt to scale impossible heights, but he literally feels the need to pour out this element in himself.

233   20 October. We called on Wolzogen, whose essay on the Stage Dedication Festival pleased R. greatly, except he said to me that he had gone too far in calling Parsifal a representation of the Saviour: 'There was no thought of the Saviour in my mind.'

20 November. Richard exclaimed once again: 'I do not leave a single person behind me who knows my tempo.'

21 November. Richard said: 'If I wrote about the Jews again, I would say there is nothing to be held against them, only they came to us Germans too soon, we were not stable enough to absorb this element.'

29 November. Over coffee he talked about his work to me: 'Sometimes it's just a few bars that hold one up dreadfully, until the key one needs is introduced unobtrusively, because I tend more and more to avoid anything that sounds strange or jarring; perhaps four or five different possibilities will present themselves at one time, and I have to find the one which will make the transition gently! So I adjust a fold (in the curtain), find something to play with, until I've solved it.' 'Painters are lucky, they have so much time, but you're right, I suppose, what I'm always looking for is the equivalent of Titian red.'

1879

17 June. R. has a more and more vivid conviction of the inevitable collapse of things as they are, and believes that only the worker justified, as it were, his right to live.

Today he described the consequences of the emancipation of the Jews to the children (Daniela), how it had oppressed the middle class and corrupted the rest of the nation. The revolution had brought down feudalism but had replaced it with Mammonism.

29 June. . . . During a conversation about vivisection R. said a link ought to be forged between religion and compassion for animals; relations between humans are too difficult, they are so malicious, everyone puts himself first and the sublime teaching of Christianity hardly has a chance; but a start might be made with patient dumb beasts, and anyone who felt compassion for animals would surely not be cruel to people either. 'Let's preach a new religion, you and I.'

23 September. During the evening Richard played us the prelude to *Parsifal*, which he calls a preface or preamble, like the preamble to a sermon, because the themes are simply stated one after another.

1880

28 April. A letter from Kapellmeister Levi made him say: 'I can't let him conduct *Parsifal* unbaptized, but I'll baptize them both (Levi and Josef Rubinstein) and we'll all take communion together.'

25 June. Joukovsky has produced another sketch for the forest (Act 1 of *Parsifal*): 'One ought not to be able to see the forest for the trees', R. said.

20 August. Visited the cathedral (Siena)! R. moved to   242
tears, the greatest impression a building has ever made on him.

24 September. What my father had to say about *Parsifal* pleased R.; because of his desire to hear something from it, after supper we had almost the whole of the third act, played by my father and sung divinely by Richard.

1881

14 April. This evening R. told our friends of his dismay at the costume designs; innocence should be the keynote   248-250
of everything, but instead: 'staled women'. 'Everything in my work is chaste', he can proudly boast.

13 November. R. spoke of three pages he had scored and mentioned how reluctant he was to have jarring effects, and how he always tried to mitigate them, make them assimilable, rather than leave the harshness to make its own effect, and he picked out Gurnemanz's line 'Kalt und starr', and said how pleased he was with today's idea of accompanying it with muted horns. He said he was delighted, listening to the 'Nibelungen', by the way the boldest steps he had been driven to take did not force themselves upon the attention as such. With such subjects as his it was essential to use an unconventional palette, '*Notte giorno faticar*' was not good enough; but the skill consisted in disguising its unconventionality.

18 December. 'For Parsifal's entry (Act 3) I have horns and trumpets; horns on their own were too soft, not

ceremonial enough, trumpets on their own were to strident, too tinny – in these cases one has to experiment, and moreover I insist that they play it well.'

20 December.   R. returned to his preoccupation with the instrumentation of the close of the work, which means he needs a lot more instruments, like the alto oboe he is having made, all the wind sections will have to be enlarged, since he needs to have them play divided – I could have no conception of the agony it gives him.

1882

5 April.   R. ended the evening's conversation about religion with the remark that *Parsifal* would certainly have to be his last work, the fellowship of the Grail knights expressed the idea of communion. *Die Sieger* could only repeat it in a less meaningful, enfeebled form.

4 July.   R. wants to show Levi how to control the baton, as he finds he uses his arm too much in conducting, while it all ought to be done with the wrist.

22 July.   Final dress rehearsal. R. found that the tempi dragged rather a lot in the first act. . . . he remarked to me privately that if he were playing in the orchestra he wouldn't like to be directed by a Jew.

1883

16 January.   Late at night he read me the first two conversations of Faust and Mephisto, with inexpressible admiration, joy and delight. 'That is German,' he said. 'Shakespeare shows us the world as it is, Goethe shows how a free spirit can rise blithely above it.'

19 January.   He played the opening of the [Beethoven] 9th! He compared it to an improvisation and said: 'This sublime naivety! How long it takes to attain it! In the early symphonies Beethoven is still reaching for it.'

22 January.   Riding in a gondola, R. said, à propos of Bach's fugues: 'Chaos becomes harmony in them.' Conversation this evening, which R. brought to a close with the Shepherd's Song and Pilgrims' Chorus. He said he owed the world another *Tannhäuser*.

Bayreuther Blätter, 1936, 1937, 1938

ABBREVIATIONS OF DOCUMENTARY SOURCES

Bayreuther Briefe Carl Friedrich Glasenapp (ed.), *Richard Wagners Briefe in Originalausgaben*, vol. 15: 'Bayreuther Briefe', 2nd ed., Leipzig 1912.

Burrell-Briefe John N. Burk (ed), *Richard Wagner, Briefe: Die Sammlung Burrell*, Frankfurt/Main 1953.

Familienbriefe *Familienbriefe von Richard Wagner*, Berlin 1907.

Gautier-Briefe Willi Schuh (ed.), *Die Briefe Richard Wagners an Judith Gautier*, Zurich and Leipzig 1936.

Kietz *Richard Wagner in den Jahren 1842–1849 und 1873–1875.* Recollections of Gustav Adolph Kietz, recorded by Marie Kietz, Dresden 1905.

Königsbriefe *König Ludwig II und Richard Wagner, Briefwechsel*, compiled by Otto Strobel, 5 vols, Karlsruhe 1936–39.

Lippert Woldemar Lippert, *Richard Wagners Verbannung und Rückkehr*, Dresden 1927.

Mein Leben Richard Wagner, *Mein Leben*, first authentic publication, presented by Martin Gregor-Dellin, Munich 1963.

Meysenbug Malvida von Meysenbug, *Memoiren einer Idealistin*, 2nd ed., Stuttgart 1877.

Röckel-Briefe La Mara (ed.), *Richard Wagner, Briefe an August Röckel*, Leipzig 1894.

RWA Richard-Wagner-Archiv, Bayreuth

RWG Richard-Wagner-Gedenkstätte der Stadt Bayreuth.

Sämtliche Briefe Gertrud Strobel and Werner Wolf (ed.), *Richard Wagner, Sämtliche Briefe*, by direction of the Richard Wagner Family Archive, Bayreuth, 2 vols, Leipzig 1967, 1970.

Schriften-Erstausgabe Richard Wagner, *Gesammelte Schriften und Dichtungen*, 10 vols, Leipzig 1871–83.

Schriften-Volksausgabe Richard Wagner, *Sämtliche Schriften und Dichtungen*, Volksausgabe (popular edition), 16 vols, Leipzig (n.d.).

Wesendonck-Briefe Wolfgang Golther (ed.), *Richard Wagner an Mathilde Wesendonck, Tagebuchblätter und Briefe*, 3rd ed., Berlin 1904.

Wille-Briefe Eliza Wille, *Fünfzehn Briefe von Richard Wagner mit Erinnerungen und Erläuterungen*, 3rd enlarged edition, Munich–Berlin–Zurich 1935.

CHRONOLOGICAL TABLE: DATES OF COMPOSITION AND FIRST PERFORMANCE OF THE PRINCIPAL OPERATIC WORKS

	Prose sketch	Poem	Composition sketches	Autograph score	First performance
Die Feen	Autumn/winter 1832	Completed January 1833	20 February–27 December 1833	Spring 1833–6 January 1834	29 June 1888, Munich
Das Liebesverbot	June 1834	August–October 1834	23 January 1835–January 1836	Spring 1836	29 March 1836, Magdeburg
Rienzi, der Letzte der Tribunen	July 1837	Completed 5/6 August 1838	7 August 1838–October 1840	8 September 1838–19 November 1840	20 October 1842, Dresden
Der fliegende Holländer	Spring 1840	18–28 May 1841	July–5 November 1841	Completed 19 November 1841	2 January 1843, Dresden
Tannhäuser und der Sängerkrieg auf Wartburg[1]	22 June–early July 1842	Summer 1842–April 1843	July 1843–January 1845	Completed 13 April 1845	19 October 1845, Dresden
Lohengrin	July–3 August 1845	Completed 27 November 1845	May 1846–29 August 1847	1 January–28 April 1848	28 August 1850, Weimar
Das Rheingold	23–31 March 1852	15 September–3 November 1852	1 November 1853–14 January 1854	1 February–26 September 1854	22 September 1869, Munich
Die Walküre	17–26 May 1852	1 June–1 July 1852	28 June–27 December 1854	January 1855–23 March 1856	26 June 1870, Munich
Siegfried[2]	24 May–1 June 1851	3–24 June 1851	Summer/autumn 1856–9 August 1857 (Acts I, II) 1 March–5 August 1869 (Act III)	11 October 1856–31 March 1857 (Act I) 22 December 1864–2 December 1865 (Act II) 25 August 1869–5 February 1871 (Act III)	16 August 1876, Bayreuth
Götterdämmerung[3]	Completed 20 October 1848	12–28 November 1848	2 October 1869–22 July 1872	3 May 1873–21 November 1874	17 August 1876, Bayreuth
Tristan und Isolde	Begun 28 August 1857	Completed 18 September 1857	1 October 1857–19 July 1859	February 1858–August 1859	10 June 1865, Munich
Die Meistersinger von Nürnberg	1) Completed 16 July 1845 2) November 1861	Late December 1861–25 January 1862	March 1862–5 March 1867	3 June 1862–24 October 1867	21 June 1868, Munich
Parsifal	1) 27–30 August 1865 2) 25 January–23 February 1877	14 March–19 April 1877	September 1877–26 April 1879	23 August 1879–13 January 1882	26 July 1882, Bayreuth

[1] Revised in 1847 and in 1860–61
[2] First entitled 'Der junge Siegfried'; text revisions in 1852 and 1856
[3] First entitled 'Siegfrieds Tod'; text revisions in 1849, 1852 and 1856

Index

Figures in bold type refer to illustration numbers; figures in italics denote mentions in explanatory captions in the illustration section (pp. 17–144). Wagner's operatic works are listed under their respective titles, while his other musical compositions and literary works appear under his name.